Humanitarian Intervention, Colonialism, Islam, and Democracy

This book offers a critical analysis of the European colonial heritage in the Arab countries and highlights the way this legacy is still with us today, informing the current state of relations between Europe and the formerly colonized states.

The work analyses the fraught relationship between the Western powers and the Arab countries that have been subject to their colonial rule. It does so by looking at this relationship from two vantage points. On the one hand is that of humanitarian intervention—a paradigm under which colonial rule coexisted alongside "humanitarian" policies pursued on the dual assumption that the colonized were "barbarous" peoples who wanted to be civilized and that the West could lay a claim of superiority over an inferior humanity. On the other hand is the Arab view, from which the humanitarian paradigm does not hold up, and which accordingly offers its own insights into the processes through which the Arab countries have sought to wrest themselves from colonial rule. In unpacking this analysis the book traces a history of international and colonial law, to this end also using the tools offered by the history of political thought.

The book will be of interest to students, academics, and researchers working in legal history, international law, international relations, the history of political thought, and colonial studies.

Gustavo Gozzi has been full professor of History of Political Doctrines and History of International Law at the University of Bologna, Italy, where he is currently professor of Justice, Multiculturalism, and Human Rights, as well as a member of the advisory board of the King Abdulaziz Chair in Islamic Studies. He is also professor of Colonial Heritage, Euro-Mediterranean Relations, Migrations, and Multiculturalism at the Breyer Center for Overseas Studies in Florence, Stanford University.

Law, Ethics and Governance Series

Recent history has emphasized the potentially devastating effects of governance failures in governments, government agencies, corporations and the institutions of civil society. "Good governance" is seen as necessary, if not crucial, for economic success and human development. Although the disciplines of law, ethics, politics, economics, and management theory can provide insights into the governance of organizations, governance issues can only be dealt with by interdisciplinary studies, combining several (and sometimes all) of those disciplines. This series aims to provide such interdisciplinary studies for students, researchers, and relevant practitioners.

Series Editor: Charles Sampford, Director, Institute for Ethics, Governance and Law, Griffith University, Australia

Recent titles in this series

Positive Social Identity
The Quantitative Analysis of Ethics
Nick Duncan

Global Governance and Regulation
Order and Disorder in the 21st Century
Edited by Leon Wolff and Danielle Ireland-Piper

The Implementation of the Paris Agreement on Climate Change
Edited by Vesselin Popovski

Humanitarian Intervention, Colonialism, Islam, and Democracy
An Analysis through the Human-Nonhuman Distinction
Gustavo Gozzi
Translated by Filippo Valente

For more information about this series, please visit:
www.routledge.com/Law-Ethics-and-Governance/book-series/LEAG

INSTITUTE FOR
ETHICS,
GOVERNANCE
& LAW

Humanitarian Intervention, Colonialism, Islam, and Democracy

An Analysis through the Human-Nonhuman Distinction

Gustavo Gozzi
Translated by Filippo Valente

Routledge
Taylor & Francis Group
LONDON AND NEW YORK

First published 2021
by Routledge
2 Park Square, Milton Park, Abingdon, Oxon OX14 4RN

and by Routledge
605 Third Avenue, New York, NY 10158

Routledge is an imprint of the Taylor & Francis Group,
an informa business

Originally published in Italian as *Umano, non umano: Intervento umanitario, colonialismo, "primavere arabe."* Copyright © 2015 by Società editrice il Mulino, Bologna. The Italian edition has been published with funding from the Bologna University Cultural Heritage Department and the EU AMITIE project on migration, development, and human rights through local partnerships.

British Library Cataloguing-in-Publication Data
A catalogue record for this book is available from the British Library

Library of Congress Cataloging-in-Publication Data
Names: Gozzi, Gustavo, 1947- author. | Valente, Filippo, translator.
Title: Humanitarian intervention, colonialism, Islam, and democracy : an analysis through the human-nonhuman distinction / Gustavo Gozzi ; translated by Filippo Valente. Other titles: Umano, non umano. English Description: Milton Park, Abingdon, Oxon ; New York, NY : Routledge, 2021. | Series: Law, ethics and governance | Includes bibliographical references and index.
Identifiers: LCCN 2020048583 (print) | LCCN 2020048584 (ebook) | ISBN 9780367478551 (hardback) | ISBN 9781003036937 (ebook) Subjects: LCSH: Humanitarian intervention--History. | Imperialism--History. | Europe--Colonies--History. | Arab Spring, 2010- | Europe--Foreign relations--Mediterranean Region. | Mediterranean Region--Foreign relations--Europe. | Democracy--Religious aspects--Islam. Classification: LCC JZ6369 .G6913 2021 (print) | LCC JZ6369 (ebook) | DDC 341.5/84--dc23
LC record available at https://lccn.loc.gov/2020048583
LC ebook record available at https://lccn.loc.gov/2020048584

ISBN: 978-0-367-47855-1 (hbk)
ISBN: 978-0-367-75524-9 (pbk)
ISBN: 978-1-003-03693-7 (ebk)

Typeset in Galliard
by KnowledgeWorks Global Ltd.

Contents

A note on the criteria for transliterating the Arabic terms x
Introduction xii

PART I
Intervening for humanity 1

1 The origins of humanitarian intervention 3

1.1 What legitimation for humanitarian intervention: A historical reconstruction 3
1.2 The theory of humanitarian intervention: Barbarous humanity and the civilization of European peoples 5
1.3 Natural law and "Human law": Western humanity's principle of solidarity 9
1.4 The Eastern question 11
1.5 Partitioning the empire 17

2 Civilization and power: Developing the colonial paradigm 21

2.1 Colonial thinking: Tocqueville and the "Eastern question" 21
2.2 Algeria: Domination and colonization—outlines of a paradigm 24
2.3 Tocqueville's Qur'ān 27
2.4 Representing the colonized: The contribution of psychiatry—a "Muslim psychiatry" 29
2.5 Frantz Fanon: Decolonizing the "Mental illness" of the colonized 30
2.6 Human and nonhuman: "How to make men out of those who are not yet men?" Colonialism and an inferior humanity 34

3 Deconstructing the concepts of humanity and human nature 40

3.1 The Western paradigm: Human nature and cultural differences 40
3.1.1 Human nature and Western hegemony 40
3.1.2 The condition of slavery of the Indios: A different humanity 41
3.1.3 The conquest of humanity 41
3.1.4 What barbarism? Cannibalism and the force of customs; reason and common sense 42
3.1.5 Hume: The science of man and human nature 43
3.1.6 Rousseau: Human nature as identification with the other 45
3.1.7 From civilization to civilizations 46
3.1.8 Human egoism and human nature 47
3.1.9 International law and Western civilization 47
3.2 A relation of complementarity between psychic universalism and cultural plurality: Human life, psychic unity, and cultural diversity 48

4 The responsibility to protect, humanitarian intervention, and neocolonial policies 53

4.1 The international community and sovereignty: An irreversible crisis? 53
4.2 War, humanitarian intervention, and the function of law 56
4.3 Humanitarian intervention and the "responsibility to protect" 57
4.4 Hegemonic logics and forms of neocolonialism 59
4.5 More on sovereignty: How to redefine it? A standing hypocrisy? 63
4.6 Hegemonic techniques, constitutionalism, and international law 65
4.7 Excursus: Humanity—history of an idea 68
4.7.1 Humanity and dignity 68
4.7.2 Humanity, international law, and international human rights law 72

PART II
New democracies? 77

5 Anticolonial nationalism and Arab nationalism 79

5.1 Anticolonial nationalism 79
5.2 Anticolonial nationalism, nation, and state 81
5.3 The nationalist mission 82
5.4 Arab nationalism 83

6 **The system of Arab states and the persistence of traditional social structures** 88

6.1 The system of Arab states 88
6.2 Traditional structures and nation-state building 89

7 **Colonial law and the formation of the nation-state** 92

7.1 Colonial law 92
7.2 The colonies' political and administrative organization 94
7.3 The colonial government of Tunisia and Algeria 97
7.4 The reception of French law in the Muslim world 99
7.5 The failed attempt of the *Code Morand* 102
7.6 Importation, cross-fertilization, assimilation 105

8 **Democracy in Islam and Western democracy: Convergences and divergences** 108

8.1 Constitutional transformations 108
8.2 Independence and constitutions 110
8.2.1 Al-Sadāt's "Permanent constitution" 112
8.3 An Islamic constitutionalism? 116
8.4 Islam and democracy: How to tackle the problem? 117
8.5 Islamic reformism 117
8.6 The Islamic concept of the civil state: Ethics and religion 120
8.7 Two democracies, Western and Islamic: What divergences? 122
8.8 The sovereignty of God and the sovereignty of the people 125
8.9 Legitimacy and validity 126
8.10 Which sovereignty? 127
8.11 Excursus: Interpretation 128
8.12 One more excursus: Muslim law and religion 130
8.13 Democracy and *shūrā* 131
8.14 Colonialism, nationalism, secularization 133
8.15 One final excursus: An interpretation of Islamic reformism 135
8.16 The perspective of liberal and democratic reformism 137

9 **Tunisia and Egypt: Two constitutional models** 143

9.1 Constitutionalism and revolutions 143
9.2 The Tunisian case: A model for a path towards democracy 144

9.3 Egypt: A postcolonial revolution 148
9.4 The Egyptian constitutional model 150
9.5 The new Egyptian constitution: The Janus-faced nature of the Egyptian state 153
9.6 Tunisia: A democratic future 159
9.7 Tunisia: At long last the first elections in the new democracy 164
9.8 The Arab Springs in the destabilized landscape of the Middle East 165
9.9 Tunisia: What prospects for the future? 166
9.10 Can the compromise stand? 168
9.11 The challenges ahead 171

10 The Arab Springs: An analysis of its roots and causes 175

10.1 The causes of the uprisings 175
10.2 From revolt to revolution: The people reclaiming their dignity 178
10.3 The civil war in Libya 181
10.4 After the fall of the regime 186
10.5 Autumn after spring? 188
10.5.1 What peace for Libya? 189
10.5.2 Europe's role 190
10.6 Revolt and revolution in Tunisia 192
10.7 The crisis of the Arab Spring in Egypt 196
10.8 The end of the Arab Spring in Egypt 200
10.9 What future for Egypt? 203

11 Democratization and development in the Arab countries of the Mediterranean area 210

11.1 The Europeanization of the southern Mediterranean countries 210
11.1.1 A Short reconstruction of relations between the two shores of the Mediterranean 210
11.1.2 Beyond Barcelona 211
11.1.3 The Europeanization of North African countries 213
11.1.4 New prospects for cooperation 214
11.2 The complex relation between Islam and democracy 216
11.2.1 Democracy and Islam in the Mediterranean 216
11.3 The relation between democracy and development 219
11.3.1 Democracy as a condition of economic development 219
11.3.2 Immigration, development, and European policies 220

11.4 Europe's challenges in fostering democracy along the Mediterranean's southern shore 221
11.4.1 The European Union, human rights, and democracy 221
11.4.2 The state's security and human security as a new prospect for cooperation 223
11.4.3 A new development model 225
11.5 What next? 229
11.5.1 The Arab Spring revolutions and the possible future of Euro-Mediterranean relations 229
11.5.2 Migrations across the Mediterranean and Europe: What does the future hold? 232

Index 241

A note on the criteria for transliterating the Arabic terms

As a general rule, Arabic terms have been transliterated on a technical basis, with special glyphs for long vowels, emphatic consonants, and other phonetic phenomena specific to the Arabic language. In treating a sizable number of graphemes, however, and in keeping with a practice that is also established in linguistics, it has been decided to resort to digraphs rather than to special glyphs. Thus, for example, the letter *shīn*, ش, pronounced /ʃ/, as in *shock*, is transliterated using an *sh* rather than an *š*. This will make it easier for non-Arabist readers to understand the corresponding pronunciations, and this is the principle behind the correspondence table accompanying this note.

In treating the grapheme *tāʾ marbūṭa* (ة), used as a feminine singular suffix, it was decided—also in keeping with well-established linguistic practice—to omit its transliteration in all contexts in which the letter is voiceless. Thus we have *khalīfa* and not *khalīfah* or *khalīfat*: for phono-syntactic reasons, the final *t* will be used only in contexts in which the letter is voiced. So, for example, in the word *khalīfa*, the *tāʾ marbūṭa* is voiceless if isolated or if followed by a word that begins with a consonant, whereas it is voiced as a /t/ (in the manner of the voiced *t* in English) when connected with a word that begins with a vowel, as in *khalīfat Allāh* (deputy of God).

The proper names of historical figures and scholars have likewise been transliterated according to the criteria just outlined, except when a different spelling has gained widespread use—so much so that a strictly technical transliteration would have made it unintuitive to recognize the person in question—or when it was felt necessary to adhere phonetically to the name in question (as with Habib Bourguiba, Ben Ali, Tariq Ramadan, or Heba Ezzat). This simplifying criterion was used particularly in spelling Tunisian anthroponyms, whose pronunciation is markedly different from that of the corresponding words in classic Arabic.

A different matter is the bibliography. Here both personal names and all Arabic words contained in the titles of works appear exactly as they are used in the sources themselves, so as to make it easier to locate these sources. The fundamentalist thinker al-Mawdūdī, for example, is identified by the technical transliteration method as *Abū l-ʿAlāʾ al-Mawdūdī* in the run of text, in discursive footnote matter, and in the titles of works published in Arabic, but in the titles of works published in English the simplified spelling *Abul A'la Mawdudi* is used so as not to alter the original title.

Giuseppe Cecere

Correspondence table used in transliterating Arabic terms

ā	أ	ṭ	ط
b	ب	ẓ	ظ
t	ت	ʿ	ع
th	ث	gh	غ
j	ج	f	ف
ḥ	ح	q	ق
kh	خ	k	ك
d	د	l	ل
dh	ذ	m	م
r	ر	n	ن
z	ز	h	ه
s	س	w/ū	و
sh	ش	y/ī	ي
ṣ	ص	ʾ	ء
ḍ	ض		

Introduction

The title of this book introduces to us what I am calling the human-nonhuman distinction. This is an allusion to the long history that has set the West in opposition to peoples belonging to other civilizations and cultures, for in this history these peoples have been understood to partake of a different, and indeed inferior, humanity.

Humanitarian intervention, theorized in the latter half of the nineteenth century, was conceived for the purpose of countering "barbarism" with what were purported to be the laws of humanity. But in fact this was no more than an ideological statement concealing the hegemonic designs of the Western powers, and it was closely connected with the forms of domination that prevailed in the colonial era.

Proceeding on a "scientific" basis, colonialism got to the point of proclaiming a different human nature of the colonized so as to legitimize its own civilizing mission. The degree of violence so inflicted could only be met with the violence of peoples who endure oppression and ultimately see their own dignity being denied.

The historical snapshot just outlined frames the issues addressed in Part One of this book, which argues that humanitarian intervention reveals itself to be a "hegemonic technique" through which its own interests are represented as *universal*, when in fact they are *unilateral.*

Part Two of the book reconstructs the complex path the Arab nations embarked on once they freed themselves of colonial domination, rebuilding the state by reclaiming their own cultural identity and lifting the dead hand of the colonial past. But the account offered in Part Two also highlights the continuity between colonial rule and the national governments that replaced the colonial ones in the wake of independence.

The point of departure for these so-called Arab Springs is to be found in the attempt to give birth to democratic forms of government capable of keeping in check the autocratic elites that were wielding power in the Arab countries, but also in the emphasis placed on the Islamic tradition and in its controversial relationship to Western political culture.

The analysis we will be making of the Arab Springs—sometimes (as in Chapter 10) in the manner of reporters witnessing an unfolding story—proceeds from a recognition that their outcomes are still unforeseeable, and so we will be highlighting the plurality of solutions that are open.

The book underscores the peculiarity of Muslim cultural identity and the original forms of government it can give rise to, thus taking a perspective that cannot be reduced to that of the Western tradition. The analysis we will make of forms of government in Arab countries is accordingly comparative, bringing out the degree to which these forms of government diverge from Western ones, as well as the possible ways in which the two may converge.

Finally, we will look at Euro-Mediterranean relations, pointing out the part that Europe has played in protracting the process that sees the countries of the Mediterranean's southern shore moving towards democracy and towards forms of development that do not simply amount to a consolidation of power in the hands of the elites in government.

In this discussion we will be looking beyond the facile and mystifying conclusions asserting that it is impossible for Arab countries to achieve democratic forms of government, and in so doing (as just mentioned) we will be underscoring the role the West has had in stifling the emancipation of these peoples.

Some of the sources used in this book have been found at the Max Planck Institut für europäische Rechtsgeschichte in Frankfurt am Main. Invaluable insights have also been gleaned from the investigations in the history of law carried out by Luigi Nuzzo and Eliana Augusti. I am especially grateful to Yadh Ben Achour and Hamadi Redissi for the suggestions they have offered and for the stimulating conversations we have had on the question of democracy and constitutionalism in the Arab Islamic world, and particularly in Tunisia. The overall approach used in thrashing out the issues addressed in this book owes an important debt to Martti Koskenniemi.

I am deeply grateful to Professor Giuseppe Cecere, whose excellent training as an Arabist and a student of the Muslim civilization has been determinative in revising the text and transliterating the Arabic terms used in it. And, finally, I'd like to thank my translator, Filippo Valente, for his tireless work in smoothing out the text and making sure it was thoroughly and accurately sourced.

Part I

Intervening for humanity

1 The origins of humanitarian intervention

1.1 What legitimation for humanitarian intervention: A historical reconstruction

The doctrine of humanitarian intervention can be said to have had its first fully developed statement in the thought of Francisco de Vitoria (1483–1546). His works, considered to be among the classics of *jus gentium*, were rediscovered after World War I and are now being once more debated in the age of multiculturalism and of military intervention for the protection of human rights, and clearly outlined in these works is a paradigm that has shaped the history of *jus gentium* and its subsequent reformulation as international law.

This paradigm is built stepwise in Vitoria's *De Indis insulanis relectio prior* (1539), first framing the problem, then constructing a picture of relations among peoples, and finally systematically laying out the criteria on which basis humanitarian intervention can be justified. The problem Vitoria was tackling came into focus with the discovery of the New World, which in turn prompted the question of the nature of its native inhabitants.

The debate thus sparked by the "discovery" of New World peoples has been masterfully reconstructed by Tzvetan Todorov (1984), who traces its development from the denial of their humanity (Juan Ginés de Sepulveda) to a statement asserting their superiority (Bartolomé de las Casas). Vitoria, for his part, building on a foundation of Stoic philosophy, recognized the human nature of the Indios and argued that over their lands they exercised a coequal *dominium* with Christian peoples. From which it followed that they could not be deprived of their goods, as if they were not their true owners.[1]

Not even the diversity of customs, as exemplified by the native practice of human sacrifice, could serve as grounds for authorizing an intervention against the Indios, or a "just war" against them, considering that their manifest cruelty

1 "The conclusion of all that has been said," writes Vitoria, "is that the barbarians undoubtedly possessed as true dominion, both public and private, as any Christians. That is to say, they could not be robbed of their property, either as private citizens or as princes, on the grounds that they were not true masters (*ueri domini*)" (Vitoria [1539] 1991, question 1 [On the Dominion of the Barbarians], § 23, Conclusion, pp. 250–51).

was certainly no more brutal than the violence in which Christian peoples engaged in their own wars of religion.

Through this paradigm, Vitoria thus took on the question of the grounds for intervening in the territories inhabited by the Indios. He systematically distinguished nonlegitimate grounds (*tituli non legitimi*) from legitimate ones and proceeded to lay out what the latter might be for the Spanish conquest of the New World. Thus, while on the one hand the diversity of customs, no matter how savage they might be, could not justify intervention, it was on the other hand argued to be legitimate to intervene in order to protect the lives of the innocent who were subject to such violence. To establish this legitimate ground, Vitoria looked to Scripture, where the imperative is found that the innocent are to be delivered from the infliction of death.[2]

This first paradigm addresses a question that can only improperly be called "humanitarian intervention"—an idea that, as we will see, does not fully take shape until the nineteenth century (Rougier 1910, 472). It is instead the idea of a "just war" that frames the problem at this early stage, and in Vitoria the argument is thus built by identifying certain "just causes" or legitimate grounds. It is in this way, by relying on the just causes built into this paradigm, that *jus gentium* sought to justify the West's colonization of New World peoples.

The historical transformations this paradigm would go through are essentially tied to the need to adapt its forms of legitimation to a variety of changing historical contexts. Thus in the history of *jus gentium*, a century after Vitoria set out his theses, his original paradigm was already secularized through and through. This can be appreciated in the work of Hugo Grotius, whose concern was with the problem of the limits that might be imposed on national sovereignty within the system of states, by this time fully established.

Grotius made an argument in favour of sovereignty, to this end relying on a theory of rights under which a right, understood as a power (*facultas*) over goods, can be distinguished as either private or public. A private *facultas* is one that *individuals* exercise over their own interests; a public *facultas*, by contrast, is exercised by the *sovereign* to protect the common good or welfare. Implicit in this distinction, according to Grotius, is the tenet of the superior status of sovereignty, and on this basis he also argues that no right of resistance exists against any exercise of sovereignty, even in the face of cruelty by a sovereign acting in violation of the common good.

But that conclusion, on this line of reasoning, only applies to the sovereign's own subjects. It does not make it illegitimate for a foreign sovereign to take up arms so as to put an end to persecutions which a sovereign prince carries out against his own people, thereby imperilling their lives (Grotius [1720] 2005, bk. II, chap. XXV, § VIII, 1159–62; orig. pub. 1625). Here, in *De Jure Belli*

2 Vitoria quotes the Book of Proverbs (24:11): "Deliver them that are drawn unto death, and forbear not to deliver those that are ready to be slain" (Vitoria [1539] 1991, question 3, article 5, § 15, p. 288).

ac Pacis, Grotius looks not to Scripture but natural law. It is equally clear, however, that so-called just causes can be instrumental and can thus be invoked to advance hegemonic aims. In fact, they can conceal the deepest injustice within a system of states fundamentally driven by the pursuit of their own power.

It appears equally clear that different forms of legitimation are closely linked to the institutional configurations that define relations among peoples and states. Thus in Vitoria the criteria of "just war" find their foundation in the still premodern reality of the *respublica christiana*; in Grotius sovereignty instead finds its limits in the relations that make up the states-system, and newer criteria of legitimation would henceforth be established by reference to the institutional frameworks that would subsequently take shape.

Thus in the wake of World War I a new international order took shape with the creation of the League of Nations, which some observers saw as heralding a new system of relations among states. In the work of Georges Scelle, for example, the League of Nations was conceived as a federative system that had given birth to a suprastate social organization. In this new federative phenomenon, for Scelle, lay the foundation of possible intervention—military or humanitarian—whose legitimacy was to be found in the need to preserve the international suprastate order.[3]

From a historical perspective, then, there clearly emerges (however, much within the limits of this sketchy and perhaps even cursory reconstruction) that the criteria of legitimation are closely bound up with the forms of institutional organization that solidify among states. In Chapter 4, we will see how this relation of legitimacy unfolds in the modern reality. But there is a basic paradigm that over the course of time has consistently been used to assert the legitimacy of humanitarian interventions, and it is to the task of blocking out this paradigm that we now turn.

1.2 The theory of humanitarian intervention: Barbarous humanity and the civilization of European peoples

In a critical essay of the early twentieth century, the French jurist Antoine Rougier (1910, 473) observed that in the sources of international European law in the latter half of the nineteenth century, explicit reference was made to the "laws of humanity" (*lois de l'humanité*),[4] which were set in contrast to the logic of "savage" and "partially civilized" peoples.

Thus, James Lorimer, a Scottish internationalist of the second half of the nineteenth century, proceeded on the basis of natural law to divide humanity

3 Scelle (1934, 31) wrote that the purpose of intervention was to maintain public international order and to secure the establishment of law, and paradigmatically this was the purpose of humanitarian intervention (*intervention d'humanité*).

4 The essay offers a broad and deep reconstruction of the theory of humanitarian intervention in the nineteenth century.

into three concentric spheres—civilized (Europe and the states in the American continent that had gained their independence from the Europeans), barbarous (Turkey and the Asian states that had not become European dependencies), and savage ("the residue of mankind")—to which three kinds of recognition would attach: "plenary political recognition," "partial political recognition," and "natural or mere human recognition," respectively (Lorimer 1883, vol. I, bk. II, chap. II, p. 101–2). This, he took to be the foundation for the unequal treaties that were in effect between different states.

In states regarded as falling within the sphere of "barbarous humanity," power could be wielded only by recourse to the force of arms. It was on the basis of this "argument from barbarousness" that European governments sought to legitimize their foreign policy positions. This was the argument that France, for example, used in the late nineteenth century to speak against an African sovereign's attempt to count human sacrifice as an institution sanctioned by the state, as well as against the torture to which a Moroccan sultan treated its political adversaries. These customs "appeared intolerable to the conscience of European peoples, who had been formed in the cult of morality and law" (Rougier 1910, 469; my translation). This is an assessment that Rougier offered without any sense of self-criticism. Which looks like an even greater moral failing if we consider that these comments were being made at a time when Western colonialism was at its zenith. Rougier went on to identify "not only a right but also a duty" to prevent such forms of barbarism, in that European peoples had committed to the "noble mission of bringing a germ of civilization to barbarous lands" (ibid.). In these words we have the constitutive elements of humanitarian intervention.

A state that acted contrary to the laws of humanity would be placed under international scrutiny, and this would in turn trigger a right of intervention on the part of any number of foreign states. At the same time, this paradigm supported a new conception of the international society as a hierarchy of powers entrusted with enforcing the principles of justice.

In the name of the international society, then, this doctrine recognized the right of one or more states to intervene in response to the sovereign acts of a foreign state that might violate the human rights of its own people. On this basis, an intervening state could request the annulment of sovereign acts subject to criticism or could work to prevent such acts from happening again in the future, or again it could take urgent precautionary measures designed to forestall any action the foreign government might take, all the while momentarily replacing the latter's sovereignty with its own (ibid., 472).

The humanitarian intervention that was beginning to come into form in the latter half of the nineteenth century looked rather different from the scenarios envisaged in the theories through which authors like Vitoria and Grotius sought to legitimize recourse to armed force by one state acting against the tyranny of another. Indeed, whereas these classic theorists of *jus gentium* rested their doctrines on a *moral* foundation, the new paradigm was essentially *juridical* in its makeup.

In the background of the idea of humanitarian intervention was mainly the so-called question of the East, for it was in response to the actions taken by the

Ottoman government that international diplomacy was set in motion with the first uses of the doctrines based on this juridical paradigm. Indeed, among the grounds of legitimate humanitarian intervention was the notion of "reason of humanity" (*raison d'humanité*), which in the context of the 1860 Civil War in Syria (or Mount Lebanon Civil War) was invoked to justify the French expedition to help pacify that region (at the time an Ottoman province).

The French intervention continued by diplomatic action, and its effect was to enable control over the internal sovereignty of the Ottoman Empire, forcing the Sublime Porte to reform its administrative organization. This intervention, creating a sort of special public law governing relations between Europe and the Ottoman authorities, became the object of an analysis that underscored the new kind of limitation of sovereignty which it put into place.

While states were recognized as having a legitimate interest in intervening abroad to guarantee their own self-preservation—protecting their own citizens by acting to contain the threat posed by a foreign power—or to protect their own financial interests, or again to enforce treaty provisions, humanitarian intervention was, by contrast, cast as disinterested: it was indeed said to take the (presumably universal and objective) "laws of humanity" as its foundation.

This right to intervene forms the subject of a revealing essay that appeared in 1876 in the *Revue de Droit International et de Législation Comparée*, giving a good sense of all the misconceptions and ambiguities which at the time accompanied the study of international law. The author of the essay, the jurist Rolin-Jaequemyns, was the journal's editor-in-chief, and in it he published a letter that had been sent to him by Prof. Arntz of Brussels, taking a position in favour of the principle of nonintervention but pointing out two exceptions to it.

The grounds identified as exceptions to nonintervention could easily lend themselves to instrumental uses. The first such exception, according to Arntz, emerged when a state violated or threatened to violate the rights of one or more other states, making it impossible for these states to coexist on regular terms,[5] and giving the aggrieved states a right to intervene in their own self-defence. But the idea that a threat or even a perceived threat was enough to justify intervention clearly brings to light the way in which one or more states could leverage their own power to limit the power of another state.

Even more problematic is Arntz's second exception, under which it would have been legitimate to intervene in the sovereign affairs of a state that should violate the rights of humanity with such a degree of injustice and cruelty as to offend Western customs and civilization (in Rolin-Jaequemyns 1876b, 675).

The scenario envisaged by Arntz was that of a conflict between sovereign rights and the rights of humanity or of human society. But concepts so vague

5 Letter by E. R. N. Arntz, reproduced in Rolin-Jaequemyns 1876b. On the debate between Arntz and Rolin-Jaequemyns, see Heraclides 2014, 33 and 41ff. The essay offers a complete and systematic analysis of the debate on humanitarian intervention that international lawyers were engaged in from the first half of the nineteenth century to the early twentieth century.

as that of humanity or fictive entities like that of human society could easily be invoked by any state looking to advance its own power interests, or they could be let go of if they did not serve such interests.

To appreciate how problematic and still inadequate this conception was, consider that Arntz developed it on the basis of a faulty analogy between individual liberty, subject to the limits of law and custom, and "the states' individual liberty," subject to the limits imposed by the rights of human society.

Finally, Arntz's paradigm revealed itself to be Eurocentric in its view that the right of intervention could not be exercised individually by a single state but rather belonged jointly to the greatest number of civil states, for it was best understood as a right of collective intervention carried out in the name of humanity. Arntz's conception appears even more loaded if we consider that, by his own recounting, it had been developed with an eye to the situation in the Ottoman Empire.

In reply to Arntz's letter, Rolin-Jaequemyns stated that he certainly did agree on the soundness of the first ground on which Arntz based the right of intervention, for on this basis intervention could be framed as a case of legitimate defence (ibid., 677). But the fundamental problem with the right of intervention had to do with *second* ground adduced by Arntz, arguing that this right could legitimately be exercised to redress the injustices or serious wrongs a state might inflict on its own people or on humanity.

In constructing a counterargument, Rolin-Jaequemyns studiously reconstructs the classics of *jus gentium* so as to identify in them the criteria by which humanitarian intervention might be legitimized. He concludes that the foundation for this kind of intervention is to be found especially in the *De Jure Belli ac Pacis* (1625), where Grotius argues that violations of justice could legitimately be met with intervention on the basis of a *jus humanae societatis* (or "right of human society") deriving from natural law.[6]

Grotius's theses came under the utilitarian criticism of Emer de Vattel, who argued that a sovereign can claim the right to punish offences against natural law only on the condition that these offences violate the sovereign's own rights or threaten the sovereign's own security.[7] So here, instead of advancing a ***normative*** conception predicated on the need to redress violations of morality on the

6 "But if the Injustice be visible, as if a *Busiris*, a *Phalaris*, or a *Thracian Diomedes* exercise such Tyrannies over Subjects, as no good Man living can approve of, the Right of human Society shall not be therefore excluded" (Grotius [1720] 2005, bk. II, chap. XXV, § VIII.2, p. 1161). The Latin original: "Si quis Busiris, Phalaris, Trax Diomedes ea in subditos exerceat, quae aequo nulli probentur, ideo praeclusum erit ius humanae societatis?" (Grotius [1646] 1913, lib. II, cap. XXV, § VIII, p. 414; see also lib. II, cap. 20, § 40).

7 "What led him [Grotius] into this error, was his attributing to every independent man, and of course to every sovereign, an odd kind of right to punish faults which involve an enormous violation of the laws of nature, though they do not affect either his rights or his safety" (Vattel [1797] 2008, bk. II, chap. I, § 7, p. 265). The French original: "Il [Grotius] est tombé dans cette erreur, parce qui'l attribue à tout homme indépendant, et par là même à tout souverain, je ne sais quel droit de punir les fautes qui renferment une violation énorme du droit de la nature, même celles qui n'intéressent ni ses droits ni sa sûreté" (Vattel [1758] 1916, liv. II, chap. I, § 7, p. 263).

basis of principles of justice, Vattel is giving us a *realistic* conception predicated exclusively on the need to protect the state's security.

Rolin-Jaequemyns looks at these two conceptions in comparison and finds that Vattel's is too limiting, precisely because it reduces the right to punish to the need to protect a state's right to its own security. Grotius, by contrast, was prescient because, as Rolin-Jaequemyns reads him, he foresaw the direction that modern legal science would take. Specifically, Grotius's modernity could be appreciated in his having identified a right of human society, even if he did not go far enough in developing this idea, in that he understood this as an *individual* right and not yet as a right that states should exercise *collectively*.

But in reality, even if Vattel did take issue with Grotius by making a *principled* statement against the morally laden conception, the practical *application* of the two conceptions made the distinction between them less significant in practice than it might in theory. In fact, as Vattel argued, "if there were a people who made open profession of trampling justice under foot—who despised and violated the rights of others whenever they found an opportunity—the interest of human society would authorise all the other nations to form a confederacy in order to humble and chastise the delinquents" (Vattel [1797] 2008, bk. II, chap. 5, § 70, p. 297). So even Vattel envisaged situations in which nations would be legitimated in banding together in the name of "human society" (*la société humaine*) (Vattel [1758] 1916, vol. I, liv. II, chap. V, § 70, p. 308). This may look a lot like the scenario envisioned by Grotius, in that both thinkers invoke the protection of human society as the basis on which states may intervene in the affairs of other states. But there is an important difference, in that this human society, on Vattel's conception, is understood *realistically* as a coalition of interests and not yet as an ideal legal community or polity: on the one hand, with Vattel, we are looking at a reality of contending parties who might find some common ground despite their opposing interests; on the other hand, with Grotius, we are aspiring to construct an international community based on principles of law serving as clearly stated criteria in light of which to (a) determine whether a violation of rights has been committed and, if so, to (b) justify intervening in order to redress the violation.

1.3 Natural law and "Human law": Western humanity's principle of solidarity

If in the seventeenth and eighteenth centuries the principles of natural law served as a reference point for Grotius and Vattel, in the nineteenth century the very *concept* of natural law came under criticism as a construct that, being "much more moral than legal, did not make it possible to achieve an adequate degree of accuracy in determining which acts this supreme rule permitted and which it prohibited" (Rougier 1910, 490; my translation). This sentiment was widely shared in the nineteenth century; indeed, as is known, this was the century of legal positivism, which saw that the certainty of law it cherished could not be guaranteed on a natural law foundation.

Thus natural law was displaced by the more legalistic conception of law as a *human* construct. We found this in authors like Arntz and Rolin-Jaequemyns, but also writing in this vein was Antoine Pillet (professor of international law at the University of Grenoble), who saw the peoples of the world as being organized on three levels: that of (1) *national* society, where we are concerned with relations among individuals within the same national boundaries; that of (2) *international* society, within which we are to frame relations among states; and that of (3) *human* society, where the essential relationship is that which exists among human beings without regard to the polity or nation they belong to. Each of these three levels of society, according to Pillet, was governed by its own law: we thus have (1) national or domestic law, (2) international law, and (3) the law of human society.[8] This human law, Pillet explained, consists in "a set of obligatory principles which in the quality of our being human finds a sufficient ground of application" (ibid.; my translation).

In commenting on Pillet's definition, Rougier attempted to clarify the scope of his human law by describing it as the highest source of law, for it answered "the deepest and most durable needs of human nature." As such it had to "necessarily seep into national as well as international law," for it was concerned to protect the human rights (*droits humains*) of everyone who belongs to a national society or the international society (Rougier 1910, 492; my translation).

This human law could be observed at work in the course it charted on both the national and the international level: it lies behind the political liberties recognized by the states, and in international law, it led to the protections recognized for prisoners of war, the end of the slave trade, and the establishment of international arbitration, among other developments. This makes it possible to identify the foundation that, from the nineteenth-century debate onward, human law was understood to rest on, namely, the principle of solidarity among humans. Rougier pointed out that the same view had previously been expounded by Léon Duguit, whose investigation of public law (Duguit 1901) led him to the conclusion that in social or human solidarity lay the fundamental legal principle, which positive law needed to embody if it was to be recognized as legitimate. In short, "human law is the most general expression of human solidarity" (ibid., 493; my translation). But as E. H. Carr (2001, 79) would later comment, and as Martti Koskenniemi (2004, 201) quotes him approvingly, "pleas for international solidarity and world union come from those dominant nations which may hope to exercise control over a unified world."

But what *content* did human law need to take if it was to serve as the ultimate foundation of positive law? Human solidarity required *all* human activities and interests to be protected, and human law accordingly needed to encompass the right to life and liberty and to the rule of law, understood as the right to a legal system under which these human rights would be recognized and guaranteed.

In the Western debate of the nineteenth century, human law and the rights it encompassed were introduced as an aim recognized by all "civilized states," and thus was closed the circle that outlined the paradigm of humanitarian

8 In Pillet's (1894, 13) own words: "Nous arrivons ainsi au troisième et dernier échelon de notre progression. A la plus générale des trois formes de société doit correspondre le plus général des tous les droits; à la communauté humaine, un droit humain."

intervention: the West had depicted this community of states as a community committed to the principle of human solidarity—a principle whose legal embodiment was that of human law—and now this conceit became the foundation on which to legitimize humanitarian intervention. It was thus a specific depiction or *representation* of Western humanity that served as the criterion by which to judge other peoples as nonhuman. Indeed, as Rougier concluded:

> When violations of human solidarity are [...] the work of a barbarous or semi-civilized state [*État barbare ou mi-civilisé* ...], the civilized powers are duty-bound to resort to a more energetic mode of control aimed more at *preventing* the harm than at suppressing or redressing it. Simple intervention will in that case be replaced by a permanent right to protect: this is the right the Western powers have claimed for themselves vis-à-vis the Ottoman Porte. (Rougier 1910, 497; my translation)

According to this doctrine, this kind of protection could be exercised even more strictly—to the point of establishing a protectorate—or it might have enabled the European states to claim the "right to civilize" the most "backward" tribes of Africa: this is what in the *Code de droit international* Johann Caspar Bluntschli called *droit de la civilisation* (see Bluntschli 1895, livre IV, art. 280, 174–75), though it was, in the end, a way to camouflage the annexation of territories (Rougier 1910, 497).

1.4 The Eastern question

In the second half of the nineteenth century, the problem of humanitarian intervention was brought paradigmatically into focus by the so-called Eastern question. With the crisis of the Ottoman Empire, the European powers saw an opportunity to justify their call for intervention. But a joint European initiative could not be justified without theoretical backing, and to that end, the internationalists of the time were entrusted with constructing an appropriate set of concepts and principles.

In the *Revue de Droit International et de Legislation Comparée*, Rolin-Jaequemyns devoted a long article to the Eastern question, arguing for a sense of responsibility and a consequent duty incumbent on Europe to intervene collectively. By recourse to stereotypes that would now be recognized as racist, and by positing an insuperable clash between civilization and religion, Rolin-Jaequemyns depicted the Turks as "Shiites (the original inhabitants of Scythia) or Tartars, whose blood is mixed with that of slaves, and who are rejected by all nations" (Rolin-Jaequemyns 1876a, 298; my translation): they were distinguished by a "roughness and pride" of character (ibid.) that ran contrary to the spirit of progress. Their position he set in contrast to that of the Christian peoples of the European continent, who formed a natural and historical group which in certain circumstances had a right as well as a duty to act collectively with a single voice. This had happened at the time of the Crusades, when all intra-European rivalries were set aside for the sake of the common interest of Christian civilization, and everyone found unity under a single idea which was neither military nor theocratic but simply human, and which could have been pursued either peacefully or by recourse to war, depending on the available means and opportunities (ibid., 300–1).

In the second half of the nineteenth century, the Ottoman Empire could still claim to be in the vanguard of Islam, but since it had been losing strength as a military power, it could rule its subjects only by repressive means. It was in this context that a growing number of voices in Europe began to reject the idea of the balance of power in favour of a policy relying on a system of international law under which the shifting interests of players seeking their own advantage would yield to the permanent interests of humanity (ibid., 301). We have here an example of what Koskenniemi (2004, 199) has termed the *hegemonic technique*, which consists in taking a partial viewpoint (here the conception of international law and policy advocated by Europe) and presenting it as universal. Which is to say that, in pretending to universality, a conception is most likely to conceal an imperialist motive (Jouannet 2007, 396).

This takes us back to the declining Ottoman Empire, which in the 1520s was expanding and reaching the peak of its power—gaining control over half of Hungary in 1526, and then laying siege to Vienna in 1529—but by the second half of the nineteenth century, it could no longer strike any sense of fear into the European powers. In fact, its weakness made it a prey, destined to be broken up by the European powers—an enterprise that would be accomplished while parading an array of grand-sounding concepts like "humanity," "justice," and "history"!

Rolin-Jaequemyns reconstructs the treaties that served as stepping stones to that gradual conquest, reading them not in that light (as treaties marking successive phases of conquest) but, more nobly, as markers of a progression in which foreign policy would increasingly be guided by principles of law (*maximes de droit*). Thus in the 1827 Treaty of London, signed on July 6, under which the United Kingdom, France, and Russia acted jointly to remove Greece from Turkish control, we find it stated, in the preamble, that the signatories "have resolved to combine their efforts, and to regulate the operation [of the state of affairs involving the Greeks vis-à-vis the Ottoman Porte], by a formal Treaty, for the object of re-establishing peace between the contending parties, by means of an arrangement called for, no less by sentiments of humanity, than by interests for the tranquillity of Europe" (cf. Rolin-Jaequemyns 1876a, 311). But by the terms of a secret pact, if the Ottoman Empire refused to recognize Greek sovereignty over its own territory, the three signatories would take measures in support of the Greek claims to independence. One outcome of this pact was the Battle of Navarino of October 20, 1827, in which the combined British, French, and Russian fleet destroyed the Egyptian fleet commanded by Ibrahim Pasha, which had been sent to aid the Ottoman forces. And another outcome was the French Morea expedition.[9]

9 The Morea is the Peloponnese, which France occupied in October 1828 in the wake of Navarino. On the naval Battle of Navarino and on French policy in Greece, see Ancel 1931, 65–89.

Next came the 1856 Treaty of Paris, which settled the Crimean War, in which Britain, France, and the Kingdom of Sardinia allied ostensibly to protect the Ottoman Empire against Russian efforts to expand into its territory. What the war gave rise to instead was a sort protectorate which the European powers exercised over the weakening empire. Indeed, as much as these powers, under Article VII of the Treaty, agreed to "declare the Sublime Porte admitted to participate in the advantages of the Public Law and System (Concert) of Europe," they included this provision only after the Sublime Porte issued a *firmān* (or decree) that, in addition to introducing measures designed to ensure good governance, fight corruption, and the like, also established a principle of religious, military, and civil equality under which the different religious groups within the empire were enabled to exercise their rights of personal status.[10]

These commitments the Ottoman Empire made had been held out by the European powers as a necessary condition for bringing the empire into the fold of civilized states.[11] At the same time, however, they acted as "tripwires," for

10 On February 18, 1856, under the Ottoman reform movement known as Tanẓīmāt, the empire issued an Imperial Reform Edict (*khatt-i hümâyûn*) granting equal rights to Muslim and non-Muslim subjects alike and expanding the rights previously recognized under the Gülhane Imperial Edict of 3 November 1839. In the latter—also known as Noble Edict of the Rose Chamber (*khatt-i cherîf* or *khatt-i hümâyûn*), named for the place where it was proclaimed, namely, Gülhane Park, adjacent to the Topkapı Palace in Istanbul—we find the recognition of "guarantees ensuring a perfect security for our subjects as regards their life, their honour, and their fortune" (Collas 1864, 414; my translation). Further on we find the right to property: "Each individual will be able to own property of any nature and will be able to use it freely, without hindrance from anyone" (ibid., 416). And then we have a principle of equality and generality: "These imperial concessions are granted to all individuals, whatever religion or sect they may belong to; everyone can enjoy them without exception" (ibid.). The 1856 edict guaranteed life and security and freedom of conscience, to which it added a menu of specific equal-protection guarantees, requiring Ottoman courts to recognize the validity of testimony given by Christians, for example, or prohibiting tax discrimination on account of religion. On the disputed question of the import of these normative innovations—whether they are to be understood as modernization processes or as measures designed to win the European powers' support against the threat of Russian expansionism—see the excellent Augusti 2013, 56–62 and 84–93. See also Testa Bappenheim 2006, 412–13. On the Tanẓīmāt period, see Dumont 1989, 459–522.

11 Not until the nineteenth century did European law begin to interact with Ottoman law. As Esin Örücü (1992, 40) observes: "Europe did not expand into the Ottoman Empire, except for voluntary borrowings, imitations and adaptations, albeit sometimes under pressure, because no part of the Ottoman Empire was ever a colony [...]. Even in the nineteenth century, when changes were introduced into the Ottoman legal system partly as a result of Western political demands and pressures, they were not impositions but rather imposed receptions, that is, not thrust from without, but received voluntarily by the appropriate organs of the legal system within."

Only under Maḥmūd II (1808–39) did modernization movements begin to affect the empire's legal system. With the help of the grand vizier Mustafa Reşid Paşa, Maḥmūd II gave start to the Tanẓīmāt reform process (see note 10), through which the Ottoman legal system was Westernized through the adoption of (Western) foreign codes (ibid., 44).

if the empire failed to live up to them, the European powers could take that as grounds for collective intervention, which is precisely what on several occasions happened after the 1856 Treaty of Paris was signed.

We can see this, for example, with the Mount Lebanon civil war of 1860, when thousands of Christians were slain by the Druze, who were backed by the Ottoman Empire. This prompted Napoleon III to intervene with an expeditionary force,[12] which put an end to the killing and set up an independent administrative entity: a *mutaṣarrifiyya* headed by a Christian administrator supported by officials representing other religious and ethnic groups.[13]

By the time we get to the Mount Lebanon civil war, then, we have a clear picture of the elements, both legal and factual, that in the eyes of the European

12 In 1860, an anti-Christian revolt broke out that claimed no less than a thousand lives. As a result of the equal status that Christians had gained under the Tanẓīmāt reforms of 1839 and 1856 (see note 10), Muslims increasingly became resentful, coming to view the reforms as the outcome of a Christian conspiracy (see Traboulsi 2007, 36). In a bid to restore its own authority over Lebanon, the Sublime Porte sent its foreign minister Fu'ad Pasha, who had the governor of Beirut placed under arrest, and in Damascus had the governor of the city arrested and executed. Despite these measures, Napoleon III felt it necessary to militarily intervene in Lebanon—which he did in August 1860, sending a fleet of 6,000 troops there under the command of General Beaufort d'Hautpoul. The task assigned to the military expedition was to work alongside the Ottoman authorities, restore peace, come to the aid of Christians, and protect the interests of French capital invested in silk farming, making it possible for the workers engaged in this sector to resume their work (ibid., 38; cf. Rodogno 2011, 175ff.). This French intervention was functional to Napoleon III's plan to expand into the Near East (in this regard, see Dumont 1989, 503–4; see also Herren 2012). Napoleon III's intent was to establish an Arab kingdom serving as a buffer state between Anatolia and the Suez Canal (Traboulsi 2007, 38).

13 After the French militarily intervened in Lebanon, a commission was set up in Beirut by Great Britain, France, Prussia, Russia, and Austria: it met from October 1860 to March 1861, overseeing the post-civil war reconstruction and reshaping the social, political, and legal system of Mount Lebanon, which had been established in the early sixteenth century as a province of the Ottoman Empire. On June 9, 1861, a *Règlement Organique* was signed making Mount Lebanon into a *mutaṣarrifiyya* enjoying a limited political and administrative autonomy within the empire. Behind its semi-independence stood the *règlement*'s European signatory powers, which Italy joined in 1867 (see Traboulsi 2007, 43). The *mutaṣarrifiyya*, formed out of two preexisting administrative units called *Qa'im maqāmiyyatayn*, was headed by a non-Arab Ottoman Christian administrator who answered directly to the Sublime Porte and included an administrative council made up of twelve elected officials, six of whom were Christian and six Muslim. Subsequently, in 1864, this balance was tipped in favour of the Christian membership, with seven Christian councillors against five Muslim ones (ibid.). The *mutaṣarrifiyya*'s semi-independence was the outcome of a compromise struck between the Ottoman Empire and France, which agreed to abandon its project to establish an Arab kingdom and to instead support a colonial model that "encouraged provincial and ethnic autonomy in the development of a world division of labour" (ibid., 41; see also Gordon 1980, 45).

powers justified them in intervening collectively against a foreign power, and specifically, in the case at hand, against the Ottoman Empire.[14]

We can unpack this idea by going back to Rolin-Jaequemyns, for on the one hand, he points out that "modern international law rightly disallows intervention in a state's domestic affairs" (Rolin-Jaequemyns 1876a, 369; my translation). But on the other hand, he immediately qualifies this principle by introducing two gaping caveats. For one thing, he comments, "the state in question needs to be worthy of its name, meaning that it should embody the rational conception of a harmonic whole, embracing all peoples who form a single territory, and who do not fall subject to the organized domination of one nation over several others" (ibid.). And, for another thing, "the state in question needs to be capable of living, and cannot simply be a political cadaver in decomposition" (ibid.). In granting that this is a dangerous qualification apt to be abused, he nonetheless holds it up as an "incontestable truth," to this end quoting Bluntschli, who in *Das moderne Völkerrecht* commented that "the law of peoples only protects viable states. [...] 'Only the living can have rights.'"[15]

Having stipulated these two conditions, he proceeds to argue that the Ottoman Empire fails in both respects and thus forms an exception to the principle of non-intervention. Indeed, for one thing, "the Ottoman Empire is not a state in the modern sense of the word" but rather exists as "the historical superimposition of one Muslim people over a multiplicity of Christian peoples" (Rolin-Jaequemyns 1876a, 369),[16] considering that the Turks as a nation accounted for no more than a fourth of East Thrace, or European Turkey (about 2,210,000 Turks out of 8,396,000 inhabitants), and that Muslims "of all races" did not even account for half the population (ibid., 370). And, for another thing, turning specifically to Turkey, the country "finds itself in a state of moral and financial bankruptcy" (ibid., 374), so much so that it lacks the means by which to pull itself up by its own bootstraps: "it can only sink deeper, not only to its own detriment but to

14 Consider in this regard the assessment made by Friedrich Martens, professor at the University of Saint Petersburg and member of the Institut de Droit International: "It is Russia that until now has been the best safeguard for the interests of humanity in behalf of the oppressed populations of Turkey," and which "absent an agreement among the European powers, has always been ready to act on its own to put an end to the Turks' excesses against Christians [...]" (Martens 1877b, 50; my translation). Similarly appealing to the high principle of the rights of humanity as a basis of intervention was the French diplomat Édouard Engelhardt, commenting that "intervention can be legitimized only when a state threatens the security and legitimate interests of another, when by persistent action it threatens to upset a balance, or when it commits a 'gross violation' of the rights of humanity" (Engelhardt 1880, 10–11; my translation).

15 My translation from the German original: "Das Völkerrecht schützt nur lebensfähige Staten. [...] 'Nur der Lebende hat Recht'" (Bluntschli 1868, § 61).

16 In presenting this part of Rolin-Jaequemyns's argument, I will ignore the distinction (which he appears to ignore) between a nation-state (a single nation formed into a state) and an empire (typically multinational).

that of the entire world" (ibid.). It is in this in landscape that the "rights" ascribed to the so-called Concert of Europe (*concert européen*) were forged.

The Concert of Europe, as dissected by Rolin-Jaequemyns, consisted in the concerted action of those "self-proclaimed" great powers that "on many occasions have claimed for themselves the right to interpose their mediation or their intervention to reestablish peace in Europe, act in the interest of humanity, and, more to the point, [...] *to represent the whole of Europe in its relations with Oriental peoples*" (Rolin-Jaequemyns 1876a, 368; italics in the original).

Having lucidly identified the problem, he ties himself into a knot trying to provide a foundation for the legitimacy of European intervention. He begins with a factual premise by noting that if the international society "were completely organized, it would be headed by a regularly constituted authority capable of deliberating and acting on a permanent basis according to certain well-defined principles." But this is not yet "a perfect state," and so it is "headed by the authority, at once imperfect and intermittent, of the most powerful of its members. Its authority has already manifested itself in the form of conferences, congresses, and even interventions" (ibid., 368–69). What is striking, at this point, is that the state of affairs he is describing in the second half of the nineteenth century looks exactly like the state of international relations such as they now exist in the contemporary age.

But even more striking, perhaps, is how, on this premise, he builds the foundation on which to justify a right of intervention. For the next remarks, in relation to the authority exercised under this system: "We will not say that it has always manifested itself in the wisest or most correct way. But we must not confuse a right (*le droit*) with its more or less reasonable exercise" (ibid., 369). And then he qualifies this statement by ascribing a duty to the great powers who take it upon themselves to intervene under this authority: "Corresponding to any right (*tout droit*)," he comments, "is a duty incumbent on the very entities that possess that right (*le droit*). The duty of the great powers is, on the one hand, not to use their international authority beyond its proper limits and, on the other hand, to use this authority effectively when the interests of humanity, and generally of peace, clearly require it" (ibid.). So the right of humanitarian intervention rests on the duty of the great powers to exercise it wisely within its proper limits and effectively in the interests of peace.

We will see that the basic elements of this paradigm will come up again in the contemporary doctrine of the responsibility to protect: the terminology will be different, to be sure, and so will the international scenario to which it will apply, but there is a case to be made that the "discourse" through which, in the second half of the nineteenth century, Western values were expressed as universal laws of humanity is still very much with us, propounding different forms of universalism that can still be analysed as expressions of Western values, as can be appreciated if we only consider the universality claimed for human rights today.

At the end of the nineteenth century, the European powers entrusted to themselves the historical task of putting an end to the "unjust" supremacy which the Ottomn Empire pretended to exercise over the Christian peoples subject to Turkish rule. The time had come for magniloquent words and idealities! The

Concert of Europe needed to act unilaterally as a collective body "for the cause of humanity, liberty, justice" (ibid., 385).

In reality, the European powers wanted to bring the Ottoman Empire under their hegemony, proceeding to gradually dismantle it by increasingly conferring administrative or political autonomy on the Ottoman provinces—a process brought definitively to completion with the close of World War I.

1.5 Partitioning the empire

The process just outlined, however, traces its origins to a much earlier time than World War I. For the Ottoman Empire had long before entered a slow decline that had already prompted the European powers to draw up plans by which to carve it up among themselves. In a 10 September 1782 letter sent to the Holy Roman Emperor Joseph II of Austria, Catherine the Great of Russia proposed rebuilding the Byzantine Empire by dissolving Turkey.

Under the plan, Austria and Russia would not have had to share a border, and Catherine the Great accordingly envisaged the birth of a new independent state, namely, Dacia, which would have comprised the provinces of Moldavia, Wallachia, and Bessarabia under the rule of a sovereign of Greek religious faith. The Ottoman Empire would then have been partitioned between the two allies under an equal distribution of territorial gains. In this way, the empress hoped to "deliver Europe from the enemy of Christians by throwing him out of Constantinople" (quoted in Kamarowsky 1896, 405; my translation). But the death of Joseph II put an end to this attempt to break up the Ottoman Empire.

The project was revived by Nicholas I of Russia, who in 1833 drew up a plan to rebuild the Byzantine Empire on the ruins of the Turkish Empire. But this plan met with the firm rejection of Austria's foreign minister, Klemens von Metternich, who unequivocally stated that Vienna would have done everything in its power to preserve the status quo, since an end to the Ottoman Empire would have been contrary to the interests of both Austria and Russia (ibid., 407).

Clearly displayed in this exchange is the contradiction of the great powers. For, on the one hand, as we have seen, in taking note of the Turkish decline, they instrumentally declare it to be morally debased, while also taking it as axiomatic that Islam is incompatible with Christianity,[17] but on the other hand they revealed themselves to be incapable of joint action, since they were divided by "the deeply conflicting political interests [...] of Russia and western Europe" (Kamarowsky 1896 403; my translation). "The great powers fear and firmly reject the notion that Russia should establish itself in the Balkan Peninsula. They are so blinded by passion that they refuse to recognize the rights of the Balkan peoples, elevating the fact of the existence of the Sublime Porte to the status of an immutable 'international dogma' (ibid.).

17 "The experience of the centuries," Friedrich Martens commented, "demonstrates that Islam and Christianity, Turks and Christians, the Turkish regime and the Christian communities cannot in any way live in peace" (Martens 1877a, 42–43; my translation).

In summarizing his thinking on the "Eastern question," Kamarowsky, an internationalist at the University of Moscow, noted that if "the preservation of Turkey as an independent power among Christian nations has become an anachronism, this is due only to the rivalries by which the great powers are most regrettably divided" (ibid, 427–28). For an adequate solution to this situation, he argued, it was necessary to rely on international law, which represented "the path of moral duty and justice—the only path that befits powers that call themselves 'great' and 'Christian'" (ibid., 428). And "what must the great powers do to proceed along this path?" Kamarowsky asks. He answers that "having in point of fact been the *family of civilized nations*, they have to form a *legal organization*. While preserving these powers' internal independence, this organization will enable them, by their joint effort, to solve in short order all the great problems [...] that currently beset humanity" (ibid.; italics in the original), and that applied to the Eastern question as well, thereby putting an end to the "anachronistic" reality of the Ottoman Empire.

As it turned out, the great powers never managed to work out their conflicting interests. Still, that did not prevent them from proceeding to dismember the Ottoman Empire, nor could the process be stopped once set in motion. Thus new political entities were formed within the empire, as happened with Montenegro, Serbia, and Romania under the 1878 Treaty of Berlin,[18] while other territories were placed under occupation, as in the case of Cyprus, which Great Britain took administrative control of in negotiating the same treaty, and Egypt, which it occupied in 1882.

Also in sight was the occupation of the Turkish territories of the Middle East and North Africa. Likewise in southern Africa, for it was regarded as a place "where an inferior civilization reigns," and the intention was to make it into "an extension of the countries that lie north of the Mediterranean" (ibid., 426).

We can see, then, that the ideology of humanitarian intervention revealed itself to be entirely instrumental, for it was functional to the Western powers' aims of colonial expansion.[19]

In the next chapter, we will look at the political struggle for supremacy that engaged the great powers in the frame of the Eastern question, showing how humanitarian intervention, along with other ostensibly good policies, was in fact a technique designed to achieve hegemony by concealing partial interests under principles of purportedly universal application.

18 Under Article XXVI of the Treaty, "the independence of Montenegro is recognized by the Sublime Porte and by all those of the High Contracting Parties who had not hitherto admitted it." Under Article XXXVI, "Serbia receives the territories included in the following delimitation: [...]." Under Article XLIII, "the High Contracting Parties recognize the independence of Romania [...]." And under Article I, "Bulgaria is constituted an autonomous and tributary Principality under the suzerainty of His Imperial Majesty the Sultan. It will have a Christian government and a national militia." Source: US Department of State, Office of the Historian, "Papers Relating to the Foreign Relations of the United States, Transmitted to Congress, with the Annual Message of the President, December 2, 1878" (Document 523).

19 In this regard see the reconstruction offered in Augusti 2013, 306.

Works Cited

Ancel, Jacques. 1931. *Manuel historique de la Question d'Orient (1792–1930)*. Paris: Librairie Delagrave.

Augusti, Eliana. 2013. *Questioni d'Oriente: Europa e Impero Ottomano nel diritto internazionale dell'Ottocento*. Naples: Edizioni Scientifiche Italiane.

Bluntschli, Johann Caspar. 1868. *Das moderne Völkerrecht der civilisirten Staten als Rechtsbuch dargestellt*. Nördlingen: Drück und Verlag der C. H. Beck'schen Buchhandlung.

Bluntschli, Johann Caspar. 1895. *Le droit international codifié*. Translated from the German by Charles Lardy. 5th ed., rev. and enl. Paris: Guillaumin.

Carr, E. H. 2001. *The Twenty Years' Crisis, 1919–1939*. With a new introduction and additional material by Michael Cox. Basingstoke, UK, and New York: Palgrave. (Orig. pub. 1939.)

Collas, M. B. C. 1864. *La Turquie en 1864*. Paris: E. Dentu.

Duguit, Léon. 1901. *L'État, le droit objectif et la loi positive*. Paris: Albert Fontemoing.

Dumont, Paul. 1989. "La période des *Tanzîmât* (1839–1878)." Chap. XII in *Histoire de l'Empire Ottoman*, edited by Robert Mantran, 459–522. Paris: Fayard.

Engelhardt, Édouard. 1880. *Le droit d'intervention et la Turquie: Étude historique*. Paris: A. Cotillon.

Gordon, David C. 1980. *Lebanon: The Fragmented Nation*. London: Croom Helm; Stanford, CA: The Hoover Institution Press.

Grotius, Hugo. (1646) 1913. *De Jure Belli ac Pacis Libri Tres, in quibus Jus Naturæ & Gentium, item Juris Publici præcipua explicantur*. Vol. I, reproduction of the 1646 edition (orig. pub. 1625). Washington, DC: Carnegie Institution of Washington.

Grotius, Hugo. (1720) 2005. *The Rights of War and Peace*. Edited by Richard Tuck, from the 1720 edition by Jean Barbeyrac. Indianapolis: Liberty Fund.

Heraclides, Alexis. 2014. "Humanitarian Intervention in International Law 1830–1939: The Debate." *Journal of the History of International Law/Revue d'Histoire du Droit International* 16, no. 1: 26–62.

Herren, Pascal. 2012 "A 'Humanitarian Intervention' in Syria—150 Years Ago." *Voltaire Network*, December 13, 2012. www.voltairenet.org

Jouannet, Emmanuelle. 2007. "Universalism and Imperialism: The True-False Paradox of International Law?" *The European Journal of International Law* 18, no. 3: 379–407.

Kamarowsky, Comte L. 1896 "La Question d'Orient." Translated from the Russian. *Revue Générale de Droit International Public* III: 397–428.

Koskenniemi, Martti. 2004. "International Law and Hegemony: A Reconfiguration." *Cambridge Review of International Affairs* 17, no. 2: 197–218.

Lorimer, James. 1883. *The Institutes of the Law of Nations: A Treatise of the Jural Relations of Separate Political Communities*. Edinburgh: William Blackwood and Sons.

Martens, Friedrich. 1877a. *Die Russische Politik in der Orientalischen Frage*. St. Petersburg: Verlag der Kaiserlichen Hofbuchhandlung H. Schmitzdorff (C. Röttger).

Martens, Friedrich. 1877b. "Étude historique sur la politique russe dans la Question d'Orient." *Revue de Droit International et de Législation Comparée* IX: 49–77.

Örücü, Esin. 1992. "The Impact of European Law on the Ottoman Empire and Turkey." In *European Expansion and Law: The Encounter of European and Indigenous Law in 19th- and 20th-Century Africa and Asia*, edited by W. J. Mommsen and J. A. de Moor, 39–58. Oxford, UK, and New York: Berg.

Pillet, Antoine. 1894. "Le droit international public: Ses éléments constitutifs, son domaine, son objet." *Revue Générale de Droit International Public* I: 1–32.

Rodogno, Davide 2011. "The 'Principles of Humanity' and the European Powers' Intervention in Ottoman Lebanon and Syria in 1860–1861." Chap. 7 in *Humanitarian Intervention: A History*, edited by Brendan Simms and D. J. B. Trim, 159–83. Cambridge: Cambridge University Press.

Rolin-Jaequemyns, Gustave. 1876a. "Le droit international et la phase actuelle de la Question d'Orient." *Revue de Droit International et de Législation Comparée* VIII: 293–400.

Rolin-Jaequemyns, Gustave. 1876b. "Note sur la théorie du droit d'intervention: À propos d'une lettre du M. le professeur Arntz." *Revue de Droit International et de Législation Comparée* VIII: 675–89.

Rougier, Antoine. 1910. "La Théorie de l'intervention d'humanité." *Revue Générale de Droit International Public* 17: 468–526. Also published as an extract, Paris: A. Pedone Éditeur.

Scelle, Georges. 1934. *Droit constitutionnel international. Deuxième partie of Précis de droit des gens: Principes et systématique*. Paris: Librairie du Recueil Sirey.

Testa Bappenheim, Stefano. 2006. "La libertà religiosa nel periodo del Mandato Britannico in Palestina (1918–1948)." *Diritto e religioni* I, no. 1/2: 411–26

Todorov, Tzvetan. 1984. *La conquista dell'America: Il problema dell'"altro"*. With an introduction by Pier Luigi Crovetto. Turin: Einaudi.

Traboulsi, Fawwaz. 2007. *A History of Modern Lebanon*. London: Pluto Press.

Vattel, Emer de. (1758) 1916. *Le Droit des Gens, ou Principes de la Loi Naturelle, appliqués à la Conduite et aux Affaires des Nations et des Souverains*. Vol. I, photographic reproduction of books I and II of the first edition (1758). Vol. II, photographic reproduction of books III and IV. Vol. III, translation of the 1758 edition by Charles G. Fenwick. Washington, DC: Carnegie Institution of Washington.

Vattel, Emer de. (1797) 2008. *The Law of Nations, or, Principles of the Law of Nature, Applied to the Conduct and Affairs of Nations and Sovereigns*. Edited by Béla Kapossy and Richard Whatmore, translated by Thomas Nugent (based on the London 1797 edition). Indianapolis: Liberty Fund.

Vitoria, Francisco de. (1539) 1991. "On the American Indians (*De Indis*)." Chap. 6 in *Vitoria: Political Writings*, edited by Anthony Pagden and Jeremy Lawrance. Cambridge: Cambridge University Press. Published in Latin under the title "De Indis insulanis relectio prior," in *Relectiones Theologicae XII,* tomus primus (Lugduni: Iacobum Boyerium, 1557).

2 Civilization and power: Developing the colonial paradigm

2.1 Colonial thinking: Tocqueville and the "Eastern question"

In the crisis of the Ottoman Empire the Western powers found fertile ground for their expansionist designs, and it was under the ideological banner of humanitarian intervention that, in that crisis, the same powers proceeded to carry out their hegemonic policies. This ideological formula in which the West's power politics were enveloped was complex, for its underlying logic (that of "humanitarian intervention") interlocked with the forms of legitimation of colonial domination,[1] this within a paradigm in which "humanitarian" policies coexisted with an imperious will to "civilize" peoples labelled as barbaric.

In this scenario the Western states also advanced their hegemonic strategies through the cynical game of pitting their powers against one another. A paradigmatic expression of this power play can be observed in the politics of nineteenth-century France, as well as in its colonial policy.

In the late 1830s, the so-called Eastern question also attracted the interest of Alexis de Tocqueville, who took up this question from the perspective of international relations and with a view to providing support for France's power politics. On July 2, 1839, when he first addressed the Chambre des Députés on

1 The coupling between the logic of humanitarian intervention and colonial domination had been clearly envisioned since the early modern age in the thought of Vitoria, who listed the protection of innocent lives as the fifth title legitimizing intervention, and for whom such protection therefore acted as a ground on which to justify Spanish colonial domination. As he put it: "THE NEXT TITLE could be either on account of the personal tyranny of the barbarians' masters towards their subjects, or because of their tyrannical and oppressive laws against the innocent, such as human sacrifice practised on innocent men or the killing of condemned criminals for cannibalism" (Vitoria [1539] 1991, question 3 ["The Just Titles by Which the Barbarians of the New World Passed under the Rule of the Spaniards"], article 5 ["Fifth Just Title, in Defence of the Innocent against Tyranny"], § 15, p. 287–88). Vitoria goes on to comment: "The barbarians are all our neighbours, and therefore anyone, and especially princes, may defend them from such tyranny and oppression" (ibid., 288). And then: "If they refuse to do so, war may be declared upon them, and the laws of war enforced upon them; and if there is no other means of putting an end to these sacrilegious rites, their masters may be changed and new princes set up" (ibid.).

the Eastern question, his speech was mainly taken up with the clash between the sultan Maḥmūd II and his vassal, the pasha of Egypt Muḥammad ʿAlī.

In 1833, Muḥammad ʿAlī's troops were marching across Anatolia towards Constantinople under the command of his first-born son, Ibrāhīm. But the march across the desert was arrested by the intervention by the Russian troops and fleet, which were arrayed in defence of the Bosphorus. Ibrāhīm was thus forced to retreat, while the sultan ended up accepting a Russian protectorate under the Treaty of Hünkâr İskelesi, signed in the outskirts of Constantinople on July 8, 1833.[2] In 1839, at the urging of the British ambassador to the Sublime Porte, Lord Ponsonby, the sultan Maḥmūd II resumed hostilities and, in the face of this deployment of forces, the French government decided it could not just idly watch.

It was in this international scenario that Tocqueville weighed in, aggressively defending the interests of France: "We do not ask to govern the affairs of the East on our own, and yet we have the same rights as Russia, for we have an interest equal to hers, however much it may be of a different nature. But we do ask and demand that the affairs of the East not be governed without us" (Tocqueville [1839] 1985b, 264; my translation). Tocqueville is thus asserting the French nation's power interests. There appears to be no need to rest this assertion on any ground of legitimacy: power simply justifies itself! Indeed, while he does mention the "natural law of nations" (***droit naturel des nations***) and "international European law," he does not explain how this law might support the proposition he is asserting: the connection is tenuous, if not irrelevant, and he simply asserts that this law is consistent with the role he is claiming for France.

In the first half of the nineteenth century the Mediterranean became a theatre of constant clashes among European powers never at rest. It was in these clashes that their colonial ventures played out.

On July 15, 1840, unbeknownst to France, Great Britain, Russia, Austria, and Prussia signed a treaty with the Ottoman Empire (the Convention of London of 1840) whose essence lay in an ultimatum demanding that the pasha of Egypt withdraw from Adana, Crete, and Syria: only under these conditions would the pasha be able to maintain his sovereignty over Egypt and his control over the Eyalet of Acre. The pasha rejected the ultimatum, and as a result, on September 11 of the same year, a British fleet bombarded Beirut, while Acre was occupied.

2 Article 3 of the treaty reads as follows: "In consequence of the principle of preservation and mutual defence, which forms the basis of the present alliance treaty, and by reason of the most earnest desire to ensure the permanence, maintenance, and complete independence of the Sublime Porte, His Majesty the Emperor of all Russias undertakes to supply as many troops and armed forces as the two High Contracting Parties will deem necessary in the event that circumstances should arise compelling the Sublime Porte to once more request Russia's naval and military aid, even if, God willing, no such thing is likely to happen. And it is accordingly agreed that, in such an unlikely circumstance, what land and sea forces the Sublime Porte may request will be made available to it" (Barié et al. 2004, 113; my translation). Cf. Mantran 1989, 447–48, and Ancel 1931, 111–12.

This turn of events was received with great alarm in French public opinion, and King Louis Philippe I took a nonaggressive attitude, rejecting the interventionist urgings of his prime minister, Adolphe Thiers, and instead heeding the more appeasing restraint advocated by François Guizot. Against this backdrop Tocqueville delivered his second address on the Eastern question, this time clearly signalling a greater awareness of the stakes. Indeed, the Eastern question was here presented by Tocqueville as the scenario in which Europe was gearing up to conquer and dominate Asia, and in which the prevailing European power would take home the biggest prize: "Do you know what is happening in the East?" he asked the Chambre des Députés on November 30, 1840.

> It is an entire world that is being transformed. From the riverbanks of the Indus to the shores of the Black Sea an immense space stretches out in which all societies are in motion, all religions are wilting away, all nationalities are disappearing, all lights are going out—the ancient Asiatic world is vanishing, and in its place there can be seen the gradual rise of the European world. Present-day Europe is not assailing Asia from a single point, as it did at the time of the Crusades: it is attacking from the North, the South, the East, the West, from all sides; it is branding, enveloping, taming Asia. (Tocqueville [1840] 1985c, 290; my translation)

This is the manifesto that heralds colonial conquest. Indeed, the greatness of the European nations will be measured precisely on the basis of their ability to establish a foothold in this new immense space: "Do you therefore believe," Tocqueville continues, "that a nation that wants to preserve its greatness can look on at such a spectacle without joining in?" The "greatness" of nations makes it necessary to be in the vanguard in this carving up of an entire land mass, even if the competition has by now turned deadly. It is inconceivable that two other European peoples—the British and the Russians—should be allowed to take possession of "this immense inheritance." "And rather than stand for it," Tocqueville concludes, "I will tell my country with energy, with conviction: better that we go to war" (ibid.).

Thus, on the one hand, Tocqueville recognizes the full import of the July 15 Convention of London, as a result of which Beirut has been shelled and the Eyalet of Acre occupied, but at the same time, because this is a treaty under which France is left out of the action, he comes to the conclusion that the country should forcefully assert its place in the international scenario that is taking shape. Specifically, France should side with the pasha of Egypt, Muḥammad ʿAlī, against the designs of the sultan of Constantinople, who on September 14, 1840, decreed that he should be deposed.

In reality, Tocqueville cynically reasons, there is nothing that France stands to gain from an interest in the fate of Muḥammad ʿAlī. Instead, the country should train its eye on the growth of British power in the Mediterranean: this is a threat to be subdued, being "an additional weapon aimed at France." *Thus the European powers' strategies and their colonial ventures are inextricably bound up in a bitter clash in which the fate of non-European peoples is merely instrumental to the aims of conquest and the growth of power.*

In some of the notes in which Tocqueville sets down his ideas in preparation for his second speech addressing the Chambre des Députés on the Eastern question, he outlines the shape of European colonial expansion, proposing to define the objectives that France ought to pursue in the context of the European engagement with the Eastern world. It was inconceivable for France to sit idly by, for the East was undergoing a deep transformation: "Disarray across the whole of Asia, from the Indus River to the Black Sea. Depopulation. Anarchy. Religious and political ties coming apart. A movement of the European race toward Asia. It is the movement of the century" (Tocqueville 1985a, 279; my translation).[3] A nation that were to watch from the sidelines, while the others moved to aggrandize themselves, would end up being dependent on them. France therefore had to join the colonial venture and build its own system of alliances in view of this objective. "The Eastern question," Tocqueville concluded, "is the question of the century: it dwarfs all other questions, which must all be made subordinate to it" (ibid., 280). The question of colonialization had by then taken centre stage, and Tocqueville took it up with the aim of preserving the "greatness" of France.

2.2 Algeria: Domination and colonization—outlines of a paradigm

The analysis that Tocqueville offered of the French presence in Algeria was geared towards conquest and the means by which to achieve it. Once more, then, the problem was how to increase France's power. "I do not believe," Tocqueville wrote, "that France can seriously think of leaving Algeria: that would be tantamount to unequivocally signalling France's decline to the rest of the world" (Tocqueville [1841] 1962c, 213; my translation).[4]

The lens through which he looked at the problem was that of the relation between domination and colonization. The objective to be pursued was that of total domination coupled with partial colonization. Indeed, domination without colonization would have been fruitless, while colonization without domination would certainly have been precarious. The objective of domination over Algeria was framed by Tocqueville on the basis of Western stereotypes, and with the ruthlessness that a Westerner had to be moved by in dealing with "barbarians."

In his first letter on Algeria, Tocqueville identified what he considered to be the distinguishing traits of the Arab "race": it is a "roving and untameable race, which loves physical pleasures, but which places liberty above all pleasures and will flee in the sands of the desert rather than vegetate under a master" (Tocqueville [1837] 1962b, 135; my translation). It is still a barbarian "race,"

3 The editor of Tocqueville's *Discours Politiques*, André Jardin, notes that it is not easy to date these remarks. But the way in which Tocqueville characterizes France's position within the international landscape suggests that he was writing before the crisis that in July 1840 would lead to the Convention of London.

4 On Tocqueville and Algeria see the excellent Letterio 2011 and Re 2012. See also Boulbina 2003.

similar to all peoples who are half-savage (*à moitié sauvages*), whose vices and virtues belong to "the period of civilization in which they find themselves." Tocqueville further elaborates on these characteristics as follows: "Being that they do not value life much and look down on commerce and the arts, [...] they especially love war, overemphasis, and noise." Thus they are "often excessive in their actions, and always more inclined to feel than to think" (ibid.).

In this summary snapshot of the Arab world, stereotypes and prejudices mix under the certainty of European superiority and the influence the European model of civilization is bound to exert on that semi-savage civilization. Indeed, Tocqueville comments that "the great works we have already done in Algeria, the examples of our arts and ideas, of our power, have powerfully shaped the spirit of the very populations who are fighting us" (Tocqueville [1841] 1962c, 216). So if in the future Algeria should fall back into the hands of the Muslims, it would do so as a different nation, for the people would be open to contacts with Christian nations and would be led by one of them—such was the Western civilization's presumption of superiority! "Africa has now joined the movement of the civilized world and will not fall away from it" (ibid.), Tocqueville concludes with the sure-footed presumption of the inevitable Europeanization of the world.

The French colonial army was to crush the resistance of the emir ʿAbd al-Qādir, who had managed to turn the Arab tribes against the French occupiers. It was religion, Tocqueville observed, that gave the different tribes the "common passion" by which they could be united. But these were "small barbarian tribes" whose fighting techniques were different from those of the Europeans, in that they shirked from clashing in an open battlefield. The Western armies, by contrast, had to protect the population, the cities, the capital, whereas the Arabs took everything with them, and so there was nothing that compelled them to fight.

Tocqueville, however, thinks it possible to divide them, insofar as "semi-civilized men" (*les hommes à moitié civilisés*) can make decisions that run contrary to their habitual inclinations. Indeed, he comments, "the heart of the savages is like a constantly storm-tossed sea, but where the wind does not always blow in the same direction" (ibid., 225).

Tocqueville is looking for some categories through which to interpret the Arab ways: those that differ from the European ways he thus qualifies as "barbaric," and the various manifestations of the Arabs' behaviour he conceptualizes as earlier stages of Western civilization. This is what we see, for example, in his account of the manner in which ʿAbd al-Qādir formed his army. Even though the emir had no notion of what happened in France in the fifteenth century, Tocqueville thinks he dealt with the tribes in just the same manner that Charles VII tackled the problem of the feudal system, namely, by depriving the aristocracy of its power, thereby concentrating power into his own hands. Regardless of how Tocqueville may have explained the process, however, the consequences he draws are stark: against barbaric nomads (*barbares nomades*) or semicivilized peoples it is legitimate, he thinks, to wage a kind of war that Western armies do not engage in, for they make war against governments and not against peoples.

The unvarnished ruthlessness of Tocqueville's analysis does not fully come out, however, until he points out the means by which he proposes to break the Arab resistance. It is necessary, he argues, to act on two fronts, on the one hand cutting off trade so as to deprive the Arabs of their livelihood, while on the other securing the territory by force: "I believe," he counsels, "that the law of war authorizes us to lay waste to the country, and that we should do this by both destroying crops at harvest time and by engaging in a campaign of constant rapid incursions, or raids aimed at taking possession of men and matériel" (ibid., 228).

To be sure, French domination could not be an end in itself but needed to be functional to colonization. To this end, however, it was necessary to change the social conditions on the ground, so that French colonizers settling next to "part-barbaric, part-nomadic" tribes could do so in security. This issue became a concern because, according to the stereotypes that informed Tocqueville's thinking, "the Arabs have been used to being ruled by foreigners for three centuries now," but they cannot accept to see a new territorial settlement of new arrivals: this would be perceived by them as an act of expropriation, a conflict "between races."

Colonial settlement would be achieved by conquest or by confiscating the lands of Arab tribes that might have put up resistance against the French army, or it could have been achieved by purchasing lands the local population would agree to sell and then selling that land to settlers at a discount. Indeed, only with the arrival of settlers from France would it be possible to make the conquest permanent by securing full control over the territory.

Finally, according to Tocqueville, the domination and colonization project would not be complete without a deep institutional reform.

Before the French conquest, the Ottoman Empire had left the social structure of Algeria intact. The country had been divided into three districts, each of which, governed by a bey, was home to several tribes. The Turks introduced a system of territorial control based on forming alliances with some Arab tribes against others: in exchange for this support, the allied tribes would be granted privileges, and in this way the Ottomans managed to govern the Arabs.

Not so under the strategy envisioned by Tocqueville, who thought it necessary to introduce a strongly centralized administration headed by a civil governor[5] or by an official who would answer directly to the governor but enjoyed a reasonable amount of leeway from Paris when it came to applying general rules, appointing subordinates, and so on. He further envisioned a specific ministry for Algeria.[6] In short, Tocqueville held it necessary to centralize government in Paris and the administrative apparatus in Algiers. This marked the birth of the centralizing apparatus of the French administrative state imposed on a social and cultural reality to which it was completely extraneous, but which would serve as the blueprint for the nation-state the Arab states would later use upon gaining independence.

5 A civil governor for Algeria was installed in 1879, at the time of the Third Republic.

6 Under the Third Republic, when Léon Gambetta was prime minister, an undersecretary for the colonies was appointed.

2.3 Tocqueville's Qur'ān

Tocqueville's political thinking was thus geared towards consolidating the French conquest of Algeria. The colonial conquest was to be achieved by superimposing the French institutional model onto the cultural, social, and economic reality of the Arab world. The representation Tocqueville offered of that reality was not the result of an effort on his part to come to an understanding and appreciation of it, but was rather the result of his bringing to it some mental constructs rooted in the biases of the time. To see this, we can look at his reading of the Qur'ān, an effort he undertook in 1838, but which he gave up after studying only a few of the suras in that sacred book.

Tocqueville used a 1783 translation (Savary 1783). He singled out some elements of Islam that would suggest its continuity with other monotheistic religions, but he especially focussed on the potential clash of civilizations that Islam could fuel. His analysis of the first eighteen suras turns to some key aspects in that regard: Islam's relation to other religions, its punishments for crimes, personal relationships, its dietary prescriptions, and the central issues in the law of war.

Tocqueville underscores that encapsulated in the Qur'ān are all the general principles of morality we find in the other monotheistic religions, but he comments that Islam is especially indebted to the conceptions expressed in the Old Testament, "to which it presents itself as a follow-up." He comments that the Muslim religion draws mainly on the figure of Moses, and it does not stray from the Ten Commandments except by adding to it the prescriptions of almsgiving. At the same time, however, he injects some highly critical remarks about Muhammad, stating that he "is much more concerned to elicit belief in himself than in giving the laws of morality. And there is no motivating factor he leverages more than terror" (Tocqueville [1838] 1962a, 160; my translation).

Even the respect the Qur'ān advocates for the "People of the Book," that is, for all those who follow a monotheistic religion, appears inauthentic to Tocqueville. For, although sura 5 provides reassurance for everyone in this group,[7] subsequent verses—as Tocqueville interprets them—only apply to those who have converted to Islam.[8]

Also condescendingly disdainful, finally, is Tocqueville's analysis of sura 15, in which the greatness of God is exalted and those who do not believe in

7 "For the [Muslim] believers, the Jews, the Sabians, and the Christians—those who believe in God and the Last Day and do good deeds—there is no fear: they will not grieve" (Qur'ān, *The Feast*, 5:69, as translated in Abdel Haleem 2005, which will be the source for all translations of the Qur'ān).

8 Tocqueville is alluding to Qur'ān 5:83: "These people are not given to arrogance, and when they listen to what has been sent down to the Messenger, you will see their eyes overflowing with tears because they recognize the Truth [in it]. They say, 'Our Lord, we believe, so count us amongst the witnesses. [...]'"

the prophets are threatened: "Nothing here that is noteworthy or practical," Tocqueville ([1838] 1962a, 161) remarks in commenting on these verses.

He is strictly descriptive in the report he gives of the Qur'ān's dietary restrictions (suras 2 and 6) and the punishments it sets out for crimes (suras 2, 5, and 17), as well as its framing of personal relationships, particularly as concerns the traditional representation of man's superiority over woman in the Muslim world (suras 2 and 4).

Much more attentive, of course, is his commentary on the question of war. He brings into focus some aspects of Islam he considers to be fundamental in this regard. In the first place, he underscores the "sanctity of the holy war" in sura 2, commenting that it is "spurred on with energy and violence" (Tocqueville [1838] 1962a, 155).[9] In the second place, he dwells on the verses of the Qur'ān that place emphasis on the resoluteness of believers who fight in the holy war and the happiness of those who die fighting for their faith.[10] The same point is made in the negative by pointing to the verses that thunder against those who fail to act in the face of disbelievers.[11]

In Tocqueville's rendition, then, what passes between the Muslim and Christian worlds is an all-out, inexorable clash in which the force that drives those who believe in Islam will be magnified to infinity by God against the enemies of that true faith.[12]

Tocqueville's hermeneutical effort—superficial, ideologically charged, and hence devoid of any critical spirit—grinds to a halt at sura 18 and does not proceed any further. Indeed, as we saw, his interpretation is aimed at consolidating the French conquest and making Algeria thoroughly "French." We also saw that these objectives were to be achieved by reshaping the conquered territory on the basis of the institutional model imported from France. Accordingly, any interest in the culture of the Algerian people was bound to be either irrelevant or entirely functional to the objective of French domination.

9 Tocqueville is referring to two verses in the Sura of the Cow: "Fight in God's cause against those who fight you, but do not overstep the limits" (Qur'ān 2:190). And: "Fight them until there is no more persecution, and worship is devoted to God" (Qur'ān 2:193).

10 "[Prophet], do not think of those who have been killed in God's way as dead. They are alive with their Lord, well provided for, happy with what God has given them of His favour; rejoicing that for those they have left behind who have yet to join them there is no fear, nor will they grieve [...]" (Qur'ān, *The Family of ʿImrān*, 3:169–70).

11 "Believers, when you meet the disbelievers in battle, never turn your backs on them: if anyone does so on such a day—unless manœuvring to fight or to join a fighting group—he incurs the wrath of God, and Hell will be his home, a wretched destination!" (Qur'ān, *The Battle Gains*, 8:15–16).

12 "Prophet, urge the believers to fight: if there are twenty of you who are steadfast, they will overcome two hundred, and a hundred of you, if steadfast, will overcome a thousand of the disbelievers, for they are people who do not understand" (Qur'ān, *The Battle Gains*, 8:65).

2.4 Representing the colonized: The contribution of psychiatry—a "Muslim psychiatry"

Tocqueville's thinking clearly illustrates the complexity of the tradition of political liberalism and its inherent relativism—a relativism predicated on the centrality of the Western world forged out of Europe.

Within this frame of thinking, the colonized were represented as the negative of the anthropological image of the West, with a view to legitimizing colonial domination. To this end it was necessary to press the sciences into service, and so a "scientific" paradigm was created that would provide the arguments to be deployed in support of the image in the negative.

So, in this endeavour to represent "the other" as inferior—as lagging behind in the march that led to the achievements of Western civilization—science increasingly came to play a supporting role, providing a basis on which to justify the European domination over an "inferior" humanity. And one of the "sciences" enlisted in this effort was psychiatry.

This started 1912, when the Congrès des Aliénistes et Neurologistes de France was held in Tunis, marking the beginning of a *colonial psychiatry* intended to serve as a basis on which to train colonial, civil, and military psychiatrists in the service of colonial power ("Le regard colonial" 2005). Proposing to advance the study of the so-called indigenous mentality, Antoine Porot founded the Algiers School, which trained an entire generation of psychiatrists.

That mentality forms the subject of a 1918 article tellingly titled "Notes de psychiatrie musulmane," in which Porot underscores its constitutive separateness from the Western mentality. Porot offers a portrait of the affective life of a Muslim, describing it as governed by an automatism inscribed in nature—a mentality constrained by "basic instincts, necessary to life and its preservation, and satisfied by this regulative automatism that nature has devised as the basis of their satisfaction" (Porot 1918, 378; my translation). The conception he puts forward is thus deterministic, and it paints a picture of a human nature that is different from that of the West, for it is destined to wallow in an irremediably backward condition.

This mindset from which Porot was working necessarily led him to construct a constellation of stereotypes revolving around the Western representation of Muslim humanity, which was accordingly distilled down to its being passive,[13] given to stasis,[14] gullible,[15] and superstitious.[16]

Finally, by combining these stereotypes he set the foundation for the "discovery" of a human nature that was different from the Western one, and on

13 In this Muslim humanity, "passivity is the manifestation of a temperament that is often atonic, lacking in vitality" (ibid.).

14 In the Muslim man "the static personality smothers the dynamic personality" (ibid., 380).

15 "The spirit of the indigene predisposes him to credulity and makes him suggestible in the extreme" (ibid., 381).

16 He is "shaped by submission and is given to religious docility, and falls prey to all manner of superstitions" (ibid., 381).

this basis he set out a theory of primitivism that depicted Muslims as "primitive spirits" or "primitive men" irremediably marked by a "mental childishness." Their mentality was devoid of "scientific craving" and "general ideas." In fact, as seen through the lens of Muslim psychiatry, this mentality was only good for formulating "simple syllogisms, occasionally stupid in their conclusions" (ibid., 383). In short, "these primitives, deeply ignorant and prone to credulity," lived "worlds apart from our mentality," and they had never even fleetingly been touched by "the minutest of our moral qualms" (ibid., 377).

This interpretive scheme even formed the basis for diagnosing diseases. The Muslims brought in to the Centre Neuro-Psychiatrique d'Alger were observed to suffer from a mental frailty (*débilité mentale*) that manifested itself in "violent and brutal hysteric spells, deaf-muteness, and forms of astasia-abasia" (ibid., 380).

In a subsequent development, this colonial psychiatry would go so far as to identify the purportedly scientific foundations on which to rest the representation of the whole native population of North Africa. Indeed, Porot and his school even claimed that the behaviour patterns of Maghrebins were to be explained by pointing to the stunted evolution of their cerebral cortex and to the predominant role played by the activity of their diencephalon (Porot and Sutter 1939; cf. "Le regard colonial" 2005). Finally, once all these elements were bundled together, they translated into the assertion that there existed a distinctly North African mentality entirely unlike the European mentality.

This paradigm rounded out the historiographical reconstructions of the colonial period by providing the scientific support needed for a definitive legitimation of the colonial enterprise (see, e.g., Mercier 1875).

2.5 Frantz Fanon: Decolonizing the "Mental illness" of the colonized

In a 1955 essay titled "Considérations ethno-psychiatriques,"[17] Frantz Fanon probed critically into Porot's work and the Algiers School, tracing the transformations that had marked the "psychiatric approach to the *Muslim*" (Fanon 2018a, 406).

While in the previously discussed "Notes de psychiatrie musulmane," Porot (1918) confined himself to underscoring the presumed social "characteristics of the North African native" (Fanon 2018a, 406), in a talk delivered at the *Congrès des Médecins Aliénistes et Neurologues de Langue Française*, held in Brussels in 1935, he made the claim "that the native, a big mental retard, whose higher and cortical activities are little developed, is above all a primitive being whose essentially vegetative and instinctive life is above all regulated by his diencephalon" (ibid., 406–7), thus launching the effort to set a "scientific" foundation for his representation of the North African native as a person essentially determined by a set of primitive traits.

17 Translated into English as "Ethnopsychiatric Considerations" (Fanon 2018a). Translated into Italian as "Considerazioni etnopsichiatriche" in Fanon 2011. With great accuracy Roberto Beneduce's foreword to the latter book reconstructs the story behind Fanon's essay, which appeared unsigned in the periodical *Consciences Maghrébines*.

The effort was further pursued in a 1939 article in which this "native primitivism" was theorized as a social condition: "Primitivism is not a lack of maturity, a pronounced cessation in the development of the individual psyche, it is a social condition that has reached the end of its evolution" (ibid., 407). In addition, it was stressed that this condition "is adapted in a logical fashion to *a life that is different from ours*" (ibid.; italics added). And, most disturbingly for us today, Porot and his colleague, Doctor Jean Sutter, concluded that if primitivism was a social condition fundamentally different from ours, its foundation was biological: "it has far deeper foundations [than a special education] and we even think that it must have its substratum in a particular disposition of the architectonics, of at least the dynamic hierarchizing of the nervous centres" (ibid.).

Fanon observes that by positing a "diencephalic dominance" (ibid.) in the North African native, the Algiers School laid the groundwork for yet another thesis it wanted to advance, namely, that "on the psychophysiological level, the Black African greatly resembles the North African—the African is a unity" (ibid.). And the same conclusions would later be reached by John Colin Carothers in an ethnopsychiatric study of the Black African he conducted for the World Health Organization (Carothers 1954/1970).

In Fanon's analysis, the primitivism theorized by this biological racism was subjected to a radical criticism that sought to demystify this conception by pointing out that it was in fact functional to colonial domination: he identified it with the colonial misrepresentation of the colonized North African mind.

In a study of the attempts made to reform the psychiatric services delivered to the Muslim men admitted into the Blida psychiatric hospital, Fanon reconstructs the frustrations that followed the initiatives undertaken to subject these patients to forms of social therapy. The study investigates the reasons for these failures and finds their root cause in the therapies' neglect for the patients' cultural background.

> We [...] believed we had adapted to this Muslim society the frames of a particular Western society at a determinate period of its technological evolution. [...] By virtue of what impairment of judgment had we believed it possible to undertake a Western-inspired social therapy in a ward of mentally ill Muslim men? How was a structural analysis possible if the geographical, historical, cultural and social frames were bracketed? (Fanon 2018b, 362)

These initial questions led Fanon to see the need for a different approach, one in light of which he came to recognize that colonial domination sought to "assimilate" North Africans by denying their culture. In this mindset of the colonizer Fanon identified the reason why the therapies administered by the psychiatric service failed. The natives needed to be "understood in their cultural originality" (ibid.), embracing a "cultural relativism" (ibid., 363) that would reject the whole premise of assimilation. It was accordingly necessary to "grasp the North African social fact [...] in its totality (ibid.), rejecting the separation of "the biological, the psychological and the sociological," for they are "tied indistinctly together" (ibid.). The Algerians, in short, needed to be understood in light of their "cultural existence" (ibid.).

Gradually, Fanon expanded his new approach until he rejected any form of biological reductionism, embarking on an investigative path that led him to explore the sociological reality behind the phenomena he was seeking to understand, thereby recognizing the cultural peculiarity of the patients taken in for treatment at the psychiatric hospital. His thought could now take in the entire field of social and anthropological research, which led him to broaden the scope of his investigation: a study specifically concerned with the dysfunctions of the psychiatric service provided to Muslim patients grew into a comprehensive endeavour to understand the various ways in which colonial domination was affecting the traditional structures of the Algerian Muslim society.

In this process, Fanon enriched his writing with other concepts he needed in order to describe the tragically painful advance of the steamroller of colonization, with its incremental destruction of traditional social bonds. As Fanon explains, Muslim society was "gerontocratic":

> The father is the one that steers the life of the family and he—or in his absence the eldest brother or even the uncle—must be consulted for all decisions of some importance. The family is incidentally very ramified [and] tends to be identified with the clan, which is the true natural group of Muslim Algeria. [...] There did not in fact exist, at least not until in recent years, a veritable national community, but instead a familial, clan community. (Ibid., 364)

The French conquest of Algeria wrought deep changes in the traditional social structure, which revolved around collective ownership of the land belonging to each village. With the French conquest, ownership was divided among village members, who thus became small proprietors making a subsistence living next to the large landholdings of the French colonizers. This condition of social imbalance lay at the origin of a process through which many North African natives were uprooted, so they migrated to the cities in search of work. This breakup of the tribal structure, with the internal nomadism it set in train, meant that people had to find ways to adjust to changes that were not of their own making. And it was this condition of social maladjustment that may have been at the root of the mental distress.

With this new understanding of what was at play, Fanon could reject any idea of a presumed Algerian primitivism and "indigenous mentality," which was instead to be ascribed to the devastation of conquest, with the violence through which the French colonizers had sought to assimilate the Algerian population, that is, by wiping out the traditional forms of social organization.

Now, in light of this new understanding, even the therapies could have some measure of success, not by imposing extraneous practices on Algerian customs (games and theatre) but by relying on the figure of the Arab storyteller, who would travel from village to village bringing stories or events to the people in ways they could easily understand, or by celebrating Muslim festivities, or again by providing the hospital with a Moorish café where patients could meet.

Any naturalistic determinism dissolves against Fanon's discovery of the extent to which colonial power can transform the social, cultural, and psychological life of the North African natives.

These are themes that Fanon, after all, had explored a few years earlier in a work titled *Peau noire, masques blancs* (Fanon 1952), translated as *Black Skin, White Masks* (Fanon 1967; 2008). Among the questions he analyses in this book is the so-called dependency complex of colonized peoples (Fanon 2008, chap. 4), subjecting to sharp criticism the work of Octave Mannoni, and in particular his *Psychologie de la colonisation* (Mannoni 1950; 1964; 2001), a book that investigates colonial relations in Madagascar. Fanon agrees with Mannoni that for a full understanding of the problem of colonization, we need to look not only at the objective and historical conditions in which colonization takes place, but also at the subjective attitude that people develop under such conditions. And yet, as Fanon points out, Mannoni ignores and contradicts his own premise, for in positing an inferiority complex which the "primitive" man experiences in relation to the "civilized" man, he presents this complex as "something that antedates colonization" (Fanon 2008, 62).

It is this contradiction that provides the initial cue for Fanon's inquiry, in which he rejects the notion of an original cultural condition of the native—the idea that "the germ of the [inferiority] complex was latent in him from childhood" (Mannoni 2001, 40). The psychological condition of the native population should instead be understood in light of the relational structure that was set up by the colonizers, taking into account all the ideas of Western civilization with which it is imbued. The colonizers destructured the cultural life of the native population: in so doing they represented the native population as inferior to themselves, thereby framing between the two a relationship that was functional to the project of colonial domination.

From this analysis follows Fanon's conclusion: "The feeling of inferiority of the colonized is the correlative to the European's feeling of superiority. Let us have the courage to say it outright: *It is the racist who creates his inferior*" (ibid., 69; italics in the original).[18] This unambiguous pronouncement is all-encompassing, for it arraigns the whole of European civilization under the charge of colonial racism. Under this sweeping language, there is no more room for any distinction between the venturing colonizers and the "best representatives" (ibid., 67) who speak for the European peoples, for they are all equally responsible, whether they have had a direct hand in bringing about the ills of colonization or whether they have done so by way of a tacit and wilful negligence.[19]

18 The French original: "L'infériorisation est le corrélatif indigène de la supériorisation européenne. Ayons le courage de le dire: *c'est le raciste qui crée l'infériorisé*" (Fanon 1952, 75).

19 The same judgment is expressed by the French anticolonialist philosopher Francis Jeanson, who like Fanon, and using the same language of neglectful blindness, makes the point that the remove the average Frenchman may be able to achieve by turning a blind eye to the dirty business of colonialism does not make him any less guilty than those who are actually engaged in that business: "Et si vous parvenez, apparemment, à ne pas vous salir, c'est que d'autres se salissent à votre place. *Vous avez des hommes de main*, et tout compte fait c'est vous les vrais coupables: car sans vous, sans votre négligeant cécité, de tels hommes ne pourraient poursuivre une action—qui vous condamne autant qu'elle les déshonore" (Jeanson 1950, 625–26; italics in the original).

The European world and its culture, its lofty ideals, the civilization of law and rights it celebrates—all these achievements find themselves deprived of any substance in the face of a judgment from which there is no appeal. A civilization that has taken part in the colonial venture cannot be held up as a higher model: it can only be called into question in light of the damage which it has done, and which its grand ideals have been powerless to prevent.

2.6 Human and nonhuman: "How to make men out of those who are not yet men?" Colonialism and an inferior humanity

Frantz Fanon compellingly showed that the way the West was constructing the colonized bore no connection to reality but served the only purpose of legitimizing what the colonizer presented as a civilizing mission. And precisely in this relation to reality the Western construction has shown itself to be *ambivalent* in the extreme. This concept of ambivalence is brought into focus by the excellent internationalist Nathaniel Berman, who describes it as "the inability of an individual, a group, or a culture to rid themselves of ideas, passions, or relationships that they nevertheless also claim to condemn or deny" (Berman 2012, 414). Ambivalence so understood has historically been used in international law to legitimize the exercise of power, and it can also be seen as an attitude the West takes towards the rest of the world.

This ambivalence has informed colonial discourse and practices since the era of protectorates; it continued to do so in the era of the mandates set up through the League of Nations, and it has carried into the contemporary period of the measures and interventions provided for in Chapter VII of the United Nations Charter. There is an argument to be made that the ambivalence of colonialism, just like the interventions legitimized under the UN Charter, has essentially been devised as a *technology of power* (ibid.).

For an illustration of the ambivalence of colonial discourse, Berman points us to a 1944 article by Pierre-Olivier Lapie, who served as French governor of Chad from 1940 to 1942. In the article, Lapie (1944) outlines for France a new colonial policy that had been coming into shape in the 1940s. At the origin of the new policy was an appreciation that when France had been at its most vulnerable, facing an existential threat in its struggle to drive back the Nazi advance, the colonial population under French control gave a demonstration of loyalty by joining the war effort on the French side. This loyalty was recognized and rewarded by pledging to support the establishment of independent states, as had happened with Syria and Lebanon. In this way, the colonized lands could be moulded into states *in the likeness of France itself.*

However, Lapie reasoned, *before you can have a country, you need to have citizens, and in order to forge citizens, you first need to forge men.* To be sure, the African people in the French colonial empire were French citizens, and among them were representatives elected to the French Chamber of Deputies. But, in Lapie's judgment, there were also people living in conditions of great backwardness. And so he asked: "How are we to create men out of those who are not yet men, and then to make citizens out of them and the others who are already more advanced in civilization?" (ibid., 106).

These pronouncements belong to a discourse cast in a "classic liberal colonialist fashion," and they bring out its inherent ambivalence, for on the one hand this discourse represents the colonized as partaking of an inferior humanity ("not yet men"), but at the same time it sees the possibility of transforming these people into human beings proper, and sees this as a feat that can be accomplished in light of the "universal" values of French republicanism (Berman 2007, 142).

The non-European was thus constructed as being at once human and non-human (Berman 2012, 423). And through the assimilationist effort undertaken by the European colonizer, this Janus-faced being would achieve a condition of "equality" understood as loyalty to the colonizer—a loyalty predicated on the idea of an alliance between "primitive" and "advanced" humanity (ibid.).

Also of great interest is the analysis Berman carries out as he turns to the *Décrets de Nationalité en Tunisie et au Maroc* of 8 November 1921. These were introduced with the aim of creating a "continuous nationality" across all Tunisian and Moroccan territories subject to the French protectorate. In a *Mémoire* submitted in 1922 to the Permanent Court of International Justice, the French government cited two international instruments—namely, the Treaty of Casr-Said of 12 May 1881 (between France and Tunis) and the Treaty of Fez of 30 March 1912 (between France and Morocco)—and pointed out that the two countries were still "thoroughly penetrated by a theocratic civilization" (Mérillon and Lapradelle 1922, 3). On that basis, the government argued, France was entrusted with a mission "to guide them in the paths of civilization and progress": this was in fact a "duty," and it would be fulfilled by introducing in those countries "the *free*, *independent*, durable, and stronger idea of a nationality, detached from all religious *contingencies*, which would evolve [...] in the broader framework of Western conceptions" (Berman 2012, 423–24).[20]

In the *Mémoire* we find it stated that the Muslim countries had no notion of nationality, in that they made up a single nation and a single nationality. It followed that whatever Muslim country a Muslim happened to live in, he or she was a subject of the sovereign who ruled over that country: if that Muslim were to leave that Muslim country for another one, he or she would become subject to a new sovereign. Hence, "once the French Protectorate is set up, the ancient principles had to evolve." It was accordingly "a duty of the Protector to progressively guide the Protectorate toward conceptions proper to modern civilization and, henceforward, toward the assertion of the concept of nationality, the basis and substance of the independence of the state" (Mérillon and Lapradelle 1922, 4).

20 The same idea—that it was incumbent on France to chaperone non-European peoples to a higher civilization—had previously been put forward at the 1908 Congrès de l'Afrique du Nord. We can see it in particular in the speech delivered by the French ambassador René Millet, who in recognizing the past glory of Islam qualified that statement by declaring that it was "necessary to extend a firm hand to our Muslim populations, taking them along with us as we set them on the path to civilization" (Millet 1909b, 22; my translation). This, he remarks elsewhere in the same conference, would make possible "the construction of a *French Africa* that is not just a faraway settlement, of more or less questionable merit, but an extension of the Mother Country across the Mediterranean" (Millet 1909a, 69; my translation, italics added).

What these policy statements also supported was an *institutional design* for the countries that were subject to the colonialization process. Which meant remaking the colonized countries into nation-states—even though, as we will see, this model was completely foreign to Muslim countries—while at the same time also thrusting on them an ideology of nationality by which to mould a sense of belonging and dependence in relation to the new nation-state form. Accordingly, the *Mémoire* reads: "Henceforth, for all individuals who are born either in Tunisia or abroad to a Tunisian father or, if the father is unknown, to a Tunisian mother, they will be Tunisian and will therefore be subject to French diplomatic protection" (ibid., 5).[21]

The ambivalence of colonial discourse thus reveals itself in full in what Berman characterizes as a "decoupled" relation. For, on the one hand, this discourse was aimed at constructing non-European natives so as to make them into "human" beings and then into citizens proper; on the other hand it identified the path a non-European country would have to follow in order to make a claim to independence in an international community governed by European international law, but this could only happen once the colonized was subjected to that law and was fully assimilated to the colonizer.[22]

21 France thought it could also impose French nationality on British subjects in Tunisia and Morocco. Great Britain objected to that view, and France resorted to the Permanent Court of International Justice, asking it to recognize that French law on nationality was a matter that fell exclusively within the scope of its domestic jurisdiction. But the court rejected the French claim (PCIJ 1923, 32).

22 The assimilationist case was presented by the French government in its final conclusions, which in 1923 D. Mérillon and A. de Lapradelle submitted to the Permanent Court of International Justice, basing their argument on the following premises: "Considering that it is of the highest importance [...] that a complete code of rules [*un statut complet*], or at least, that a general principle applicable to the various protectorates [...] be laid down by means of the authoritative opinion of the Court of Justice; / Whereas this general principle should above all be based upon the lofty aims of a protectorate, which does not, in the mind of the Protector, constitute an annexation in disguise, but is above all a work of civilisation, which in the domain of the economic and social intercourse of the world increases the resources of the whole body of nations, a matter in which all have an equal interest; / That, in order to obtain this result, it appears necessary that the consent of the nations, by means of a simple recognition of the protectorate, should be obtained, for all measures intended fruitfully to combine the legislation of the Protector and the Protected, and *the progressive assimilation of the customs and laws of the Protectorate to those of the protecting country*" (Mérillon and Lapradelle 1923, 242; italics mine). Cf. Berman 2007, 152; 2012, 432.

These conclusions by the French government are reported critically by Berman, who accordingly edits as follows the literal English version of the text submitted by Mérillon and deLapradelle: "On the basis of these arguments [!], no reason of international law can be opposed to the primordial principle of [French] territorial sovereignty [in Morocco] ... and therefore that nationality questions in Morocco are 'an exclusively domestic {French} matter']" (Berman 2007, 151; 2012, 432). "France," Berman goes on to comment in irony, "ruled in North Africa not simply as a sovereign dominating another, but as an agent of universalism: French rule was '*a work of civilisation ... a matter in which all [nations] have an equal interest*'" (Berman 2012, 432; italics in the original).

Works Cited

Abdel Haleem, M. A. S., trans. 2005. *The Qur'an: A New Translation.* Oxford: Oxford University Press.

Ancel, Jacques. 1931. Manuel historique de la Question d'Orient (1792–1930). Paris: Librairie Delagrave.

Barié, Ottavio, et al., eds. 2004. "La prima crisi egiziana: Trattato di Unkiar Skelessi tra Russia e Impero Ottomano (Costantinopoli, 8 luglio 1833)." Sec. 84 in *Storia delle relazioni internazionali: Testi e documenti (1815–2003).* Bologna: Monduzzi.

Berman, Nathaniel A. 2007. "Les ambivalences impériales." In *Impérialisme et Droit International en Europe et aux États-Unis,* edited by Emanuelle Jouannet and Hélène Ruiz-Fabri, 131ff. Paris: Société de Législation Comparée.

Berman, Nathaniel A. 2012. "Imperial Ambivalences: Scenes from a Critical History of Internationalism." Chap. 9 in *Passion and Ambivalence: Colonialism, Nationalism, and International Law.* Leiden and Boston: Marinus Nijhoff Publishers. (Originally published as Berman 2007.)

Boulbina, Seloua Luste. 2003. Foreword to *Sur l'Algérie,* by Alexis de Tocqueville. Paris: Flammarion.

Carothers, John Colin. 1954/1970. *The African Mind in Health and Disease: A Study in Ethnopsychiatry.* Geneva: World Health Organization; New York: Negro University Press.

Fanon, Frantz. 1952. *Peau noire, masques blancs.* Paris: Seuil.

Fanon, Frantz. 1955. "Considérations ethno-psychiatriques." In "Aperçus sur le racisme: Un fait divers ... un article médical." Dossier, *Consciences Maghrébines* 5.

Fanon, Frantz. 1967. *Black Skin, White Masks.* Translated by Richard Philcox. New York: Grove Press.

Fanon, Frantz. 2008. *Black Skin, White Masks.* Translated by Lam Markmann, forewords by Ziauddin Sardar and Homi K. Bhabha. London: Pluto Press. (1st ed. 1986.)

Fanon, Frantz. 2011. *Decolonizzare la follia: Scritti sulla psichiatria coloniale.* With a foreword by Roberto Beneduce. Verona: Ombre Corte.

Fanon, Frantz. 2018a. "Ethnopsychiatric Considerations" (1955). Chap 14 in *Alienation and Freedom,* edited by Jean Khalfa and Robert J. C. Young, translated by Steven Corcoran, 405–8. London: Bloomsbury. Originally published as *Écrits sur l'aliénation et la liberté*: Textes réunis, introduits et présentés par Jean Khalfa et Robert Young (Paris: Éditions La Découverte, 2015).

Fanon, Frantz. 2018b. "Social Therapy in a Ward of Muslim Men: Methodological Difficulties" (1954). Chap. 10 in *Alienation and Freedom,* edited by Jean Khalfa and Robert J. C. Young, translated by Steven Corcoran, 353–72. London: Bloomsbury. Originally published as *Écrits sur l'aliénation et la liberté*: Textes réunis, introduits et présentés par Jean Khalfa et Robert Young (Paris: Éditions La Découverte, 2015).

Jeanson, Francis. 1950. "Cette Algérie, conquise et pacifiée." *Esprit* 4 (April): 613–35.

Lapie, Pierre-Olivier. 1944. "The New Colonial Policy of France." *Foreign Affairs* 23, no. 1 (October): 104–11.

"Le regard colonial de l'École psychiatrique d'Alger." 2005. Les deux rives de la Méditerranée: Les "populations" de l'Algérie coloniale. *LDH Toulon,* February 24.

Letterio, Domenico. 2011. *Tocqueville ad Algeri: Il filosofo e l'ordine coloniale.* Bologna: il Mulino.

Mannoni, Octave. 1950. *Psychologie de la Colonisation.* Paris: Seuil.

Mannoni, Octave. 1964. *Prospero and Caliban: The Psychology of Colonization.* New York: Praeger.

Mannoni, Octave. 2001. *Prospero and Caliban: The Psychology of Colonization.* With a new foreword by Maurice Bloch. Ann Arbor, MI: Ann Arbor Paperback. (1st ed. 1990.)

Mantran, Robert, ed. 1989. *Histoire de l'Empire Ottoman.* Paris: Fayard.

Mercier, Ernest. 1875. *Histoire de l'établissement des Arabes dans l'Afrique septentrionale selon les documents fournis par les auteurs arabes et notamment par l'"Histoire des Berbères" d'Ibn Khaldoun.* Algiers: Juillet-Lager; Paris: Challamel.

Mérillon, D., and A. de Lapradelle. 1922. "Mémoire présenté au nom du Gouvernement de la République Française" (Paris, 24 November 1922). In *Publications of the Permanent Court of International Justice.* Series C. Second (extraordinary) session (January 8–February 7, 1923), *Nationality Decrees in Tunis and Morocco*, pp. 1–32. Leiden: A. W. Sijthoff's Publishing Company.

Mérillon, D., and A. de Lapradelle. 1923. "Final Conclusions Submitted by the French Government" (translation). In *Publications of the Permanent Court of International Justice.* Series C. Second (extraordinary) session (January 8–February 7, 1923), *Nationality Decrees in Tunis and Morocco.* Part II, "Speeches and Documents Read before the Court. Sec. 5 (Annex 8), pp. 240–44. Leiden: A. W. Sijthoff's Publishing Company.

Millet, René. 1909a. "Banquet de clôture du congrès." In tome 1 of *Congrès de l'Afrique du Nord, Tenu à Paris du 6 au 10 Octobre 1908: Compte Rendu des Travaux*, edited by Charles Depincé, 56–72. Paris: Comité d'Organisation des Congrès Coloniaux.

Millet, René. 1909b. "Si l'Islam est incompatible avec la civilisation moderne." In tome 1 of *Congrès de l'Afrique du Nord, Tenu à Paris du 6 au 10 Octobre 1908: Compte Rendu des Travaux*, edited by Charles Depincé, 19–36. Paris: Comité d'Organisation des Congrès Coloniaux.

PCIJ. 1923. Permanent Court of International Justice, second (extraordinary) session, 7 February 1923. Advisory Opinion No. 4 (File F. c. V., Docket II.1). Published in Series B: *Collection of Advisory Opinions (1923–1930).*

Porot, Antoine. 1918. "Notes de psychiatrie musulmane." *Annales Médico-Psychologiques* 9: 377–84.

Porot, Antoine, and Jean Sutter. 1939. "Le primitivisme des indigènes nord-africains: Ses incidences en pathologie mentale." *Sud Médical et Chirurgical*, April 15.

Re, Lucia. 2012. *Il liberalismo coloniale di Alexis de Tocqueville.* Turin: Giappichelli.

Savary, Claude-Étienne. 1783. *Le Coran, traduit de l'Arabe, accompagné de notes et précédé d'un abrégé de la Vie de Mahomet tiré des écrivains Orientaux les plus estimés, par M. Savary.* 2 vols. Paris: Knapen & Fils & chez Onfroy.

Tocqueville, Alexis de. (1838) 1962a. "Notes sur le Coran (Mars 1838)." In *Écrits et Discours Politiques*, edited by André Jardin, tome III, vol. 1, of *Œuvres Complètes.* Paris: Gallimard.

Tocqueville, Alexis de. (1837) 1962b. "Première lettre sur l'Algérie (23 Juin 1837)." In *Écrits et Discours Politiques*, edited by André Jardin, tome III, vol. 1, of *Œuvres Complètes.* Paris: Gallimard.

Tocqueville, Alexis de. (1841) 1962c. "Travail sur l'Algérie (Octobre 1841)." In *Écrits et Discours Politiques*, edited by André Jardin, tome III, vol. 1, of *Œuvres Complètes.* Paris: Gallimard.

Tocqueville, Alexis de. 1985a. "Ordre des Idées: Politique Générale." In *Écrits et Discours Politiques*, edited by André Jardin, tome III, vol. 2, of *Œuvres Complètes.* Paris: Gallimard.

Tocqueville, Alexis de. (1839) 1985b. "Premier discours sur la Question d'Orient, 2 juillet 1839." In *Écrits et Discours Politiques*, edited by André Jardin, tome III, vol. 2, of *Œuvres Complètes*. Paris: Gallimard.

Tocqueville, Alexis de. (1840) 1985c. "Second discours sur la Question d'Orient, 30 novembre 1840." In *Écrits et Discours Politiques*, edited by André Jardin, tome III, vol. 2, of *Œuvres Complètes*. Paris: Gallimard.

Vitoria, Francisco de. (1539) 1991. "On the American Indians (*De Indis*)." Chap. 6 in *Vitoria: Political Writings*, edited by Anthony Pagden and Jeremy Lawrance. Cambridge: Cambridge University Press. Published in Latin under the title "De Indis insulanis relectio prior," in *Relectiones Theologicae XII*, tomus primus (Lugduni: Iacobum Boyerium, 1557).

3 Deconstructing the concepts of humanity and human nature*

3.1 The Western paradigm: Human nature and cultural differences

3.1.1 Human nature and Western hegemony

Stoic philosophy, stretching from Roman antiquity to the early modern age, held that there was only one nature common to all human beings—a single human nature that all humans share on the material side and the spiritual side alike. But with the discovery of the New World, the incommensurable diversity of customs became apparent for all to see, and this led to the view that some peoples still found themselves at an initial stage of development,[1] and that it was therefore legitimate for the Spanish conquerors to guide the Indios along the long path to civilization—the *only* conceivable civilization, that of the West. Hence the rights of peoples—among which ***dominium***, namely, the right to ownership of land—were conceived from the start as qualified, and needed to be refashioned in such a way as to fit the model of Western civilization. The legitimate grounds of conquest were thus found to lie in the need to protect the right to life (an entirely instrumental protection), the universal right of free movement (in the lands of the Indios), and the right to spread the Christian faith in the New World. What came into shape, then, was a paradigm predicated on the uniformity of human nature and the different degrees of civilization as a criterion by which to legitimize Western hegemony—and it was this paradigm that would be coercively reproduced throughout the age of colonialism, fully establishing itself in the nineteenth century.

* This chapter was originally published in 2011 under the title "Abbandonare la natura umana? Verso una democrazia multiculturale" (Gozzi 2011). It was subsequently republished with substantive revisions in Gozzi 2015, and in that version it now appears in translation.

1 In an attempt to explain why the New World Indios appeared not to have reached an advanced stage of civilization, Francisco de Vitoria resorted to the Aristotelian distinction between potentiality (*potentia*) and actuality (*actus*). The Indios, he conjectured, certainly had the use of reason (*habent pro suo modo usum rationis*), but any such potential that failed to express itself in actuality was vain (*frustra est potentia, quae non reducitur ad actum*). See Vitoria (1539) 1991, § 23, p. 250.

3.1.2 The condition of slavery of the Indios: A different humanity

As is known, the discovery of the New World put front and centre a whole set of issues in a debate that brought competing conceptions of humanity into play.

One such paradigm—representing the Indios in such a way that conquest could then be legitimized—was the one put forward by Juan Ginés de Sepúlveda. In *Democrates Secundus*, a work thought to have been written between 1544 and 1545, he starts off with a description of the differences that separate the customs and institutions of New World peoples from those of Christian peoples. Through this faming device, the Indios are represented as "homunculi in whom you would be hard put to it to find any vestiges of humanity" (Sepúlveda [1544/45] 2009, 55; my translation). They "have no doctrine, but neither do they make use of writing, [...] nor do they have any historical memory." What is more, "they have no written laws, only certain barbarous institutions and customs." They "indulge in all sorts of intemperance and dishonest lust." And, finally, "they eat human flesh and make war with such savageness that they are almost constantly fighting one another" (ibid.). Such was the diminished humanity Sepúlveda saw in the Indios that he even felt compelled to liken their architecture to the mechanical constructions of bees and spiders (and not in any complimentary way).[2]

One might think that, having so described the Indios, Sepúlveda should inevitably have seen fit to cast them as a people meant for the condition of natural slavery theorized by Aristotle. But in reality the debates of the time, and Vitoria's *Relectiones Theologicae*, led Sepúlveda to introduce a different perspective.[3] He distinguishes the views of the philosophers, who construe slavery as the consequence of an "inborn obtuseness and inhumane and barbarous customs,"[4] from the views of the jurists, who frame it by reference to the law of peoples and civil law, and the principle that might makes right. On what basis, then, does Sepúlveda argue for the conclusion that conquest is legitimate?

Here Sepúlveda develops his paradigm by dogmatically endorsing the natural law theory of the Christian Catholic tradition. Indeed, when he looks at the condition of the Indios he sees as a constant violation of the laws of nature, which he identifies with those of God. It is this premodern and dogmatic vision that ultimately becomes the foundation for conquest.

3.1.3 The conquest of humanity

Sepúlveda's *Democrates Secundus* is a work of great erudition that avails itself of the Catholic Church's doctrinal tradition to legitimize the subjugation of the

2 See the excellent introduction to *Democrates Secundus* that Domenico Taranto provides in Sepúlveda (1544/45) 2009 at p. XXXVIII.

3 See the introduction to *Democrates Secundus* in Sepúlveda (1544/45) 2009 at p. XLI.

4 Ibid.; my translation.

Indios. And it is Saint Augustine in particular that Sepúlveda looks to in seeking to justify Western domination over non-Western peoples, regarded as sinners. As Augustine reflects in his letter to Marcellinus, "it is quite useful to conquer one who has been stripped of the freedom to sin, while nothing is more unhappy than the happiness of sinners."[5]

So therein lies the work of Christian charity: in lifting sinners from their condition of sin, in bringing their nature into line with the laws of nature, that is, with the laws of God, by which is meant the God of Christianity. Christian charity thus becomes the means through which to conquer humanity and make it true: once the Indios are made into "worshippers of the true God," they will "change from barbarians into humans, or almost so, that is, into human and civil people according to their capacities" (Sepúlveda [1544/45] 2009, 97; my translation).

The design is thus complete: if those barbarians should refuse "the command of Christians," they could "by rights" be put down, on the ground of the despicable offences they commit and of their acts of inhumanity, and they could therefore achieve the highest good if they pay obedience to good men—ones who are "human and practice the true religion"—in such a way that they can be restored to "integrity, humanity, and piety" (ibid., 89). In virtue of Christian charity, sinners who act contrary to the laws of nature can be brought "under our power," so that they can be snatched up before they fall "over the cliff, even against their will" (ibid.).

3.1.4 *What barbarism? Cannibalism and the force of customs; reason and common sense*

A little more than three decades after Sepúlveda wrote his *Democrates Secundus*, Michel de Montaigne upended the question of the legitimacy of the conquest of the New World by introducing a different, and completely new, way of looking at the matter. He did so in his well-known essay "Of Cannibals," written in 1579–80, the year of the first edition of the *Essays*: it is here that Montaigne relativizes the concept of barbarianism (cf. Montaleone 2011, 138).

While in the eyes of Sepúlveda barbarianism consisted in violating a law of nature dogmatically taken as true in virtue of its belonging to the tradition of Catholic Christian natural law, according to which the law of nature is the law of God, Montaigne took a sceptical view of the world that sees it as "always

5 Augustine, Letter 138 (AD 412), chap. 2, § 14. Quoted in the introduction to *Democrates Secundus* in Sepúlveda (1544/45) 2009 at p. 97; my translation. Here is the passage as translated in Cunningham 1886 at p. 485: "For the person from whom is taken away the freedom which he abuses in doing wrong is vanquished with benefit to himself; since nothing is more truly a misfortune than that good fortune of offenders, by which pernicious impunity is maintained, and the evil disposition, like an enemy within the man, is strengthened."

multiplex and ambiguous" (ibid., 150; my translation), which in turn led him to instead look for what common ground there may be beneath the differences that give the appearance of irreconcilability (ibid., 147).

The essay "Of Cannibals" opens with a quotation that Montaigne attributes to King Pyrrhus of Epirus, the words he uttered on beholding the formation of the army that Rome had sent out against him: "'I know not,' said he, 'what kind of barbarians' (for so the Greeks called all other nations) 'these may be; but the disposition of this army that I see has nothing of barbarism in it.'"[6] Montaigne invites us to take away from this remark the lesson that "we are to judge by the eye of reason, and not from common report" (Montaigne 1842, 87).

And in that opposition—between reason and received opinion—lies the central theme that runs all through the short essay: in opposition to common sense, which structures our convictions and transforms them into habits, reason needs to be able to make its own independent judgments by a constant effort not to accept opinions, doctrines, and theories without first having assessed their foundation.

In this way the essay anticipates the conclusion that will famously be arrived at through the principles that will underpin the new discipline of cultural anthropology, namely, "that there is nothing barbarous and savage in [the New World], excepting that every one gives the title of barbarism to everything that is not in use in his own country" (ibid., 89). Conversely, "we have no other level of truth and reason than the example and idea of the opinions and customs of the place wherein we live: there is always the perfect religion, there the perfect government, there the most exact and accomplished usage of all things" (ibid.). Exemplified in this reflection is an extraordinary appreciation for the relativism we have come to recognize in our understanding of cultures, and it prompts Montaigne to consider how unfortunate the "barbarous horror" is by which we are seized as we judge the cruel actions of others, "seeing so clearly into their faults" while remaining "so blind to our own" (ibid., 91).

3.1.5 Hume: The science of man and human nature

In the age of the Enlightenment, an effort was made to set the concept of human nature on a scientific footing, but this did not come without contradictions that ended up favouring the discourse of the presumed superiority of the West.[7]

More to the point, from the Scottish Enlightenment there sprang some approaches that called into question some of the central concepts of seventeenth-century natural law, particularly the concepts of the state of nature and the law of nature: these were found to be unscientific, and the emphasis

6 Montaigne, *Essays*, bk. I, chap. XXX, in Montaigne 1842, 87, citing Plutarch, *Life of Pyrrhus*, c. 8.

7 I understand *discourse* here in the Foucauldian sense of the term.

accordingly fell on the concept of human nature.[8] As we read in the introduction to the *Treatise of Human Nature* (1739–40), Hume's intent was to establish a rigorous science of man based on observation and experience. This science was to explain the principles of human nature on the basis of a cautious observation of human life, that is, of the way humans behave in company, in business, and in pleasure. On this foundation, Hume thought, a new science could be aspired to that would be as certain as any other science of human understanding and no less useful (Hume [1739–40] 1969, 46), and that would form a solid basis for other sciences closely connected with human nature (logic, morality, critical reasoning, and politics). The focus of investigation thus shifted from humans in the state of nature to humans in society, to the individual as a member of an organized social group. As Edward Keene observes, however, this new interest inevitably also led to a shift in attention from the laws of nature and natural rights, understood as universal, to the differences and contrasts that could be observed between *civilized* and *barbarian* peoples. And so, paradoxically, the very interest in investigating human nature on an empirical basis—with a view to uncovering its sameness—drew attention to the *differences* that existed among peoples according to where they fell in the march of progress towards a common civilization (Keene 2005, 136). This paradox comes through especially clearly in the work of Hume: "It is universally acknowledged," he asserts, "that there is a great uniformity among the actions of men, in all nations and ages, and that human nature remains still the same, in its principles and operations" (Hume 1894, sec. VIII, pt. I, § 65, p. 83). On this approach, it was history that would inevitably bear out the thesis of the uniformity of human nature. But in fact the argument proceeds *a priori* (Keene 2005, 150), for Hume does not even consider the possibility of any real difference among peoples. As he puts it:

> Should a traveller, returning from a far country, bring us an account of men, wholly different from any with whom we were ever acquainted; men, who were entirely divested of avarice, ambition, or revenge; who knew no pleasure but friendship, generosity, and public spirit; we should immediately, from these circumstances, detect the falsehood, and prove him a liar, with the same certainty as if he had stuffed his narration with stories of centaurs and dragons, miracles and prodigies. (Hume 1894, sec. VIII, § 65. pt. I, p. 84)

We should instead look to "ambition, avarice, self-love, vanity, friendship, generosity, public spirit": it is these passions, says Hume, that can be observed to drive the actions of people across nations and over time. "Mankind," in other

8 Keene 2005, 136. On the idea of human nature in the age of the Enlightenment and the possibility of universalizing the Enlightenment principles on the basis of a uniform human nature, see Berlin (1947) 2013.

words, "are so much the same, in all times and places, that history informs us of nothing new or strange in this particular" (ibid., 83).

And yet what empirical analysis brought to light were some undeniable differences that needed to be accounted for. In Hume we find the important distinction between physical causes (as in Montesquieu) and moral causes,[9] to which he gave greater weight in explaining the diversity of peoples. On these bases Hume, disconcertingly for us, came "to suspect the negroes, and in general all the other species of men [...] to be naturally inferior to the whites."[10] This made for a contradiction that was destined to remain unresolved—a contradiction between the claim that there existed a uniform human nature and the observation that there existed different degrees of development among peoples. And it is against the backdrop of this ambivalence that in the following century the paradigm of Western primacy would be asserted.

3.1.6 Rousseau: Human nature as identification with the other

It would be remiss on our part if, in looking at the Enlightenment thinkers, we were to neglect the complexity that distinguishes the thought of Jean-Jacques Rousseau, who on the one hand underscored the uniformity of sentiments inherent in human nature, while on the other hand he shone a spotlight on the forms of abuse and oppression that had originated as a result of denying those universal sentiments.

It was on the idea of a sentiment common to all people that Rousseau rested the universality of human nature. This universality he set in contrast to the alterations and deformations that human nature undergoes as a result of our living in civil society. In a masterly reconstruction of Rousseau's thought, Claude Lévi-Strauss takes this universality as the origin and foundation of ethnology. Humans partake of a universal or "essential faculty which possesses originally and immediately

9 As Hume put it: "Different reasons are assigned for these *national characters*; while some account for them from *moral*, others from physical *causes*. By *moral* causes, I mean all circumstances, which are fitted to work on the mind as motives or reasons, and which render a peculiar set of manners habitual to us. Of this kind are, the nature of the government, the revolutions of public affairs, the plenty or penury in which the people live, the situation of the nation with regard to its neighbours, and such like circumstances. By *physical* causes, I mean those qualities of the air and climate, which are supposed to work insensibly on the temper, by altering the tone and habit of the body [...]. / That the character of a nation will much depend on *moral* causes, must be evident to the most superficial observer; since a nation is nothing but a collection of individuals, and the manners of individuals are frequently determined by these causes" (Hume [1772] 1994, 78–79; cf. Keene 2005, 152).

10 Hume (1772) 1994, 86. Even Montesquieu stated: "Those concerned are black from head to toe, and they have such flat noses that it is almost impossible to feel sorry for them. / One cannot get into one's mind that god, who is a very wise being, should have put a soul, above all a good soul, in a body that was entirely black. / [...] It is impossible for us to assume that these people are men because if we assumed they were men one would begin to believe that we ourselves were not Christians" (Montesquieu [1748] 1989, pt. 3, bk. 15, chap. 5 ["On the Slavery of the Negroes"], p. 250).

some contradictory attributes," a faculty "both natural and cultural, affective and rational, animal and human" (Lévi-Strauss 1983, 37). "This faculty—Rousseau did not neglect to repeat—is compassion, deriving from the identification with another who is not only a parent, a relative, a compatriot, but any man whatsoever, seeing that he is a man, and much more: any living being, seeing that it is living" (ibid., 38). Compassion, as conceived by Rousseau, is a *natural universal virtue* which can "soften in certain circumstances the ferocity of his pride [*amour-propre*], or before the birth of that pride, his desire for self-preservation," and which "serves to moderate the ardour he has for his own wellbeing by giving him an innate repugnance against seeing a fellow creature suffer" (Rousseau [1754] 1984, pt. 1, p. 99). This virtue is all the more universal considering that it precedes all reflection. Lévi-Strauss brings out the depth of Rousseau's thought by underscoring that it was Rousseau who introduced the principle that *humans identify not only with other human beings but also with all that is living and is liable to suffer.* When this original bond was severed, a vicious cycle was set in motion that progressively separated humans from one another and placed an increasingly small group of people in a position of superiority, excluding all the rest from the claim to equality. This exclusionary mechanism was compellingly denounced by Rousseau, who rejected it on the basis that there exists a single human nature whose original thrust was to identify itself with all forms of life. Hence the conclusion that Lévi-Strauss reaches by elaborating on this teaching of Rousseau: "In an organized society there could be no excuse for the only crime which man cannot expiate: the belief in his lasting or temporary superiority and his treating other men like objects, be it in the name of race, of culture, of conquest, of mission, or simply of expediency" (Lévi-Strauss 1983, 42).

3.1.7 From civilization to civilizations

As the brief reconstruction just offered clearly suggests, two opposite lines of investigation were brought together in the making of Enlightenment thought: on the one hand was a *normative* investigation that sought to evaluate social and political systems against the benchmark of a universal human nature; on the other was an empirical investigation that sought to analyse human nature such as it could be observed in its own reality. This opened up a new horizon for Western civilization, which in the very diversity that could empirically be observed among peoples found the basis on which to legitimize its interventions aimed at exercising control over the processes through which other peoples evolved. In a seminal study in the history of concepts, Lucien Febvre traces the history of the concept of civilization. The first appearance this concept makes is in French sources in the second half of the eighteenth century, when it was introduced to capture the idea of an ascent towards reason, as well as towards a standard of justice. During the French Revolution the term gained currency and came to form the kernel of a philosophy of progress. But in the first half of the nineteenth century, with the development of the natural and ethnographic sciences, and with the great voyages and accounts of famous travellers and explorers, the idea of civilization found itself being relativized, and in its place came the idea of *civilizations* in the plural. This new approach, writes Febvre, "represented, for natural scientists, the beginning of the long specialization process and the great relativist development of the '*universelles*' ideas of the eighteenth century, which was to take place, in parallel fashion, in the fields of history, ethnography and linguistics" (Febvre [1930] 1973, 237). Finally, the concept of civilization forked into two directions, one pursuing its empirical study, the other its scientific study: on the former approach, civilization was thought to belong to every each human group; on the latter, the assumption was that it only belonged to the white peoples of Europe and North America, conceived as superior to all others (ibid., 247).

3.1.8 Human egoism and human nature

These two approaches can easily be identified in utilitarianism. The utilitarians proceeded from the assumption of certain unchangeable principles of human nature. These had their source not in the idea of natural rights, but in the universal inclination to seek pleasure and avoid pain (Burrow 1968, 24). These theses can be found, for example, in James Mill's ([1820] 1937) *Essay on Government*, in which the immutable trait of human egoism is set in contrast to historically shaped habits (regarded as secondary). On these premises Mill outlined the philosophy of history that informs his *History of British India*. The principle of utility thus became the gold standard against which to measure the degree of civilization reached by different societies, at whose apex he set the Europe of his own time. By the same criterion he accordingly thought he could assess the degree of civilization achieved by Hindu society, which he characterized as stationary.[11] He also thought that there was a single path which all nations inevitably must follow in their evolution (Burrow 1968, 47).

Indeed, one of the recurrent themes in nineteenth-century legal and political thinking on the problem of civilization lies in the distinction between civilization as an event, that is, as a condition already attained, and civilization as a process towards a goal yet to be achieved (Keene 2002, 114). Civilization as an event was seen to be embodied in the European countries and the American states-union, which accordingly were fully legitimized in their endeavour to bring good government to peoples who had yet to achieve civilization, as well as to promote trade as a means towards economic and technological progress. The argument, in short, was that it was in the best interest of the world's civilization to give universal currency to the freedoms, legal principles, and order proper to the world and to Western civilization (ibid.).

3.1.9 International law and Western civilization

What in this way came into form was the vision that drove the rise of Western colonialism, whose legitimacy rested on the idea of the "civilized peoples" of Europe

11 As Mill put it, the "Hindus have, through all ages, remained in a state of society too near the simplicity and rudeness of the most ancient times" (Mill [1817] 1997, vol. 1, p. 173). On the significance of *The History of British India* as a work that helped to shape the "discourse" through which to legitimize British colonial rule in India, see Giuliani 2008.

and North America. Civilization could only be ascribed to those in the community of peoples who subscribed to the principles of international law, regarded as the embodiment of the consciousness of European peoples. Such international law was understood to be universal and could accordingly be extended to all peoples—or rather, it could be *imposed* on them—regardless of their distinctive cultures and religions. This vision accordingly denied any claim to universality that might be advanced by other great legal traditions, such as the Islamic tradition and the Chinese. In reality, as was made explicit at the Berlin Congress of 1884–85, it was the path of trade and commerce that needed to be pursued if Western civilization was to extend its reach across the globe (see Onuma 2000, 1–66).

There were some major consequences that would follow from the West's engagement with the "otherness" of non-Western peoples and cultures. For, on the one hand, international law as an expression of the scientific outlook embraced by Western states came to be restricted in its scope to this very system of states, and the contrast was therefore highlighted that set their system of law apart from others. Thus, for example, the claim was made that international law belonged to Christian nations and could not be extended to Muhammadan ones (Wheaton 1836, 45). On the other hand, while the stance was taken that asserted the superiority of European international law—Christian and Aryan—revolving around the idea of the sovereignty of the state, it was felt that "noncivilized" peoples were deserving of "humanitarian" treatment, and native peoples were accordingly recognized as entitled to enjoy the rights of man. But what this meant, in short, was that in the nineteenth century the rights of peoples did not express the recognition of each people's right to self-determination—much less was it recognized that different peoples had a right of ownership over their own natural resources: they were only accorded a right to humanitarian treatment.

The phases just briefly outlined—from the early modern age to the Enlightenment to the colonial age—were ultimately capped by the demise of colonialism. This in turn dragged into crisis the paradigm that had sought to couple the certainty of a universal human nature with the recognition of the cultural differences that were observed to exist among peoples. In fact this paradigm was predicated on a Eurocentric understanding of human nature in light of which other peoples could be cast as backward, in such a way as to legitimize Western hegemony over them. With the end of the colonial age came a recognition of the inherent value of other cultures and civilizations: this made it necessary to part with the idea of human nature conceived according to Western criteria, and to construct a new foundation on which to represent cultures and understand their relations. It is this new approach that we will now turn to.

3.2 A relation of complementarity between psychic universalism and cultural plurality: Human life, psychic unity, and cultural diversity

In the sphere of international relations, the end of colonialism brought into focus the need to achieve a lasting peace in the face of the plurality of different legal and political systems. This inevitably meant taking an intercivilizational approach to the problem of the relation among such systems, proceeding from the premise of a mutual understanding among the civilizations out of which those systems have sprung. Now, much the same point can be made about the sphere of domestic law, where the plurality of values and cultures we are now confronted with can be enabled to coexist only by singling out a foundation that everyone can share, making it possible to set in motion a process of integration and mutual recognition. But what might that foundation look like? This is a problem that Ronald Dworkin turned to in the early 2000s as he set out to answer the question, is democracy possible in a pluralist society? In answering that question, he identifies two principles of human dignity that democracy ought to take as its shared foundation, or common ground.

The first of these he calls the principle of intrinsic value: it "holds that each human life has a special kind of objective value. It has value as potentiality; once a human life has begun, it matters how it goes" (Dworkin 2006, 9). The second is a principle of personal responsibility: it "holds that each person has a special responsibility for realizing the success of his own life, a responsibility that includes exercising his judgment about what kind of life would be successful for him" (ibid., 10).

These two principles together act as necessary conditions for the dignity of each human being. The first one corresponds to the ideal of equality, the second to that of liberty (ibid.). And the first one can be said to be the condition for the second one. If we recognize the *objective value inherent in every human life*, regardless of ideological or cultural interpretations of it, we will not introduce the kinds of discriminations that derive from denying the associated rights, such as the right to *citizenship*.

The implications of such a denial are quite serious, for a denial of rights introduces a condition of inferiority that inevitably translates into a judgment of anthropological inferiority, which amounts to claiming that someone has no rights because they are not like us. *Recognition of the objective value of each individual life* instead acts as the condition enabling everyone to freely choose the kind of life they want to live, even if this life is culturally different from those of the people who make up the majority.

Recognition of the objective value of each individual life is what protects each person's dignity, and it means that everyone is owed *the same consideration and respect*. The recognition of dignity so conceived means that equality is not merely a *formal* concept—the idea of equality as equal treatment under the law, which does nothing to address the disparity of conditions—but should rather be understood as *substantive* equality, meaning that all persons are to be treated as equals, with the same concern and respect for everyone, regardless of how different they may be from us.

Unlike the formal conception of equality, the substantive conception takes account of differences, such as we find in our understandings of health and sickness, and it requires that the delivery of care be mainly aimed at overcoming conditions of inequality. It is on this basis, then, that we need to tackle problems of inequality, such as we find them, for example, in health care.

On the basis of the substantive concept of equality just mentioned, this conception intends to specify the conditions that will make it possible to overcome all forms of racism, discrimination, and marginalization. *But the Western organization of knowledge tends to apply and impose its own criteria.* As Foucault has observed, this organization has its own *discourse*, that is, a paradigm of its own that frames a specific conception of health and sickness, of normality and pathology.

This mindset—a vestige of the colonial era—has not been entirely overcome, such that certain conditions that by our own criteria count as disease are in fact understood to be entirely physiological in other cultures. Indeed, in the West, the physician looks at the patient's body in strictly biological or medical terms, without in any way considering the patient's cultural background (Quaranta and Ricca 2012). That is because this biomedical reductionism counts as irrelevant "the meaning that patients attach to their own experience of illness" (ibid., 25; my translation).

Illness conjures up a tight-knit web of words, conceptions of reality, and images of the body. This suggests the need to critically reflect on the concept of culture, a concept that, as has been compellingly argued in cultural and medical anthropology, is best understood not in essentialist terms but in processual ones: culture, in other words, is a process that unfolds within a web of relations. It is therefore within this same web that patients live their sickness, along with their loved ones and caregivers, and medical practitioners need to be mindful of that fact as they approach the patient.

This complex biological and cultural reality needs to be taken into account as we *train doctors, psychologists, psychiatrists, social workers, and government administrators*, in such a way that we can ultimately come to appreciate the *normality of diversity*. It is certainly a difficult road that needs to be travelled to get to that stage, but not an impossible road.

This desirable outcome brings out the paradox of multiculturalism, in that the *relativistic* approach it calls for—the equal legitimacy that ought to be bestowed on the different cultural outlooks and practices—is *predicated on a universal principle, that is, on an appreciation for the equal value that ought to be recognized for the life of every human being*. This same approach underpins a fundamental discipline, namely, ethnopsychoanalysis, which recognizes the complementary relation that exists between *psychical universality* and the *plurality of cultural constructs*.[12]

Indeed, according to Georges Devereux, the father of complementarist ethnopsychoanalysis, there is a complementary relation that holds between the individual and society: "The human psyche and culture are methodologically and functionally inseparable concepts." (Devereux 1953, 630). At the foundation of this conception we find a couple of tenets: the first is "the psychic unity of mankind, which includes its capacity for extreme variability" (Devereux [1955]

12 One of the leading exponents of this discipline, Marie Rose Moro, writes as follows in this connection: "In effect, from a theoretical point of view, there is a postulate without which ethnopsychoanalysis could not have been built, and that is the postulate of *psychical universality*, referring to the basic unity of the human psyche [Devereux 1980]. This postulate means that *the same ethical status, as well as the same scientific status*, needs to be accorded to all human beings, to their cultural and psychical constructs, and to their way of living and thinking, regardless of how different and divergent they may be. [...] The universal is the point of view towards which all knowledge tends in the human sciences without ever having the certainty that it has been attained" (Moro 2005, 128; italics mine).

1976, 83); the second is the influence exerted by different cultures, which can shape a great variety of behaviours.

In short, both psychoanalysis and ethnology are branches of anthropology, defined by Devereux (1953, 634) through the words of Kant as "the science of that which is distinctively human in man." With these elements in place—meaning an understanding of psychical universality and a recognition of the value inherent in every human life, coupled with a willingness to embrace the plurality of its manifold cultural expressions—we have a basis on which to build a society capable of appreciating how important and rich coexistence in diversity can be.

Works Cited

Berlin, Isaiah. (1947) 2013. "The Decline of Utopian Ideas in the West." In *The Crooked Timber of Humanity: Chapters in the History of Ideas*, edited by John Banville, 21–50. Princeton, NJ: Princeton University Press.

Burrow, J. W. 1968. *Evolution and Society: A Study in Victorian Social Theory.* Cambridge: Cambridge University Press.

Cunningham, J. G. 1886. *Letters of St. Augustin.* In *The Confessions and Letters of St. Augustin, with a Sketch of His Life and Work*, 209–619. Vol. 1 *of A Select Library of Nicene and Post-Nicene Fathers of the Christian Church*, edited by Philip Schaff. Buffalo, NY: The Christian Literature Publishing Company.

Devereux, Georges. 1953. "Cultural Factors in Psychoanalytic Therapy." *Journal of the American Psychoanalytic Association* 1, no. 4: 629–55.

Devereux, George. (1955) 1976. "Culture and the Unconscious." Chap. 4 in *A Study of Abortion in Primitive Societies: A Typological, Distributional, and Dynamic Analysis of the Prevention of Birth in 400 Preindustrial Societies*, 76–89. New York: International Universities Press.

Devereux, Georges. 1980. *Basic Problems of Ethnopsychiatry.* Translated by Basia Miller Gulati and Georges Devereux. Chicago and London: University of Chicago Press. Originally published as *Essais d'ethnopsychiatrie générale*, translated from the English by Tina Jolas and Henry Gobard (Paris: Gallimard, 1970).

Dworkin, Ronald. 2006. *Is Democracy Possible Here? Principles for a New Political Debate.* Princeton, NJ: Princeton University Press.

Febvre, Lucien (1930) 1973. "Civilisation: Evolution of a Word and a Group of Ideas." In *A New Kind of History: From the Writings of Febvre*, edited by Peter Burke, translated by K. Folca, 219–57. London: Routledge and Kegan Paul.

Giuliani, Gaia. 2008. *Beyond curiosity: James Mill e la nascita del governo coloniale britannico in India.* Rome: Aracne.

Gozzi, Gustavo. 2011. "Abbandonare la natura umana? Verso una democrazia multiculturale." Chap. 7 in *Indagine sulla natura umana: Itinerari della filosofia contemporanea*, edited by Matteo Galletti and Silvia Vida. Rome: Carocci.

Gozzi, Gustavo. 2015. *Umano, non umano: Intervento umanitario, colonialismo, "primavere arabe."* Bologna: il Mulino.

Hume, David. 1894. "An Enquiry Concerning Human Understanding." In *An Enquiry concerning the Human Understanding, and an Enquiry concerning the Principles of Morals*, reprinted from the posthumous edition of 1777, edited by L. A. Selby-Bigge, 5–165. Oxford: Clarendon Press.

Hume, David (1739–40) 1969. *A Treatise of Human Nature: Being an Attempt to Introduce the Experimental Method of Reasoning into Moral Subjects.* Edited by Ernest C. Mossner. New York: Penguin Books.
Hume, David (1772) 1994. "Of National Characters." Chap. 12 in *Political Essays*, edited by Knud Haakonssen. Cambridge: Cambridge University Press.
Keene, Edward. 2002. *Beyond the Anarchical Society: Grotius, Colonialism and Order in World Politics.* Cambridge: Cambridge University Press.
Keene, Edward. 2005. *International Political Thought: A Historical Introduction.* Cambridge: Polity Press.
Lévi-Strauss, Claude. 1983. "Jean-Jacques Rousseau, Founder of the Sciences of Man." Chap. II in *Structural Anthropology*, Vol. 2, translated by Monique Layton, 33–43. Chicago: University of Chicago Press.
Mill, James (1820). 1937. *Essay on Government.* With an introduction by Ernest Baker. Cambridge: Cambridge University Press.
Mill, James. (1817) 1997. *The History of British India.* Reprint of the 1858 edition. London: Routledge.
Montaigne, Michel de. 1842. *Essays.* Translated by Charles Cotton. In *The Complete Works of Michel de Montaigne*, edited by William Carew Hazlett. London: John Templeman.
Montaleone, Carlo. 2011. *Oro, cannibali, carrozze: Il Nuovo Mondo nei Saggi di Montaigne.* Turin: Bollati Boringhieri.
Montesquieu, Charles-Louis de Secondat. (1748) 1989. *The Spirit of the Laws.* Translated and edited by Anne M. Cohler, Basia Carolyn Miller, and Harold Samuel Stone. Cambridge: Cambridge University Press.
Moro, Marie Rose. 2005. *Bambini di qui venuti da altrove: Saggio di transcultura.* Milan: FrancoAngeli.
Onuma, Yasuaki. 2000. "When Was the Law of International Society Born? An Inquiry of the History of International Law from an Inter-civilizational Perspective." *Journal of the History of International Law* 2: 1–66.
Quaranta, Ivo, and Mario Ricca. 2012. *Malati fuori luogo: Medicina interculturale.* Milan: Raffaello Cortina.
Rousseau, Jean-Jacques. (1754) 1984. "Discourse on the Origins and the Foundations of Inequality among Men." In *A Discourse on Inequality*, translated with an introduction and notes by Maurice Cranston, 77–138. London: Penguin Books.
Sepúlveda, Juan Ginés de. (1544/45) 2009. *Democrate secondo, ovvero sulle giuste cause di guerra*, edited with a foreword by Domenico Taranto (an Italian translation of *Democrates secundus sive de justis belli causis*). Macerata: Quodlibet.
Vitoria, Francisco de. (1539) 1991. "On the American Indians (*De Indis*)." Chap. 6 in *Vitoria: Political Writings*, edited by Anthony Pagden and Jeremy Lawrance. Cambridge: Cambridge University Press. Published in Latin under the title "De Indis insulanis relectio prior," in *Relectiones Theologicae XII*, tomus primus (Lugduni: Iacobum Boyerium, 1557).
Wheaton, Henry. 1836. *Elements of International Law: With a Sketch of the History of the Science.* Philadelphia: Carey, Lea & Blanchard.

4 The responsibility to protect, humanitarian intervention, and neocolonial policies*

In this chapter we take up the question of the responsibility to protect (RtoP). This means (a) inquiring into the changes that have transformed the sovereignty of states in the contemporary age, (b) seeing if we can understand the new makeup of international relations, and (c) attempting to draw the ambivalently shifting line that threads its way through the avowed aims of "humanitarian" intervention, the reality of the superpowers' new policies of hegemonic advance, and the new forms of neocolonialism.

4.1 The international community and sovereignty: An irreversible crisis?

The transformations that have taken place in international relations have been analysed from different vantage points. Particularly significant among these is the one that traces these transformations to the crisis of national sovereignty. It is in the context of this crisis that I propose to assess the modern upshot of humanitarian interventions, and in particular of the doctrine that goes by the name of RtoP.

In a pathbreaking work, Anne-Marie Slaughter describes the present-day world order as "an intricate three-dimensional web of links between disaggregated state institutions" (Slaughter 2004, 15). This new order is a system made up of horizontal and vertical networks that make it possible to gather and share information, coordinate policies, cooperate, deliver aid, and even enact new legal frameworks.

On this new interpretation of international relations, the state is not disappearing but is rather breaking apart into the institutions that make it up and increasingly interact with the their counterparts beyond state borders. From this breaking up of the state there emerge horizontal and vertical transgovernmental networks (Cohen 2004, 5).

* This chapter was first published in 2012 under the title "*Responsibility to Protect* e crisi della sovranità" (Gozzi 2012). It has since gone through substantive revisions with several additions, and in that updated version it now appears in translation.

Examples of horizontal regulatory governmental networks include the G-7, the G-8, and the G-20. These networks operate by way of government officials who act without claiming to represent the state as a whole. Examples of vertical networks "the relationship between the European Court of Justice (ECJ), the International Criminal Court (ICC), and the courts of their respective member states" (ibid., 6). To be sure, Slaughter (2004, 9) is

> not arguing that a new world order of government networks will replace the existing infrastructure of international institutions, but rather complement and strengthen it. States can be disaggregated for many purposes and in many contexts and still be completely unitary actors when necessary, such as in decisions to go to war.

It can be objected, however, that this unitary configuration of states can hold together only in virtue of the stronger states, and that it cannot be held up as a model for the weaker ones. This raises the problem of how humanitarian intervention and RtoP fits into the disaggregated picture that seems to describe the new reality of relations among states. In the post-WWII period a conception of the international community took hold under which states could join this community so long as they subscribed to the broad principles of the equal sovereignty of states and the protection of human rights (as happened with the states that joined the United Nations), and on this basis it was understood that the states in the community would commit to mutual recognition and nonintervention.

Membership in the international community entailed what Cohen (2004, 20) refers to as the "'democratization' of external sovereignty," through which we arrive at the sovereign equality of states, and from which follows the states' commitment to refrain from making war, as well as the criminalization of wars of aggression (ibid., 19).

It is on this basis that states have in principle accepted limitations on their sovereignty in international relations. It thus appears evident that the concept of sovereignty does not refer to any single, uniquely specified reality. For while in the domestic sphere the states' sovereignty is limited by principles of constitutional law, in the international sphere sovereignty is disaggregated, being spread out across myriad networks of intergovernmental relations, and being limited as well by the principles of international law.

It is in this context that there arises "the problem of what to do in the case of dictatorial authoritarian regimes that overthrow democratic institutions or block their emergence" (ibid., 21). A case in point is the "decision taken in 1997 by the Organization of American States (OAS) to amend its charter to permit suspension of a member whose democratic government is overthrown"—an "example of a set of rules agreed upon by sovereign states aimed at linking recognition of state sovereignty to the protection of internal popular sovereignty" (ibid.).[1] This

1 The OAS Charter can be found at www.oas.org/juridico/english/charter.html.

is also an example of how a regional union can be made up of states agreeing that no democracy can be overthrown by force and recognizing the *necessary link between popular sovereignty and external sovereignty.*

In the world of international relations, however, there are no powers capable of putting a check on a superpower that should unilaterally decide to militarily intervene in the affairs of another state on "humanitarian" grounds (so as to prevent genocide, ethnic cleansing, or crimes against humanity). In this sense, there is certainly some truth to the "'political realist' stance" (ibid., 4) taken by Carl Schmitt, arguing that "cosmopolitan" law is utopian and ideological.

There is no "right to humanitarian intervention" in international law (ibid., 22). We are therefore left with only the vague moral "cosmopolitan" discourse of human rights (to life, security, and so on), which lends itself to the worst kinds of instrumental uses designed to unilaterally advance power interests. The principles of international law, and in particular the recognition of sovereign equality, are constantly being violated under a "political instrumentalization of 'law' (cosmopolitan right)" (ibid., 3). In short, "cosmopolitan" law can be used to legitimize violations of international law.[2]

2 Compare the discussion in "'The Lady Doth Protest Too Much,'" where Martti Koskenniemi (2002) introduces in the analysis of law the Schmittian "distinction between the normal and the exceptional" (ibid., 159) and the view that "legal normality" depends "on the power of the one who could decide on the exceptional" (ibid., 171).

On the topic of NATO's 1999 bombing campaign in Serbia, Koskenniemi underscores that the bombing "was the exception that revealed, for a moment, the nature of the international order which lay not in the Charter of the United Nations nor in principles of humanitarianism but in the will and power of a handful of Western civilians and military leaders. The sacrifice of 500 civilians would then appear as a violent reaffirmation of the vitality of a concrete international order created sometime after the second world war and in which what counts as law, or humanitarianism, or morality, is decided with conclusive authority by the sensibilities of the Western Prince" (ibid.). Koskenniemi is here trying to isolate international law from the ability of superpowers to instrumentally use it to advance their own ends: "Even as law now arrogates to itself the right to speak the language of universal humanitarianism, it is spoken only by a handful of experts fascinated about matters military and technological, the targeting of missiles and press conferences with uniformed men who speak clearly. Should *their* moral sensibilities now be the lawyers' greatest concern?" (ibid., 173; Koskenniemi's italics).

In this article, Koskenniemi is unequivocal in his point that recourse to morality as a basis on which to legitimize humanitarian intervention in Serbia was an essentially political act, "a politics by those who have the means to strengthen control on everyone else" (ibid.). Against this practice Koskenniemi sets the "culture of formalism" (ibid., 174), which is "about setting limits to the impulses—'moral' or not—of those in decision-making positions in order to fulfil general, instead of particular, interests; because it casts decision-makers as responsible to the political community; and because it recognises the claims made by other members of that community and creates the expectation that they will be taken account of" (ibid.). While conceding that this is a tenuous solution that may well succumb to the steamroller of hegemonic power, it does nonetheless express a "strategy of resistance, and of *democratic hope*" (ibid.; italics mine).

4.2 War, humanitarian intervention, and the function of law

It is no easy task to set out the relation under which international law interfaces with sovereignty and its prerogatives. And yet—if we are to clarify the meaning of humanitarian intervention and the new definition it has received under RtoP—we will need to pin down the way international law relates to the recourse made to force on ostensibly humanitarian grounds.

In an in-depth study, Nathaniel Berman has put forward an extraordinarily original thesis, claiming that the role law plays in relation to force, and in particular to war, does not consist in *limiting* or *preventing* recourse to it: its role is rather one of "*construction*—the facilitation of war through the establishment of a separate legal sphere immunizing some organized violence from normal legal sanction and, inevitably, privileging certain forms of violence at the expense of others" (Berman 2004, 1; Berman's italics). In other words, "rather than *opposing violence*, the legal construction of war serves to *channel violence* into certain forms of activity engaged in by certain kinds of people, while excluding other forms engaged in by other people (ibid., 5; Berman's italics).

Berman further observes that "the forms of this legal construction of war are highly contingent, both in the sense of having varied historically and in the sense of having been contested within each period" (ibid., 6): "The contours of the legal construction of war have been contested, defended, transformed, and reconstructed" in the interaction "between people fighting for powers great and small, for Europeans and those they colonized, and for state armies and guerrilla forces of every political, ethnic, and geographical variety" (ibid.). This pattern has continued even in the aftermath of 9/11, which gave way to an effort to instrumentalize the distinction between war and nonwar and between prisoners of war and criminal defendants (ibid., 7). The role of law in relation to war can thus be framed as one of *construction*, *contestation*, or *instrumentalization* (ibid., 8).

In this connection, Berman revisits the categories through which the relation between law and war has classically been framed, namely, the categories of *jus ad bellum* (regulating recourse to war) and *jus in bello* (regulating the waging of war and the treatment of prisoners and civilians). He suggests that "*jus in bello* could only be fully established once the medieval *jus ad bellum* doctrine, that of 'just war,' had been abandoned (ibid., 5, n. 9). And now "the more recent renaming of *jus in bello* as 'international humanitarian law' appears to reflect a persistent discomfort about the semantic conjunction of law and war. This discomfort," he comments, "may be seen in the strikingly euphemistic [...] use of the term 'humanitarian' to describe a body of rules one of whose key doctrines is the 'combatants' privilege'—the provision of *legal immunity* for certain kinds of large-scale violence" (ibid., 3; Berman's italics).

The use of force in *jus in bello* is legitimized by legally restructuring it in the initial phase of military intervention or in the later phases of occupation, or by restructuring it in still a different way, whether this is done by the occupying powers or by resistance forces, insurgents, and so on. Berman cites an example from 1961 in India, when Krishna Menon, the country's defence minister, "declared that even a centuries-long colonial occupation should be viewed as an ongoing 'permanent aggression'" (ibid., 27). As Berman notes, while this "the notion of 'permanent aggression' captures much of the political and experiential dimensions of at least some colonial situations at least some of the time" Menon's use if it was instrumental to the aim of legitimizing "anticolonial military action—specifically, the invasion of Goa by India after 450 years of Portuguese rule" (ibid.).

This approach moves decisively beyond the traditional conception of law as a tool for limiting the use of force, for it enables us to appreciate that the legal construction of humanitarian intervention, military intervention, or war lends itself to a strategic instrumentalization designed to legitimize, *not limit, the use of force.* Let us see, then, on the basis of these premises, if we can unpack the complex paradigm that provides the conceptual framework for the concept of RtoP.

4.3 Humanitarian intervention and the "responsibility to protect"

The concept of RtoP can be traced, at its origin, to a few documents in which it was first blocked out. The first of these is a report so titled (*The Responsibility to Protect*) issued in 2001 by the International Commission on Intervention and State Sovereignty, which had been set up at the initiative of the Canadian government (ICISS 2001). The concept was subsequently developed by the UN's High Level Panel on Threats, Challenges and Change in its 2004 report titled "A More Secure World: Our Shared Responsibility" (UNGA 2004). The following year the theses set out in this report were taken up and developed in another UN report, this one signed by the secretary general, titled "In Larger Freedom: Towards Development, Security and Human Rights for All" (UNGA 2005a). And finally, in September 2005 the concept of RtoP was further developed in the UN document titled "World Summit Outcome" (UNGA 2005b).[3]

These documents sought to give an answer to the humanitarian disasters in Somalia, Bosnia and Herzegovina, Rwanda, Kosovo, and Darfur, identifying new forms of legitimacy for humanitarian intervention. The first document (ICISS 2001) reframed the conception of sovereignty, no longer as a state's control over its own territory and population, on the Westphalian model, but as responsibility exercised both internally and externally—the former towards the population, the latter in the face of serious human rights violations in other geopolitical contexts (Focarelli 2008, 320).

3 On this reconstruction see Stahn 2007.

Central to this first document by the International Commission on Intervention and State Sovereignty was the distinction between humanitarian intervention and RtoP. In the first place, the new concept of responsibility was meant to address "the dilemma of intervention from the perspective of the needs to those who seek or need support [...], rather than from the interests and perspectives of those who carry out such action (entities asserting 'the right to intervene')" (Stahn 2007, 103). In the second place, the International Commission, by so relativizing the concept of sovereignty, introduced an approach on which "responsibility is shared by the national state and the broader international community" (ibid.). Finally, the concept of responsibility was given an expanded meaning under which "an effective response to mass atrocities requires not only reaction, but ongoing engagement to prevent conflict and rebuild after the event" (ibid.).

Underpinning this approach is a constant critical reflection on the concept of sovereignty. Indeed, as Stahn points out, the International Commission drew a distinction between a state's internal responsibility and its external one, recognizing in the former case that states are "responsible for the safety, life, and welfare of their citizens" (ibid., 104), to whom they are accountable, and in the latter case that they also answer to the "international community through the United Nations" (ibid.). If this "dual responsibility" is violated and certain specific circumstances obtain, there comes into play a "'residual responsibility' of the broader community of states" (ibid.).

Also worthy of note is the manner of identifying the institutional entities entrusted with stepping in if a state should prove incapable of protecting its own population or should itself commit crimes and atrocities. In the International Commission's report, this "residual responsibility" may be assumed not only by the UN Security Council but also—"if the Security Council rejects a proposal or fails to deal with it in a reasonable time" (ICISS 2001, XIII)—by the General Assembly or by regional organizations or coalitions of states.

In the report, this latter option is phrased as "action within area of jurisdiction by regional or sub-regional organizations under Chapter VIII of the Charter, subject to their seeking subsequent authorization from the Security Council" (ibid.). And as Noam Chomsky has sarcastically remarked, this phrasing brings out "the skeleton in the closet," in that "the powerful unilaterally determine their own 'area of jurisdiction'" (Chomsky 2011, 14). This applies in particular to NATO, which "unilaterally determined that its 'area of jurisdiction' includes the Balkans," and that it "extends to Afghanistan, and beyond" (ibid.). In short, according to Chomsky, because the "expansive rights accorded by the International Commission are in practice restricted to NATO alone," the commission's report sets the stage "for resort to R2P as a weapon of imperial intervention at will" (ibid.).

Finally, the International Commission specified the criteria that need to be satisfied before the "responsibility to protect" can have a legitimate basis. These criteria fall under six headings as follows: right authority, just cause, right intention, last resort, proportional means, and reasonable prospects (ICISS 2001, § 4.16; cf. Stahn 2007, 104).

4.4 Hegemonic logics and forms of neocolonialism

The complex paradigm that has been built around the concept of RtoP reflects the transformation that sovereignty has undergone in recent history, and it answers to the need to set a foundation on which to legitimize the placing of limits on sovereignty. But what are these limits?

In the international landscape marked by globalization, unilateral action by the great powers, and the shaky ground on which stands international human rights law, it is difficult to accommodate a foundation on which to compellingly legitimize efforts to impose limits on the sovereignty of another state. The International Commission's 2001 report claims that RtoP is "supported by a wide variety of legal sources" (ICISS 2001, § 2.26), among which it lists "fundamental natural law principles" (ibid.). But the report makes no argument for these principles, nor does it clarify what they are (one may speculate that the drafters are referring to the principles of seventeenth- and eighteenth-century natural law theory), and by that fact alone we can appreciate how difficult it is to set this new paradigm on any solid foundation. Even the reference the report makes to just cause as a necessary condition for an intervention to be legitimate anchors the RtoP doctrine to the "just war" paradigm of the sixteenth and seventeenth centuries (Focarelli 2008, 234). Contrary to that paradigm of the modern age, however, the report neither clarifies how "just causes" relate to their natural law foundation nor defines the criteria of justice that ought to justify recourse to force.

Just causes are essentially those that involve extreme human rights violations, as in mass killing and ethnic cleansing.[4] These are unspeakable crimes, of course, betokening a contempt for humanity so alarming that the threat it poses to peace triggers Chapter VII of the UN Charter ("Action with respect to Threats to the Peace"), authorizing the Security Council to "take such action by air, sea, or land forces as may be necessary to maintain or restore international peace and security" (Art. 42).

That much is true. However, the *legal construction* of humanitarian intervention once a decision is made to act on RtoP inevitably lends itself to instrumentalization. In the debate that took place in the UN General Assembly on the secretary general's "In Larger Freedom" report (UNGA 2005a), many states expressed concern that the new basis for legitimizing humanitarian intervention—its basis under the RtoP doctrine—was no more than a device the great powers could use to further their own interests and impose their own values on the weaker states (Focarelli 2008, 331). As has been argued by many Third World or developing countries, including Algeria, Egypt, Colombia, Vietnam, Venezuela, Iran, Cuba, Syria, and Tanzania, the RtoP doctrine

4 From the "World Summit Outcome" document (UNGA 2005b) it clearly emerges that the RtoP doctrine was endorsed by the UN general Assembly and that a consensus had formed among the states on what counts as grounds for an RtoP intervention (genocide, war crimes, ethnic cleansing, and crimes against humanity). Cf. Focarelli 2008, 337.

essentially serves the purpose of placing the stronger states in a position where they do not have to take the interests of the weaker states into account,[5] all the while *legitimizing neocolonial policies*.[6] This is what happened, for example, with the military intervention in Libya under Security Council Resolution 1973 (2011) 25, which on the premise that the Libyan authorities' "attacks [...] against the civilian population *may* amount to crimes against humanity" (UNSC 2011, 1; italics added), provided the basis on which to justify the West's neocolonial response—the basis on which the Security Council, "reiterating the *responsibility* of the Libyan authorities to *protect* the Libyan population" (ibid.; italics added), "authorizes Member States [...] to take all necessary measures [...] to protect civilians and civilian populated areas under threat of attack" (ibid., § 4).[7]

Other countries, like the Russian Federation, ruled out that RtoP could amount to a new principle of international law, for if it did, it would have had to gain broad consensus within the international community, but that was not the

5 See UN General Assembly, 59th session, 86th plenary meeting (6 April 2005), UN doc A/59/PV.86; 87th plenary meeting (7 April 2005), UN doc A/59/PV.87; 89th plenary meeting (8 April 2005), UN doc A/59/PV.89; and 90th plenary meeting (8 April 2005), UN doc A/59/PV.90. As an example of these positions, consider the speech delivered by the Syrian representative, Mr. Mekdad, who spoke thus (in translation): "In earlier statements on the report of the High Level Panel, Arab States have emphasized their rejection of the right to resort to humanitarian or other intervention which has no basis in the Charter or in the international law. [...] In accordance with the principle of non-interference in the internal affairs of States, and in order not to undermine the peace, stability or sovereignty of States, which are safeguarded by the Charter, we believe that we should not use the pretext of the needs of the twenty-first century to restrict the concept of state sovereignty so as to allow intervention. Neither should the concept of sovereignty revert to its nineteenth-century definition so as to relax restrictions on the use of force and allow so-called preventive action" (UN doc A/59/PV.90, p. 19).

6 Anne Orford highlights the colonial stereotypes and ambivalence embedded in the discourse of humanitarian intervention. Colonial discourse at once underscored racial difference and disavowed that difference by constructing the conceit of the "reformable native," in such a way as to mask the same difference (Orford 2003, 182, quoting Bhabha 1994, 74). Likewise, the narrative of humanitarian intervention deploys colonial stereotypes that "include the representation of Yugoslavs, Rwandans, Somalis and East Timorese as childlike, unable to govern themselves, barbaric and unruly" (Orford 2003, 182), and at the same time it advocates the use of force to stop human rights violations and make the same people governable, just as it seeks to legitimize the presence of intervening powers (for broader context see Orford 2003, 182–85).

7 In commenting on UNSC Resolution 1973 (2011), Karim Mezran observes that military intervention "quickly morphed from a targeted action aimed at protecting the civilian population into a regime-change action aimed at overthrowing Muammar Gaddafi. The legitimacy of the intervention therefore remains, to this day, doubtful," especially in view of the hegemonic and neocolonial aims it sought to achieve under the guise of a "humanitarian war" (Mezran 2012, 172; my translation).

case.[8] Here, then, is an example illustrating how ***international law shows itself to be a construction that lends itself to instrumentalizations of power within the complex international relations system.***

In short, as concerns the RtoP doctrine, it does not have the backing of any shared *opinio juris*, nor does it clearly identify the authority entrusted with the decision to intervene. One commentator (Strauss 2011) has observed that, while the UN General Assembly resolution of 2005 (UNGA 2005b) did gain broad consensus around the concept of RtoP, it was nonetheless no more than a recommendation: it did not introduce a new legal principle. This is because UN Assembly General resolutions can gain the status of international customary law only if they are backed by an *opinio juris* in their favour—which, as just noted, is precisely what did not happen here.

But, as mentioned, RtoP also envisions *regional* solutions. This is what we see in the 2005 "World Summit Outcome" document, which at Paragraph 139 provides for precisely that option, in accordance with Chapter VII of the UN Charter.[9] An example of such regional initiatives is what we saw in Liberia in 1990—nine years before the NATO intervention in Kosovo—when the Economic Community of West African States (ECOWAS, established in 1975) received a request for help and agreed to intervene.[10] Also, four years before the RtoP doctrine was adopted, some of the states in the African Union recognized a right of intervention in response to grave humanitarian emergencies (see Williams 2007).

However, absent a clear *legal framework* for this doctrine (cf. Focarelli 2008, 342), we still face the risk of humanitarian interventions serving only to advance the interests of the great powers sitting at the UN Security Council. In this regard, the movement of nonaligned states has underscored that RtoP may be exploited to legitimize coercive unilateral interference in the internal affairs of other states (Bellamy, Davies, and Glanville 2011, 11). Indeed, and here I am

8 This is how the point was made (in translation) by the representative of the Russian Federation, Mr. Denisov: "The Secretary-General and the High-Level Panel define the concept of 'responsibility to protect' as an 'emerging norm.' Strictly speaking, the establishment of an international norm presupposes that there is wide support within the international community for such a norm. However, that is not the case here." UN General Assembly, 59th session, 87th plenary meeting (7 April 2005), UN doc A/59/PV.87, p. 6.

9 Here is the specific language of the "World Summit Outcome" document (under the heading "Responsibility to Protect Populations from Genocide, War Crimes, Ethnic Cleansing and Crimes Against Humanity"): "we are prepared to take collective action, in a timely and decisive manner, through the Security Council, in accordance with the Charter, including Chapter VII, on a case-by-case basis and in cooperation with relevant organizations as appropriate, should peaceful means be inadequate and national authorities manifestly fail to protect their populations from genocide, war crimes, ethnic cleansing and crimes against humanity" (UNGA 2005b, § 139; cf. Bellamy, Davies, and Glanville 2011, 10).

10 In 1990, in response to the military coups attempted by Charles Taylor's National Patriotic Front of Liberia, the Liberian president, Samuel Doe, appealed to ECOWAS requesting a military intervention to protect the government.

borrowing an expression from Martti Koskenniemi, RtoP reveals itself to be a *hegemonic technique*, giving the great powers a tool with which to make a case for their hegemonic designs by pointing to grave human rights violations, and hence to grave attacks on human dignity. In other words, as Emmanuelle Jouannet (2007, 386) has pointed out, human rights are an expression of "modern legal humanism" (referring to the values informing the "human rights proclaimed in the 'Universal' Declaration of 1948"), and they can accordingly provide a basis that can be instrumentally invoked when territorial sovereignty is violated.

In these transformations we can appreciate the full ambivalence of international law. In fact, as Koskenniemi has rightly pointed out, when exceptional situations arise, as in the case of serious human rights violations, the purpose or point of the rule of international law, namely, to prevent human rights violations, upstages and outweighs its formal validity. What this means, in other words, is that the *form* of law ceases to act as a check on the use of force to avert or prevent mass killing, genocide, or ethnic cleansing. As Koskenniemi expresses this point, "the need to uphold the formal validity of the law cannot be compared to the weight of *the impulse to act now*. If the rule does not allow this, *so much worse for the rule*" (Koskenniemi 2002, 169; italics mine)—even if the violation of the rule is entirely instrumental.

In these transformations Koskenniemi sees a "deformalization" of law "accompanied by a turn to ethics" (ibid., 160).[11] But the appeal to ethics clearly amounts to a political choice: behind it are the decisions the hegemonic powers make in a state of exception (ibid., 171). As a counterweight to the potential for this discretionary decision-making, Koskenniemi points to the constraints of formalism: "In such a situation, insistence on rules, processes, and the whole culture of formalism now turn into a strategy of resistance, and of democratic hope" (ibid., 174). In fact formalism, in his assessment, can place limits on decision-makers, making them accountable to the political community. The formalist approach would at the same time make it possible to take into account the claims advanced by the other members of the community, so that their voice may be heard.

But can formalism actually work as a counterpoise to the hegemonic tendencies of the great powers? Can formalism prevent violations of sovereignty, like the one that took place with the 1999 NATO bombing of Serbia?

In reality, I submit, the formalist approach cannot prevent the RtoP doctrine from being used as a hegemonic technique—one that, as the movement of nonaligned states has stressed, can be deployed to legitimize coercive unilateral interference in the internal affairs of states (Bellamy, Davies, and Glanville 2011, 11). Because this risk has in fact materialized on plenty of occasions,[12] it

11 Jouannet (2007, 389), for her part, sees the rise of a "substantive universalism."

12 RtoP was in point of fact made a legitimate basis for humanitarian intervention in 2006 with UN Security Council Resolution 1674 (2006), on the protection of civilians in armed conflict, under which the Security Council "reaffirms the provisions of paragraphs 138 and 139 of the 2005 World Summit Outcome Document [UNGA 2005b] regarding the responsibility to protect populations from genocide, war crimes, ethnic cleansing and crimes against humanity" (UNSC 2006, § 4).

becomes incumbent on us to reconsider the import and limitations of a concept whose role in political history and in the history of international law has been decisive, and that is the concept of sovereignty. A brief historical overview will thus enable us to see how this concept has been a mere *formal construction*, constantly changing under the shaping hand of the dominant powers.

4.5 More on sovereignty: How to redefine it? A standing hypocrisy?

An authoritative jurist like José E. Alvares concedes that the time has come to rethink some fundamental documents like the 1948 Genocide Convention (UNGA 1948) by adding a protocol clearly setting out what is within the signatory states' rights to do in the face of genocides taking place in other signatory states.[13] And Anne-Marie Slaughter even argues that UN member states at best enjoy "conditional sovereignty" (as distinct from a "Westphalian ideal of absolute autonomy") (Slaughter 2005, 628), and that a state retains the rights accorded to it under the UN Charter only so long as it fulfils its "responsibility to respect the dignity and basic rights of its citizens," internally, and "the responsibility to respect the sovereignty of other states," externally (ibid.).

The RtoP principle would seem to offer a solution to the problem of addressing serious crimes against humanity: it would do so by recasting sovereignty as responsibility. But, as Alvarez points out, while there is no denying that restrictions can be placed on the sovereign rights of a state that commits crimes like genocide and ethnic cleansing, "when the largest military and economic power seems all too ready to deploy the 'preventive' use of force anywhere and everywhere, [...] old-fashioned notions of un-impeachable sovereignty and non-intervention against overweening power retain their traditional appeal" (Alvarez 2008, 279).

These considerations suggest that sovereignty is a *relative concept*. What this means, on a first approximation, is that it should be gauged against the economic, military, and political power that different states wield. "Smaller and weaker states, particularly those that have suffered colonialism, are more prone to interpret sovereignty in territorial terms. Some powerful states, including most pointedly the United States, tend to see sovereignty in terms of freedom of policy choice and hence are reluctant to accept any interpretation of RtoP that implies an automaticity of response" (Luck 2009, 11). This observation connects to the question of the *political* implications of sovereignty, and it was Hans Kelsen who previously saw the need to engage with these implications, arguing that Jean Bodin's famous definition of sovereignty boiled down to the

13 Alvarez, however, has also aimed criticism at the RtoP principle, noting that this principle "by its nature is grounded in a more 'flexible' or permeable view of the legal rights of sovereigns (including their rights to territorial integrity)" (Alvarez 2008, 279; also published as Alvarez 2009).

French sovereigns' effort to free themselves of the hegemony exercised through the *imperium* bestowed on the German emperors (Kelsen 1920, §§ 1–2).

In grappling with the complexity of the problem of the plural interpretations the concept of sovereignty is open to, it will be useful to turn to Stephen D. Krasner's (1999) book *Sovereignty: Organized Hypocrisy*, noting that "the term *sovereignty* has been commonly used in at least four different ways." We have

- *domestic sovereignty*, referring to the organization of public authority within a state and to the level of effective control exercised by those holding authority;
- *interdependence sovereignty*, referring to the ability of public authorities to control transborder movements [the flow of information, ideas, goods, people, pollutants, or capital across the borders of their state];
- *international legal sovereignty*, referring to the mutual recognition of states or other entities; and
- *Westphalian sovereignty*, referring to the exclusion of external actors from domestic authority configurations. (Krasner 1999, 9; italics and line breaks added; phrase within square brackets quoted from p. 4)

In this breakdown of the meanings of sovereignty we also have an outline of the concept's historical transformations within a systematic frame that brings together its domestic implications and its outward projections. The RtoP doctrine—mainly concerned with the fourth, Westphalian meaning—has only *formally* changed the meaning of sovereignty, while leaving intact what Krasner argues to be its substance as an example of "organized hypocrisy," which continues to be its main defining trait. That the transformations of the concept of sovereignty have not changed its substantive meaning is something that can be appreciated by briefly going through its history.

In the history of political thought, the concept of sovereignty in the domestic relations system has mainly been investigated through the problem of its *limits*. In its international setting, by contrast, sovereignty has consistently been construed as *unlimited*, as an exercise of authority in something like a state of nature. We can see this in the work of Thomas Hobbes and John Locke. Thus in Hobbes's doctrine, domestic sovereignty found its basis of legitimation in the principles governing the state of nature, which required individuals to forsake their natural rights for the (natural) right to life and limb, all the while securing this latter right by an agreement to keep covenants (*stare pactis*). On this absolutist approach, a symmetric scheme was thus set up that would provide a dual guarantee, ensuring respect for the sovereign's authority, all the while protecting the sovereign's subjects in the security of their person.

While domestic sovereignty is the sovereignty of authority, interdependence sovereignty (as we saw) is a state's ability to control movement across its own borders. As Krasner points out, the loss of control that comes with globalization does not necessarily entail a loss of authority, nor does it entail a loss of legal recognition (international legal sovereignty). What *can* happen, by contrast—and indeed what we have seen—is that the loss of control, as in transportation and communication, "has prompted states to enter into agreements (an exercise of international legal sovereignty) to create international institutions, some of which have compromised their Westphalian sovereignty by establishing external authority structures" (Krasner 1999, 13–14) that undermine their ability to prevent foreign intervention in their own territory.

This takes us to sovereignty in Krasner's third meaning of the term, namely, international legal sovereignty. As Krasner notes, this idea is built on the "classic model of international law," which analogizes states to individuals. Indeed, on this model, writes Krasner (1999, 14), "states are equal in the same way that individuals are equal." But this is a spurious analogy: whereas individuals formally enjoy the equal protection of the laws, states are not all equal under a single supranational legal system. Their juridical equality in the international arena can only be based on their mutual recognition, and in this setting a state's recognition or nonrecognition of another state serves as an instrument of political leverage in conditions of material or ideological conflict—an instrument with which to weaken or strengthen the position of another state.

But it is the fourth meaning of sovereignty in the context of international relations that best enables us to clarify the import of humanitarian intervention and of RtoP.

4.6 Hegemonic techniques, constitutionalism, and international law

Through a careful historical reconstruction, Krasner radically demystifies Westphalian sovereignty. He points out, to begin with, that this conception essentially boils down to the "rule of nonintervention in the internal affairs of other states" (Krasner 1999, 20), but that this rule—though it may be associated with the 1648 Peace of Westphalia—"was not clearly articulated until the end of the eighteenth century" (ibid.). Quite accurately, Krasner traces the first statements of the nonintervention principle to the works of Christian Wolff and Emer de Vattel, but he compellingly shows that the grounds of nonintervention have in reality been systematically ignored.

Wolff invoked the *natural liberty of nations* as a basis on which to exclude all violations of sovereignty.[14] At the foundation of Wolff's conception was certainly his normative idea of a *civitas maxima*, within which peoples would be recognized as enjoying the same rights and as bound by the same duties. But Wolff

14 Writes Wolff in this regard: "Sese immiscere regimini alieno, quomodocumquetandem fiat, libertati naturali Gentium adversatur, vi cujus prorsus independens est a voluntate aliarum gentium in agendo" (Wolff [1749] 1934, vol. I, cap. II, § 256, p. 92. In translation: "To interfere in the government of another, in whatever way indeed that may be done, is opposed to the natural liberty of nations, by virtue of which one is altogether independent of the will of other nations in its action" (Wolff [1749] 1934, vol. II, chap. II, § 256, p. 131).

himself thought that all peoples belonging to the *civitas maxima* should be able to intervene coercively against any people who might disavow the central aim of this international society, namely, "to promote the common good" (Wolff [1749] 1934, vol. II, Prolegomena, p. 14, § 13; cf. vol. I, Prolegomena, p. 5, § 13).

Vattel was likewise emphatic in asserting the nonintervention principle as a guarantee of the liberty and independence of nations.[15] Equally central to Vattel's conception, however, was the idea of the *balance politique*, "the political balance, or the equilibrium of power; by which is understood such a disposition of things, as that no one potentate be able absolutely to predominate, and prescribe laws to the others" (Vattel [1797] 2008, bk. III, chap. III, § 47, p. 496; cf. Vattel [1758] 1916, vol. II, liv. III, chap. III, § 47, p. 40). And the need to preserve this equilibrium—especially in a legal-positivist world that had already moved beyond the ideal of natural law—meant that when a state acted to upset the balance of power among sovereign states, there was no way to escape the obligation to intervene against that state. As Vattel put it: "The safest plan, therefore, is to seize the first favourable opportunity when we can, consistently with justice, weaken that potentate who destroys the equilibrium (§ 45)—or to employ every honourable means to prevent his acquiring too formidable a degree of power" (Vattel [1797] 2008, bk. III, chap. III, § 49, p. 498).[16] So, even as Vattel gave pride of place to the nonintervention principle, he set a limit to it in the interest of preserving the balance of power: whenever that balance came under threat, in other words, it became legitimate to intervene. This balance-of-power conception would later be developed by Ludwig Dehio, who reframed it through the dialectic between balance and hegemony: Dehio showed that in the period spanning from the end of the fifteenth century to World War II, all attempts at hegemony within the European states-system were met with a counter-response from the other powers, in such a way that a balance could be restored (Dehio [1948] 1962).

15 Wrote Vattel: "It is an evident consequence of the liberty and independence of nations, that all have a right to be governed as they think proper, and that no state has the smallest right to interfere in the government of another" (Vattel, Emer de. [1797] 2008, bk. II, chap. IV, § 53, p. 289). And he concluded that any interference in another state's internal affairs was tantamount to an injustice: "If any intrude into the domestic concerns of another nation, and attempt to put a constraint on its deliberations, they do it an injury" (ibid., bk. I, chap. III, § 37, p. 96). The two passages in the French original: "C'est une conséquence de la Liberté & de l'indépendance des Nations, que toutes sont en droit de se gouverner comme elles le jugent à propos, & qu'aucune n'a le moindre droit de se mêler du Gouvernement d'une autre" (Vattel [1758] 1916, vol. I, liv. II, chap. IV, § 54, p. 297). "Si quelqu'une s'ingère dans les affaires domestiques d'une autre, si elle entreprend de la contraindre dans ses délibérations, elle lui fait injure" (ibid., vol. I, liv. I, chap. III, § 37, p. 38). For a reconstruction of the nonintervention principle outlined in this section, see Thomas and Thomas (1956, 5ff.).

16 The French original: "Le plus sûr est donc d'affoiblir celui qui rompt l'équilibre, aussi-tôt qu'on en trouve l'occasion favorable, & qu'on peut le faire avec justice (§ 45); ou d'empêcher par toute forte de moyens honnêtes, qu'il ne s'élève à un degrè de puissance trop formidable" (Vattel [1758] 1916, vol. II, liv. III, chap. III, § 49, p. 41).

As should be clear from the foregoing reconstruction, at the same time that nonintervention doctrines have constructed this concept as a principle, they have also unfailingly ended up carving out an exception to it on one basis or another. As Ann Van Wynen Thomas and A. J. Thomas have commented, "if one turns to history and views the practices of states it becomes difficult to escape the conclusion that intervention is the rule and non-intervention is the exception" (Thomas and Thomas 1956, 3).

Historically, intervention has taken on different meanings reflected in the different ways in which its basis of legitimacy has been construed in different geopolitical contexts, and here a contrast can be highlighted between two main contexts, namely, that of relations among European states and that of relations between Western and non-Western states: whereas intervention within the European system found its justification in the need to guarantee the principle of equality among states (Wolff) or to preserve the balance of power (Vattel), when it came to non-European peoples its basis became that of the system of Western values, with the simultaneous repudiation of non-Western normative systems. And so it was that the Spaniards appointed themselves as judges of the Inca emperor Atahualpa and sentenced him to capital punishment on the basis of Spanish law.[17]

It clearly emerges, then, that over the course of history the nonintervention principle has been bent to serve the interests of the most powerful states; and, conversely, as Krasner (1999, 21) observes, "weaker states have always been the strongest supporters of the rule of nonintervention." We can thus say, with Krasner (1999, 24), that even though Westphalian sovereignty is supposed to exclude foreign interference in a state's domestic affairs, "the principles associated with [it] have always been violated."

Humanitarian intervention and the RtoP doctrine are only the contemporary development of the continuing effort to legitimize foreign intervention, and they are only compounding the crisis of Westphalian sovereignty, once more revealing its nature as a form of "organized hypocrisy" (ibid., 25).

To be sure, the ambivalences embedded in the RtoP principle are undeniable, so much so that, as Noam Chomsky has argued with his realist sense of analysis, we should be led to think that the principle only works to the advantage of a "favored list of the powerful." Even so, the principle "can be a valuable tool, much as the Universal Declaration of Human Rights has been," for it "serves as an ideal that activists can appeal to in educational and organizing efforts, often effectively." In finding cause for such optimism, he points to "the civilizing effect of popular movements," as a result of which "the maxims that largely guide international affairs [...] have become considerably less harsh over the years" (Chomsky 2011, 16).

17 This historical event is reported by Vattel (quoted in Krasner 1999, 21), commenting that by their action "the Spaniards violated all rules" (Vattel [1797] 2008, bk. II, chap. IV, § 55, p. 290).

We have seen, then, that RtoP is essentially a hegemonic technique. But as Martti Koskenniemi (2004b, 214) points out, "although international law [...] is a hegemonic politics," its language and vocabulary nonetheless points in the opposite direction: the ideas expressed through it—"'self-determination,' 'fundamental rights,' 'division and the accountability of power,' and so forth"—"contest the structural biases of present institutions and politicize what otherwise appears as routine administration" (Koskenniemi 2007, 34). In other words, the concepts that international law has acquired from the constitutionalist tradition make it possible to "express a fundamental critique of present politics" (ibid., 35). Inherent in law, then, is a normative force that sustains the formation of a critical public opinion and frames expectations of change with the potential to unhinge the organization of political power, as happened with the French Revolution at the end of the eighteenth century.

In short, the language of international law can challenge the governance conducted by the hegemonic powers. It can do so by serving as the form through which "groups whose interests are not well represented in governance bodies receive a voice" (Koskenniemi 2004a, 253). In this way, the pure form of law—its "empty form"—provides a platform for "constructing a public space" or a legal "community, a *Rechtsgemeinschaft*" (ibid.) through which "***particular*** grievances may be articulated as ***universal*** ones" (ibid., 254; italics added), thereby breaking the scheme of the governance model built on the Schmittian opposition between "friend" and "enemy."

This brings to light the paradox of contemporary international law, with the two contrary strains that coexist within it: the realist one of power struggle, and the Kantian one that looks to the ideal of a cosmopolitan society. For if international law is undoubtedly the legal form through which the powerful states dominate and exploit the weaker ones, it also provides a space in which to work towards cooperation, solidarity, and emancipation (Jouannet 2007, 406–7).

4.7 Excursus: Humanity—history of an idea

If there is a common element between the concept of human rights—understood as rights that belong to every human being—and that of humanitarian intervention, it is the idea of humanity they both implicitly appeal to. This idea is meant to be universal in its scope, and should serve as the basis for the claim that all individuals and peoples ought necessarily to be recognized as having basic rights worthy of protection (Teitel 2011, 20). But, as noted, the same idea can be used to legitimize unilateral intervention and power politics. Let us therefore attempt a genealogical reconstruction of the idea of humanity, tracing its historical transformations so as to arrive at an understanding of the origins of humanitarian intervention and the foundation of human rights.

4.7.1 Humanity and dignity

In this genealogy, we will start out with the concept of *humanitas romana*, whose fullest statement comes to us from the Scipionic Circle of the second century BC.

As conceived by Cicero, *humanitas* was the complex of the highest moral and intellectual powers we put to use when moved by an awareness of moral duty. This view rested on the idea of man as endowed with reason, which in turn equipped him with a knowledge of duty and placed him above all other living beings.[18]

In Stoic philosophy, the concept of *humanitas* was expanded so as to encompass universal fellow feeling among human beings. Seneca underscored the common foundation of humankind, from which came the sense of sociability among all humans.[19]

With the rise of Christianity the idea of humanity came to be understood in light of its contrast to that of divinity.

Only with the humanists did the idea come to be re-evaluated in its own terms. Which is to say that it was used to describe humans as beings endowed with reason and so as capable of self-determination. This newfound sense of the human condition comes through clearly in the words of Pico della Mirandola, who in *De Hominis Dignitate* (written in 1486 and published posthumously in 1496) wrote that "man is an animal of diverse, multiform, and destructible nature. But why all this? In order for us to understand that, after having been born in this state [...] [,] we may be what we will to be" (Pico della Mirandola 1998, 6–7).[20]

18 Writes Cicero (*De Officiis* 1.107): "We must realize also that we are invested by Nature with two characters, as it were: one of these is universal, arising from the fact of our being all alike endowed with reason and with that superiority which lifts us above the brute. From this all morality and propriety are derived, and upon it depends the rational method of ascertaining our duty. The other character is the one that is assigned to individuals in particular" (quoted from Cicero 1913, bk. I, par. 107, p. 109). The Latin original: "Intellegendum etiam est duabus quasi nos a natura indutos esse personis; quarum una communis est ex eo, quod omnes participes sumus rationis praestantiaeque eius, qua antecellimus bestiis, a qua omne honestum decorumque trahitur et ex qua ratio inveniendi officii exquiritur; altera autem, quae proprie singulis est tributa." On Cicero's thought, see Heinemann 1931, 300ff..

19 Writes Seneca (*Letter* 5.4): "The very first thing philosophy promises is fellow feeling, a sense of togetherness among human beings. By becoming different, we will be cut off from this" (quoted from Seneca 2015, 31–32). The Latin original: "Hoc primum philosophia promittit, sensum communem, humanitatem et congregationem, a qua professione dissimilitudo nos separabit." Cf. Nybakken 1939, 412.

20 Compare the text in its fuller context as rendered in Pico della Mirandola 2012, 133–35: "Hence that saying of the Chaldeans [...], 'Man is by nature diverse, multiform and inconstant.' Yet, why go on about this? So that we may understand that we (having been born into this condition; that is, *born with the possibility to become what we wish to be*) must take the greatest care, lest people say of us that we [...] that we had turned ourselves into brutes and mindless beasts of burden" (italics added). The Latin original: "Hinc illud Chaldeorum [...], idest 'homo variae ac multiformis et desultoriae naturae animal.' Sed quorsum haec? Ut intelligamus (postquam hac nati sumus conditione, ut id simus quod esse volumus) curare hoc potissimum debere nos, ut illud quidem in nos non dicatur, cum in honore essemus non cognovisse similes factos brutis et iumentis insipientibus" (ibid., 132–34).

As noted in Chapter 1.2, Hugo Grotius, working within the Stoic tradition, invoked the "right of human society" (*jus humanae societatis*) as the foundation on which the sovereign was authorized to intervene against another sovereign who should oppress his own people. As he reasoned in *De Jure Belli ac Pacis*:

> It is another Question, *Whether we have a just Cause for War with another Prince, in order to relieve his Subjects from their Oppression under him.* True it is, that since the Institution of Civil Societies, the Governors of every State have acquired some peculiar Right over their respective Subjects [...].
>
> But if the Injustice be visible [...], as no good Man living can approve of, the Right of human Society shall not be therefore excluded. [...]
>
> And indeed tho' it were granted that Subjects ought not, even in the most pressing Necessity, to take up Arms against their Prince [...] we should not yet be able to conclude from thence, that others might not do it for them. (Grotius [1720] 2005, bk. II, chap. XXV, § VIII.1–3, pp. 1159–62; italics in the original)

In Grotius's conception, Hersch Lauterpacht (1946, 46) sees "the first authoritative statement of the principle of humanitarian intervention—the principle that the exclusiveness of domestic jurisdiction stops where outrage upon humanity begins." Indeed, Grotius held that sovereigns were accountable not only to their own people but also to the whole of humanity.[21] However, in laying out this vision, on which the idea of humanity encompasses the whole of humankind, Grotius strikes an ambiguous balance between the sovereignty of the state and the natural rights of individuals, this by failing to clarify what status individuals enjoy in relation to the state (Vincent 1992, 246).

It was Kant's philosophy that would introduce the primacy of the rights of man relative to political power, pointing to the idea of humanity as the locus of the dignity of man. As Kant wrote in the *Metaphysics of Morals*:

> Humanity itself is a dignity [*Würde*]; for a man cannot be used merely as a means by any man (either by others or even by himself) but must always be used at the same time as an end. It is just in this that his dignity (personality) consists [...]. But just as he cannot give himself away for any price [...], so neither can he act contrary to the equally necessary self-esteem of others, as men, that is, he is under obligation to acknowledge, in a practical way, the dignity of humanity in every other man. Hence there rests on him a duty regarding the respect that must be shown to every other man. (Kant [1797] 1991, "Doctrine of the Elements of Ethics," § 38, p. 255 [AA 6:462])

21 Grotius wrote "that kings who measure up to the rule of wisdom make account not only of the nation which has been committed to them, but of the whole human race [*totius humani generis*], and that they are [...] not 'friends of the Macedonians' alone, or 'friends of the Romans,' but 'friends of mankind'" (Grotius [1646] 1925, Prolegomena, § 24, p. 18).

Earlier in the same work Kant asserts that man is endowed with an original right to freedom *in virtue of his humanity*.[22] The dignity of humanity, recognizing the objective value inherent in every human being, means that certain rights to freedom need to be guaranteed so that that dignity can be realized. And indeed *The Metaphysics of Morals*, conceived in the late eighteenth century, can be understood as a work that celebrates the rights of man and the universal value of the humanity that is to be recognized for every human being. This is a universalistic vision that leads Kant to condemn any denial of rights, along with all the abuses and violence of colonialism.

But the ensuing nineteenth century instead marked the *triumph* of colonialism, on the part of Western powers that rejected any universalistic conception of humanity and established the superiority of a distinctly "European humanity." This hierarchical conception positing a superior humanity was clearly recognized by Carl Schmitt, who pointed out that international law between the nineteenth and twentieth centuries was "a specific *European* international law" (Schmitt 2006, pt. IV, chap. 2, A, p. 228; italics in the original). As he went on to observe:

> This was also true of such worldwide, universalist concepts as *humanity*, *civilization*, and *progress*, which determined the general concepts of the theory and vocabulary of diplomats. However, the whole picture thereby was understood to be Eurocentric to the core, since by "humanity" one understood, above all, *European* humanity. "Civilization" was self-evidently only *European* civilization, and "progress" was the linear development of *European* civilization. (Ibid.)

This ideology became the basis for legitimizing the conquest, occupation, and domination of the colonial period. The "laws of humanity" and the "reason of humanity" in whose name the Ottoman Empire was progressively carved up were in reality the laws and reason of "European humanity." Accompanying this assertion of a superior humanity was a manifest violence driven by a resolve to subdue populations regarded as belonging to an inferior humanity stuck in a backward civilization. But this violence could only beget more violence, in a vortex where only violence could quell the violence. The colonizer denied the humanity of the colonized. As Frantz Fanon (2004, 7–8) observes, the colonized

> is reduced to the state of an animal. And consequently, when the colonist speaks of the colonized he uses zoological terms. [...] In his endeavours at description and finding the right word, the colonist refers constantly to the bestiary. [...] The colonized know all that and roar with laughter every time they hear themselves called an animal by the other. For they know they are not animals.

22 "There is only one innate right," he argues: "*Freedom* (independence from being constrained by another's choice), insofar as it can coexist with the freedom of every other in accordance with a universal law, is the only original right belonging to every man by virtue of his humanity" (ibid., "Division of the Doctrine of Right," B, p. 63 [AA 6:238]; italics in the original).

Fanon further comments that the "violence" and "aggressiveness" with which the colonizers seek to impose the "supremacy of white values" results in an outcome that is contrary to its design. For it elicits in the colonized an awareness of their own humanity. "And at the very moment when they discover their humanity," he comments, "they begin to sharpen their weapons to secure its victory" (ibid., 8).

At this point, when the colonized alight on their own humanity, the colonizer's humanity faces the full force of its opposition, and an irresistible emancipation process is thereby set in motion. *The crisis and end of colonialism can thus be said to have originated out of the discovery the colonized made that in them was a humanity that had been denied to them.* They accordingly proclaimed a free humanity that pridefully rejoiced in its cultural identity, capable of forging its own destiny, and in this way they pushed back the imperious violence of "European humanity." The humanity of the colonized finally wrested itself from the chokehold of the colonizer's inhumanity.

4.7.2 Humanity, international law, and international human rights law

In the second half of the nineteenth century, when international humanitarian law (*jus in bello*) first came into form, its purpose was to protect human beings from the ravages of war. The first step in this direction came on August 12, 1864, with the First Geneva Convention, which sought to protect the victims of armed conflict by establishing an international standard and framework that held valid above and beyond the sovereignty of the states.

The subsequent Hague Convention of 1899 explicitly appealed to the laws of humanity as a standard in light of which to place constraints on the waging of war (in this regard see Teitel 2011, 26). In its preamble, the convention stated:

> Until a more complete code of the laws of war is issued, the High Contracting Parties think it right to declare that in cases not included in the Regulations adopted by them, populations and belligerents remain under the protection and empire of the principles of international law, as they result from the usages established between civilized nations, from the laws of humanity, and the requirements of the public conscience. (Hague Convention 1899, preamble)

If these developments marked an advance in international humanitarian law, or *jus in bello*, the UN Charter of 1945 and the UN's 1948 Universal Declaration of Human Rights sought to set limits on *jus ad bellum* (covering the justification or reasons for war) by positing human rights as the necessary condition that needs to be met to guarantee peace and justice.

As the Universal Declaration of Human Rights says in its preamble, its intent, against the backdrop of World War II, was to protect these rights against the "disregard and contempt" for them that had "resulted in barbarous acts which [...] outraged the *conscience of mankind*" (italics added). Only the protection of human rights, then, in the declaration's own understanding, could ward off the danger of yet more wars and prevent the wartime atrocities that had shocked the "conscience of mankind."

As Hedely Bull (2002, 146) has commented, "the doctrine of human rights and duties under international law is subversive of the whole principle that mankind should be organised as a society of sovereign states": it "left open [the way] for the subversion of the society of sovereign states on behalf of the alternative organising principle of a cosmopolitan community."

The relation between state sovereignty and human rights has been insightfully analysed by Anne Peters (2009, 513), who argues that this relation "should not be approached in a balancing process in which the former is played off against the latter on an equal footing, but should be tackled on the basis of a presumption in favour of *humanity*" (italics mine), adding that such a "humanized state sovereignty implies responsibility for the protection of basic human rights and the state's accountability." With this "humanization of sovereignty," she further argues, "the focus is shifted from states' rights to states' obligations towards natural persons." In short, "sovereignty implies responsibility" (ibid., 522), absent which a state is no longer entitled to recognition by the international community.

But as Carl Schmitt points out in *The Concept of the Political*, "the concept of humanity is an especially useful ideological instrument of imperialist expansion," this with "incalculable effects, such as denying the enemy the quality of being human and declaring him to be an outlaw of humanity; and a war can thereby be driven to the most extreme inhumanity" (Schmitt 2007, 54; cf. Zolo 2000). Indeed,

> when a state fights its political enemy in the name of humanity, it is not a war for the sake of humanity, but a war wherein a particular state seeks to usurp a universal concept against its military opponent. At the expense of its opponent, it tries to identify itself with humanity in the same way as one can misuse peace, justice, progress, and civilization in order to claim these as one's own and to deny the same to the enemy. (Schmitt 2007, 54)

Works Cited

Alvarez, José E. 2008. "The Schizophrenias of R2P." Chap. 8 in *Human Rights, Intervention, and the Use of Force*, edited by Philip Alston and Euan Macdonald, 275–84. Oxford: Oxford University Press.

Alvarez, José E. 2009. "The Schizophrenias of R2P." Paper presented at the 8th Hague Joint Conference on Contemporary Issues of International Law, The Hague, 28–30 June 2007. Published as *Criminal Jurisdiction 100 Years after the 1907 Hague Peace Conference*, edited by Willem J. M. van Genugten, Michael P. Scharf, and Sasha E. Radin, 212–18. The Hague: T. M. C. Asser Press.

Bellamy, Alex J., Sara E. Davies, and Luke Glanville. 2011. "Introduction." In *The Responsibility to Protect and International Law*, edited by Alex J. Bellamy, Sara E. Davies, and Luke Glanville. Leiden and Boston: Martinus Nijhoff.

Berman, Nathaniel. 2004. "Privileging Combat? Contemporary Conflict and the Legal Construction of War." *Columbia Journal of Transnational Law* 43, no. 1: 1–71.

Bhabha, Homi K. 1994. *The Location of Culture*. London and New York: Routledge.

Bull, Hedley. 2002. *The Anarchical Society: A Study of Order in World Politics*. 3rd. ed. With forewords by Stanley Hoffmann and Andrew Hurrell. Houndmills, Basingstoke, UK, and New York: Palgrave Macmillan. (Orig. pub. 1977.)

Chomsky, Noam. 2011. "The Skeleton in the Closet: The Responsibility to Protect in History." Chap. 2 in *Critical Perspectives on the Responsibility to Protect: Interrogating Theory and Practice*, edited by Philip Cunliffe. Abingdon, Oxon: Routledge.

Cicero. 1913. *De Officiis*. With an English translation by Walter Miller. Loeb Classical Library 30. London: William Heinemann; New York: G. P. Putnam's Sons.

Cohen, Jean L. 2004. "Whose Sovereignty? Empire versus International Law." *Ethics & International Affairs* 18, no. 3: 1–24.

Dehio, Ludwig. (1948) 1962. *The Precarious Balance: Four Centuries of the European Power Struggle*. Translated by Charles Fullman. New York: Alfred Knopf. Originally published in German under the title *Gleichgewicht oder Hegemonie: Betrachtungen über ein Grundproblem der neueren Staatengeschichte* (Krefeld: Scherpe, 1948).

Fanon, Frantz. 2004. "On Violence." Chap. I in *The Wretched of the Earth*, translated from the French by Richard Philcox, with commentary by Jean-Paul Sartre and Homi K. Bhabha. New York: Grove Press. Originally published as *Les damnés de la terre* (Paris: François Maspero, 1961).

Focarelli, Carlo. 2008. "La dottrina della 'responsabilità di proteggere' e l'intervento umanitario." *Rivista di diritto internazionale* 2: 317–46.

Gozzi, Gustavo. 2012. "*Responsibility to Protect* e crisi della sovranità." In *Crisi della legittimità e ordine internazionale: Lo scontro sui principi costitutivi della società internazionale*, edited by A. Colombo, 113–32. Milan: Guerini e Associati.

Grotius, Hugo. (1646) 1925. *De Jure Belli ac Pacis Libri Tres* (orig. pub. 1625). Vol. II, a translation of the 1646 edition by Francis W. Kelsey, with the collaboration of Arthur E. R. Boak, Henry A. Sanders, Jesse S. Reeves, and Herbert F. Wright, and an Introduction by James Brown Scott. Oxford: Clarendon Press; London: Humphrey Milford.

Grotius, Hugo. (1720) 2005. *The Rights of War and Peace*. Edited by Richard Tuck, from the 1720 edition by Jean Barbeyrac. Indianapolis: Liberty Fund.

Hague Convention. 1899. Convention (II) with Respect to the Laws and Customs of War on Land and Its Annex: Regulations concerning the Laws and Customs of War on Land. The Hague, 29 July 1899.

Heinemann, Isaak. 1931. "Humanitas." In *Paulys Realencyclopädie der classichen Altertumswissenschaft*. Supplement V. Stuttgart: Alfred Druckenmüller.

ICISS. 2001. *The Responsibility to Protect: Report of the International Commission on Intervention and State Sovereignty*. Also issued in French under the title *La responsabilité de protéger*. Ottawa: International Development Research Centre. http://www.iciss-ciise.gc.ca/report2-en.asp (now archived, captured by Wayback Machine on 31 July 2007)

Jouannet, Emmanuelle. 2007. "Universalism and Imperialism: The True-False Paradox of International Law?" *The European Journal of International Law* 18, no. 3: 379–407.

Kant, Immanuel. (1797) 1991. *The Metaphysics of Morals*. Introduction, translation, and notes by Mary Gregor. Cambridge: Cambridge University Press.

Kelsen, Hans. 1920. *Das Problem der Souveränität und die Theorie des Völkerrechts: Beitrag zu einer reinen Rechtslehre*. Tübingen: J. C. B. Mohr / Paul Siebeck.
Koskenniemi, Martti. 2002. "'The Lady Doth Protest Too Much': Kosovo, and the Turn to Ethics in International Law." *The Modern Law Review* 65, no. 2: 159–75.
Koskenniemi, Martti. 2004a. "Global Governance and Public International Law." *Kritische Justiz* 37, no. 3: 241–54.
Koskenniemi, Martti. 2004b. "International Law and Hegemony: A Reconfiguration." *Cambridge Review of International Affairs* 17, no. 2: 197–218.
Koskenniemi, Martti. 2007. "Constitutionalism as Mindset: Reflections on Kantian Themes about International Law and Globalization." *Theoretical Inquiries in Law* 8, no. 1: 9–36.
Krasner, Stephen D. 1999. *Sovereignty: Organized Hypocrisy*. Princeton, NJ: Princeton University Press.
Lauterpacht, Hersch. 1946. "The Grotian Tradition in International Law." *British Year Book of International Law* 23: 1–53.
Luck, Edward C. 2009. "Sovereignty, Choice, and the Responsibility to Protect." *Global Responsibility to Protect* 1, no. 1: 10–21.
Mezran, Karim. 2012. "La rivolta." Chap. VIII in *Libia: Fine o rinascita di una nazione?*, edited by Karim Mezran and Arturo Varvelli, with a foreword by Lucio Caracciolo, 157–76. Rome: Donzelli.
Nybakken, O. E. 1939. "Humanitas Romana." *Transactions and Proceedings of the American Philological Association* 70: 396–413.
Orford, Anne. 2003. "The Constitution of the International Community: Colonial Stereotypes and Humanitarian Narratives." Chap. 5 in *Reading Humanitarian Intervention: Human Rights and the Use of Force in International Law*, 158–95. Cambridge: Cambridge University Press.
Peters, Anne. 2009. "Humanity as the A and Ω of Sovereignty." *European Journal of International Law* 20, no. 3: 513–44.
Pico della Mirandola. 2012. *Oration on the Dignity of Man: A New Translation and Commentary*. Edited by Francesco Borghesi, Michael Papio, and Massimo Riva. Cambridge: Cambridge University Press.
Pico della Mirandola, Giovanni. 1998. *On the Dignity of Man*. Translated by Charles Glenn Wallis. Indianapolis, IN: Hackett Publishing Company.
Schmitt, Carl. 2006. *The Nomos of the Earth in the International Law of the Jus Publicum Europaeum*. Translated by G. L. Ulmen. New York: Telos Press Publishing. (Orig. pub. 1950.)
Schmitt, Carl. 2007. *The Concept of the Political*. Expanded edition. Translation and introduction by George Schwab, foreword by Tracy B. Strong, notes by Leo Strauss. Based on the 1932 edition of *Der Begriff des Politischen*. Chicago and London: University of Chicago Press.
Seneca, Lucius Annaeus. 2015. *Letters on Ethics*. Translated and with an introduction and commentary by Margaret Graver and A. A. Long. Chicago: University of Chicago Press.
Slaughter, Anne-Marie. 2004. *A New World Order*. Princeton, NJ, and Oxford: Princeton University Press.
Slaughter, Anne-Marie. 2005. "Security, Solidarity, and Sovereignty: The Grand Themes of UN Reform." *The American Journal of International Law* 99, no. 3: 619–31.
Stahn, Carsten. 2007. "Responsibility to Protect: Political Rhetoric or Emerging Legal Norm?" *The American Journal of International Law* 101, no. 1: 99–120.

Strauss, Ekkehard. 2011. "A Bird in the Hand Is Worth Two in the Bush: On the Assumed Legal Nature of the Responsibility to Protect." In *The Responsibility to Protect and International Law*, edited by Alex J. Bellamy, Sara E. Davies, and Luke Glanville, 25–57. Leiden and Boston: Martinus Nijhoff.

Teitel, Ruti G. 2011. *Humanity's Law*. New York: Oxford University Press.

Thomas, Ann Van Wynen, and A. J. Thomas, Jr. 1956. *Non-intervention: The Law and Its Import in the Americas*. Dallas: Southern Methodist University Press.

UNGA (UN General Assembly). 1948. "Prevention and Punishment of the Crime of Genocide: Adoption of the Convention on the Prevention and Punishment of the Crime of Genocide." Resolution 260 A (III) adopted on 9 December 1948, third session, 179th plenary meeting. UN doc A/RES/3/260.

UNGA (UN General Assembly). 2004. "A More Secure World: Our Shared Responsibility." Report of the High-Level Panel on Threats, Challenges and Change (2 December 2004). UN doc A/59/565.

UNGA (UN General Assembly). 2005a. "In larger freedom: towards development, security and human rights for all." Report of the Secretary-General (21 March 2005). UN doc A/59/2005.

UNGA (UN General Assembly). 2005b. "World Summit Outcome." Resolution adopted on 16 September 2005 (24 October 2005). UN doc A/RES/60/1.

UNSC (UN Security Council). 2006. Resolution 1674 (2006). Adopted by the Security Council at its 5430th meeting (28 April 2006). UN doc S/RES/1674 (2006).

UNSC (UN Security Council). 2011. Resolution 1973 (2011). Adopted by the Security Council at its 6498th meeting (17 March 2011). UN doc S/RES/1973 (2011).

Vattel, Emer de. (1758) 1916. *Le Droit des Gens, ou Principes de la Loi Naturelle, appliqués à la Conduite et aux Affaires des Nations et des Souverains*. Vol. I, photographic reproduction of books I and II of the first edition (1758). Vol. II, photographic reproduction of books III and IV. Vol. III, translation of the 1758 edition by Charles G. Fenwick. Washington, DC: Carnegie Institution of Washington.

Vattel, Emer de. (1797) 2008. *The Law of Nations, or, Principles of the Law of Nature, Applied to the Conduct and Affairs of Nations and Sovereigns*. Edited by Béla Kapossy and Richard Whatmore, translated by Thomas Nugent (based on the London 1797 edition). Indianapolis: Liberty Fund.

Vincent, R. J. 1992. "Grotius, Human Rights, and Intervention." Chap. 8 in *Hugo Grotius and International Relations*, edited by Hedley Bull, Benedict Kingsbury, and Adam Roberts. Oxford: Clarendon Press.

Williams, Paul. D. 2007. "From Non-interference to Non-indifference: The Origins and Development of the African Union's Security Culture." *African Affairs* 106, no. 423: 253–79.

Wolff, Christian. (1749) 1934. *Jus Gentium Methodo Scientifica Pertractatum*. Vol. I, Photographic reproduction of the 1764 edition. Vol. II, English translation by Joseph H. Drake. Oxford: Clarendon Press.

Zolo, Danilo. 2000. *Chi dice umanità: Guerra, diritto e ordine globale*. Turin: Einaudi.

Part II

New democracies?

5 Anticolonial nationalism and Arab nationalism

The first part of this book sought to shed light on the ambiguities of humanitarian intervention. It did so by scrutinizing colonial thought in an analysis that keyed in on the Western conceit of the presumed superiority of Western civilization and the inferiority of non-Western humanity—a presumption that formed the backdrop against which the European powers set out on a "civilizing mission" intended to shepherd that humanity towards what they saw as the higher standard of their civilization. But the mission backfired, as we saw, when the colonized recognized their own humanity, along with the colonizers' *inhumanity*, thereby setting in train a process of emancipation. So, if we have so far looked at the problem by dissecting the *Western* mindset, we will now switch sides and look at it from the vantage point of the "colonized," in an exploration that will take us to the formation of the independent Arab states and the season that has come to be known as the Arab Spring.

5.1 Anticolonial nationalism

Let us enter into this analysis by turning to the case of French Algeria. The transformations the country went through as a result of the French conquest have been analysed by the sociologist Abdelmalek Sayad, who notes, to begin with, that the aims of this colonial venture were the ones that had been described by Montesquieu, namely, to gain control over the country's raw materials and open a market for the goods produced in the mother country (Sayad 2003, 22).[1]

Following various attempts at growing exotic produce in a Mediterranean climate, the decision was finally made to introduce viticulture under an agricultural system based on the French colonists' appropriation of land. This colonial system was violent, for in addition to being based on armed conflict and land appropriation, it wiped out traditional agriculture, thereby radically modifying the Algerian people's system of social and cultural relations. "In the outcome" Sayad observes, "the whole of the colonized society was massively disrupted, with a complete destructuring of all social units at all levels" (ibid., 25; my translation). More to the point, a proletarianization process was set off based on the commodification of labour in the metropolis.

Sayad deepens the analysis of the conditions that explain the relationship between the colonized and the colonizer. He reconstructs this as a "passional" relationship

1 Sayad died in 1998, before completing the manuscript, which was published posthumously under the editorship of Salvatore Pallida and Nino Recupero. Cf. Montesquieu (1748) 1989, pt. 4, bk. 21, chap. 21, pp. 391–93.

enmeshed in history, and in whose formation both sides played a part—both the dominant party (France) and the dominated one (Algeria). This was a colonial relationship that set up a relational structure of reciprocal influences. When it proved just too difficult to arrive at the "essence" of colonization, the notion was introduced of "passional relationships" (ibid., 35), in which only one party is understood to be possessed of rationality, while the other party is thought to lack precisely this capacity.

Sayad seeks to break the barrier in which these representations are encased, so as to grasp the dialectic underpinning the interactive relationships that were forged in the era of colonization. Through his analysis, centred on the political outcome of colonization, he outlines the process that led to the formation of an "anticolonial" or "anticolonialist" nationalism which nonetheless never managed to throw off the yoke of colonial domination. In this process, a movement was mounted to resist colonial power, but this movement "never managed to free itself of the bonds of the colonial condition so as to be able to think of itself as fully independent, with its own worldview" (ibid., 42). This inability of Algerian nationalism to shape its own identity can be ascribed to its having been a "child of colonization": it was in reaction to colonization that this movement took shape, but in a process marked by contradictory impulses, for even as it rejected the colonial set-up, it continued to mimic the colonial mindset in a way that shaped the movement itself down to the core.

At the same time, this nationalism was not all assimilationist, for it sprang up in a Muslim country and "charted its own path toward religion, sacralizing itself in a literal sense, merging the political sphere with the cultural, and more specifically with the religious one, in such a way as to make religion the essential linchpin of national identity" (ibid., 44).[2]

2 The process through which Arab-Islamic nationalism came into shape has accurately been reconstructed in depth by Antonino Pellitteri in an extensive analysis that identifies three main aspects of it. In the first place, there are no concepts of race or blood in this stream of thought, which instead looks to the idea of an Arab nation unified by its language and capable of tapping into the rich store of its complex civilization (see Pellitteri 2012, 28).

In the second place—and in making this argument Pellitteri draws especially on the work of the Algerian historian Abū l-Qāsim Saʿd Allāh—it is to Algeria that we can trace the birth of Arab nationalism, for this is where the Arab resistance to French occupation was mounted, and in this fight for Algerian liberation two conceptions of nationality confronted each other: the French conception (with its principle of *laïcité*) and the Arab Islamic conception claimed for Algeria (ibid., 32).

In the third place, the idea of an Arab nation emerged out of the complex relation between Arabism and Islam. Following the Algerian thinker, Pellitteri states that "Arab resistance in Algeria was at the same time Arab and Islamic" (ibid.; my translation).

In offering this analysis, Abū l-Qāsim Saʿd Allāh rejects the Eurocentric narrative that identifies three moments in the development of Arab nationalism: its birth, traced to the eighteenth-century formation of Wahhabism in the Arabian peninsula; a second stage, descried in the anti-Ottoman policy that in the early nineteenth century was carried forward by Muḥammad ʿAlī; and then a further resurgence with the Arab revolt that in 1916 al-Ḥusayn of Mecca led against the Ottoman Empire. But in reality, as Abū l-Qāsim Saʿd Allāh observes, none of these three moments were tied to Arab nationalism: the Wahhabite movement was essentially concerned to purify Islam; the policy championed by Muḥammad ʿAlī was a form of expansionism encroaching on the Ottoman Empire; and far from advancing the cause of Arab nationalism, al-Ḥusayn's revolt cleared the way for the advance of colonialism and Zionism (ibid., 34).

According to Sayad, this cross-fertilization between the political and the religious is reflected in two aspects of the "sacred": on the one hand there could be observed a "religious sacred" that enveloped Muslim society in its every manifestation; on the other there emerged a "nationalist sacred" that first sacralized the political concept of nation and then the cause of political nationalism. In this sense, religion can be said to have been bent to the service of nationalism.

This "nationalist sacred" that emerged in reaction to colonization thus set itself up against the "sacred of the civilizing mission." But the two worlds remained inextricably bound up even so, in that the colonization that gave rise to Algerian nationalism never ceased to exert a power of obsession over that movement. Indeed, as Sayad observes, even in his own time the identity of nationalism continued to be the "negative" one that had been impressed on it by colonization, just as there continued to be an unresolved overlap between the two spheres of the religious and the political. Sayad gives even greater scope to his inquiry by arguing that in trying to understand these unresolved issues that come to light through his analysis, we should not be looking at them in the context of this or that specific country but should rather proceed on an ideal-typical Weberian approach that makes it possible to "take a different perspective on colonialization (though not on colonialism) as a phenomenon both general and universal, a phenomenon incident to civilization itself (but in a different way than is understood by those who speak of the 'civilizing mission' of colonization)" (Sayad 2003, 50).

Sayad's reflection is fully consonant with that of other commentators—such as Bassam Tibi (1996)—who have underscored that the concept of nation is extraneous to the Muslim tradition, central to which is not the nation but the community of believers (*umma*).

5.2 Anticolonial nationalism, nation, and state

Sayad's analysis of anticolonial nationalism develops in two directions, being geared towards clarifying the relation that nationalism bears, on the one hand, to the nation and, on the other, to the nation-state.

We just saw that in identifying the contents of colonial nationalism, Sayad looks to the aims of the anticolonial struggle and to the mimetic relationship that pulls the colonized into the logic of colonization. Not so straightforward, by contrast, is the path he follows in defining the concept of nation. Where to look in tracing its origin? Sayad cannot pin down the moment of creation, that is, a specific time when the myth of the nation was actually forged.

There are two reasons for this impossibility. The first of these is that there is nothing in the Muslim world like the Western concept of nation understood as an entity set in a prelegal state of nature in which a "national" community comes into form whose members we consider to be our forebears. The second reason has to do with the history and ideology of colonization, which deprived the Algerian people of the possibility of even constructing a national myth. This was done by promoting a view of Algerian history as the history of a people who had always been subject to one domination after another. This process, Sayad (2003, 63) writes, "is exemplified by the Arab conquest and the Islamification of the country, which melded into each other and were reduced to simple expeditions of troops and nomadic tribes." Even the Ottoman regency of Algiers was a moment in this continuous series of "conquest after conquest." Thus the "French conquest, occupation, and colonization [...] took on the meaning of a historical foundation, for the Algerian lands were constructed as being colonial by vocation: the colony of the East or that of the West—all territories that thereby lacked an independent political or national existence" (ibid.).

Hence the central thesis that Sayad extracts from his analysis—namely, that Algerian nationalism, anticolonial in its thrust, is *nationless* in spirit and in its self-understanding.

In fact, all the components of Algerian society—the village, the tribe, the federation of tribes, the brotherhoods—jealously guarded the myth of their own origin and legitimation. It is this social fabric, *and not an inexistent Algerian nation*, that formed the seedbed of Algerian nationalism, which sprang up as the child of colonization and embraced the ideals of French colonialism.

Whereas Algeria's "negative" nationalism took hold only as a movement of opposition to colonial domination, the French nation-state, initially imposed on an Algeria set up as a "French department," continued to provide the model for the Algerian state after independence: France continued to act as "the institutional benchmark, representing the state's omnipotence in every sector of national life, which logically can be powerfully seductive for a state aspiring to an existence in its own right." France, in other words, acted as "the organizational vantage point," as a model for organizing the many aspects of the state's life: "territorial, administrative, social, economic, etc." (ibid., 57).

5.3 The nationalist mission

The core problem that Sayad is trying to solve is that of the institutional makeup of the postcolonial state and the basis of its legitimacy.

To be sure, the colonial state was "violent, arbitrary, profoundly unjust, and inegalitarian." But it was, at the same time, the only form of political authority that Algerian society had known until independence. The independent state could only point to a single source of political legitimacy, namely, its reaction to colonial domination, but it didn't manage to construct a basis of legitimacy independent of the history of colonization. Its claim to "political legitimacy," in other words, bore no relation to any "social legitimacy." Indeed, having originated exclusively out of the anticolonial struggle, it did not establish any connection with "the ordered edifice of social relationships," with the needs of daily life, with the "sense of social life." And so it was that, as Sayad comments, "before militancy and nationalism, no doubt genuine at first [...], could even put themselves to the test of power, they gave way to the most self-serving nepotism, to clientelism, to a vassalage system that pandered to the party—all of which beclouded that selfsame militancy and nationalism, while also tarnishing their prestige" (ibid., 76). Here Sayad compellingly outlines the birth of postcolonial autocratic regimes, tracing out their ***ideal-typical configuration***—thus applying to postcolonial developments the same approach that informs his analysis of colonization—while never losing sight of the specificities of each single country.

In the effort to gain political legitimacy, the postcolonial regimes donned the ideological mantle of anticolonial nationalism, but what this resulted in were forms of state in which political and military power formed a close alliance and governed by clamping down on the people in increasingly repressive ways. This made democracy impossible, an outcome that can accordingly be ascribed to the progressive curtailment of freedoms and the protection of the law, both of which ceased to be unconditional and universal. Sayad's sociological approach enables him to diagnose the postcolonial forms of government as states in which an immovable wedge is driven between the people, on the one hand, and an autocratic regime, on the other, with the coterie of acolytes it depends on for its own survival.

The nationalist mission, Sayad concludes, collapsed into reason of state, and thus ended up justifying all the forms of repression and the abuses that in the name of nationalism were perpetrated by the regimes that had just gained independence from colonialism (ibid., 94).

With these sociological insights that Sayad offers in describing the political and social relationships that took shape in the newly independent states, he can proceed to his analysis of the constitutional forms of contemporary Arab regimes. But before we can turn to the question of constitutionalism in the Islamic world, we will have to dwell a little longer on the meaning of Arab nationalism.

5.4 Arab nationalism

The nationalism that took shape in the Middle East from the late eighteenth to the early twentieth century can be distinguished into three main types: there was a religious nationalism, where people would form a political community under the banner of a single faith; a "territorial patriotism," uniting all peoples within a given territory; and a nationalism based on the idea of a common culture and language. It was this third type that became dominant in the Middle East, overshadowing the others.[3] Even so, prevalent among thinkers who championed Arab nationalism was the idea that it could not be separated from the Islamic community.[4]

3 This nationalism of common heritage (drawing on a common culture, language, and literature) received particular emphasis in the debate that took place at the *Congrès des Écrivains Arabes* held in Cairo in 1957. Thus Ṭāhā Ḥusayn, the official representative of Egypt, remarked that it was literature that had enabled "Arab nationalism to flourish, develop, and fill the world with science, culture, and light." He went on to observe: "As early as two centuries after the birth of Islam, Arab nationalism spread out from Arabia, which then fell back into its nomadism, and culturally it overtook the occupied countries. Arabic spontaneously replaced the autochthonous languages and became the language not only of government but also of literature and science. [...] Islam thus created a new nation, the Arab nation—Arab in its language, way of thinking and feeling, civilization (*ḥaḍāra*), science, culture, and literature" (Ḥusayn 1957, 330–31; my translation).

4 See Hourani 1998, 343, which will be the main source for this section.

Arab nationalism drew on two main sources. One of these was "the liberal secularism of nineteenth-century England and France" (Hourani 1998, 343). It was first embraced by al-Bustānī, who passed it on to Luṭfī al-Sayyid and his "school of Egyptian nationalists [...]. It was secularist in the sense that it believed that society and religion both prospered best when the civil authority was separate from the religious" (ibid.).

"The second source," Hourani explains, "was the Islamic 'reformism'" (ibid. 343–44) propounded by Muḥammad ʿAbduh (1849–1905) and Rashīd Riḍā (1865–1935), who sought to revive the Islamic tradition "under the stimulus of European liberal thought" (ibid., 344): this "led to a gradual reinterpretation of Islamic concepts so as to make them equivalent to the guiding principles of European thought of the time" (ibid.), which in turn ushered in "a *de facto* separation of the sphere of civilization from that of religion," in such a way as "to open another door to secular nationalism" (ibid.).

The main objective of this second strand of nationalism was to achieve independence. But the attitude it took to Europe was ambivalent. For the generation that was coeval with ʿAbduh and Riḍā, as well as those who followed in their footsteps in the interwar period, found it natural to "look to the west as the repository of modern civilization and teacher of the ways of thought and techniques on which it depended" (ibid., 347–48).

In the countries subject to French colonial occupation—Algeria since 1830, Tunisia since 1881, and Morocco since 1912—nationalism took a particular form. Whereas the Ottoman Empire left social structures intact in the Arab lands they conquered, the French occupation came with a centralized administration "geared to the needs of the French communities more than of the indigenous population" (ibid., 362). Thus "in Algeria the old bourgeoisie and the class of artisans [...] largely disappeared during the period of French occupation; it was only after 1860 that a new middle class began to appear,"[5] and it was "only after the reform of the educational system in the late 1880s that there emerged [...] a class of Algerians with a mastery of French methods of thought. In Tunisia also a similar class appeared only after a generation of French rule" (ibid.).

As Hourani goes on to explain, it was from these groups that there emerged the "first new movement of political thought" (ibid.), and it did not call for independence but was rather aimed at "convincing the French that Tunisians and Algerians would be loyal to the existing regime only if they had a better position within it" (ibid.). In Tunisia this movement found expression through the newspaper *Le Tunisien* (published from 1907 to 1912), which served as an outlet for the views of a group that came to be called the Young Tunisians (ibid.). As Hourani reiterates, "what they claimed was not full independence but a better position within the protectorate" (ibid., 363): "Tunisians should be enabled to rise to the highest posts in the administration."[6] They also demanded a constitution, a fair share of the land that "was being distributed to the [French]

5 Here Hourani points to Berque 1948 as his source.
6 Here Hourani points to *Le Tunisien*, issues xvii (30 May 1907), xxxv (3 October 1907), and xxviii (27 August 1908).

colons," and economic support for "their industry and agriculture" (ibid.). And they wanted "modern schools" that would give them a "French education" in "the sciences of the age," including the economic sciences (ibid.).[7]

But the French administration was unresponsive to these claims. As a result a nationalist movement sprang up even before the outbreak of World War I, and "when the war ended nationalist feeling came more openly to the surface" (ibid., 364); "in Tunisia nationalist feeling found expression in a party, the Destour (*Dustur*), and a programme. Embodied in a book published in French, *La Tunisie martyre* (1920) [Thaʿalibī 1920], the programme still fell short of asking for independence: it demanded [...] that the *colons* should no longer have privileges but be considered as Tunisian citizens [...]; that the rights of individuals should be guaranteed, the judiciary be free, and Tunisians have the same right as Frenchmen to buy State domain" (Hourani 1998, 364).

"The leader and spokesman of the Destour was ʿAbd al-ʿAzīz al-Thaʿalibī [...]. But within a decade or so his leadership was being challenged by a younger group organized in the Neo-Destour, and with the aim of using the pressure of mass opinion and action to achieve complete independence" (ibid., 364–65). Thus "effective control of Tunisian nationalism passed into the hands of its founder and chief, Habib Bourguiba.[8] From then until 1955 the struggle for independence was directed [...] by men for whom to be independent meant to enter the new world and the community of modern European culture" (ibid., 365).

Thus Bourguiba recognized that "French presence has contributed to accelerating the country's material progress," despite the fact that "the French administration has been unable or unwilling to adapt to the evolution in the thinking of men, or to their new needs." But above all he underscored that it was France that had "taught the world the principles on which we act, and which we are forced to invoke against her" (Bourguiba 1954b, 207). Indeed, once independence was achieved, in 1956, the newly established Tunisian state was modelled after French democracy and the principles of liberty that Bourguiba had absorbed in France.

In that same vein, "his nationalism was territorial rather than ethnic" (Hourani 1998, 366), and this, too, was an idea reflected in the Tunisian state. As he put it: "We need to do away with the tribal life that runs rampant across the country and that, sustaining the spirit of the clan, works against the establishment of a

7 Here Hourani points to *Le Tunisien*, issues xi (18 April 1907) and xcvi (14 January 1909).

8 In the April 15, 1933 issue of *Action Tunisienne*, Bourguiba openly denounced the French protectorate asking: "What is the claim made by this absurd regime, which has no regard for the egalitarian aspirations that lie deep in every thinking, reflective human being? What enables it to last if not the use of force?" It was in asking this question that Tunisian nationalism set the French occupation in contrast to the higher standards of its own moral grounds: "Against this brute, essentially capricious force we try to hold up a moral force that will sooner or later enable the just causes to triumph" (Bourguiba 1954a, 48–49; my translation).

Subsequently, in a statement he made in Cairo on August 9, 1947, this sentiment became overtly anticolonial: "You will have to rid yourselves of the old colonial mentality, which is an essentially racist mentality; you will have to get used to the idea that we are human beings just like you—that we feel, think, and suffer just like you, that like you we have a sense of dignity and of national honour" (Bourguiba 1954b, 212; my translation).

true civilization."[9] Accordingly, he did not "believe that the laws of religion, too strictly applied, should be allowed to obstruct acts designed to further human welfare; in his criticism of the fast of Ramaḍān, he maintained that the principles of Islam should be interpreted flexibly" (ibid., 367).

So, while there was certainly an "Islamic element" (ibid.) in Bourguiba's political thought, it was tempered and qualified by the need to grow Tunisia economically, and Bourguiba was indeed "the most consciously secular and modern of Tunisian politicians" (ibid.). "In other North African countries," however, "the religious element was important in the formation of nationalist movements" (ibid., 368). Thus "in Libya, the resistance to Italian rule was organized by the Sanūsiyya, a reforming order which had obtained great influence in Cyrenaica before the Italians came, and was the only force solid enough to stand against them" (ibid.).

The end of World War II gave new impetus to the process towards independence for the countries that had been subject to Western domination, and their link to the West was rejected as a hangover from the colonial age. This is what happened, for example, in Egypt, where the revolution of 1952 was led by men who rejected the primacy of the West.

Further, a new line of thinking emerged on the birth of a new Arab society, which could no longer be built on a system of norms rooted in the legacy of the colonial past. For it was, after all, the case that law codes based on the European model had been introduced in Turkey, Egypt, and Tunisia going back to the nineteenth century.

In the intellectual debate, too, fissures began to develop reflecting the complexity of the transformations that were afoot. Thus the Egyptian writer Khālid Muḥammad Khālid "sketched the outlines of a social revolution in Egypt: it would involve the division of large estates and fixing of agricultural rents, the nationalization of resources and protection of the rights of labour, the emancipation of women and birth-control. *But it would also involve the creation of a real parliamentary democracy and political parties; the revolution should be a democratic one*" (ibid., 353–54; italics added).

"A similar change took place in the idea of Arab nationalism, under the impact of a seminal disaster, the loss of Palestine. The creation of the State of Israel [1948], the defeat of the Arab armies and expulsion of the Arab population had indeed a profound effect on Arab nationalist thought and started a far-reaching debate on the reasons for the Arab failure" (ibid., 354).[10] This failure was set down to the fact that "there did not exist an Arab nation in the real sense" (ibid.), making it urgent to bring about "a unified State" (ibid.) "and *a reformed system of government, truly constitutional*, rational in its policy and scientific in its administration, and concerned for the welfare of the people" (ibid., 355; italics added).[11]

9 Habib Bourguiba, *Le Président Bourguiba dans le sud tunisien* (Tunis, 1959), p. 53, quoted in French in Hourani 1998, 366; my translation.

10 On the Arab defeat in Palestine and the rebirth of the pan-Arabic movement alongside that of Palestinian nationalism, see Charif 2018, 23ff.

11 This was part of the policy proposal the Palestinian leader Musa al-ʿAlami laid out as a way to fight back the advance of Zionism (see ʿAlami 1949, cited in Hourani 1998, 355).

It finally bears mentioning that another movement emerged whose aim was to couple nationalism with socialism under a "comprehensively Arab" banner (ibid., 357). The idea was promoted by the Baʿth Party, which was founded in 1940 by Michel ʿAflaq in Damascus, and which in 1958 led to the formation of the United Arab Republic (ibid., 357). This movement advocated Arab independence and unity and sought to achieve social justice by steering Arab nationalism towards socialism.

With this overview of Arab nationalism, we should now have a sense of its complexity, with the multiple paths the Arab states followed as they fought to achieve independence from the colonial regimes.

Works Cited

ʿAlami, Musa al. 1949. "The Lesson of Palestine." *Middle East Journal* 3, no. 4: 373–405. Originally published under the title *ʿIbrat Filastin* (Beirut: Dar al Kashshaf, 1949).

Berque, Augustin. 1948. "La Bourgeoisie algérienne, ou à la recherche de Cesar Birotteau" (dated 1946). *Hespéris: Archives Berbères et Bulletin de l'Institut des Hautes Etudes Marocaines* XXXV: 1–29.

Bourguiba, Habib. 1954a. "Tradition coloniale" (1933). In *La Tunisie et la France: Vingt-cinq ans de lutte pour une coopération libre*, 45–49. Paris: Juilliard.

Bourguiba, Habib. 1954b. "Je ne suis pas un ennemi de la France" (1947). In *La Tunisie et la France: Vingt-cinq ans de lutte pour une coopération libre*, 206–12. Paris: Juilliard.

Charif, Maher. 2018. *Storia del pensiero politico palestinese.* Edited by Ignazio De Francesco, foreword by Massimo Campanini, translated by Paola Pizzi. Marzabotto, Bologna: Zikkaron.

Hourani, Albert. 1998. *Arabic Thought in the Liberal Age, 1798–1939.* Cambridge: Cambridge University Press.

Ḥusayn, Ṭāhā. 1957. Speech delivered at the *Congrès des Écrivains Arabes*, Cairo, December 9–16. Institut Dominicain d'Études Orientales du Caire. *Mélanges* 4 (1957). Cairo: Dar Al-Maaref.

Montesquieu, Charles-Louis de Secondat. (1748) 1989. *The Spirit of the Laws.* Translated and edited by Anne M. Cohler, Basia Carolyn Miller, Harold Samuel Stone. Cambridge: Cambridge University Press.

Pellitteri, Antonino. 2012. *La formazione del pensiero nazionale arabo: Matrici storico-culturali ed elementi costitutivi.* Milan: FrancoAngeli.

Sayad, Abdelmalek. 2003. *Algeria: Nazionalismo senza nazione.* Edited by Salvatore Pallida and Nino Recupero. Messina: Mesogea.

Thaʿalibī, ʿAbd al-ʿAzīz al. 1920. *La Tunisie martyre: Ses revendications.* Paris: Jouve.

Tibi, Bassam. 1996. *Das arabische Staatensystem: Ein regionales Subsystem der Weltpolitik.* Mannheim: Bibliographisches Institut Taschenbuchverlag.

6 The system of Arab states and the persistence of traditional social structures

6.1 The system of Arab states

The Syrian-born political scientist Bassam Tibi observes that nationalism is an ideology that Arabs and other Muslims acquired from the West and introduced into their own relations. Even the nation-state is a politico-institutional construct that originates out of European history (Tibi 1996, 50). It will therefore be necessary to investigate how the institutional makeup has changed as a result of transposing the ideology of nationalism and the form of the nation-state into the religious, social, and cultural relations by which the Arab world is structured.

As just suggested, the Western concept of the nation is foreign to the Muslim world. Indeed, its closest Islamic equivalent—the *umma*—is defined neither by ethnicity nor by nationality. As was discussed in the last chapter, it was through the anticolonial struggle that nationalism took hold in the Muslim world, and it was through colonialism that the model of the nation-state was imported into this world. This model was built around the institutional forms of the European world (ibid., 54). But these institutional forms were overlaid onto the social, cultural, and religious fabric of the Muslim world, whose organizational structure differed in profound ways from that of the European countries.

For a proper analysis of the nation-building process in the Arab world—and more specifically in the Maghreb, the main focus of this analysis—we need to turn to interpretive categories that make it possible to grasp the specificity of that geopolitical context and the peculiarities of its forms of nation-building. And the question that needs to be answered through that theoretical lens is the following: *why is it that Maghrebi society, which did not lag behind Europe's feudal society in the Middle Ages, did not manage in the Renaissance or in the modern age to break away from the structures of the medieval period and lay the groundwork for the birth of nations in the modern sense of the term?* (Zghal 1971, 467).

This question has been tackled from two different angles, with some authors taking an orientalist approach and others a Marxist one. The leading orientalist thinker until World War II was Émile-Félix Gautier (1952), according to whom the lack of state-making in the Maghreb is to be explained by pointing to the clash between sedentary and nomadic farmers. Only in the tenth century did an opportunity emerge for the Maghreb to form into a nation: this came with the rise of the Fatimid Caliphate, whose people were the Kitāma, a tribe of sedentary farmers who had settled in Kabylie. But the Fatimid endeavour was cut short by the nomadic tribes of the Banū Hilāl, who invaded from Egypt in the mid-eleventh century.

Marxists writers, for their part, have compared the social structures of medieval Maghreb to those of the European feudal system, arguing that the Maghrebi people's state-making inability was owed to the economic decline the region entered into once it lost control of trade routes between Sudan and Egypt (Lacoste 1966).

But as Abdelkader Zghal argues, neither the Marxist approach nor the orientalist one hits the mark, for they both pretend to understand medieval Maghrebi society on the basis of (Western) interpretive categories that fail to take the specific features of that society into account. So it is a *different* set of categories that we need for a proper analysis of the problem.

6.2 Traditional structures and nation-state building

The first characteristic by which medieval Maghrebi society was distinguished from European society lay in its *close kinship relations.* In the European world, by contrast, these relations were much looser, which made it necessary to establish a system under which to afford the kind of protection they could otherwise ensure, and this was the feudal system. A second characteristic, also marking a profound difference from Europe, is that *there was no distinction in medieval Maghrebi society between peasants and warriors*: unlike in the Western world, the Arab peasant could have arms and horses at his disposal. In virtue of this different social reality, local communities in the Maghreb could retain a great degree of autonomy, their economic life never being subject to the control exercised by a central power. And it was this instability of central power that characterized the Maghrebi social system from the Middle Ages down to the dawn of colonization (Zghal 1971, 472).

In an accurate reconstruction of this social system, Zghal notes that the geography of precolonial Maghreb was divided into two broad areas: the Bled Siba (*bilād al-sība*) and the Bled Makhzen (*bilād al-makhzan*). The latter was inhabited by communities that accepted to pay taxes to a central authority, the Makhzan. The Bled Siba, by contrast, was the area of dissidence, mainly inhabited by Berber tribes that could not easily be brought under the control of centralized power. In fact, their heartland consisted of mountainous terrain (including the Rif and the Anti-, High, and Middle Atlas in Morocco, and the mountain region of the Kabylie and the Aurès Mountains in Algeria) and the predesert regions inhabited by nomadic tribes. Zghal observes that the Bled Siba is "the ideal terrain for ethnological research" (ibid., 473; my translation), from which there emerges "a fact of central importance for understanding the state-making process in the Maghreb" (ibid.). Which is that, "apart from the particularisms that distinguish Berbers and Arabs, and apart from the differences between the nomadic tribes' ways of life and those of sedentary peasant communities, we can observe, in the final analysis, the same structural forms in familial and political organization across the different Maghrebin peasant communities" (ibid.).

In the social structure there could be found "two types of identification: with the extended family and with the Muslim community at large (the umma)" (ibid., 474). Between these two reference points there existed a plurality of intermediate groupings.

Zghal recognizes the importance of the research conducted by Ernest Gellner, who introduced "the notion of a segmentary society" (Gellner 1969, 41ff.), describing the Berber tribal structure in such a way as to explain the plurality of conflicts that "can break out at all levels and mobilize groupings of all sizes" (Zghal 1971, 475). Thus, in a segmentary society, it may happen that groups of common lineage may be fighting one another at one level, all the while forming an alliance under a higher unit in conflict with a homologous group (ibid., 475–76, quoting Balandier 1967).

This social organization excluded the possibility of an absolute authority, in that power was distributed across the tribal structure (Zghal 1971, 476, quoting Evans-Pritchard 1949). So the lords who wielded power were subject to the control of their own tribal assemblies, made up of all adult males.

On top of this social structure came the politico-military organization of French colonization, which managed to also subdue the areas of traditional dissidence (the Bled Siba) (ibid., 477–78). However, by the time the three Maghrebin countries gained their independence, they had undergone internal changes that set them apart in consequential ways: in Tunisia and Morocco, which had been protectorates and not colonies, the city elites were in a position to spearhead the movement for national liberation; in Algeria, which by contrast had existed as a French department, the internal conditions worked *against* the emergence of a modern nation (ibid., 478).

As Zghal observes, however, "the three countries' gaining of independence [...] provided the occasion to reactivate segmentary structures, and was accompanied by a reappearance of the ancient *sība* in the areas of traditional dissidence (the pre-desert mountains and regions)" (ibid., 479). While "in Tunisia this reactivation of segmentary structures was tempered by the existence of a very old political party whose roots in the country ran deep, in Algeria the absence of a political party like the Tunisian Néo-Destour explains the internal clashes without ideological foundation which the clans fell into at the moment of independence, with the seizing of political power by the army, the only organization with a relatively stable structure" (ibid., 480). Likewise, "in Morocco, the traditional legitimacy of the Alawite dynasty, coupled with the reactivation of segmentary structures at the level of the political elites (Waterbury 1970), seemed to hamper the functioning of institutions and set the stage for an explosive situation further down the line" (ibid.).

Hence, the building of a nation-state—a process that had been set in train in the colonial age—was conditioned by elements belonging to the legacy of traditional structures.

It is on top of this structure—shaped by colonization but influenced by tradition—that a constitutional organization was formed. But how was this organization configured? In order to answer this question, we need to reconstruct the forms of colonial organization and their effect on the construction of state structures.

Works Cited

Balandier, Georges. 1967. *Anthropologie politique*. Paris: Presses Universitaires de France.

Evans-Pritchard, E. E. 1949. *The Sanusi of Cyrenaica*. Oxford: Clarendon Press.

Gautier, Émile-Félix. 1952. *Le passé de l'Afrique du Nord: Les siècles obscurs*. Paris: Payot. (1st ed. 1937.)

Gellner, Ernest. 1969. *Saints of the Atlas*. London: Weidenfeld and Nicolson.

Lacoste, Yves. 1966. *Ibn Khaldoun: Naissance de l'histoire, passé du Tiers Monde*. Paris: Maspero.

Tibi, Bassam. 1996. *Das arabische Staatensystem: Ein regionales Subsystem der Weltpolitik*. Mannheim: Bibliographisches Institut Taschenbuchverlag.

Waterbury, John. 1970. *The Commander of the Faithful: The Moroccan Political Elite; a Study in Segmented Politics*. London: Weidenfeld and Nicolson.

Zghal, Abdelkader. 1971. "L'édification nationale au Maghreb." *Revue Internationale des Sciences Sociales* XXIII, no. 3: 465–81.

7 Colonial law and the formation of the nation-state

7.1 Colonial law

As the history just surveyed suggests, a proper understanding of nation-building in the Arab world requires that we delve deeper into the question of how the structures of the nation-states built in the postcolonial era were shaped by the different forms of colonization to which they were subject. In this deeper probing of the question, colonial law provides us with a vantage point from which to gain insight into both the organizational blueprint used to achieve domination and the ideology deployed to legitimize the same endeavour.

One place we can turn to for such a vantage point is a textbook the Italian jurist Santi Romano wrote in 1918 in which, with characteristic clarity, he lays out the basic principles of colonial law. With analytical and "scientific" detachment, Romano maps out a taxonomy of forms of colonization, weighing in with commentary only when he feels sympathetic to the aims of the colonial process.

Romano distinguishes three types of colonization based on its different aims, all of them involving "a social body, a specifically organized collectivity" undertaking to "nurture [*coltivare*], populate, subjugate, etc." another country (Romano 1918, 8–9; my translation).[1] These activities can be carried out by public or private entities (ibid., 9), but Romano restricts his investigation to the public: he is only concerned with activities undertaken by means of public powers, that is, by means of the state. He further restricts his field of view to what he refers to as external state colonization, describing it as the activity a state undertakes in a foreign country or in territories deemed to be *nullius*, which remain such (ibid., 9).

But external colonization also includes cases in which one country appropriates or subjugates another one, as Italy did in Eritrea, Somalia, and Libya (ibid., 10). As Romano explains, the reason why colonization counts as external in these cases, too, is that the legal-political order of the colonizing country, or metropole, remains clearly distinct from that of the subjugated country. In

1 In this regard see the perspicuous analysis in Nuzzo 2012, 266ff.

short, the colonizing power makes a unilateral decision establishing a distinct regime for the conquered country.

This point holds a place of particular significance in Romano's exposition, for it is here that Romano makes explicit the ideological reason why the metropole should refuse to effect a fusion with the colonized country: "the country held in subjection as a colony," he explains, "is marked by an inferior civilization, and for this reason is chosen by the colonizing state as the theatre of its colonizing activity" (ibid.).

But as Romano also points out, "civilization" is a *relative* concept, not an absolute one, for it may happen that a colony's civilization is not inferior to that of the metropole, as is the case with certain colonies of England. This means that "the concept of civilization and that of barbarism are not amenable to any absolute determination, for they can only be assessed by looking at two countries in comparison—a comparison that can be made from points of view that may be subjective and hence, in a sense, arbitrary" (ibid., 11). If this comparison should reveal a difference in the degree of civilization—in economic, intellectual, or social terms—then the conditions are in place for a country of "inferior civilization" to become a colony.

In a display of intellectual honesty, however, Romano goes on to remark that the purpose of colonization is not to civilize, "for colonization is a phenomenon of *political expansion*, its primary purpose residing in the advantage of the metropole" (ibid., 12; italics added). He does say that the metropole's colonial venture may "tend not only to its own interests but also to those of the colonized territory," but he is quick to point out that "this latter purpose is subsidiary and complementary to the former" (ibid.). Indeed, as he also clarifies, the concern of colonization rests not with the people but with the territory, whose resources it wants to exploit, and that is why the development of the colonized country's civilization can only be a secondary effect, certainly not its primary purpose. In short, colonization "is not a work of protection and charity toward inferior peoples; it is instead an assertion of power and domination" (ibid., 13).

Having laid this theoretical groundwork, Romano can now proceed to a classification of the various forms of state colonization: these can be (i) colonies for trade and commerce, (ii) resource-exploitation or industrial colonies; (iii) population colonies, meaning that they are meant to be populated by people emigrating from the mother country; and (iv) military, penal, or deportation colonies (ibid., 14–15).

Romano next turns to "colonial science," noting that this is actually a plural science comprising a multitude of "colonial disciplines" reflecting the complexity of colonial phenomena, the disparity between the metropole and its colonies, and the multiplicity of the purposes of colonization. And so, according to Romano, these disciplines were best distinguished "not so much by subject matter as in light of the special point of view from which colonization is investigated" (ibid., 16–17), which can be that of the physical and natural sciences, of the economic sciences, of the social and political sciences, or of legal science (ibid., 16–21).

The political science of colonization is a "practical doctrine" (ibid., 19), concerned "in the first place with examining the advantages and disadvantages of colonization, its dangers, and so forth, relative to the state's other aims" (ibid., 20). This science is further concerned with analysing the colonies' organizational forms, meaning the *administrative* machinery with which the colonial power needs to equip the colonized power, considering that colonial policy needs to be based on *principles that are specific to the colonies* and different from those that govern in the mother country (ibid.).

More complex is the discussion Romano devotes to the sciences in the last group, analysed under the broad rubric of colonial law, which he describes as a "heterogeneous" body of law, in that "the provisions it consists of are not all of the same nature but can be made to fall under the many branches into which the legal encyclopaedia is divided [...]. Indeed, colonial law takes in elements from international law, especially in what concerns the acquisition or loss of colonies [...]; constitutional law, insofar as the acquisition or loss of colonies brings about changes in the state's territory [...]; administrative law, which governs the way colonies are to be organized; [...] ecclesiastical law, which is of great importance here because religion cuts across a large swath of colonial life, and sometimes even pervades it entirely. And even judicial law plays an important part in colonial law." Indeed, "the administration of justice is perhaps the activity of the state that is most pertinent to the indigenous populations, in dealing with which it is, in this area, indispensable to respect their traditions and customs" (ibid., 21–22).

Santi Romano defines colonial law as "*special law*: this means that it consists of a complex of *particular provisions* distinct from those forming the common law of the state, which governs the metropole" (ibid., 22; italics added). He then turns to the *sources* of colonial law, in an analysis that reveals how complex this law is. Indeed, part of colonial law falls under international law, whose source lies in the "concordant will of a plurality of states" (ibid., 24). Another source of colonial law lies in the "will of the state to which the colony belongs" (ibid.), and sometimes even in "legal norms that are not laid down by the state the colony is dependent on but are anterior to, and thus preexist, the acquisition of the colony" (ibid.). Colonial law can indeed contain "a sizable part of the *Muslim law* that was in effect before occupation" (ibid.; italics added) by the colonizing power, whose laws can make express reference to it.

7.2 The colonies' political and administrative organization

In 1900, on the occasion of the Exposition Universelle held in Paris, two inspectors for the French colonies, Alain Arnaud and Henry Méray, published a book devoted to the colonies' administrative, judicial, political, and financial administration (Arnaud and Méray 1900). The two authors pose the question of the best model under which to govern the colonies, proceeding from the premise that because the colonies do not enjoy the same "level of maturity" as the mother country, they need to be brought under a different set of organizational forms. Indeed, colonial law is "marked by instability," a characteristic owed to the multiplicity of the situations that fall within its scope.

The French inspectors single out three models that can be introduced to organize the colonies: *subjugation*, *autonomy*, and *assimilation*.

On the first model, the colony is to be exploited to the exclusive benefit of the metropole. This model is meant only for the initial period of colonial settlement, after which time it needs to be phased out, transitioning to one of the two other models. At the time the book was being written, subjugation was in effect only in the Sunda Islands, under Dutch colonial rule.

The two other models—autonomy and assimilation—correspond to the forms of colonial organization favoured by the British and the French, respectively. Institutionally, the autonomy model takes the form of a local assembly set up in the colony and charged with enacting *special legislation*. Arnaud and Méray make no secret of the admiration they have for the "marvellous achievements" obtained by British colonization, and with that appreciation in the background they set out to analyse the French system of colonies.

Assimilation is an ideologically driven model aimed at progressively working the colonizing element into the indigenous element under a nation's plan to "bring civilization to a new nation" (Arnaud and Méray 1900, 4). However, the assimilationist project often comes into contradiction with the great diversity of colonial situations and with the colonized countries' plurality of customs and institutions, which can be a source of conflict with the colonizing nation's character and attitudes.

Arnaud and Méray understand the assimilationist model as going back to and extending the forms of Roman colonization. But in reality, as Romano points out, "one thing is the assimilationist system such as it is practiced today—a formal system mainly reflected in the legal order—and quite another was the practice of the Romans, who sought to transform the conquered country in such a way that the Latin civilization could flourish in it" (Romano 1918, 111; my translation).

However, once the problems and conflicts engendered by the assimilationist model became apparent, economists, publicists, and politicians in France began to question its basic premises and thus pivoted towards the autonomy model (cf., e.g., Leroy-Beaulieu 1886, 735ff.). It was on the basis of this new thinking, for example, that the assimilationist model for annexing Algeria came under criticism. This policy shift was formally enacted by the Department for the Colonies, which in 1889 introduced forms of administrative autonomy in some settlements of the Western coast of Africa. But this meant breaking away from the traditional assimilationist policy that had been inaugurated under the French Revolution, when it was enshrined into law that the colonies "form an integral part of the French empire" (Arnaud and Méray 1900, 7).

In the assimilationist tradition of republican France, the colonies were governed by "special laws" on which basis the legislative branch delegated its own powers to the executive branch, which could thus govern the colonies under the system of ***rule by decree***. This institutional form lasted through the restoration period. Indeed, according to the Constitutional Charter of 1814, the colonies were to be governed under "special laws and regulations,"[2] which made it possible for the government to make wide use of decrees in organizing the colonies. This resulted in an ***authoritarian institutional system*** under a governor, through whom the metropole exercised its central power in the colony, supported by three deputy governors entrusted with specific administrative tasks: there was an *ordonnateur*, in charge of administering war; a ***director of the interior***, in charge of local services; and an ***attorney general***, charged with overseeing the judicial service (Arnaud and Méray 1900, 7).

Even the Constitution of 1848 contained language firmly securing the assimilationist policy introduced under the revolution, with special regulations providing that "the territory of Algeria and of the Colonies is declared to be French territory, and shall be governed by their separate laws until a special law shall place them under the provisions of the present Constitution" (Art. 109). "But," as Girault (1929, 4) points out, "this special law was never enacted" (my translation).

Under the Constitution of 1852 an imperial decree was issued (the *sénatus-consulte* of 3 May 1854) that divided the colonies into two groups: the first one governed by law, the second one by decree. As Arnaud and Méray point out, the first scheme was reserved only for the colonies of Martinique, Guadeloupe, and Réunion. This made rule by decree the prevalent institutional form, even if it meant placing the colonial possessions in a condition of abject uncertainty.[3]

The characteristics of this prevalent institutional form were clearly identified by Alexis de Tocqueville in his 1841 "Travail sur l'Algérie." As he put it, the government of Algeria is violent, arbitrary, and tyrannical, all the while being weak and ineffectual. It is easy to identify the reason for this phenomenon.

> The government is arbitrary and tyrannical because the citizens have no guarantees against the actions taken by the authorities' agents; and it is weak and ineffectual because there is no centralized power in the colony. (Tocqueville [1841] 1962, 255; my translation)

According to Tocqueville it was therefore necessary to act on two fronts, on the one hand limiting the governor's arbitrary power, and on the other centralizing power in such a way as to restrict the ability of each chief executive to act independently within the scope of his charge. Furthermore, in his view, it was

2 On these aspects of colonial legislation, see Girault 1929, 1–2. Article 73 of the Constitutional Charter of 4 June 1814 reads as follows: "Les colonies sont régies par des lois et des règlements particuliers." As Girault explains, this meant that the laws and regulations in effect in the metropole did not apply to the colonies.

3 On the need to gradually move beyond the decree system and ensure for the colonies a right of representation in the French parliament, see the debate that took place at the International Colonial Congress of 1889 (Congrès International 1889, 33).

necessary for Paris to loosen its centralized control over administrative functions so as to make it possible for the colony to be managed more effectively. Indeed, the system under which administrative control was centralized in Paris made for a paradoxical situation, in that the governor could issue general orders applying across the entire colony, often appealing to a case of urgency (*cas d'urgence*), but then each administrative measure needed to be authorized by Paris. In short, Tocqueville concluded in regard to the governor's powers, "it can be said about him, with greater reason than is the case with the king, that while he may govern, he does not administer, which surely runs contrary to what is sensible" (ibid., 259).

The colonial government, then, was arbitrary, imposing measures that were deemed necessary to further the aims of colonization, even if the local authorities were dysfunctionally dependent on Paris for all administrative tasks. This organization of power ended up imposing on the colonies a political-administrative model irredeemably disconnected from the social organization of Arab society.[4] It will therefore be necessary to take a closer look at the administrative and legislative organization of French colonial government.

7.3 The colonial government of Tunisia and Algeria

For deeper insight into French colonial government we can look in particular at the case of Tunisia and Algeria. Their two realities are compared against each other in a work titled *Principes de Colonisation et de Législation Colonial* (1908), which forms part of the vast scholarship of Arthur Girault, who was doyen of the law school at the University of Poitiers, as well as a member of the International Colonial Institute based in Brussels.

Before the French protectorate in Tunisia was established—under the Treaty of Bardo, signed on 12 May 1881 (Abadi 2013, 327–28)—the bey ruled as an absolute sovereign, concentrating the legislative, executive, and judicial powers in himself. The only limit on his power was that of the Qur'an, whose prescriptions he was bound to obey. The central administration was called *Ouzara*, and it was organized into three branches: one was entrusted with the country's internal administration, another with civil and criminal justice, and the third with relations with foreign powers. The protectorate modified but did not suppress this governmental organization: as Girault observes, "the previous central administration survives with some amputations and some additions" (Girault 1908, 386; my translation). Girault's reconstruction shows how *the French state crept deeper and deeper into the bey government's administrative organization, ultimately taking full control of it.* Gradually, the ancient *Ouzara* grew with the accretion of technical services delivered under dedicated directorates headed by executive chiefs: thus to the

4 On the colonial powers' creation of the administrative system in the colonized countries of the Middle East, see Owen 2004.

administrative apparatus were added a *direction générale des travaux publics*, a *direction générale des finances*, a *direction générale de l'agriculture*, a *direction de l'enseignement public*, and an *office des postes et télégraphes*. These directorates were set up as small ministries, as is evidenced by the fact that the chief executives were part of a council of ministers chaired by a *résident général* in whom, under the establishing decree of 23 June 1885, "all the powers of the Republic in the Regency are vested."

By thc time this apparatus was fully in place, the bey's powers had been reduced to little more than nominal powers. His ability to issue *décrets beylicaux* was subject to the approval of the *résident général*. His power was no longer limited only by the Qur'an, but now also by an obligation to honour international commitments, particularly towards France. At the same time, there was also a semblance of *autonomy* that the system maintained, considering that, as Girault (1908, 390) points out, "Tunisian law is made in Tunis and not in Paris"—and therein lies "the whole secret to the success of the Tunisian protectorate" (ibid., 390).

Quite different, by contrast, was the colonial reality of Algeria, where the metropole's attempt to *assimilate* the colony made it difficult to tell the difference between the colonial legislator and the Algerian legislator. Many and sundry were the sources of Algerian law that had been introduced since the occupation: the *arrêtés* (orders) of the field marshal in charge of the expeditionary corps; the *arrêtés* of the *intendant civil*; the *ordonnances royales* and the subsequent *décrets*; the *arrêtés* of the governor-general of Algeria; the *arrêtés* of the minister of war; the *sénatus-consultes*; and the laws of the legislative chambers. Of all these sources of law, only two—statutes and decrees—were still in use when Girault published his 1908 *Principes*. But the main source was that of decrees, and with these, Girault critically comments, "there is no guarantee or security." What Algeria instead needs, he argues, is "an organic law that identifies the essential points of its constitution and enumerates the matters that can only be governed by statute" (ibid., 186).

There was uncertainty as well about whether the laws in effect in the mother country were also applicable in Algeria. In Algerian legal scholarship, a distinction was drawn between the laws passed before annexation—under the ordinance of 22 July 1834—and those passed afterward under French occupation. It was the 1834 ordinance that set out the framework for administering the new Algeria: it did so by establishing a governor-general subordinate to the French minister of war, who in turn was entrusted with general command and administration of French possessions in North Africa.[5] By effect of the conquest, all the laws passed in the mother country before

5 This set-up is introduced as follows in the 1834 ordinance: "Le commandement général et la haute administration des possessions françaises dans le nord de l'Afrique (ancienne régence d'Alger) sont confiés à un gouverneur général. Il exerce ses pouvoirs sous les ordres et la direction de notre ministre de la Guerre" (quoted in Girault 1908, 82).

1834 were now fully applicable in Algeria as well. As for post-1834 laws, they could each include a provision that made them applicable in Algeria; absent such a provision, however, the president of the republic retained the right to legislate by decree.

In short, two systems were taking shape: "an Algeria subject to all the laws in force in France, and an Algeria entirely governed by special legislation" (ibid., 191). But the legislature had never made a choice between the two systems, with the result that, as we have seen, it was the system of rule by decree that wound up prevailing, within the framework of a colonial enterprise that, having proclaimed Algeria "French territory," deprived it of any semblance of autonomy.

7.4 The reception of French law in the Muslim world

In the nineteenth and twentieth centuries, French civil law spread its influence to the southern Mediterranean, especially through its reception in the Near East (Mousseron 1968, 48). For the Arab states that were formed in the wake of World War I, the experience of Muslim law coming into contact with Western European law was not new. In fact, that process had been underway since the mid-nineteenth century (Tyan 1963, 18).

The modernizing forces set in motion by new trade relationships and the redefinition of the function of credit, among other factors, made it necessary to "reduplicate" the law of the Near East, that is, to develop the positive law alongside traditional Muslim law, whose rigidity was in fact incompatible with the flexibility needed to respond to a changing environment. It was the proclaimed divine origin of Muslim law that accounted for its rigidity, ruling out the very idea that it might be subject to change. There was also another reason for this understanding of Muslim law, having to do with the way Islamic jurisprudence witnessed a loss of cohesion in the seventh and eighth centuries, branching into four main schools—the Shafiʿi, Mālikī, Ḥanafī, and Hanbali schools—therefore raising fears of a possible dissolution of Muslim law into plural streams of thought (Mousseron 1968, 51). And there was, finally, a third reason for the rigidity of Muslim law, namely, the need to recognize the authority (*taqlīd*) of past generations—an aspect of Muslim law that excluded any independent exegesis in interpreting the sources of law. And yet the transformations brought about by social and economic evolution forced deep changes in the legal system.

All subject matter relating to personal status continued to find its legal basis in the sacred texts, but other areas—including business law, criminal law, the law of civil procedure, and maritime law—fell under the scope of positive law, thereby developing independently of Muslim law. As Mousseron (1968, 58) points out, it was in this way that Muslim law underwent a process of *secularization*.

This process can be observed through the modernization the Ottoman Empire underwent in the latter half of the nineteenth century, in the era of the Tanẓīmāt reforms, through which Western codes were introduced: the French commercial code in 1850, as well as the French codes of criminal law in 1858;

maritime law in 1864; and commercial, civil, and criminal procedure in the 1880s (ibid., 59).[6]

Between 1870 and 1877, the contrast between the reception of the French codes and the common Muslim law led to the drafting of the Mecelle, or Majalla,[7] "the first original code enacted by a Muslim country in modern form, but whose content is exclusively religious" (Velidedeoğlu 1960, 164; my translation).

After the fall of the Ottoman Empire, Atatürk's reforms introduced a radical Westernization process with the 1926 enactment of the Italian criminal code and the German commercial code. Then, in 1927, came the Swiss code of civil procedure, and in 1929 the German code of maritime trade. All provisions that stood in contradiction to the new codification were repealed, starting from the Mecelle, or Majalla.

The Westernization process spread across the entire Muslim world. If the Turkish republic looked to the Italian, Swiss, and German codes, Egypt and Lebanon instead looked to the French codes. This is what happened with the Egyptian codification of 1875, and then again—after Egypt gained its independence, in 1922—with the civil code of 1948. Egypt's civil codification, based on the French model, in turn established itself as the prevailing model across the Arab world.

According to Mousseron (1968), in order to understand the reasons why the Near East embraced Western law, and French law in particular, we have to look at the "ideologies" behind this process.[8] French law is certainly a

6 Through technological, administrative, and institutional innovation the Sublime Porte, Egypt under Muḥammad ʿAli, and Tunisia under Ahmed Bey sought to "contain and govern European expansion in their own territories" for the purpose of "protecting and reinforcing their own 'sovereign' power" (Trentin 2012, 284; my translation).

7 Majalla is its better-known Arab form, whose full name in Turkish is *Mecelle-ʾi Aḥkām-ʾi ʿAdlīye*, corresponding to the Arab *Majallat al-aḥkām al-ʿadliyya*, a collection or code of legal provisions whose literal translation is "provisions of justice" (note by Prof. Giuseppe Cecere). The Mecelle, or Majalla, was a civil code that sought to systematize the principles of the *sharīʿa* governing loans, property, and trial law in keeping with *fiqh* (Islamic jurisprudence). It came in response to social, legal, and economic changes posing a challenge that could not be met under existing law. It consists of a prologue and sixteen books comprising 1,851 articles. Contained in the first one hundred of these are the general principles of Islamic law. In view of the sources used in the code, it is fair to say that the notion that the Majalla was drafted under the influence of the *Code Napoleon* or of Roman law has never been accurate (Akgündüz and Öztürk 2011, 515). This Ottoman civil code was completed in 1876 and became law not only in Turkey (within its present-day borders) but also across a broader area that included Egypt, the Hejaz, Iraq, Syria, Jordan, Lebanon, Cyprus, Palestine, and Israel. It remained in force in Albania and in Bosnia and Herzegovina until 1928 and in Kuwait until 1984. Some of its provisions are still in effect in Israeli law (ibid., 516).

8 Mousseron makes reference to the concept of ideology formulated by René David, who understands it as a complex of criteria of justice and morality (see David and Jauffret-Spinosi 2002, 16).

secularized law, but it is not indifferent to moral reasons. These reasons can also be found in Near Eastern law. In both French and Near Eastern law, for example, Mousseron finds the concept of "consension" (understood as a meeting of the minds), harm (specifically understood as an unfair imbalance in the contracting parties' rights and obligations), equivalence of prestation (akin to adequacy of consideration), frustration of purpose (when unforeseeable circumstances come to pass which make it unreasonably burdensome to perform the original contract), and civil responsibility (making one liable for an injury caused by abusing another's rights). It has also been speculated that these concepts find their source in Christian morality such as it can be distilled from the work of the medieval canonists and theologians—a morality that in many respects is seen to overlap with Islamic morality. In short, Mousseron (1968, 78) makes the argument that Western legal technique is compatible with Islamic ideology.

> It was the French legal model that dominated the colonial scene in the Middle Eastern (and African) countries. Even Egypt, an otherwise British protectorate, opted for that model. Nor is it difficult to see why this should have been the case. One of the most salient features of the nation-state is its totalistic appropriation of the domain of law, an appropriation that presupposed centralization and bureaucratization of the legal system. [...] A strong colonialist regime (and later nationalist governance) thus required the *code*, the *statute* and the *act* as tools of total control. (Hallaq 2009, 119; italics added)

However, the Western powers' effort to impose their legal model on the colonies did not go so far as to attempt to reshape the Islamic family into the nuclear one proper to the Western state. That is because "the quintessential project of colonialism" was not to assert the ideology of the Western state but rather to use the colonies for "material exploitation" (ibid., 120). Even so,

> when France developed the unique colonial idea of absorbing Algeria into the French nation, it repeatedly attempted to alter the personal laws of the Shari'a and replace them with what were seen as more progressive and civilized rules. From the middle of the nineteenth century onward, the French attempted to enforce many codes and decrees, most notably the *Code Morand*, a code that was devised, inter alia, to redesign the Muslim family along the lines conceived by the *état suprême* of post-Revolutionary France.[9]

9 On May 27, 1905, the Commission de Codification du Droit Musulman Algérien formed a subcommission chaired by the French jurist Marcel Morand, doyen of the Faculté de Droit at the University of Algiers, as well as a member of the Institut Colonial International, based in Brussels. The subcommission was entrusted with the task of drafting a code of Algerian Muslim law. This draft, titled *Avant-Projet de Code du Droit Musulman Algérien*, was published in 1916 but never became law, even if it would often be cited as a source in the courts' case law. In this regard, see Borrmans 1986. On the failure of the *Code Morand* to make it into law, see Powers 1989, 551.

> In the end it was due to the determined resistance of the Algerians that such attempts resulted in failure, and surely not to the lack of French effort.[10] (Hallaq 2009, 120–21; cf. 114)

7.5 The failed attempt of the *Code Morand*

In the report submitted to the Commission de Codification du Droit Musulman Algérien, published in 1916 as the preface to the *Avant-Projet de Code du Droit Musulman Algérien*, Morand clarifies the aims of the *Avant-Projet*, and in so doing enables us to glean the reasons why this draft code was never passed into law. The first task entrusted to the Moran subcommission was to provide a comprehensive picture of the efforts that had been undertaken in foreign countries and in French possessions to codify Muslim law, as well as future plans that had been announced towards that end. The second task was to recommend whether the code ought to apply only to orthodox Muslims or to all populations in Algeria, including those in Greater Kabylia (the mountainous region close to the Tunisian border between Algiers and Béjaïa) and in Mzab (the Algerian region in the Northern Sahara Desert).

Under the first task, the subcommission surveyed the codification efforts made in Turkey and Egypt, in that both countries were ruled by Muslim sovereigns: this meant looking at the Mecelle (the Ottoman Civil Code previously discussed) and the Egyptian code of personal status and inheritance. However, as Morand observes, the Ottoman Civil Code did not encompass the whole of private law but was confined in its scope to covering civil and commercial obligations. Much more important for the subcommission was the Egyptian code, even if, as Morand points out, next to it there existed other codes—the so-called indigenous codes—that contained rules of private civil and commercial law, as well as rules of criminal law and procedure. But these codes had been fashioned after the European codes, especially the French one, and thus could not bear pertinently on the project to draw up a specifically Algerian code.

10 In a speech delivered in 1889 at the *Congrès International Colonial* in Paris, Gustave Le Bon turned to the question of the local resistance offered to the effort to introduce the French educational model in Algeria, coming to the conclusion that it was futile to attempt to export Western civilization to the Algerian colony: "We must therefore realize," he remarked, "that we are powerless to translate our own civilization for the benefit of peoples whose living conditions and beliefs come into such stark contrast with those of our West. The only institutions, the only religions that can have any effect on them are those that, in virtue of their simplicity, remain within the ken of their spirit, still half-lit, and do not touch their form of existence: whence the deep influence that Islamism has had on barbarian peoples [...]. Let us leave the indigenes to their customs, their laws, their religions. Let us drastically draw down our boundless legion of colonial functionaries, and let us be on guard against simplistic and humanitarian theories!" (Le Bon 1889, 28; my translation).

As for other Muslim-populated countries subject to the rule of European powers, such as British India and the Dutch East Indies, it was found that none had had any codification of Muslim law. It could therefore be gloatingly asserted, as Morand did, "that none of these powers except France has so far thought to codify Muslim law in the interests of its Muslim subjects" (Morand 1916b, 7; my translation).

Morand's report also points to the commission established in 1896 in French Tunisia, underscoring its role in the drafting of a Tunisian civil and commercial code. The work done by the commission was valued for the collection of public documents and bibliographic sources it turned up, as well as because it captured "in broad outline the spirit of Muslim law."

The second task assigned to Morand, recall, was to determine whether there should be a single Algerian code of orthodox Muslim law—considering that the majority of the Algerian population adhered to one of the four main traditions of Islamic thought—the Shafiʿi, Mālikī, Ḥanafī, and Hanbali traditions (most people were either Malikites or Hanafites)—or whether there should also be two regional codes: one for the people of Greater Kabylia, who accepted Islam as the religious law but not as their civil law, and another one for the people of Mzab, who followed Ibadi Islam (Ibāḍiyya), a movement that had spun off from the heretic Khawarij sect.

This problem, Morand concluded, was distinctly political in nature, and so it was up to the public authorities to decide whether it was best to also draw up a code specific to the customs of Greater Kabylia and another one specific to Ibadi Islam. Either way, there was no doubt, in his opinion, that a widespread application of Muslim law would be a mark of "true progress," for this law appeared "more humane" than the customs of Kabylia in matters such as the status of women. *This is where the French project for a code of Algerian Muslim law begins to look like an attempt to statutorily control the Algerian population.*

This comes through even more clearly if we consider that the scope of Muslim law would gradually be reduced by effect of a French decree of 17 April 1889 that under Articles 1 and 3 provided that "Muslims residing in Algeria are subject to Muslim law only in what concerns their personal status, certain kinds of immovable property, and evidence of obligation" (ibid., 12). And corresponding to this narrowing of the scope of Muslim law was a gradual expansion of French law. We can see this, for example, where the *Avant-Projet* proposes to regulate "the ways in which real estate can be purchased": in the preliminary observations to Title III of the *Avant-Projet* it is stated that insofar as "unowned real estate in Algeria belongs to the French state, it follows, pursuant to Article 713 of the French Civil Code, that such property can only be purchased according to the rules of French law. Hence there is no reason to codify Muslim law governing the occupation and use of unowned lands (*terres mortes*)."[11]

11 *Avant-Projet de Code du Droit Musulman Algérien*, livre III ("Statut réel immobilier"), titre III ("Des modes d'acquérir les droits réels immobiliers: Observations préliminaires"). Morand 1916a, 381; "my translation."

But the intent behind the project for a code of Algerian Muslim law was not just to restrict the scope of Muslim law: it was also, according to Morand, "to clearly set out the *true principles* of Muslim law in methodical order" (Morand 1916a, 13; italics added). This meant laying claim to the right to exercise discretion over the opinions formulated by the Muslim lawyers, choosing from among these opinions those which the French occupiers found to be "*most in keeping with morality or equity,*" and "in closest harmony with the social status of our indigenes and with their true economic interests" (ibid.; italics added).

The discretionary power the French occupiers claimed for themselves went so far as to pretend to determine which interpretation of Muslim law was best suited to the Arab peoples subject to French rule. Thus Morand took the view that, even though the Algerian Muslims are prevalently Mālikī, the French codification of Muslim law should tend to favour Ḥanafī provisions, in that they were often "more humane" and "more tolerant" (ibid.).[12] This, according to Morand, would make the French codification of Muslim law "an instrument of progress," in that, like the Ottoman Mecelle, it would align the law with "the interests of the public and the needs of the time" (Morand 1916a, 15).

But the French attempt to limit the scope of Muslim law, to change the customs of large segments of the Algerian population, and even to dictate the "authentic" interpretation of Muslim law ended in failure. This was due to the unrelenting resistance put up by the Algerians.[13] But this was *before* independ-

12 In other cases the French codifiers of Algerian Muslim law instead chose to discretionarily go with the Mālikī interpretation of Muslim law. We can see this, for example, with the way they chose to interpret the legal concept of *ḥubus*, or *waqf*. This was a typical institution of Muslim law, an arrangement under which "property is granted in usufruct for a pious [*pieux*] purpose or for the public welfare, so long as this property remains sequestered [*séquestré*], as far as both the bare ownership and the usufruct are concerned, for the purpose of ensuring that the income derived from the property is used according to the grantor's wishes." Among the interpretations of this institution, the Morand subcommission chose the one, consistent with Mālikī doctrine, according to which to grant a *ḥubus* was no more than to grant a usufruct, while bare ownership remained with the grantor (meaning that ownership reverts to the grantor once the usufruct has expired). See *Avant-Projet de Code du Droit Musulman Algérien*, livre II ("Statut successoral"), titre III ("Habous: Dispositions générales") (Morand 1916a, 285–86). On the nature of the institution of *ḥubus*, or *waqf*, and on its three main historical forms, see Castro 2007, 64–68.

13 But the attempt to codify an "indigenous law" met with criticism from France, too. Thus, for example, Arthur Girault observed that these codification projects were bound to come up against some roadblocks that needed to be taken into account. The first of these lay in the instinctive tendency to fashion these codes after the Western model, with the consequence of "completely denaturing indigenous law." He also pointed out the risk of failing to appreciate "the importance of certain original institutions that have no equivalent in our codes." Some, he went on to comment, "see this codification primarily as a means by which to mould indigenous law into the shape of our European institutions." But above all, the upshot of these codification efforts was to impart to native customs a rigidity that wasn't proper to them. Indeed, he concludes, codification processes "delay a natural evolution that would likely happen upon coming into contact with European domination" (Girault 1929, 387–88; my translation).

ence. Once independence was achieved, the new nationalist leadership that gained power reversed course:

> Tellingly, what this leadership had resisted under colonial rule, it would insist upon after independence. For instance, under the French, the Tunisian and Algerian nationalists vehemently opposed any change in the law of personal status, but as soon as the French were made to leave, and as soon as the former assumed power, they almost immediately embarked on a program of "reform" in this presumably sensitive legal sphere. (Hallaq 2009, 121)

The establishment of the nation-state after independence shaped the *sharīʿa* in profound ways. For "even when the law was both substantively and substantially that of the Shariʿa, it was ultimately the state that determined this fact and what part—or what combination thereof—was or was not law" (ibid., 122). This tension between tradition and modernity makes for a thorny problem that will condition the process launched by the so-called Arab Springs.

7.6 Importation, cross-fertilization, assimilation

Ben Achour has speculated that the reasons why the French model saw widespread take-up in the Muslim world have to do with its emphasis on conceptualization, formalism, and logical unity (Ben Achour 1992, 144). This is in contrast to the practice of Muslim law, which on the basis of a rule tailored to a specific case looks for the underlying rationale (*ʿilla*), thereby extracting a principle that, by analogy, can then be applied to similar cases. The difference between the formal structures ended up favouring the greater flexibility of French law.

At play was a process of importing a legal model capable of adapting the social and economic transformations underway in the Arab world. Thus the model was not extended to personal status, for this matter was more closely bound up with customs that bore the deep imprint of religion. Nor, generally, was it imported by mechanical transfer: the importation process rather proceeded by cross-fertilization between different systems of law, an aspect that Ben Achour illustrates by describing the work behind the Tunisian *Code des Obligations et des Contrats* enacted in 1899. Drafting began in 1896 under the direction of David Santillana, a jurist and professor of Muslim law who chaired the commission entrusted with the codification project. The commission, made up of French administrators and judges, drew up a project that was translated into Arabic and was submitted to six Muslim jurisconsults reviewing the work under the guidance of the sheikh al Islam. Santillana observed that wherever interpretive discrepancies came up, they were resolved by looking at what was more coherent with European law, and in particular with French law. As Ben Achour comments, the code that came out was "Islamic and Romanist in its content, and French in its form and presentation" (ibid., 139; my translation).

Whereas in civil law the process was mainly based on *importing* a foreign legal system and adapting it to the local reality by *cross-fertilization* with the domestic system, in administrative law the effort was essentially to *assimilate* domestic law into the Western model, with a view to forging administrative structures that would first serve the interests of the colonial state and then, after independence, those of the nation-state. As Ben Achour correctly observes, "regardless of the legal forms of colonization (the colony as department, protectorate, mandate, tutelage, commonwealth, and so on), colonial policy was invariably, by its nature, assimilationist, even if this fact was not officially stated" (ibid., 128). What is more, administrative law, with its hierarchical structure, turned out to be functional as well to the postcolonial state in its effort to consolidate its own authority.

At the same time, however, French law—with its emphasis on the rights of man—contributed to fostering a political culture of opposition to power, a culture that translated into the emergence of counter-powers: labour unions, human rights leagues, and the like. Ben Achour can thus diagram the legal landscape by noting that "three areas can be distinguished that were subject to French influence: civil law, serving the needs of civil society; the administrative tradition, serving the state; and the principles of constitutionalism and the rule of law, underpinning the activity of contestation" (ibid., 146).

It is a profoundly different landscape that we are looking at today in the Arab countries of North Africa. Nationalism has become more radical, and intertwined with Arabism and Islamism: while nationalism is intent on dismantling the legacy of the former colonizer, Arabism is reclaiming its own cultural identity in opposition to Western culture and Islam, the latter of which asserts itself as absolute, thereby rejecting the very possibility of relativism. These are the values and forces that have been churning in the crucible of change that has swept through the countries affected by the deeply transformative Arab Springs—a confluence of elements that is playing itself out in ways that have yet to be seen and are difficult to predict.

Works Cited

Abadi, Jacob. 2013. *Tunisia since the Arab Conquest: The Saga of a Westernized Muslim State.* Reading, UK: Ithaca.

Akgündüz, Ahmed, and Said Öztürk. 2011. *Ottoman History: Misperceptions and Truths.* Rotterdam: IUR Press.

Arnaud, Alain, and Henri Méray. 1900. *Les colonies françaises: Organisation administrative, judiciaire, politique et financière.* Paris: Challamel.

Ben Achour, Yadh. 1992. *Politique, religion et droit dans le monde arabe.* Tunis: Cérès Productions.

Borrmans, Maurice. 1986. "Le nouveau code algérien de la famille dans l'ensemble des codes musulman de statut personnel, principalement dans les pays arabes." *Revue Internationale de Droit Comparé* 38, no. 1: 133–39.

Castro, Francesco. 2007. *Il modello islamico.* Edited by Gian Maria Piccinelli. Turin: Giappichelli.

Congrès International. 1889. *Congrès international colonial tenu à Paris du 30 juillet au 3 août 1889.* Third general session, held on Friday, August 2, at the Collège de France. Paris: Imprimerie Nationale.

David, René, and Camille Jauffret-Spinosi. 2002. *Les grands systèmes de droit contemporains*. Paris: Dalloz.

Girault, Arthur. 1908. *Principes de colonisation et de législation coloniale*. Tome III, *Algérie et Tunisie*. Paris: Librairie J.-B. Sirey.

Girault, Arthur. 1929. *Principes de colonisation et de législation coloniale*. Tome II, *Notions administratives, juridiques et financières*. Deuxième partie, "Les colonies françaises depuis 1815." Paris: Librairie du Recueil Sirey.

Hallaq, Wael B. 2009. *An Introduction to Islamic Law*. Cambridge: Cambridge University Press.

Le Bon, Gustave. 1889. Speech delivered on 31 July 1889 at the first general session of the *Congrès International Colonial*, held at the Collège de France in Paris from 30 July to 3 August 1889. Paris: Imprimerie Nationale.

Leroy-Beaulieu, Paul. 1886. *De la colonisation chez les peuples modernes*. Paris: Guillaumin.

Morand, Marcel. 1916a. *Avant-projet de code, présenté à la Commission de Codification du Droit Musulman Algérien*. Algiers: Typographie Adolphe Jourdan.

Morand, Marcel. 1916b. "Rapport fait à la Commission de Codification du Droit Musulman Algérien." In *Avant-projet de code, présenté à la Commission de Codification du Droit Musulman Algérien*. Algiers: Typographie Adolphe Jourdan.

Mousseron, Jean-Marc. 1968. "La réception au Proche-Orient du droit français des obligations." *Revue Internationale de Droit Comparé* 20, no. 1: 37–78.

Nuzzo, Luigi. 2012. *Origini di una scienza: Diritto internazionale e colonialismo nel XIX secolo*. Frankfurt: Vittorio Klostermann.

Owen, Roger. 2004. *State, Power and Politics in the Making of the Modern Middle East*. 3rd ed. Abingdon, Oxon: Routledge.

Powers, David S. 1989. Orientalism, Colonialism, and Legal History: The Attack on Muslim Family Endowment in Algeria and India. *Comparative Studies in Society and History* 31, no. 3: 535–71.

Romano, Santi. 1918. *Corso di diritto coloniale, impartito nel R. Istituto di Scienze Sociali C. Alfieri di Firenze: Appunti raccolti dal Dott. Domenico Biscotti*. Rome: Athenaeum.

Tocqueville, Alexis de. (1841) 1962. "Travail sur l'Algérie (Octobre 1841)." In *Écrits et Discours Politiques*, edited by André Jardin, tome III, vol. 1, of *Œuvres Complètes*. Paris: Gallimard.

Trentin, Massimiliano. 2012. "Le distanze del Mediterraneo: Europa e mondo arabo tra sviluppo e nazionalismo." In *Il Mediterraneo attuale tra storia e politica*, edited by Ennio Di Nolfo and Matteo Gerlini, 283–304. Venice: Marsilio.

Tyan, Émile. 1963. "Les rapports entre droit musulman et droit européen occidental en matière de droit civil." *Zeitschrift für vergleichende Rechtswissenschaft* 65: 18–28.

Velidedeoğlu, Hıfzı Veldet. 1960. "Le mouvement de codification dans les pays musulmans: Ses rapports avec les systèmes juridiques occidentaux." In *Rapports généraux au Ve Congrès Internationale de Droit Comparé* (Brussels, 4–9 August 1958), tome I, 131–78. Brussels: Centre Interuniversitaire de droit Comparé.

8 Democracy in Islam and Western democracy: Convergences and divergences

8.1 Constitutional transformations

In the previous chapter we looked at the way the colonial powers imposed the structure of the Western administrative state on the countries they colonized, but we also saw that these countries were made to absorb the principles of European civil law. In this chapter, then, we will turn to the task of examining the constitutional models used in the same countries and the shape that was imparted to the forms of government introduced under these models. We will be confining our analysis to two cases—Tunisia and Egypt—highlighting the transformations that, against the backdrop of the Tunisian and Egyptian constitutional stories, have been brought about by the so-called Arab Springs.

In 1861 "the first written constitution in the Arab world" was enacted in Tunisia (Brown 2002, 16).[1] This document—called *qānūn al-dawla al-tūnisiyya* (law of the Tunisian state)—was the work of a monarchical regime that introduced limited elements of constitutionalism in an international context shaped by the presence of the European powers, especially Great Britain.

> Growing European [...] interest in Tunisia [...] led the European powers to demand that the Tunisian *bey* (hereditary governor) adopt some of the reforms recently promulgated in the Ottoman Empire. Thus, in 1857, the *bey* enacted the *'ahd al-īmān* [Charter of Faith], which promised protection of persons and property [...] and concessions to non-Muslims in the adjudication of disputes.
>
> Shortly after the issuance of the *'ahd al-īmān*, the *bey* formed a commission of Tunisian officials to study the application of Ottoman legal reforms and draft a constitution. (Ibid.)

This constitution, enacted in 1861, scarcely contained any constitutional element. It is worth pointing out in this regard that a supreme council was set up

1 Nathan J. Brown's excellent study will be the main source on which the initial sections of this chapter are based.

called (*al-majlis al-aʿlā*),[2] made up of ministers, officials, and notables. It was entrusted with protecting the rights of the people, but in reality its commixture of legislative, administrative, fiscal, and judicial functions was the very negation of the fundamental principle of constitutionalism, namely, the separation of powers, which stands as the necessary condition for the protection of rights.

As Brown points out, while the Supreme Council "was clearly conceived as representing the Tunisian population, it was not to do so through any recognizably democratic procedures" (Brown 2002, 19): "popular sovereignty was not even considered" (ibid.). In fact, "the constitution was designed to serve the political elite" (ibid., 18): "it promises no democracy and [...] authority is to be held accountable only to the existing political elite" (ibid., 19).

Brown analyses the considerations on the Tunisian constitution offered by Khayr al-Dīn al-Tūnisī, a statesman and important political thinker of the second half of the nineteenth century who envisioned an Islamic constitutionalism conceived against the backdrop of European constitutionalism. He located the essence of constitutionalism in the ability to hold those in government accountable to the people (Khayr ed-Din 1987). On the Islamic view, this accountability was to be based on the *sharīʿa*. But in reality, as will be discussed shortly, the two approaches to constitutionalism—the Western one and the Islamic one—cannot in any way be brought into comparison.

Like the Tunisian constitution, the constitution approved in Egypt in 1882 (the Fundamental Ordinance) was the work of a political elite and was promulgated in a political context very much shaped by the European presence. In Egypt in 1878 a "bankruptcy had led to the introduction of a French and a British minister into the Egyptian cabinet" (Brown 2002, 27; cf. Cecere 2012, XLIIIff.). Faced with growing tensions in the relations these two ministries held with the Consultative Council of Delegates that had convened to draft an earlier constitutional text of 1879, the Egyptian khedive (hereditary governor), Ismāʿīl Pāshā, dissolved the government and entrusted Prime Minister Muḥammad Sharīf with the task of drafting a new constitution. The draft constitution introduced a principle of "balance between royal prerogatives and parliamentary powers" (Brown 2002, 27), vested in the Consultative Council. However, the European governments took exception to this shift towards a liberal form of government, since it gave them no control over Egyptian finances, and they

2 See Abadi 2013, 283ff. "The prerogatives of the supreme council were defined in Article 63 of the constitution, which authorized it to make new laws, modify existing ones, increase or decrease expenses, [...] and interpret the law" (ibid., 284). "The sovereign's power was limited by the constitution, by the power of the legislative assembly to depose him and by tribunals that were organized according to a European model, but the constitutional regime established along these lines lasted for no more than three years" (ibid.). In fact, "the relations between the supreme council and the executive branch, which was controlled by the *bey* [...], were rarely in harmony because the bey did not seem to be able to relinquish old habits and refused to renounce his prerogatives" (ibid., 284–85).

got the sultan of Constantinople to depose Ismāʿīl "before any action could be taken on the draft" (ibid.).

The khedivate passed to his son, Muḥammad Tawfīq Pasha, who under the pressure of the national liberal movement was compelled to restart the constitutional process by calling for the election of a new Consultative Council. The Council went back to Sharīf's draft constitution and shaped it into the Fundamental Ordinance of 1882: a "fairly brief" document (ibid.) of only fifty-two articles, this constitution "provided a sounder basis for constitutionalism than the Tunisian constitution of 1861" (ibid., 28).

As Brown observes, the Egyptian constitution of 1882 placed limits on the power of the khedive, while making "ministers [...] responsible to the Council" (ibid.)—an "elected body" (ibid., 27) that in turn "was given an extensive role in legislation and in oversight of public finances" (ibid., 27–28). Indeed the Council was intent on exercising control over the share of the budget apportioned to it and over fiscal policy, thereby limiting European influence in shaping Egypt's economy and its politics.

It would be a mistake, however, to see the Fundamental Ordinance of 1882 as an exercise in parliamentary constitution-making: "The delegates [...] did not have in mind at all the establishment of a system of 'parliamentary government'" (Scholch 1981, 213, quoted in Brown 2002, 28). "Their aim was not to end all khedival prerogatives—nor did their draft even contain them all within constitutional channels—but to diminish the khedive's discretion and allow him to be as responsive to domestic as to foreign concerns" (Brown 2002, 29). In fact, "democracy was hardly an issue: the Council, though elected, was essentially a way to ensure representation primarily of the provincial notability" (ibid.). Be that as it may, "in the summer of 1882, Great Britain occupied Egypt, restored Tawfīq, and allowed the constitution to be forgotten" (ibid., 28).

As can be appreciated, the early constitutional efforts, under the heavy influence of the European governments, sought to hold competing interests together, on the one hand preserving the preexisting institutional legacy, in the person of the bey and the khedive, while at the same time giving the traditional Tunisian and Egyptian elites the ability to elect representatives in the Council. The path towards constitutionalism had just begun.

8.2 Independence and constitutions

On 15 June 1920 in Tunisia, under the French protectorate, "the nationalists formed the Constitutional Liberal Party, which they named the *Destour* (Constitution [from the Arabic *dustūr*]), and presented their demands to the *bey* (Abadi 2013, 361). They were calling for a constitutional monarchy—and hence, implicitly, for autonomy from French occupation. The politics grew more complex when onto the scene came a younger group, the Neo-Destour, which was formed in 1934 breaking off from the main party. Faced with opposition from both parties, France finally recognized Tunisia as an independent state in 1956.

This was the year when a constituent assembly was elected. It was dominated by the Neo-Destour party, led by Habib Bourguiba, and it "moved to abolish the monarchy entirely" (Brown 2002, 76).

> At this point, the work of the assembly shifted sharply in the direction of presidentialism. Parliamentarism was abandoned: an elected parliament was retained but had limited influence over the executive (ministers were appointed by and responsible to the president); and the executive was granted some legislative authority as well. (Ibid., 76–77)

But such a setup undermines a fundamental principle of constitutionalism, namely, the separation of powers—and with it the separation of the functions assigned to the different branches of government. By comparison with the constitutional traditions of Western countries, we can see here an evident anomaly of the constitutions of Arab countries, which tend to accord a primacy to the executive by reason of a sort of preconstitutional basis of legitimacy. (In the case of Habib Bourguiba this basis of legitimacy came from the role he played in the struggle for liberation from French rule.)

The primacy of the executive was maintained even under the government of Zayn al-ʿAbdīn Ben ʿAli, who in 1987 deposed Bourguiba, claiming "that Bourguiba's senility prevented him from continuing in office" (ibid., 77). That same year, having assumed the presidency, Ben ʿAli introduced some modest constitutional reforms, in particular through the establishment of a constitutional council, though restricting its powers to the exercise of a preventive constitutional review of laws, while "the authority of the president and the cabinet remains quite extensive. The opposition needs a supermajority of two thirds of the parliament before it could bring down a single minister" (ibid., 78). It was in the scenario framed by this constitutional scheme that the Arab Spring found its spark in Tunisia.

We can turn now to the complex constitutional story of Egypt once it gained independence from Great Britain in the 1950s (postponing to the next chapter a discussion of the first constitution, of 1923). This is a story in which two key moments can be singled out, marking two turning points. The first came in 1952, when "a group of army officers overthrew the Egyptian government and deposed the king. A self-proclaimed Revolutionary Command Council (RCC) maintained full authority," and it "appointed a committee of leading jurists and political figures to draft a new constitution. As they began work, the RCC issued a series of constitutional declarations" under which (among other things) "popular sovereignty was proclaimed as a principle" (ibid.). "Only after considerable delay [...] did the RCC allow the constitution to be submitted to a popular plebiscite. In 1956, Egypt finally had a fully functioning constitution" (ibid.)—one that, as in Tunisia, set up a strong presidential system. In fact the monarchy had been abolished in 1953, and with the 1956 constitution came "the replacement of the king by a president. The new presidency was not a mere substitution, however, because the constitution ensured that the cabinet would clearly be responsible to the president" (ibid., 79). In this way,

> the parliament even found its dominance of the legislative process weakened with the president's ability to issue decrees with the force of law enhanced in comparison to his royal predecessor. With the entire constitutional system under presidential domination, constitutional guarantees and freedoms [...] lost whatever limited force they had previously held. Egypt had perfected the art of writing anticonstitutionalist constitutions. (Ibid.)

The second key moment was that of Egypt's socialist turn. It came in 1958, when "the union between Syria and Egypt produced a hastily issued constitution" creating "a unified state with its capital in Cairo. Syria withdrew from the United Arab Republic in 1961; the following year Egypt abandoned the 1958 constitution" (ibid.).

> In 1962, a national congress was elected to confirm a new document, the National Charter, which President Jamāl ʿAbd al-Nāṣir presented to the delegates in draft form. The National Charter proclaimed the country's basic policy directions and the components of its political system: [...] the major change introduced by the National Charter was to elevate Arab socialism into the official ideology. The Charter was not designed to serve as a basic law, however. Egypt's new constitution was to be drawn up by a popularly elected assembly. This body was elected in 1964 and swiftly approved a provisional constitution that functioned as Egypt's governing document for the next seven years. This constitution was designed to implement the principles of the National Charter. (Ibid.)

Once more, the 1964 constitution set up a weak parliament around the central figure of the president, whose power was especially enhanced by the ability to declare a state of national emergency essentially at will. It followed that "in practice the President would exercise far more powers than the Assembly and civil rights were not always adequately protected" (ibid., 80, quoting from Boyle and Sherif 1996).

"While formally labeled a 'provisional' constitution, the 1964 constitution survived until the death of ʿAbd al-Nāṣir in 1970. His successor, Anwar al-Sadāt, sanctioned the effort to write a permanent replacement" (Brown 2002, 80), which came in 1971.

8.2.1 Al-Sadāt's "Permanent constitution"

This constitution was ambivalent. For on the one hand it reinforced presidentialism, while on the other it entrenched the principles of constitutionalism and the rule of law. So, for example, while the menu of constitutional freedoms was extensive, the executive was given broad powers to resort to emergency measures that could restrict the exercise of those freedoms.

The socialist ideology was preserved. On the other hand, as Brown observes, "not only was private ownership protected, but sequestration, nationalization, and confiscation could take place only by law and through the judicial process" (ibid., 81).

Even the judicial system turned out to be a hybrid creature. In fact, the drafting process in 1971 pitted constitutionalist and antiliberal forces against each other:

> Drafters also were forced to consider the newly established Supreme Council of Judicial Organizations. This body, headed by the president, had replaced the exclusively judicial Supreme Judicial Council, and oversaw hiring, assignment, and promotion of judges. Liberals lost a battle when the Supreme Council of Judicial Organizations was given a constitutional basis. (Ibid., 83)

On the other hand, "liberals [...] successfully argued against the abolition of Egypt's administrative courts; the establishment of this system in the 1940s was regarded as strengthening the ability of Egyptian citizens to contest adverse administrative actions" (ibid.).

Finally, and importantly, there is the question of the Supreme Court created in 1969, "a presidential-dominated body that seemed to guarantee executive oversight of the entire judicial system. The 1971 constitution transformed this new structure into the Supreme Constitutional Court but left all weighty matters concerning appointment and jurisdiction to legislation" (ibid.).[3] And when "the Supreme Constitutional Court" was "finally created in 1979," it "quickly emerged not as an instrument of executive domination but one of the strongest institutional advocates for constitutionalist values in Arab history" (Brown 2002, 83). In this regard, Brown highlights the role the Court played in the 1980s in its effort to uphold the rule of law and keep executive power in check:

> In the 1980s the Court issued a series of judgments that established it as the boldest judicial actor in restricting executive action even in cases with significant political aspects. Perhaps the two cases which involved the greatest public notice involved challenges to Egypt's electoral laws. In 1987, the Court ruled that the 1983 law governing the 1984 parliamentary elections unconstitutionally restricted the right of citizens to elect their representatives. The law, which provided for proportional representation, prevented independents from running for parliament. (Brown 1997, 104)

3 On the establishment and significance of Egypt's Supreme Constitutional Court, see Moustafa 2007, 57ff., and Brown 1997, 102ff.

> The boldness of the Court was also illustrated in a 1985 decision regarding Egypt's law of personal status. In 1979, President Sadat had decreed changes in the law, strengthening the position of women in divorce and custody cases. The Court ruled that the president had exceeded his authority by doing so. The government argued that the dire need for updating the personal status law and the paralysis of the legislature in considering changes constituted by themselves an emergency situation allowing the president, under article 147 of the 1971 constitution, to issue a decree-law. The Court rejected this reasoning, and ruled that the desire to amend existing legislation was not sufficient to invoke article 147. (Ibid., 105)[4]

Finally, in 1980 some amendments were made to the Egyptian constitution that can be placed into three buckets: the first I am calling "ideological,"

4 In considerable detail, Brown (1997) also reconstructs the controversial developments the Egyptian judicial system went through since the 1920s, as well as the persistent efforts the executive power made to exercise control over it.

After "Great Britain unilaterally declared Egypt independent in 1922" (ibid., 40), a process got underway to centralize the judicial system. This led to the 1937 abolition of capitulations (enabling Great Britain to try its own subjects in Egypt under its own law), and then, in 1949, to the abolition of the mixed courts (each chaired by a foreign judge and made up of foreign as well as Egyptian judges), whose jurisdiction was transferred to the national courts.

The push to centralize the judicial system was carried even further in the wake of the 1952 coup d'état that made Egypt into a republic. Thus in 1956 came the abolition of the *sharīʿa* and *Milli* courts: the latter had jurisdiction over non-Muslim religious communities, and both were viewed as encroaching on governmental authority. Furthermore, special courts were set up to try political cases: this is the route the regime took rather than attempting to impose its own authority over regular courts. And so it was that in 1954 "*Mahakim al-Shaʿb* (People's Courts) were established to suppress the Muslim Brotherhood in the wake of an unsuccessful assassination attempt on ʿAbd al-Nāṣir" (ibid., 80).

After enactment of the 1971 constitution and during the presidency of Anwar al-Sadāt, special courts were introduced—like the Socialist Public Prosecutor, the Court of Ethics (*Mahkamat al-Qiyam*), and the Parties Court—that "unlike the exceptional courts of the mid-1950s, were constructed with the participation of the regular judiciary" (ibid., 95). Still, despite the creation of these exceptional courts, measures were introduced that "would have had the effects of turning the vague assurances of the 1971 constitution into concrete realities" (ibid.): this was true in particular of the rule of law as the basis of government and the independence of the judiciary, and judicial power itself could finally act as a check on executive power.

Also significant are the rulings issued by the State Security Courts recognized under the 1971 constitution. As Brown points out, these courts "have used their independence since the mid-1980s to issue acquittals in cases in which defendants claim to have been tortured" (ibid., 98).

As noted, however, it is above all the Supreme Constitutional Court that through its case law has acted to keep executive power in check and to safeguard civil and political rights. As has been argued, "Egyptian constitutional justice has played a key role in both placing constraints on executive power at its highest rungs and holding back the predominant force the state in society, and has done so without going so far as to call for a judicialization of law" (Sbailò 2011, 353; my translation).

the second institutional, and the third "presidential," concerning as they do the office of the president: while these amendments strengthened the country's constitutionalism, they also at the same time made for a more powerful presidency. The ideological element comes through clearly in Article 2, under which "the principles of Islamic sharīʿa [*mabādiʾ al-sharīʿa al-islāmiyya*] are the principal source [*al-maṣdar al-raʾīsī*] of legislation," and are not just one among other sources of law. On the one hand, this "Islamification" of the system of the sources of law came in response to growing Islamist pressures in Egypt; on the other hand, the effect of identifying the *sharīʿa* as the main source of legislation was to shift power to the state. But this reform also strengthened the role of the Supreme Constitutional Court, which secured the ability to interpret the principles of the *sharīʿa* on which basis lawmakers were to enact laws.[5]

As for the institutional framework, multipartyism was allowed under a system in which the party in government holds a dominant position. But

> the 1980 amendments enhanced the authority of the president in two ways. First, they removed the two-term limit on the president, allowing him to serve indefinitely (al-Sadāt was assassinated before being able to take advantage of this change, but his successor, ḥusnī Mubārak, has been elected to four terms). Second, one third of the Consultative Assembly was to be filled by presidential appointments, allowing the president to dominate the new body. (Brown 2002, 85)

The controversial modernization policy introduced by al-Sadāt was kept in place by Mubārak, but in a political framework in which "the central position of the presidency [...] remained unchanged, and mechanisms to hold the president accountable [...] worked only at the margins" (ibid.). Indeed, in 2007 Mubārak pushed through a constitutional reform that, ostensibly to protect the system, strengthened the president's emergency powers as well as the power of the executive (see Sbailò 2012, 261ff.). These characteristics of the Egyptian regime lasted through and informed the 2010 elections, during which a presidential system was at work that, in the name of stability, felt it could legitimize the repressive measures taken against political adversaries, and mainly against those who espoused radical Islamism (ibid., 278–79).

This was the political landscape, devoid of any real constitutionalism, across which in 2011 the Egyptian Arab Spring would sweep.

5 See Sbailò 2012, 212. In 1993, the Supreme Constitutional Court "argued that the sharīʿa can be divided between fixed principles (which must be observed) and rules subject to contestable and changeable rules (in which the legislature may exercise its discretion according to changing needs and conditions)" (Brown 1997, 126). Cf. Lombardi and Brown 2006.

8.3 An Islamic constitutionalism?

As Brown notes, "Arab constitutional texts have been written primarily to enable, organize, and justify political authority" (Brown 2002, 161): from the very start, since the 1861 Tunisian constitution, ***they have essentially been conceived to legitimize existing balances of power.*** Given this background, Brown asks two central questions: "how can constitutionalism emerge in societies in which liberalism is so far from hegemonic?" And "can Islamic principles [...] be employed to build a different kind of constitutionalism? (ibid., 162).

In the late nineteenth and early twentieth centuries, several Islamic thinkers set out principles for an Islamic constitutionalism that in the *sharīʿa* located the limits of political power. They were looking to both the Islamic and the Western traditions. This, for example, was the vision espoused by both taken by Rashid Riḍā and ʿAbd al-Razzāq al-Sanhūrī (ibid., 165).

In Islamic constitutionalism, a clear distinction is drawn between human-centric views—those that locate sovereignty in human beings—and Islam, which recognizes only God as sovereign, making the *sharīʿa* the foundation of the Islamic constitutional order. However, by also keeping the *sharīʿa* distinct from *fiqh* (Islamic jurisprudence), Islamic constitutionalists accept that the sacred sources of Islamic law are open to constant reinterpretation. Brown notes in this regard that "Islamic constitutionalists can be fairly wide-ranging in their acceptance of new interpretations of law" (ibid., 171). There are likewise other commentators who, while representing a minority voice in the Muslim world, go so far as to claim that "Sharīʿa is not identical with the sources of Islam as such, but rather the way those sources were historically interpreted and applied" (An-Naʿim 1989, 12, quoted in Brown 2002, 175). On this view, "an Islamic political order must be based on the *sharīʿa*, but the *sharīʿa* must be reinterpreted" (Brown 2002, 175; cf. An-Naʿīm 1996). The problem, then, lies in interpretation (and this is a problem we will come back to it in the following sections).

At the core of the debate on modern Islamic constitutionalism is the concept of the *shūrā* (consultation), the ancient practice of deciding matters of public or communal interest in consultation with those who stand to be affected by the decision. The turn towards consultation therefore poses the problem of how the sovereignty of the people can be made consistent with that of God. This question of popular sovereignty became a central concern, perhaps irreversibly so, when in the season of the so-called Arab Springs of the early 2010s, a series of uprisings and protests broke out seeking to end the corruption of the power elites in the Arab world. These developments suggested an opening towards Western constitutional models, but this inevitably meant going against the Islamic tradition.

Closely bound up with the problem of constitutionalism is that of democracy, in that there can be no democracy without a constitution placing limits on the exercise of power. It is to these problems that we will therefore now turn.

8.4 Islam and democracy: How to tackle the problem?

For an understanding of the conflicted relation between Islam and democracy, it will be useful to do a brief *history of concepts*. This approach attempts to clarify the meaning of concepts by tracing their historical origin, in such a way as to look at them in different social contexts and see how they have been shaped in different cultures. We will focus here on the concept of democracy, which in Western constitutional history can be seen to have been interpreted under two broad conceptions: that of the "ancients" and that of the "moderns." In a word, whereas in antiquity democracy was understood as a concept of *direct participation*, in the modern age it is understood as one of *representative government*. This modern concept is the one that took shape with the revolutions of the late eighteenth century, finding concrete form in *constitutional democracy*, as in the case of the newly independent United States, or in *legislative democracy*, as in the case of revolutionary France. In neither of these two examples did religion serve as a basis of democratic government, since both democracies came into shape through a *secularizing process* under the principle of the separation of church and state. This was a long process that began in the eleventh century, found new impetus with the European wars of religion in the first half of the seventeenth century, and came into full bloom with the French Revolution—the seminal moment of Western constitutional history.

In the history of Islam, by contrast, religion and democracy have formed an unbreakable bond, in a process as a result of which there is no way to extract the full meaning and implications of the concept of democracy except by looking at it in relation to religion. Like the West, the East also went through its own wars of religion. These began in the sixteenth century, pitting Sunni Islam (practiced in the Ottoman Empire) against Shia Islam (practiced in the Safavid Empire) (cf. Khadduri 1966, 60ff.). But whereas the European wars of religion ultimately resulted in a *separation* of church and state, these Ottoman-Persian Wars resulted in the recognition of Sunni and Shia Islam as state religions.

How, then, to interpret the concept of democracy in the Muslim world? In the Western tradition, democracy is understood as *popular sovereignty*. How is the same concept understood in the Muslim tradition?

8.5 Islamic reformism

Before we can unpack the complex relation between Islam and democracy, specifically in connection with the question of sovereignty, we should outline the main streams of political thought in the Muslim world. For such an overview we can turn to Tareq Ramadan, who in a work of broad scope distinguishes four such currents: (1) traditional; (2) Western-influenced; (3) Islamic reformism; and (4) the radical thinking that advocates armed struggle to end the repression exercised under dictatorial forms of government (Ramadan 2004, 35). Of all these currents, the one that Ramadan focusses on is Islamic reformism, which he considers to be the most significant and vital development in Muslim thought, and which he clearly distinguishes from liberal reformism. This latter thinking belongs to the Western world, being thoroughly secular and hence, in his assessment, impossible to reconcile with an Islamic outlook.[6]

In contrast, Islamic reformism couples the sacred sources—the Qur'ān and the Sunnah—with a political understanding that recognizes the need to put a check on political power and ensure the participation of the Muslim community. It is this combined vision, according to Ramadan, that can achieve the form of government that is more suited to the Muslim world. The most significant articulation of this vision has come from the Muslim Brotherhood, and in particular from its founder, Ḥasan al-Bannā.[7] But Ramadan also looks at other important intellectuals who preceded al-Bannā, especially Jamāl al-Dīn al-Afghānī and his disciple Muḥammad 'Abduh.

Ramadan is unambiguous in his rejection of liberal reformism, whose secularism has led thinkers like Alī 'Abd ar-Rāziq to draw a line of separation between the political and religious spheres, a separation that Ramadan considers to be ill-suited to the Islamic tradition.[8] At the same time Ramadan moves away from the "modern Islamism" that took hold during the years of repression that Egypt saw under al-Nāṣir (from 1954 to 1970) and Sadāt (from 1971 to 1981): what grew out of this context was a radicalized form of the vision advanced by the Muslim Brotherhood.

Among the leading thinkers who preceded Ḥasan al-Bannā in giving shape to an Islamic reformist vision, Ramadan lists, as mentioned, Jamāl ad-Dīn al-Afghānī. Central to al-Afghānī's thinking was the idea of Islam, whose values and principles he saw as coming under threat from the West. Hence, for al-Afghānī, the fight against colonial rule and for independence was not an end in itself but was instead a means through which to recover the principles of Islam. In reflecting on the Eastern question, Afghānī commented that the decline of the Ottoman Empire was owed not so much to the Western powers' expansionist aggression as to "the Muslims' loss of the religious fervour that had enabled their civilization to achieve its greatness" (Rizk 1983, 147–48; my translation). In this sense Afghānī cannot be considered a nationalist; rather, his project was to go back to the authentic roots of Islam and to protect

6 "The intellectuals who adhere to it," he observes, "look to the West, to its civilization and culture" (Ramadan 2004, 27; my translation). Among the proponents of liberal reformism, Ramadan lists 'Alī 'Abd ar- Rāziq, Ḥasan Ḥanafī, and Muḥammad Arkūn (ibid., 29).

7 As we will see in Section 8.15, however, there are some commentators for whom the views propounded by the Muslim Brotherhood amount to a form of fundamentalism, or radical Islamism.

8 In 1925 'Alī 'Abd ar-Rāziq achieved controversial fame for a book he wrote titled *Al-Islām wa Uṣūl al-Ḥukm*, translated into French as *L'islam et les fondements du pouvoir* (Abderraziq 1994) and into English as *Islam and the Foundations of Political Power* (Abdel Razek 2012): it was precisely the secularized and rationalistic approach he took to the question of political power under Islam that attracted criticism.

its civilization from the encroachment of the West. This he sought to do by training and education, and through an effort to spread the ideas of Islam (Ramadan 2004, 96).

Like al-Afghānī, Ḥasan al-Bannā would oppose colonial rule and the division of the Muslim world. And like al-Afghānī, he would place emphasis on educational and social work with a view to effecting reform over the long term. Education was key to the project envisioned by Ḥasan al-Bannā, for whom the dynamics of power depended on the kind of education and training that was being promoted and provided in society. Central to this vision was, here too, the need to revive Islam and its principles: these were viewed as the linchpin of society, but not without also taking into account the historical context in which the legislation had to be enacted that would "bring about the Islamic order" (ibid., 426; my translation). In short, according to al-Bannā, it was necessary to recognize a role for humans in laying down rules for those areas of human activity and existence that fall outside the scope of the *sharīʿa* (ibid.).

The political conception advanced by the Muslim Brotherhood is particularly complex, containing a variety of elements. The movement's fountainhead, Ḥasan al-Bannā, saw the Qurʾān as a constitution for Muslims and held that men needed a form of political organization capable of translating the fundamental principles of the Qurʾān into laws. In outlining this conception, however, he rejected the idea of theocracy and thought that the form of government best equipped to apply the teachings of Islam was that of parliamentarism.

This was in contrast to the thinking of Sayyid Quṭb, an intellectual who came out of the Muslim Brotherhood but became radicalized in prison under the al-Nāṣir regime: what Sayyid Quṭb saw as forming the core of Islamic political thought is the concept of *ḥākimiyya*,[9] or divine sovereignty. On this view, any form of government must accordingly recognize the sovereignty of God and must apply God's law exclusively.

In the 1950s and 1960s this broad conception came under scrutiny as the distinction grew sharper between divine principles and their historical application. And under the Mubārak regime, the Muslim Brotherhood sought to establish itself as a political party, in such a way that "the secular principles of the civil and criminal law in effect in Egypt could be brought into dialogue with the *sharīʿa*, whose origin is, by contrast, divine" (Campanini 2007, 73; my translation). This dialogue was supposed to lay the foundation on which to bring into effect a new model of democracy in Islam, but what instead came to pass is that, under

9 As Massimo Campanini points out in this regard, Sayyid Quṭb's conception of *ḥākimiyya* drew criticism from Ḥasan al-Bannā, who had founded the Muslim Brotherhood. Even so, the Muslim Brotherhood did qualify as "a 'religious party' proper, openly committed to translating its religious outlook into political action" (Campanini 2007, 46; my translation).

the presidency of Muḥammad Mursī, an authoritarian government was installed that proved inept at engaging and interacting with all the various components of Egyptian society. Still, despite this failure, it will be useful to drill deeper into the complex political reflection that developed within the movement of the Muslim Brotherhood.

8.6 The Islamic concept of the civil state: Ethics and religion

In the late 1990s the political discourse of the Muslim Brotherhood began to increasingly foreground the concept of the civil state. One of the movement's most respected and influential figures, Sheikh Yūsuf al-Qaraḍāwī, stated that what Islamists wanted was not a religious state but a civil state within an Islamic frame of reference (Qaraḍāwī 1997; cf. Tadros 2012, 50). After the fall of the Mubārak regime, the Muslim Brotherhood submitted a request for the creation of a Freedom and Justice Party. They invoked the idea of a civil state essentially to allay the fear that they should be aiming to introduce a form of state fashioned after the Iranian model. They also took care to point out that they neither wanted a military dictatorship nor a secular state. As is clarified in Chapter 1 of the party platform: "The Islamic state by its nature is a civil state; it is not a military state governed by the army which ascends to rule via a military coup" (quoted in Tadros 2012, 52). Continuing to quote the party platform, Tadros also notes that the civil state is not

> a religious state (theocracy) ruled by a clergy. In Islam there are no religious men but specialized scholars of religion (*ʿulamā*); it cannot be ruled by divine will. There are no infallible persons who monopolize the interpretation of the Koran or who specialize in the legislation for the Umma or own the right to absolute obedience and are characterized by holiness. (Ibid.)

So, while the civil state is distinguished from any form of theocratic state, it also rejects the Western form of the secular state. This makes it necessary to clarify how the organization of powers relates to Islam. In this regard, al-Qaraḍāwī offers the following statement:

> The Islamic state is a constitution or legitimate state that has its own constitution to which it refers for governance and a law to refer to, and its constitution is represented in the principles and laws of the Sharia as came down in the Koran and the Sunna in terms of doctrine, *ʿibādāt* [religious practices], ethics and *muʿāmalāt* [social practices]. (Qaraḍāwī 1997, 32, as quoted in Tadros 2012, 56)

What can be extracted from these statements of principle is that, *even if the civil state is clearly not conceived as a theocratic state, the central role it recognizes for Islam makes it difficult to tease out what it means for this state to be characterized as "civil."* This is a point that Tariq Ramadan has made by drawing a neat distinction between morality and religion. He observes that thinkers like al-Qaraḍāwī in Egypt or Rāshid al-Ghannūshī in Tunisia have endorsed the principles of democracy without detecting any contradiction there may be with Islam as a political project. For in doing so, as we will see, these thinkers have rejected the idea of a secular state, along with its stronger sibling, the principle of *laïcité* (Ramadan 2011, 167).[10]

In fleshing out the idea of a civil state, Muslim intellectuals accept that there can be two distinct sources of authority: a political one and a religious one. According to Ramadan, referring to the doctrines advocated by the Moroccan Islamist association al-ʿAdl wa-l-Iḥsān (Justice and Spirituality), this means that "the management of the affairs of state is a matter falling within the scope of *ijtihād* (human and independent legal reasoning) and cannot be entrusted to 'divine law' in the manner understood by the Islamic thinkers, scholars, and activists who invoked the idea of *al-ḥākimiyya*" (ibid., 171), that is, the sovereignty of God (a question we will come back to shortly).

A vision so described entails reframing the relation between religion and the state. Which in turn, in a Muslim-majority society, means rethinking the role played by ethics—understood in connection with religion—in the management of the state. On this vision, religion is understood as a complex of principles and goals in light of which to guide political decision-making, but the ways in which ethics—founded on religion—ought to provide such guidance need to be independently worked out within the political itself. This makes for a civil state that looks quite different from the secular state as conceived in the West, premised on the separation between the political and religious spheres.

The civil state envisioned by Ramadan is an expression of what the Egyptian scholar Heba Ezzat calls Islamic democratic secularism (see Bechler 2005)—a formula he borrows from her to explain the essential role the civil state accords to ethics in the exercise of power. On this conception, ethics can draw on a variety of sources depending on the different cultural traditions that lie in the background, and what makes ethics essential in this connection is that when the state is severed from them, it will fall prey to corruption, patronage, and the interests of multinational corporations.

This is the same basic concern that in the West also informs the republican tradition with its idea of a "civil religion," placing the public interest ahead of private interests, so as to counteract the ills and fractious destructiveness unleashed by the factionalist spirit. In the Muslim world, the scenario that

10 On a state visit to Egypt on 13 September 2011, Recep Tayyip Erdoğan, then prime minister of Turkey, called for Egypt to enact a secular constitution. But despite his support for the Muslim Brotherhood during the Arab Springs, his proposal was rejected precisely on account of its secular ideology.

comes into view with the idea of a civil state charts a path towards forms of democratic government fully respectful of the cultural identities in Muslim societies. But unless and until it can be clarified how the political and religious orders stand in relation to each other, it is difficult to see how this idea can come to fruition.

8.7 Two democracies, Western and Islamic: What divergences?

What mainly accounted for the Muslim Brotherhood's rise to political prominence were the educational and social initiatives promoted by the movement, but the same goes for other movements as well. One example is the political party called Jamāʿat al-islāmī (Islamic Society), established in Pakistan in 1941 under the leadership of Abū al-Aʿlā al-Mawdūdī, a fundamentalist thinker who lived in British India and then in independent Pakistan. Both movements coupled social work with political action through participation in parliamentary life within a constitutional framework. Al-Mawdūdī worked out a systematic doctrine that we can look at in comparison with the Western conceptions of democracy in an attempt to deepen our analysis of the relation between Islam and democracy.[11] This comparative analysis will highlight the peculiarities of the Islamic conceptions, while showing why any attempt to "export" Western democracy is unacceptable and bound to fail.

The relation between Islam and democracy forms the subject of numerous writings by John L. Esposito, who has attacked the problem from a variety of angles and has argued that in the history of Islam we can find some concepts that can serve as a foundation on which to as construct an Islamic conception of democracy (Esposito and Voll 1996, 23). As Esposito points out, Mawdūdī "stated that the 'political system of Islam has been based on three principles, *viz*.: *Tawḥīd* (Unity of God), *Risāla* (Prophethood) and *Khilāfa* (Caliphate). It is difficult to appreciate different aspects of the Islamic polity without fully understanding these three principles'" (ibid., quoting from Mawdūdī 1967, 40).

The first concept—*tawḥīd*—is that of the unity of God, whose will acts as a guide for all men. This forms the basis for the concept of the absolute sovereignty of God (*al-ḥākimiyya*), which is incompatible with the Western concept of the sovereignty of the people. Mawdūdī makes this point emphatically: "Islam, speaking from the viewpoint of political philosophy, is the very antithesis of secular Western democracy" (Esposito and Voll 1996, 23, quoting from Mawdūdī 1976, 159–60). While the Islamic understanding of the sovereignty of God is set in opposition to a secular

11 As we will see shortly, al-Mawdūdī is considered by Hamadi Redissi (2003b, 49) not an exponent of Islamic reformism (under the classification proposed by Tariq Ramadan) but rather one who championed a kind of fundamentalism Redissi calls radical Islam.

understanding of sovereignty, it requires that the entire population act in accordance with God's will. And herein lies the democratic element inherent in the vision of Islam offered by Mawdūdī. For, as he stresses: "Every Muslim who is capable and qualified to give a sound opinion on matters of Islamic law, is entitled to interpret that law of God when such interpretation becomes necessary. In this sense the Islamic polity is a democracy" (Mawdūdī 1976, 161, as quoted in Esposito and Voll 1996, 23). Thus Islam, as construed by Mawdūdī, can be said to envision a *democracy of interpretation* based on the idea of equality, that is, on the premise that every Muslim is equal before God.

This doctrine put forward by Mawdūdī warrants further consideration, for it is radically antithetical to Western conceptions of democracy. In defining the Islamic state, he singles out its core elements as follows:

> The foundation upon which building it rests is the concept of the idea of *ḥākimiyya* of Allāh, the one and only […]. Command (*al-amr*) and rule (*al-ḥukm*) and legislation (*al-tashrī'*) are all the particular province of Allāh alone […]. There is no scope in the confines of Islam […] except for the state wherein man engages in the function of *khalīfa* Allāh. (Mawdūdī 1980, 77–78, quoted in Belkeziz 2009, 206)

It may seem that implicit in Mawdūdī's use of the concept of *khilāfa* is the recognition of a government of the human being as a representative (*bi-l-nīyāba*) of Allāh. But in reality Mawdūdī clearly "establishes the distinction between the *ḥākimiyya* of Allāh and the *ḥākimiyya* of the human being" (Belkeziz 2009, 207). He accordingly comes to the following conclusion: "It is not correct to assert the term democracy for the system of the Islamic state; rather what is a more accurate expression is the term the 'divine government' (*al-ḥukūma al-ilāhiyya*) or theocracy" (Mawdūdī 1980, 34, quoted in Belkeziz 2009, 207).

Mawdūdī's views were in large part informed by the Indian Muslims' demand for an independent Islamic state, on the premise that there could be no peaceful coexistence with the Hindu population of India in a non-Islamic state.

If we compare this doctrine with Western theories of democracy, we should be able to see that two points of contrast stand out. In the first place, these theories see the state's secularism as a necessary condition of democracy, and in the second place they frame equality not in relation to God (everyone is equal before God) but in terms of dignity (everyone is owed equal dignity as a human being). In these two elements lies the basic difference between the Western conception of democracy and the Islamic one advanced by Mawdūdī.

The second defining concept of Islamic democracy is, as mentioned, that of *khilāfa*, or representation: it traces back to the concept of *khalīfa* understood as "successor" to the Prophet Muḥammad, but has since taken on the meaning of a deputy, representative, or agent of God on Earth.[12] According to Mawdūdī, in this concept of God being represented on Earth lies "the point where democracy begins in Islam. Every person in an Islamic society enjoys the rights and powers of the caliphate of God and in this respect all individuals are equal" (Mawdūdī 1967, 43–44, quoted in Esposito and Voll 1996, 26). From this perspective, then, the construction of Islamic democracy presupposes a community of Muslim believers. And in this respect, too, a deep fissure exists that can be seen to separate Islamic democracy from its Western counterpart.

Tawḥīd and *khilāfa* are the two key concepts structuring the paradigm of Islamic democracy. Indeed, they form the basis for the "concepts of consultation (*shūrā*), consensus (*ijmāʿ*), and independent interpretive judgement (*ijtihād*)" (Esposito and Voll 1996, 27). The concept of consultation is closely bound up with that of believer as an agent of God on Earth. Believers as a community can "delegate their authority to the ruler," but their "opinion must also be sought in the conduct of state" (Esposito 1998, 154). In addition, collective decisions by the community need the latter's consensus, on which rests the legitimacy of authority. Finally, completing the paradigm is the concept of independent interpretive judgment: this element imparts a considerable degree of pliancy to

12 The semantic evolution of the term *khalīfa* has been reconstructed by John L. Esposito in a way that does not seem entirely clear (Esposito and Voll 1996, 25–26). The concept of lieutenant, representative, or agent of God is in reality Qurʾānic, appearing twice in the Qurʾān and both times in that sense. One occurrence is in *The Cow*: "I am putting a successor on earth" (Qurʾān 2:30, quoting from Abdel Haleem 2005, 7, where the point is made that "the term *khalifa* is normally translated as 'vicegerent' or 'deputy.' While this is one meaning of the term, its basic meaning is 'successor'—the Qurʾān often talks about generations and individuals who are successors to each other, cf. 6: 165, 7: 129, etc.—or a 'trustee' to whom a responsibility is temporarily given, cf. Moses and Aaron, 7: 142" [Abdel Haleem 2005, 7 n. *a*]. The same concept is rendered as "ruler" in Muhammad Ali 2010, commenting that "the word 'ruler' (*khalīfa*) here refers to the whole of mankind, which is corroborated by the Quran itself in 6:165" [Muhammad Ali 2010, 9, n. *g*], and as "(mankind) generations" in Hilālī and Khān n.d., 7]). These are words that God speaks to the angels, subsequently enjoining them to "Bow before Adam" (Qurʾān 2:34, quoting from Abdel Haleem 2005, 7). The other occurrence of the concept of *khalīfa* is in *ṢĀD* 38:26, where God invests the Prophet David with the function of serving as his "representative" on Earth and tells him what responsibilities flow from that role: "David, We have given you mastery [*khalīfa*] over the land. Judge fairly between people" (Abdel Haleem 2005, 291). Compare: "O David, surely We have made you a ruler in the land; so judge between people justly [...]" (Muhammad Ali 2010, 570). And: "O Dāwūd (David)! Verily! We have placed you as a successor on the earth; so judge you between men in truth (and justice) [...]" (Hilālī and Khān n.d., 611–12). The original text: "yā Dāwūd, jaʿalnā-ka khalīfatan fī l-arḍi, fa-ḥkum bayna l-nāsi bi-l-ḥaqqi." The use of the term *khalīfa* in these two Qurʾānic texts helps to clarify two important aspects of the concept's semantic evolution. First, considering that the concept of the *khalīfa* of Allāh makes its appearance in the Qurʾān, it precedes the concept of the *khalīfa* of Muḥammad (not only chronologically but also conceptually). And, second, the meaning "successor of Muḥammad" is simply a specific application of the more general meaning "representative/successor" that in common parlance was already forming a set phrase next to the word *khalīfa*. I should thank Professor Giuseppe Cecere for this accurate explanatory gloss.

Islamic democracy by enabling it to adapt revealed concepts to the conditions by which each different era is marked.

To be sure, this makes Islam compatible with a range of different forms of government, and so also with its democratic parliamentary form, where *ijtihād* is exercised by a representative body. But as Esposito and Voll (1996, 30) comment: "Consultation, consensus, and *ijtihād* are crucial concepts for the articulation of Islamic democracy within the framework of the oneness of God and the representational obligations of human beings." And here, too, we can see how disparate the two forms of democratic government are in view of the different foundations they rest on and the systems of values they embrace—the Western form being rooted in the secular principle of the separation of the political order from the religious, the Islamic form instead being inseparable from the idea of the truth of revealed sources.

8.8 The sovereignty of God and the sovereignty of the people

The concept of sovereignty finds itself at the core of a crucial theoretical difficulty that Muslim thought faces in dealing with the question of democracy in Islam. For on the one hand democracy comes down to popular sovereignty, that is, to the idea that the people are their own lawgivers (they are the ultimate source of authority for the laws they agree to submit to). But on the other hand Islam seems to reject the idea of popular sovereignty, instead embracing the idea of divine sovereignty, or the "sovereignty of God," an idea for which "fundamentalist Islamic thinkers often use the slogan *al-ḥākimiyya li-llāh*, which may roughly be rendered as 'sovereignty (rulership) belongs to God'" (Bahlūl 2000, 287, which will be the main source for the discussion in this section).

There is little doubt about the aim the theory of the sovereignty of God serves in Muslim thought: it can be deployed to invalidate secular conceptions that deny that God can rule over society, and hence over Muslim society. Still, some commentators have argued that the contrast between popular and divine sovereignty is more apparent than real, and that a close analysis of the meaning of the sovereignty ascribed to God will reveal this sovereignty to be actually *consistent* with democracy.

In illustrating the idea of divine sovereignty and the principles framing the forms of government based on that idea, Islamic thinkers point to the Qur'ān, and in particular to *Women* 4:53: "You who believe, obey God and the Messenger, and those in authority among you" (Abdel Haleem 2005, 56).[13] On

13 In this verse some Islamic thinkers see the makings of an Islamic state and the basis for the authority that vests in God. As Ghannūshī (1993, 119) comments, "obedience to the Messenger of God [...] is the practical form in which obedience to God expresses itself. After this comes the power which the people exercise. The legitimate scope for this power does not violate divine law which is found in the Qur'ān and the Traditions of the Messenger" (quoted in Bahlūl 2000, 288).

this understanding, then, "there is no place in Islam for a popular government which is separated from the Faith." In other words, "democracy in Islam does not mean absolute popular power, but rather popular power in accordance with *sharīʿa*" (Turābī 1987, 63–64, 67, quoted in Bahlūl 2000, 288).[14]

But this also means that "the authority of government is limited because *sharīʿa* is the higher law, just like the constitution except that it is a detailed constitution" (Bahlūl 2000, 288, quoting Turābī as quoted in Lowrie 1993, 25). Reasoning from these premises, "many Islamic thinkers want to draw an opposition between *government by people* and *government by God*" (Bahlūl 2000, 288). But this assumption of a neat separation between these two forms of government needs to be tested: as Raja Bahlūl (2000, 289) puts it, "does government by God exclude government by the people and vice versa?" Or, more to the point: "If the people freely choose to be governed by God's law, that is, if they take God's law to be their own law, are they exercising popular sovereignty, or are they subject to divine sovereignty, or both?" (ibid.).

8.9 Legitimacy and validity

In clarifying the concept divine sovereignty, Bahlūl (2000, 291) asks us to first "distinguish between 'validity' (or rightness), on the one hand, and (mere) 'legitimacy,' on the other." Legitimacy (the weaker of the two notions) is about "established rules and procedures" (ibid.). Thus, laws enacted by majority vote are certainly legitimate, but not if they "severely infringe rights and liberties" recognized for minorities (ibid.). There is no doubt that "decisions taken by solid majorities in democratic systems are expressive of the people's being sovereign," but they "cannot depart too far from justice if they are to claim legitimacy (Rawls 1993, 429). In other words, too much injustice has a corrupting effect on legitimacy" (Bahlūl 2000, 291). But in distinguishing legitimacy from validity, and likening the latter to justice, Bahlūl notes that "it is not obvious that we have access to notions of rightness and justice independent of social settings and historically conditioned arrangements to be discovered in specific political communities" (ibid., 291–92).

But what is justice? According to Kelsen ([1960] 2017), an absolute concept of justice can only be found in the sphere of religion. But if we look at the problem from a secularized perspective, then we will have to concede that there are *plural* concepts of justice, each *relative* to the particular legal system within which it has historically taken root. Very much in the same vein, Michael Walzer (1995, 314) puts forward a "local account" of justice on which "a given society is just if its substantive life is lived in a certain way—that is, in a way faithful to the shared understandings of the members" (Walzer 1995, 312–13, quoted in Bahlūl 2000, 292).

14 A theologian and politician, Ḥasan Turābī (1932–2016) served as minister of justice and foreign affairs in Sudan, where he had led the National Islamic Front, part of the Muslim Brotherhood movement.

As Bahlūl points out, this local, relativizing account of justice tends to blur the distinction between validity (which is substantive) and legitimacy (which is procedural). By contrast, "*Islamic (and other religious) thinkers do not accept collapsing the distinction between what is 'right' and what is merely 'legitimate' (on account of being passed by commonly accepted rules of procedure)*" (Bahlūl 2000, 292; italics added). They do not so much deny the legitimacy of decisions taken according to democratic procedure as they want to say that the validity of political decisions ought to conform to divine law. In doing so, they foreground the concept of divine sovereignty, thereby claiming that the attainment of equality within the political system ultimately rests on a theological foundation (Esposito and Voll 1996, 25). Bahlūl asks whether there is anything like this conception to be found in Western political thought.

In an exchange the philosopher Jürgen Habermas had in 2004 in Munich with Cardinal Joseph Ratzinger (who would soon be elected pope), the latter argued for the need to move beyond the procedural rules of democracy, for these can become an instrument through which the rights of minorities are infringed (Ratzinger 2004, 31). He stated that it was necessary to identify the moral foundations of law, claiming they could be found in the great religious traditions of humanity (ibid., 34). Habermas rebutted by making a case for the superiority of the constitution over the majority principle and arguing that lawmakers enacting legislation by majority vote should do so relying on constitutionally entrenched principles and values as their guide (Habermas 2004, 26):[15] these include individual autonomy and the basic rights and freedoms, on the one hand, and equality, on the other, and they should trump any democratic procedure based on majority rule (Dworkin 1996).

Bahlūl (2000, 292) weighs in on this discussion by arguing that "Islamic thinkers' advocacy of divine sovereignty" is best understood "as a way of trying to go beyond this purely procedural view of democracy," and "that statements such as 'Sovereignty belongs to God' [...] are to be viewed as statements about what political decisions *ought* to be like, if they are to have validity, or moral rightness. The ideal situation is when the democratic procedure functions within parameters set by divine law." He sees this theory as having parallels in Western political thought, including in the work of David Estlund (1997, 174), criticizing theories of correctness on which justice is determined by the outcome of decision-making procedures.

8.10 Which sovereignty?

In coming to a conclusion, Bahlūl takes us to the crux of the problem. He does so by pointing out that "Islamic thinkers can (and many do) admit that there are at least two ways in which the people can be said to exercise power. First, it

15 The debate between the two intellectuals has also been published in Italian in Habermas and Ratzinger 2005 and in English in Habermas and Ratzinger 2006.

is up to the people to accept or reject the divine message. [...] Second, people exercise power not just by choosing to live under 'divine law' at all but also by choosing *how* to live under such a law. Divine messages are subject to interpretation, and the interpretation is invariably carried out by human agencies, even when people attribute everything they do to divine guidance (providence)" (Bahlūl 2000, 295).

One option that is open to believers in the matter of sovereignty is to think of divine law as akin to moral laws. For even if moral laws are held to be of divine origin, "there is no reason to think that God's authorship of the moral laws means that we cannot claim them as our own" (ibid., 296).

Bahlūl finally draws a parallel between divine prescriptions and liberal principles: "All the ideas, principles, commands and injunctions that issue from 'the mouth of God' will remain inert, and utterly ineffective, so long as they do not dwell in the hearts and minds of people who are willing and able to act on them. The same applies to liberal principles, whose, validity [...] does not derive from popular acceptance" (ibid., 295). Regardless of where our basic principles come from, he points out, they "are not active agents, or forces of nature. Hence they can do nothing until they come to be espoused by living human wills, until they come to 'inform' human minds" (ibid., 295–96).

In light of this parallelism, Bahlūl can make the argument that *the people are sovereign even when the laws, norms, and principles they commit to are regarded as "objectively right" or "true."* This, according to Bahlūl, is true of the principles of liberalism and democracy, as well as of divine law. In short, he concludes, "divine sovereignty, so-called, need not conflict with popular sovereignty" (ibid., 297). This is a conclusion that flows from his central argument, namely, that the formal procedures of democracy are always so framed as to reflect principles recognized as objectively right, whether these are constitutional principles or divine laws.

Whereas, from an Islamic worldview, "objectively right" applies to divine law, from a liberal-democratic worldview it applies to constitutional principles—the latter worldview being the outcome of a secularization process, the former instead being nonsecular, and antithetical to the Western tradition.

Furthermore, democratic principles can be interpreted in different ways depending on the interplay among the political forces that confront one another over the course of history. Are divine laws amenable to multiple interpretations? Does Islam allow such plurality?

8.11 Excursus: Interpretation

The questions just posed take us to the problem of the interpretation of the Qur'ān. Here we can turn to the work of Naṣr Ḥamid Abū Zayd, a leading Muslim intellectual whose reading of the Qur'ān draws on the insights afforded by modern disciplines like textual analysis and hermeneutics (Abū Zayd 2004, 127ff.). Abū Zayd contends that those who believe that "everything that is written in the Qur'ān is binding [...] go against the word of God" (Abū Zayd 2012, 33;

my translation). This stance flows directly from his reading of the Qur'ān, a reading based on a two-pronged approach to its *prescriptions*, on the one hand, and its *aims*, on the other. Its *prescriptions*, he argues, *need to be interpreted in light of historical circumstances*. Thus, for example, the different punishments the Qur'ān prescribes need to be understood as a *historical reflection* of the punishments that were distinctive to a specific society set in a specific time and place. The *aims* of the Qur'ān, by contrast, need to be understood *independently of historical conditioning*: this can be done by extracting them from the paradigm the Qur'ān expresses as a whole. Instead of working from this premise, that is, instead of looking at the paradigm of the Qur'ān as a whole, jurists have sought to extract its aims from the customary law of the Arabian Peninsula in the seventh century.

Abū Zayd frames the problem vividly by asking: "When a form of punishment prescribed in the Qur'ān has been incorporated into it from another source, is it correct to consider this punishment Qur'ānic, and hence binding on the community of believers?" (ibid., 35). While the Qur'ān states that it is certainly legitimate to punish someone who commits a crime, the punishments it prescribes "are best understood in the context of the practices that gain acceptance in a given era" (ibid). He also claims that to elevate the historical aspects of the Qur'ān to the rank of the divine is to violate the Word of God, and that "to crystallize it in a given spatiotemporal frame is to distort it" (ibid.).

At the core of Abū Zayd's reflection we thus find the problem of identifying the true aims of the Qur'ān. Its fundamental aim, he contends, is justice: "Whatever question the Qur'ān may be turning to—the universe, the cosmos, nature, God and his works, life in society or the afterlife—the central problem is that of justice" (ibid., 39). This aim is so crucial that in a scenario of potential conflict with liberty, it is always justice that prevails. This applies, for example, to the debate on *ribā* (usury) or on polygamy.

The primacy of justice can also be appreciated in the thesis that liberty must serve the purpose of creating a just society. The nexus between justice and liberty provides the vantage point from which Abū Zayd addresses the properly political problems that come up in his reading of the Qur'ān. In this regard, there are two problems that need to be brought into focus: the concept of community and the application of the Qur'ān in light of its interpretation.

The first problem comes up in connection with the innovation the Qur'ān introduced relative to the existing tribal system of Arab society. Abū Zayd observes that "Islam established a *community* rather than a tribe—a community that transcended the bonds of the tribal system" (ibid., 70; italics added). But tribal bonds continue to play an important role in the Islamic world, underpinning relations within governments, military regimes, and royal families. Even when a modern form of government is introduced, the tribal tradition can be observed to persist. In places like Tunisia, Egypt, and Libya, these tribal and familial bonds acted as an obstacle to the full accomplishment of the Arab Springs. The forces of change unleashed under the new paradigm introduced by the Arab Springs appear to have lost their momentum, and part of the explanation may well have to do with this web of allegiances that permeates the Islamic world.

The second problem addressed by Abū Zayd is how to go about interpreting the Qur'ān and what this means for its application. This is a problem that came to the fore in the debate surrounding the uprisings that seemed to herald a radical transformation of Arab societies. One question that has yet to be answered in this connection is whether these societies will take a different turn, away from the tendency to see the word of God in what can otherwise be explained as the outcome of social forces. And another, related, question is what weight will continue to be accorded to the word of God in the making and interpretation of law.[16]

8.12 One more excursus: Muslim law and religion

Four schools of Islamic jurisprudence became established in the ninth century, each building on the work of a fountainhead. These were the Shafi'i, Mālikī, Ḥanafī, and Hanbali schools (Redissi 2003a, 97). While these four schools are in agreement on the foundations of the Islamic faith, they differ on the weight that needs to be accorded to the sources of Islamic law and on the practical solutions that are best in each branch of law. They all start out from the basic premise of the centrality of the Qur'ān, but whereas Mālik and Ibn Ḥanbal ascribe primary significance to the expanded tradition encompassing the teachings of the Prophet Muḥammad and his companions, Shāfi'ī sees the Qur'ān and the prophetic tradition as having equal standing, while Abū Ḥanīfa accords primacy to *ijtihād* (the effort of reasoning).

Once the jurisprudence stabilized into different schools, the founders' *ijtihād* became *taqlīd* (imitation), meaning that the legal solutions that had become established were no longer subject to interpretation. This system remained firmly in place until the colonial period of the nineteenth century, when the Western powers established their hegemony and Islamic law opened itself to foreign influences. *This development set off a vast modernization process.*

Central to this process was an effort to work out the relation between reason and revelation, leading thinkers like Muḥammad 'Abduh (1849–1905) in Egypt to state that in cases where reason and tradition should come into conflict, "we need to take account of the solution indicated by reason" (quoted in Redissi 2003a, 105; my translation).

Between the nineteenth and twentieth centuries, the modernization process opened Islamic law to foreign models, as happened in the Ottoman Empire,

16 This is a question that Abū Zayd tackles by pointing out the need for critical scrutiny in figuring out what it means to make law in a society for which justice is an ideal to be pursued in keeping with God's law: "Those who in the Islamic world are entrusted with legislating need to do their job with a good dose of critical thinking as they go about the task of constructing a just society, and one that is turned in the same direction as the word of God" (Abū Zayd 2012, 36).

but it also spawned independent reform efforts, as happened in criminal law, where corporal punishments were softened, and in family law. As Redissi points out, in the postcolonial states these trends led to the formation of a *composite law*, in that Islam was proclaimed the state religion, but Islamic law is not the same thing as the *sharīʿa*. "This means that the Islamic state reserves the right to enact norms that do not conform to the letter of the *sharīʿa* or to the legal tradition" (ibid., 110).

In this regard we also need to bear in mind the distinction that exists between Arab and Islamic states. This is the distinction between states that apply the *sharīʿa* and those that "in various ways apply positive law." As Redissi concludes, "the practical outcome is a composite law in which some subject matters are regulated under classic law, while others fall under classic *fiqh*" (ibid., 114), or Islamic jurisprudence. It is therefore worth considering how this legal landscape has changed as a result of the transformations set in motion by the Arab Springs.

8.13 Democracy and *shūrā*

The question of democracy in relation to *shūrā* is the focus of an extensive and multifaceted debate among Islamic thinkers, offering solutions that suggest several different paths towards democracy. In a lucid and probing study, Massimo Campanini highlights the central role the concept of *shūrā* plays in the context of Islamic democracy and the potential it holds for the achievement of democratic forms of government in the Islamic world. "Since the Middle Ages, and then especially in the contemporary age," Campanini explains, "the principle of consultation has been associated with the idea of *a limit on discretionary use of sovereign power*" (Campanini 2013, 40; my translation). If historical forces should cause this principle to be inflected "in ways that differ from the liberal or free-market democracy in vogue in the West, this would make room for a properly Islamic rereading of the political space, and this exercise should engage the minds of the most attentive Muslim thinkers" (ibid., 45–46).

Particularly significant in this regard are the theses advanced by Muḥammad Salīm al-ʿAwā, who has identified what he sees as the pillars on which an Islamic state must rest: consultation (*shūrā*); justice (*ʿadl*); liberty (*ḥurriyya*); equality (*musāwāt*); the governors' accountability and the consent of the governed; and the state's moral foundation, which lies in its promotion of the good and the suppression of evil (*al-amr bi-l-maʿrūf wa-l-nahī ʿan al-munkar*). This is a flexible conception that sets politics on a moral foundation and can make it possible to reach an institutional solution under a democratic paradigm. This approach "does not in any way require us to assume an institutional equivalence between religion and politics when it comes to implementing an Islamic state" (ibid., 46).

There are two opposing tendencies that can be highlighted in the debate on the concept of *shūrā* within the Muslim world: on one side is an interest in finding points of similarity and convergence with the democratic system; on the other is a stance that rules out the possibility of any reconciliation between the two systems (Belkeziz 2009, 179). A prominent figure in the first camp is Rāshid al-Ghannūshī, who has argued that *shūrā* is not a derivative source that might be ignored. "Rather it is a source (*aṣl*) among the *uṣūl* of the religion and dictated by the requirements of human vice-regency (*al-istikhlāf*), that is, conferral of the divine authority on the slaves (i.e., upon humans) [...] and from there, *al-shūrā* was the backbone of the political power of the *ummah* and their means of rising to rule" (Ghannūshī 1992, 109, as translated in Belkeziz 2009, 174). Al-Ghannūshī further points out that in the Islamic system,

> it is possible to put into effect the political values that Islam brought such as *al-shūrā* and the pledge of allegiance (*al-bay'a*) and consensus (*al-ijmā'*) and commanding what is just and forbidding what is unjust (*al-amr bi-l-ma'rūf wa al-nahīy 'an al-munkar*); that is, the teachings that came to establish justice and to effectuate human happiness. If so, it is possible for democratic implements, just as it is possible for manufactured implements—in the consideration that they are a human inheritance—to be employed in different cultural environs and different conceptual terrain. (Ghannūshī 1992, 88, as translated in Belkeziz 2009, 182)

On the basis of these premises, he concludes that "democracy offers the best instrument or device for rule, enabling the citizens, through its use, to practice basic freedoms, and among these are the political liberties" (Ghannūshī 1992, 75, as translated in Belkeziz 2009, 180). *What al-Ghannūshī is saying, in other words, is that the* al-shūrā *system can be made to work compatibly with a procedural, or formal, conception of democracy as a form of government.*

By contrast, his reflection on the relation between *al-shūrā* and the *substantive* aspects of democracy highlights what he considers to be the *negative* aspects of the democratic system. We can see this where he makes explicit his "*philosophical* reservation, not his *political*, about Western democracy" (Belkeziz 2009, 180), commenting that

> the point of concern (lit., disease) is not in the apparatus of democracy—elections, parliament, majority, multiplicity of political parties or freedom of the press—not to the extent that it is latent in the political philosophies of the West [...] which separate between the spirit (*al-rūḥ*) and the body (*al-jasad*)—the philosophy of Descartes—and then ignore the spirit, burying it alive; and [these philosophies] *make war on Allāh* and struggle to the utmost to displace the human being from his [rightful] place so that there does not remain anything in the universe or within the human being other than material substrate, motion, appetite and control and struggle and the legitimacy of raw force. (Ghannūshī 1992, 86–87, as translated in Belkeziz 2009, 180–81; italics added)

So, while al-Ghannūshī sees the *al-shūrā* system as compatible with the procedural aspects of Western democracy, he draws a stark contrast with its substantive aspects, on the basis that this democracy rests on forms of philosophical thought that separate body and spirit and in so doing "make war on Allāh."

But the philosophy of Western democracy can be understood as a *philosophy of relativism*, in opposition to all forms of absolutism. For the democratic process, and hence the democratic form of government, is designed to work only with values that are *relative*, being specific to the different conceptions espoused by the majority and the minorities.[17] As is known, at the origin of the democratic form of government and its philosophy is the process of *secularization*, which has led to the autonomy of reason being elevated above all forms of revealed religion and, accordingly, to the separation of church and state.

8.14 Colonialism, nationalism, secularization

From the criticism al-Ghannūshī directs at the secularization process, we can appreciate how far apart his conception of democracy stands from Western forms of democratic government. In a complex study devoted to the problem of secularization, al-Ghannūshī analyses this process from a historical perspective, highlighting all its ambivalences in relation to colonial domination and the postcolonial governments and Islamic resistance movements that came in its wake.

The colonial powers that ruled over the countries of the Maghreb introduced in these countries modernization measures informed by an explicit aim to undermine the values and traditional institutions of Muslim society. While the *ummah*, the Muslim society established more than fourteen centuries earlier, was based on a principle of liberty and voluntary cooperation and was governed by a nonrepressive authority, the colonizers attempted to suppress the values of compassion, brotherhood, and cooperation so as to promote a materialistic and individualistic outlook.

In fact, as al-Ghannūshī argues, *the governments that took power in the newly independent states in the postcolonial period maintained a continuity with the earlier forms of colonial power*: "Secular elites in these societies, who claim to be the missionaries of modernity, have inherited the role of the colonialists and have inherited their thoughts as well as their means and methods of dealing with the masses which they view as primitive and backward" (Ghannūshī 2000, 99). The indictment that al-Ghannūshī levels at the postcolonial governments contains some damning language, claiming that the "modernization" pursued by these governments consisted in an effort to "nationalize" society by imposing a "national identity" on other identities, such as Arabism or Islam, and by attempting to reshape popular mentality in the mould of so-called modern life.

17 As Hans Kelsen (1955, 38) made this point: "To legislate, and that means to determine the contents of a social order, not according to what objectively is the best for the individuals subject to this order, but according to what these individuals, or their majority, rightly or wrongly believe to be their best—this consequence of the democratic principles of freedom and equality is justifiable only if there is no absolute answer to the question as to what is the best, if there is no such a thing as an absolute good."

But this aim could only be pursued through the repressive machinery of the state, which authoritatively asserted itself in society, violating civil liberties, controlling the educational system, and impressing itself onto social institutions and religion. But is it "the West," Ghannūshī (2000, 100) argues, that "bears moral responsibility for creating and maintaining undemocratic secularist regimes in North Africa in the name of promoting modernity. One wonders," therefore, "whether the West should pride itself on having accomplished a modernity that has ended in police states whose regimes legitimise repression in the name of democracy and human rights and in the name of defending civil society against an alleged 'obscurant fundamentalist onslaught.'" In reaction against these autocracies, which al-Ghannūshī considers to be expressions of a pseudo-secularism or "pseudo-modernity, Islamists today seek genuine modernity, one that emanates from within, one that is in response to local needs and that is in conformity with the local culture and value system" (ibid.). With regard to the Tunisian reality and the Tunisian regime, "the most radically secularist in the region" (ibid., 98), he writes: "We, the Tunisian Islamists, value human dignity and civil liberties, accept that the popular will is the source of political legitimacy and believe in pluralism and in the alternation of power through free elections" (ibid., 100). In these considerations, which lay bare the responsibility of the West and the illegitimacy of the Arab world's autocratic regimes, we can find some of the deep sentiments that have sparked the Arab Springs.

In his closing remarks, al-Ghannūshī reveals all the complexity of Islamic reformism in its uneasy relationship to the idea of democracy. For on the one hand he highlights the achievements of the secularization process, noting that

> secularism in the West has succeeded [...] in awakening the Western mind from its theocratic slumber [...]. man's inalienable rights to life, to freedom freedom of expression and to participate in administering public affairs were recognized. The sovereignty of the people was recognized, and [...] peaceful alternation of power was accomplished. For the first time too, a constitutional framework to inhibit despotism [...] was formulated and this state power was restricted by the rule of law. (Ibid., 122–23)

But on the other hand, "secularism is self-contradictory" (ibid., 122), for in the process of transitioning towards a secular polity, the human being has lost sight of the values of altruism and humanity and has been reduced to an assemblage of material needs. Even so, he argues,

> until an Islamic *shūrā* (consensual) system of government is established, the second best alternative for Muslims is a secular democratic regime which fulfils the category of the rule of reason, according to Ibn Khaldūn. Under such a system of governance, it is agreed to respect the fundamental rights of all people without discrimination and without commitment to a religious frame of reference. [...] A democratic secular system of government is less evil than a despotic system of government that claims to be Islamic. (Ibid., 123)

In short, from the standpoint of al-Ghannūshī's Islamic reformism, the Western form of democratic government can only be a stepping stone on the way to an Islamic form of government. This is the path that Tunisia embarked on when the Arab Spring led to the downfall of Ben Ali's autocratic regime, for in the aftermath of this event, the al-Nahḍa (or Arab Renaissance) movement endorsed democratic procedures only as a means of forming a government whose goal was to Islamize Tunisian society.

8.15 One final excursus: An interpretation of Islamic reformism

Islamic reformism has been analysed by Hamadi Redissi from a very different perspective than that of Tariq Ramadan. Reformism (*Islah*), Redissi observes, designates a movement that from the nineteenth century to the 1930s sought to renew Islam and improve the lot of Muslims by going back to the true sources of the faith; that is, it sought to *reform Islam so as to go back to Islam* (Redissi 2020, 43; my translation, italics added).[18] In this sense reformism reveals itself to be a form of fundamentalism, insofar as it consists in "returning to the sources of the faith, purging it of all the residue and deformations that, according the proponents of this movement, derive from centuries of decadence; the original truths, once found, make possible a dialogue with the new times" (Abdel-Malek 1973, XV; my translation).

Reformism, as Redissi explains it, bears a strong resemblance to *salafiyya*, and so with the qualities associated with the "righteous ancestors." Accordingly, the words *uṣūliyya* (fundamentalism), *iṣlāḥ* (reformism), and *salafiyya* (allegiance to the ancestors) can be considered as belonging to the same semantic family (Redissi 2020, 43).

The concept of reformism takes a broad meaning, for it used in reference to thinkers whose doctrines are marked by profound differences. The idea is associated, for example, with the founder of Wahhabism, Muḥammad ibn Abd al-Wahhab (1703–1792), and the spiritual father of all fundamentalisms, Jamāl ad-Dīn al-Afghānī (1839–1897),[19] as well as with secular modernist statesmen open to the West, like Khayr al-Dīn (1810–1879) and Muḥammad ʿAbduh, the founder of modern reformism (Redissi 2020, 41).

18 On the concept of *Islah*, Mohammed Arkoun writes: "The Word of God cannot be gainsaid by history; Muslims have certainly lost touch with its meaning: we need to determine when, how, and why. And so new life is breathed into the reformist attitude, this *Iṣlāḥ*, or return to the true, original form of the Islamic teaching" (Arkoun 1975, 97; my translation).

19 In his political action, al-Afghānī sought to develop constitutional institutions in the Arab world and to free Egypt from European domination. He also sought to regenerate the Muslim religion with an infusion of philosophy and science and a return to Sufism, taking a stance against all forms of dogmatism. For a discussion see Laoust 2002, 306.

Reformism is antitraditionalist insofar as it is opposed to imitation (*taqlīd*), relying instead on *ijtihād*, that is, interpretation, and in such a way as not to fall under the sway of the established schools. Particularly significant in this sense is the previously introduced position espoused by Muḥammad ʿAbduh, who on an Averroistic rationalist approach argues for the need to take account of the solution that reason points to in cases where a conflict arises with tradition. ʿAbduh's programme was aimed at reforming justice, education, and "political institutions by looking to modern notions of parliament, public opinion, utility, and separation of powers as standards in light of which to rethink Islamic concepts like *shūrā* (consultation), *raʾy* (personal judgment), *maslahʾa* (general interest), and *ijmāʿ* (unanimous agreement)" (Arkoun 1975, 99).

As far as method and outlook are concerned, the proponents of reformism practiced "*ijtihād* and not *jihad*. Their rationalistic rereading of the Qurʾān was aimed not at revolution but at reforming the institutions" (Redissi 2003b, 48).

As for the politics of reformism, the stance it took was against despotism. We can see this, for example, in the thought of Khayr al-Dīn, as well as in the work of al-Afghānī, even if in his analysis of tyranny he conceded the possibility of a "just tyrant."

Sunni reformism has a decadent reading of history, seeing it on a course that from the righteous caliphate has backslid to forms of unjust monarchy, and a great many reformists have equated *shūrā* (consultation) with the parliamentary representative system.

Finally, in the reformist thesis Redissi sees the founding moment of modern Islam, imbuing it with the principles of humanism, with its embrace of a *jihad* solely concerned with promoting tolerance and ensuring respect for international humanitarian law.

Reformism, or first-wave fundamentalism, developed in the latter half of the nineteenth century and the early twentieth century. This was the period known as *nahdha* (rebirth), when the Muslim world reexamined itself in an effort to pinpoint the reasons why it had fallen behind the West. The explanation that found most favour was that "the West owed its power to the fact that it had felicitously wrested itself from the baneful dominance of the church, while Islam—as a synthesis of religions, a totality without remainders, the cradle of civilization, an engine of progress—owed its decline to the fact that Muslims strayed away from the church!" (Redissi 2003b, 47).

The rebirth made it possible for the Arab world in the nineteenth century to overcome its own sense of inferiority in the face of Western supremacy, and to develop the ideas with which it sought to reform Arab society. Khayr al-Dīn and Muḥammad ʿAbduh called on Muslims to fight their adversaries with their own weapons, but they were not referring to material weapons. According to ʿAbduh anything that is used in a violent or peaceful competition is a weapon, including science, commerce, industry, justice, and religion (Husry 1980, 118).

In the 1930s there emerged second-wave fundamentalism, conventionally referred to as radical Islam. Its origins trace back to the formation of the Muslim Brotherhood in Egypt in 1928 and the Jamāʿat al-islāmī (Islamic society) party founded in 1941 by al-Mawdūdī, whose political thought was previously described as placing him at the opposite end of the spectrum from Western conceptions of democracy.

The Muslim Brotherhood's motto was forthright and direct: "Allāh is our objective. The Prophet is our leader. Qur'ān is our law. Jihād is our way. Dying in the way of Allāh is our highest hope." The Muslim Brotherhood radicalized the religious themes of those who advocated allegiance to the "righteous ancestors," nor did the movement make any concession to modernism. "Islam," al-Bannā states, "is dogma and cult, homeland and nationality, religion and state, spirituality and action, Qur'ān and sabre" (Arkoun 1975, 100; my translation).

The rise of these movements can essentially be attributed to the failure of the postcolonial states, which undertook modernization processes authoritatively managed from the top down, all the while bureaucratizing the economy (ibid., 51). In response to such failures, this brand of fundamentalism asked a specific question, namely, how is it possible for Muslims to live in modernity without forsaking tradition. The answer it found was to put revelation at the service of revolution. As Redissi reminds us, Mawdūdī was the first public figure to congratulate Ayatollah Khomeini on his success in taking over as supreme leader in the Iranian Revolution of 1979 (ibid., 52).

Just how problematic the relation is between these movements and democratic parliamentary systems became apparent under Muḥammad Mursī's short-lived presidency in Egypt, which, as we will see shortly, was marked by an effort to Islamize Egyptian society and by a difficulty in coming to terms with the pluralism of democracy.

Finally, in Al-Qā'ida Redissi (2003b, 64) sees a third type of fundamentalism: not a movement, not a party, but an international terrorist network intent on waging an unrelenting total war on the West (global Islamic jihad).

8.16 The perspective of liberal and democratic reformism

Another current that needs to be taken into account in the world of Muslim thinking on democracy is that of liberal reformism. One thinker who exemplifies this stream of thought is Yadh Ben Achour. While al-Ghannūshī underscores the repressive nature of the governments that held power in the postcolonial nation-states, and shows how the secularization process has had the effect of dehumanizing the individual, Ben Achour probes deeper into the relation that in the postcolonial states settled into shape between Muslim law and state law, between religion and politics, between democracy and constitutionalism.

Even while recognizing the authoritarian nature of the governments that came into power after independence from colonial rule, Ben Achour accepts that the state has become a source of law and of legislation. This is in contrast to the legal systems of antiquity, in which a clear separation existed between the state and the law—the former acting in the realm of the temporal, the latter instead falling within the sphere of the sacred. Islam understood there to be a separation between politics, on the one hand, and law and ethics, on the other. This separation served as the basis for a hierarchy under which *sharʿ* (religion, along with ethics and law) stood above *siyāsa* (politics). Our present age, Ben Achour states, has instead sacralized the state and desacralized the law (Ben Achour 1992, 168).

In postcolonial Tunisia the Bourguiba government undertook a vast process aimed at reforming "the state and society on the basis a new ethic centred on citizenship, a sense of the value of the state, joie de vivre, work, and equality between the sexes" (ibid.). But a deep disconnect came to exist between this *ideal* of law and state and its *reality* on the ground. Indeed, corresponding to the *form* of a constitutional state—with basic liberties and universal suffrage under a system of checks and balances and the rule of law—was the *reality* of a police state.

Furthermore, the reforms did not manage to establish the primacy of state-made law over Muslim law. The latter is based on religious sources—the Qurʾān and the Sunnah—and espouses a theological vision premised on the eternity of the human being; the principle of "insufficient reason," meaning that reason cannot attain the eternal truths; and revealed law, which human beings must take as their guide in matters of faith, morality, and the law.

State-made law, for its part, and as previously discussed, is instead of Western origin and was introduced in the Muslim world in the second half of the nineteenth century. It is the outcome of the state's will, through which it shapes society. The problem of the relation between the two forms of law—the secular and the religious—has found different solutions in different political and cultural situations. Thus in Tunisia the scope of Muslim law is limited to personal status, whereas in Saudi Arabia it covers a broad range of subject areas: all criminal law is Muslim law, for example, as are family and property law. As Ben Achour casts his eye "across the diversity of all the situations" that characterize the Muslim world, he can accordingly offer a broad assessment: "it can be claimed from the outset that what exists in it is neither secularism nor absolute theocracy" (Ben Achour 2004, § 26). On this reasoning he claims that the Tunisian code of personal status can neither be described as secular nor as an application of Muslim law.

Hence, the relation between a Muslim law based on the sacred sources and a state-made law imported from the West, under the paradigm of the constitutional state, remains an open problem that lies at the origin of unresolved tensions. And in fact Ben Achour also comments that in the Arab states a shift has taken place from a "religious state" to a "state religion," that is, to a "statization of Muslim law," which, having moved into "the order of constitutionality," is no longer subject to "the order of the Muslim theory of the sources of law" (ibid., § 36). The two normative systems—that of state-made law and that of Muslim law—thus find themselves in an unstable relation in search of an equilibrium that has yet to be settled on.

It is with these considerations in place that Ben Achour introduces the problem of democracy. His analysis rightly leads him to ask the question whether democracy can be built against the background of this unresolved tension with religious tradition. He warns against the risk that democracy should translate into demagogy, that is, into the action of political leaders who draw their legitimacy from an ability to connect directly with the masses, nor can democracy be reduced to a simple procedure through which a government is formed. Instead, resorting to Baruch Spinoza's masterful *Theologico-Political Treatise* of 1670, he argues that democracy needs to be nourished by an ethic that accepts pluralism and dissidence: "This is the ethic without which democracy is reduced to a simple mechanism, or it will give way to a materialist regime (be it bourgeois or proletarian)" (Ben Achour 1992, 261). This is also why democracy is incompatible with any form of absolutism. And it also follows from his conception that politics needs to be governed by its own laws, meaning that it needs to be kept separate from religion, in that politics can only corrupt religion by bending it to its own ends. Will the Arab world be able to achieve a kind of polity so described, proclaiming the end of absolutes, or can it only expect the solution of a religious or military regime?

Works Cited

Abadi, Jacob. 2013. *Tunisia since the Arab Conquest: The Saga of a Westernized Muslim State*. Reading, UK: Ithaca Press.

Abdel Haleem, M. A. S., trans. 2005. *The Qur'ān: A New Translation by M. A. S. Abdel Haleem*. Oxford: Oxford University Press.

Abdel-Malek, Anouar. 1973. *Il pensiero politico arabo contemporaneo*. Rome: Editori Riuniti. Translated by Giuseppe Morosini. Originally published as *La pensée politique arabe contemporaine* (Paris: Éditions du Seuil, 1970; 3rd ed. 1980).

Abdel Razek, Ali. 2012. *Islam and the Foundations of Political Power*. Translated by Maryam Loutfi. Edited by Abdou Filali-Ansary. Edinburgh: Edinburgh University Press, in association with the Aga Khan University Institute for the Study of Muslim Civilisations. (Orig. pub. 1925.)

Abderraziq, Ali. 1994. *L'islam et les fondements du pouvoir*. Translated by Abdou Filali-Ansary. Paris: Éditions La Découverte; Cairo: Centre d'Études et de Documentation Économique, Sociale et Juridique (CEDEZ). (Orig. pub. 1925.)

Abū Zayd, Naṣr Ḥāmid. 2004. *Una vita con l'Islam*. Edited by Navid Kermani, translated by Jutta Mott and Massimiliano Celli. Bologna: il Mulino. Also published in German under the title *Ein Leben mit dem Islam*, edited by Navid Kermani, translated by Cherifa Magdi (Freiburg, Basel, Vienna: Herder, 1999).

Abū Zayd, Naṣr Ḥāmid. 2012. *Testo sacro e libertà: Per una lettura critica del Corano*. Edited by Federica Fedeli, foreword by Nina zu Fürstenberg. Venice: Marsilio.

An-Na'im, Abdullahi Ahmed. 1989. "Constitutionalism and Islamization in the Sudan." *Africa Today* 36, no. 3/4: 11–12.

An-Na'īm, Abdullahi Ahmed. 1996. *Toward an Islamic Reformation: Civil Liberties, Human Rights, and International Law*. Syracuse, NY: Syracuse University Press.

Arkoun, Mohammed. 1975. *La pensée arabe*. Que sais-je? series, no. 915. Paris: Presses Universitaires de France.

Bahlūl, Raja. 2000. "People vs. God: The Logic of 'Divine Sovereignty' in Islamic Democratic Discourse." *Islam and Christian-Muslim Relations* 11, no. 3: 287–97.

Bechler, Rosemary. 2005. "Meeting Heba Ezzat." *openDemocracy*, May 11. https://www.opendemocracy.net/en/article_2497jsp/

Belkeziz, Abdelilah. 2009. *The State in Contemporary Islamic Thought: A Historical Survey of the Major Muslim Political Thinkers of the Modern Era*. London: I. B. Tauris, in association with the Centre for Arab Unity Studies.

Ben Achour, Yadh. 1992. *Politique, religion et droit dans le monde arabe*. Tunis: Cérès Productions.

Ben Achour, Yadh. 2004. "L'articulation du droit musulman et du droit étatique dans le monde arabe actuel." In *Lectures contemporaines du droit islamique: Europe et monde arabe*, edited by Franck Frégosi, 101–20. Strasbourg: Presses Universitaires de Strasbourg. (Citations are to the paragraph numbers in the publisher's online edition of the article at https://books.openedition.org/pus/14730.)

Boyle, Kevin, and Adel Omar Sherif. 1996. "The Road to the 1971 Constitution—a Brief Constitutional History of Modern Egypt." In *Human Rights and Democracy: The Role of the Supreme Constitutional Court of Egypt*, edited by Kevin Boyle and Adel Omar Sherif. London, Boston, The Hague: Kluwer Law International.

Brown, Nathan J. 1997. *The Rule of Law in the Arab World: Courts in Egypt and the Gulf.* Cambridge: Cambridge University Press.

Brown, Nathan, J. 2002. *Constitutions in a Nonconstitutional World: Arab Basic Laws and the Prospects for Accountable Government*. Albany: State University of New York Press.

Campanini, Massimo. 2007. "La seconda ondata del riformismo islamico: I Fratelli musulmani." Chap. 4 in *Arcipelago Islam: Tradizione, riforma e militanza in età contemporanea*, edited by Massimo Campanini and Karim Mezran. Rome and Bari: Laterza.

Campanini, Massimo. 2013. "Le rivolte arabe: Verso un nuovo modello politico?" Chap. 1 in *Le rivolte arabe e l'Islam: La transizione incompiuta*, edited by Massimo Campanini. Bologna: il Mulino.

Cecere, Giuseppe. 2012. "La primavera incompiuta del liberalismo egiziano." *Introduction to Costituzione egiziana (1923)*. Macerata: Liberilibri.

Dworkin, Ronald. 1996. *Freedom's Law: The Moral Reading of the American Constitution*. Oxford: Oxford University Press.

Esposito, John L. 1998. *Islam and Politics*. Syracuse, NY: Syracuse University Press.

Esposito, John L., and John O. Voll. 1996. *Islam and Democracy*. New York and Oxford: Oxford University Press.

Estlund, David. 1997. "Beyond Fairness and Deliberation: The Epistemic Dimension of Democratic Authority." In *Deliberative Democracy: Essays on Reason and Politics*, edited by James Bohman and William Rehg, 173–204. Cambridge, MA: The MIT Press.

Ghannūshī, Rāshid al-. 1992. *al-Ḥurīyāt al-ʿĀmma fī al-Dawlah al-Islāmiyah*. Beirut: Centre for Arab Unity Studies.

Ghannūshī, Rashid al-. 1993. *Al-ḥurriyyāt al-ʿĀmma fī al-dawla al-islāmiyya*. Beirut: Markaz Dirāsāt al-Waḥda al-ʿArabiyya.

Ghannūshī, Rāshid al-. 2000. "Secularism in the Arab Maghreb." In *Islam and Secularism in the Middle East*, edited by Azzam Tamimi and John L. Esposito, 97–123. London: Hurst & Company.

Habermas, Jürgen. 2004. "Quel che Habermas concede a Dio (più di Rawls)." *Reset* 83 (May–June): 24–30.

Habermas, Jürgen, and Joseph Ratzinger. 2005. *Ragione e fede in dialogo: Le idee di Benedetto XVI a confronto con un grande filosofo*. Edited by Giancarlo Bosetti. Venice: Marsilio.

Habermas, Jürgen, and Joseph Ratzinger. 2006. *The Dialectics of Secularization: On Reason and Religion*. Translated by Brian McNeil. Foreword by Florian Schuller. San Francisco: Ignatius. Originally published in German under the title *Dialektik der Säkularisierung: Über Vernunft und Religion* (Freiburg: Herder 2005).

Hilālī, Muhammad Taqī-ud-Dīn al-, and Muhammad Muhsin Khān, trans. n.d. *Translation of the Meanings of The Noble Qur'an in the English Language*. Medina, KSA: King Fahd Complex for the Printing of the Holy Qur'an.

Husry, Khaldun S. al-. 1980. *Origins of Modern Arab Political Thought*. Delmar, NY: Caravan Books.

Kelsen, Hans. 1955. "Foundations of Democracy." *Ethics: An international Journal of Social Political and Legal Philosophy* 61, no. 1, pt. 2 (Foundations of Democracy): 1–101.

Kelsen, Hans. (1960) 2017. "Das Problem der Gerechtigkeit." In *Reine Rechtslehre. Mit einem Anhang: Das Problem der Gerechtigkeit*, 611–758. 2nd ed. Tübingen and Vienna: Mohr Siebeck.

Khadduri, Majid. 1966. *The Islamic Law of Nations: Shaybānī's Siyar*. Baltimore, MD: The Johns Hopkins Press.

Khayr ed-Din. 1987. *Essai sur les réformes nécessaires aux États musulmans*. Edited by Magali Morsi. Aix-en-Provence: Édisud.

Laoust, Henri. 2002. *Gli scismi nell'Islam: Un percorso nella pluralità del mondo musulmano*. Edited by Valentina Colombo, translated by Stefano A. E. Leoni. Genoa: ECIG. Originally published as *Les schismes dans l'Islam: Introduction à une étude de la religion musulmane* (Paris: Payot, 1965).

Lombardi, Clark B., and Nathan J. Brown. 2006. "Do Constitutions Requiring Adherence to Shari'a Threaten Human Rights? How Egypt's Constitutional Court Reconciles Islamic Law with the Liberal Rule of Law." *American University International Law Review* 21, no. 3: 379–435.

Lowrie, Arthur, ed. 1993. *Islam, Democracy, the State, and the West: A Round Table with Dr. Ḥasan Turābī*. Tampa, FL: The World of Islam Studies Enterprise.

Mawdūdī, Abū al-ʿAlā al-. 1980. *Naẓarīyyat al-Islām wa-hadī-h fī l-sīyāsa wa-l-qānūn wa-l-dustūr*. Beirut: Mu'assasat al-Risāla.

Mawdūdī, Abūʾl Aʿlā. 1976. "Political Theory of Islam." Chap. 10 in *Islam: Its Meaning and Message*, edited by Khurshid Ahmad. London: Islamic Council of Europe.

Mawdūdī, Sayyid Abul Aʿla. 1967. *Islamic Way of Life*. Translated by Khurshid Ahmad. Delhi: Markazi Maktaba Islami.

Moustafa, Tamir. 2007. *The Struggle for Constitutional Power: Law, Politics, and Economic Development in Egypt*. Cambridge: Cambridge University Press.

Muhammad Ali, Maulana, trans. 2010. *English Translation of The Holy Quran, with Explanatory Notes from the English Translation and Commentary of Maulana Muhammad Ali*, edited by Zahid Aziz. Wembley, UK: Ahmadiyya Anjuman Lahore Publications. (Orig. pub. 1917.)

Qaraḍāwī, Yūsuf al-. 1997. *From the Fiqh of the State in Islam*. 4th ed. Cairo: Dār al-Shurūq.

Ramadan, Tariq. 2004. *Il riformismo islamico: Un secolo di rinnovamento Musulmano*. Translated by Amina Fazio and Nourredine Beghidja. Troina: Città Aperta. Originally published in French under the title *Aux sources du renouveau musulman: D'al Afghānī à Hassan al-Bannā; un siècle de réformisme islamique* (Paris: Bayard/Centurion, 1998).

Ramadan, Tariq. 2011. *L'Islam et le réveil arabe*. Paris: Presses du Châtelet.

Ratzinger, Joseph. 2004. "Ragione e fede: Scambio reciproco per un'etica comune." *Reset* 38 (May–June): 31–34.

Rawls, John. 1993. *Political Liberalism*. New York: Columbia University Press.

Redissi, Hamadi. 2003a. "Diritto e tradizione in Islam." *Ars Interpretandi: Annuario di Ermeneutica Giuridica* 8: 89–114.

Redissi, Hamadi 2003b. "Verso un terzo tipo di fondamentalismo." In *Tradizioni culturali, sistemi giuridici e diritti umani nell'area del Mediterraneo*, edited by Valentina Colombo and Gustavo Gozzi, 37–65. Bologna: il Mulino.

Redissi, Hamadi. 2020. "Muhammad Abduh ou les limites du réformisme." In *L'invention des modernités en Islam*. Tunis: Cérès.

Rizk, Charles. 1983. *Entre l'Islam et l'arabisme: Les Arabes jusqu'en 1945*. Paris: Éditions Albin Michel.

Sbailò, Ciro. 2011. "L'Egitto, tra mutamento di regime e transizione costituzionale." *Diritto Pubblico Comparato ed Europeo* II: 341–72.

Sbailò, Ciro. 2012. *Principi sciaraitici e organizzazione dello spazio pubblico nel mondo islamico: Il caso egiziano*. Padua: CEDAM.

Scholch, Alexander. 1981. *Egypt for the Egyptians! The Socio-Political Crisis in Egypt, 1878–1882*. London: Ithaca Press.

Tadros, Mariz. 2012. *The Muslim Brotherhood in Contemporary Egypt: Democracy Redefined or Confined?* London and New York: Routledge.

Turābī, Ḥasan. 1987. *Qaḍāyā al-ḥurriyyā wa-l-waḥda wal-shūrā wal-dī mūqrāṭ iyya*. N.p.: al-Dar al-Sa'udiyya lil-Nashr.

Walzer, Michael. 1995. *Spheres of Justice: A Defense of Pluralism and Equality*. Oxford: Blackwell.

9 Tunisia and Egypt: Two constitutional models

9.1 Constitutionalism and revolutions

The Arab Springs have resulted in new constitutions under a constituent process that has tried to effect deep change in the Arab countries' constitutional traditions. As previously discussed, the initial thrust of Arab constitutions was essentially to legitimize the elites in power (Le Roy 2012, 110), so if we look at the countries of the Maghreb before these uprisings, it is hard to make the case that elements of modern constitutionalism can be detected in them (ibid., 111).

With the establishment of constitutional courts in three Maghreb countries—Algeria, Tunisia, and Morocco—a milestone was reached in the march towards constitutionalism, but this development did not in any significant way alter the existing balance of powers, which is tilted in favour of the executive. Furthermore, the relation between constitutionalism and Islamic law still looks unresolved, even in societies as secularist as those of Tunisia and Algeria. It therefore makes sense to ask, what will be the position of the *sharīʿa* in the hierarchy of sources of law?

Thierry Le Roy (2012, 115) finds that "three conclusions can be drawn about the divergence between secular law and religious-inspired law in the countries of the Maghreb: their constitutions make ample reference to Islam; but compliance of the legislation with the Sharīʿah is not explicitly required; at the same time, laws can be inspired by the Sharīʿah without meeting any constitutional obstacles."

It should also be observed that if in the constitutions of the Maghreb countries until the time of the Arab Springs there was no express provision requiring the law to be compliant with the *sharīʿa*, this requirement did exist in the constitutions of other Muslim countries, such as Egypt, Pakistan, Afghanistan, Iran, and the Persian Gulf states. This difference can be explained by pointing to the fact that the Maghreb countries have had greater exposure than other Arab-Muslim countries to the influence of the West, and that is particularly true of French influence (see Association Henri Capitant 1994; cf. CEDROMA 2005). This influence has mainly exerted itself on constitutional and public law, and less on civil law. It is this influence that can explain, for example, why religious pluralism is guaranteed in the Maghreb countries, and why the Moroccan constitution protects freedom of religion and the Algerian constitution freedom of conscience.

Still, even though "the Maghreb constitutions are built, mainly, on the model of the French constitutions, particularly the Constitution of 1958" (Le Roy 2012, 117), they confer emergency powers on the head of state in ways that the French model does not envision. And indeed, as concerns the Maghreb, "it can be said that the drawing up of constitutions has more to do with the strengthening of the state than with the definition and protection of citizens' individual rights" (ibid., 118).

Have the Arab Springs managed to turn the tide in favour of a stronger protection of rights? And will it be possible to complete the march towards constitutionalism by introducing a true separation of powers and their functions and, consequently, a system of genuine constitutional review?

9.2 The Tunisian case: A model for a path towards democracy

Will the Arab Springs be able to debunk the narrative that democracy exists only in the West? To answer this question, which can be extended to all societies across the Arab world, we can look at the constituent process in Tunisia, the place where the spark was lit that kindled the flame of the Arab Springs.

The event that sparked those uprisings happened on 17 December 2010, when a young street vendor named Muḥammad al-Bū'azīzī set himself on fire in front of a government building in the town of Sīdi Bu Zīd, Tunisia, in response to an incident in which his wares were confiscated. The youth in the streets demanded that the 1959 constitution be suspended and a constituent assembly be formed. In response, the government suspended the constitution and dissolved the chambers of parliament. Under Article 57 of the 1959 constitution, the president of the chamber of deputies became president of the republic and decreed a provisional scheme for exercising the powers of the state. This was done under Decree Law No. 14 of 23 March 2011, conferring *law-making powers* on the president. Article 57 of the 1959 constitution contained the following provision:

> Should the office of President of the Republic become vacant because of death, resignation, or absolute disability, the Constitutional Council meets immediately and certifies the definitive vacancy by an absolute majority of its members. It addresses a declaration to that effect to the President of the Chamber of Advisors and to the President of the Chamber of Deputies who shall immediately be vested with the functions of interim president of the Republic for a period ranging from 45 to 60 days. If the definitive vacancy coincides with the dissolution of the Chamber of Deputies, the President of the Chamber of Advisors is vested with the functions of interim president of the Republic for the same period.

The only organ empowered to declare a "definitive vacancy" was the Conseil Constitutionnel, which needs to be credited with having mustered the political will to make this decision, playing a "role as an unexpected liberator and saviour" (Ben Mrad 2012, 12; my translation). The *conseil* found that when a president of the republic is facing a crisis beyond his control (a state of exception), and yet is unwilling to hand over power or to step down, he can be deemed unfit for office. What appears to carry the weight of the argument, for the *conseil*, is the crisis it points to in combination with the fact that President Ben Ali fled the country: even if he did flee feeling compelled to do so under mounting pressure from the civil unrest in the streets, these protests had a legitimate basis in a "right of resistance to oppression," which Ben Mrad considers a natural and inalienable human right (ibid., 13).

On 15 March 2011, a revolutionary body was formed called the Haute Instance pour la Réalisation des Objectifs de la Révolution, de la Réforme Politique et de la Transition Démocratique, merging the Conseil de Défense de la Révolution with the Commission Supérieure de la Réforme Politique. Appointed to the helm of the Haute Instance was the jurist and intellectual Yadh Ben Achour. Making up the body were 155 members representing twelve political parties and nine trade unions, as well as nongovernmental organizations, the Tunisian Human Rights League, civil society organizations, and trade associations. These representatives had not been elected but had been selected by the government by negotiation. On June 27 the Islamist movement al-Nahḍa (Renaissance Party) announced it would withdraw from the Haute Instance, declaring that the body had fashioned itself into a parliament while lacking any electoral mandate.

The Haute Instance further proceeded to form the Instance Supérieure Indépendante pour les Élections (ISIE), which was entrusted with overseeing the electoral process. On 11 April 2011, the Haute Instance began work on rules for electing a constituent assembly, a process that lasted until October 3, ten days before the elections. These rules contained a principle of equality between men and women and a principle of proportionality designed to enable a full spectrum of political groups to participate in the democratic process. The electoral decree law of 2011 barred anyone from running for office who had served as minister under the previous Ben Ali regime,[1] and the same prohibition also extended to anyone who had held a position of authority within the Rassemblement Constitutionnel Démocratique (RCD).

The elections held on October 23 gave a relative majority to the al-Nahḍa party.

On November 22, the National Constituent Assembly met to draft a new constitution. The assembly's first act, on December 16, was to adopt a

1 Décret-loi 2011-35 du 10 mai relatif à l'élection d'une assemblée nationale constituante, Chapitre II (Candidature), Section 1 (Conditions d'éligibilité), Art. 15, in *Journal Officiel de la République Tunisienne* (JORT) no. 33 of 10 May 2011, 651–61.

provisional constitution, or *petite constitution*,[2] issued by the president of the republic, Mohamed Moncef Marzouki. Yet Article 1 of the 2011 constitution stated that "the public powers of the Tunisian Republic are provisionally established pursuant to the provisions of the present law,"[3] and this meant that in assuming the task of drafting a constitution, the constituent assembly also conferred other powers on itself, which it proceeded to list in Article 2: the power to (1) legislate (*exercice du pouvoir législatif*); (2) elect the president of the constituent assembly itself (*élection du président de l'Assemblée nationale constituante*); (3) elect the president of the republic (*élection du Président de la République*); and (4) control government action (*contrôle de l'action du gouvernement*).

Article 4 defined the manner in which the constituent assembly was to exercise legislative power, providing that the government or ten members of the assembly had the power to introduce bills and that the assembly had the power to enact organic laws by an absolute majority of its members' votes.[4]

What we can see here, then, is *a blurring of the line between the constituent function and the legislative function—a confusing overlap that no doubt significantly hindered the process of drafting a new constitution for the Tunisian republic.* In addition, the assembly expended much effort drawing up a set of bylaws laying out its own internal procedures.

In fact the debate that unfolded during the preparatory work took on a particularly bitter tone, as when al-Nahḍa pushed for the *sharīʿa* to be used as a source of law. This happened in March 2012, when a draft document attributed to al-Nahḍa began to circulate containing an Article 10 provision under which the *sharīʿa* was to count as an essential source of legislation. In addition, this draft document provided for the establishment of an Haut Conseil Chara'ique (*al-majlis al-aʿ lā li-l-iftāʾ*) entrusted with making sure that any proposed legislation was compliant with the *sharīʿa*.

It was in this context that on 20 March 2012 a protest with a hefty turnout of 25,000 people took place against these initiatives, viewed as militant expressions of religious zeal. The upshot of this outpouring of public opinion was that on March 25 Rāshid al-Ghannūshī, having met with the leadership of al-Nahḍa, announced that the *sharīʿa* plan would be scrapped, and in addition declared himself open to the possibility of rewriting Article 1 of the Tunisian

2 Loi constituante 2011-6 du 16 décembre 2011, relative à l'organisation des pouvoirs publics. Arabic original published in *Journal Officiel de la République Tunisienne* (JORT) no. 97 of 20 and 23 December 2011, 3111–15.

3 Translated into French as follows: "Les pouvoirs publics de la République tunisienne sont organisés à titre provisoire conformément à la présente loi."

4 Translated into French as follows: "Le Gouvernement ou dix membres au moins de l'Assemblée nationale constituante, ont le droit de proposer des projets de lois. L'Assemblée nationale constituante adopte les lois organiques à la majorité absolue de ses membres" (Art. 4, 2nd clause).

constitution of 1959,[5] given the statement of creed it contained: "Tunisia is a free, independent and sovereign state. Its religion is Islam, its language is Arabic and its type of government is the Republic."

On 14 December 2012 an *Ébauche de Projet de la Constitution* was published that took out Chapters 3 and 4 of the 2011 constitution (on legislative and executive power, respectively). This draft came under criticism from the Observatoire pour les Droits de l'Homme on account of the contradictions it contained when it came to freedom of expression, women's rights, the nondiscrimination principle, and freedom of thought and conscience. Even more pointed was the criticism the *observatoire* levelled at Article 4: "The state protects religion; it guarantees freedom of conscience and the practice of religion; it protects the sacred; and it guarantees the neutrality of places of worship in relation to partisan propaganda."[6] For in providing these guarantees, the draft constitution did not specify what was meant by *sacred*, nor did it say who the sacred might come under threat from. Moreover, the freedom of conscience it guaranteed did not include the freedom to change one's religion.

Also targeted as problematic was Article 37, providing that "the state guarantees the elimination of all forms of violence against women."[7] For it premised this guarantee by stating that men and women are assigned different roles: "The state guarantees equality of opportunity for men and women *so as to enable them to carry out their different responsibilities*,"[8] thereby repurposing equality of opportunity as a tool not of gender *equality* but of gender *discrimination*.

Finally, Human Rights Watch took exception to Article 15, stating that "international treaties are binding only so long as they are not contrary to the provisions contained in the present Constitution."[9] This clause was seen as an escape hatch, enabling judges and lawmakers to ignore international treaties on the pretext that they contradict the Tunisian constitution.

But, as we will see, the constitution enacted in 2014 set the future of Tunisian democracy on a solid footing.

5 See Ben Achour 2012, 7. On the resistance to introducing the *sharīʿa* as a source of legislation, see Longo 2013, 35. Strong pressures came from Salafi groups demanding that Article 1 of the constitution include the *sharīʿa* as a source of legislation. Al-Nahḍa instead took a middle-ground position, mediating between the secular front and the Salafi movements. See Houssi 2013, 64.

6 The French text: "L'État protège la religion; il est garant de la liberté de conscience et de l'exercice des cultes et le protecteur du sacré et le garant de la neutralité des lieux de cultes par rapport à la propagande partisane."

7 The French text: "L'État garantit l'élimination de toutes les formes de violence à l'égard de la femme."

8 The French text: "L'État garantit l'égalité des chances entre la femme et l'homme pour assumer les différentes responsabilités."

9 The French text: "Le respect des traités internationaux est obligatoire, tant qu'ils ne sont pas contraires aux dispositions de la présente Constitution."

9.3 Egypt: A postcolonial revolution

The Egyptian revolution began on 25 January 2011. The people of Egypt were seeking not succession from one regime to another but regime change proper. President Mubārak was overthrown through a peaceful popular uprising representing wide swaths of society, in both economic and religious terms.

Until the revolution, solid relations between Egypt and the United States had helped to guarantee regional peace in the area, but this stability soon gave way to a sense of deep uncertainty. The international situation certainly had an effect on the way the revolution would play itself out. At the urging of the American president Barack Obama, the United States Senate passed Resolution 44, calling on "President Mubārak to begin an orderly and peaceful transition to a democratic political system."[10]

The January Revolution was not without precedent. In October of 1798 the people of Egypt rebelled against the French occupation led by Napoleon. In 1882 came the British occupation of Egypt. In 1919 a popular uprising took place uniting Muslims and Christians in an effort to give birth to an independence movement that achieved its objective in 1922 and led to a constitution in 1923.[11]

Mohamed A. 'Arafa (2011, 6) contends that the Egyptian revolution of 2011 bears a historical connection to the 1919 revolution for independence from British colonial rule. The 1923 constitution marked the beginning of a new era that "established democratic institutions, which included a parliament with both a lower and upper house [Art. 24], a political system based on parliamentary democracy, and a government reflecting the parliamentary political forces"

10 A Resolution Supporting Democracy, Universal Rights, and the Peaceful Transition to a Representative Government in Egypt, S. Res. 44 112th Cong. (2011–2012).

11 See Jankowski 2000. On the 1923 constitution see Cecere 2012. The 1923 constitution was an octroyed (granted) constitution marked by the primacy of monarchical power, but it also contained elements proper to liberal constitutionalism. The task of drawing up a constitution was assigned to a panel of experts appointed by Prime Minister Tharwat Pāshā. They were charged with bringing out a constitutional text in keeping with "the principles of modern public law" (Cecere 2012, LXVI; my translation), but what came out instead was a scheme that undermined the basic principle of the separation of powers by placing executive, legislative, and judicial powers in the hands of the sovereign. Running all through the constitutional text, then, was a tension between an aspiration to provide the Egyptian nation with a representative system of government and the autocratic pull of the monarchy (ibid., LXXX). Furthermore, while the document protected basic rights—equality, freedom of conscience, freedom of religion—this protection was undercut by a provision that recognized Islam as the official "state religion" (Art. 149), making the Egyptian constitutional monarchy a confessional state. This framing of the relation between religion and the state would also be reiterated in the subsequent constitutions of 1956 and 1971, including in the latter's amended version of 1980. And the same characteristic carries through to the country's present constitutional season—from the 2012 constitution that came in the wake of the 2011 revolution to the current constitution of 2014—in which the confessional nature of the state is retained under a provision recognizing the *sharīʿa* as the main source of legislation.

(ibid., 8). But then "abuses by the monarchy and the corrupt, ruling elite led to the *Free Officers' Revolution* or *Revolution 23 July* of 1952" (ibid.; italics in the original). A military dictatorship followed whose first leader was Lieutenant Colonel Jamāl ʿAbd al-Nāṣir, followed by Colonel Anwar al-Sadāt and then Ḥusnī Mubārak.

Although "the people strongly supported the revolution" (ibid.), the military regime it ushered in "protected a corrupt class of profiteers who became an oligarchy. This corruption attained extraordinary levels within the last twenty years. The result is that just 200 families, all enabled and protected by the government, hold approximately 90% of [...] Egypt's wealth" (ibid.). It is here that ʿArafa makes the connection with Egypt's early anticolonial struggles:

> In 1907, Egypt's first political party, The Nation Party [*Ḥizb al- Umma*], was founded [...]. *For half a century after this first political party was established, Egyptians struggled for their independence and democracy, leading to the 1952 coup d'état by the Army. The Revolution 25 January could be seen as an extension of this original struggle.* (Ibid., 8; italics added)

It has similarly been argued that the Egyptians are carrying on a postcolonial revolution against a military regime which, though initially formed with the intent of liberating the people from the abuses of the monarchy, subsequently turned into an equally brutal exploitative regime (see Vatikiotis 1991; Jankowski 2000). The 2011 revolution can accordingly be framed as part of a long, intermittent struggle to achieve a democratic form of government that has yet to be fully realized.

This first step that will have to be taken in advancing towards this goal is to dismantle the police apparatus, which since the al-Sadāt regime has been used to maintain the power of a corrupt oligarchy whose abusive practices have been widely reported (see Human Rights Watch 2011). It will further be necessary to repeal the country's state-of-emergency law,[12] under which it has been possible to deprive citizens of due process rights, and it will also be necessary to repeal the law which restricts the ability to form political parties.

In the second place, and more broadly, before any process of development for Egypt can get underway, it will be necessary to get rid of corruption. As ʿArafa notes, referring to Egypt in 2011, about 40 million people, out of a population of 84 million, were estimated to be living at or below the poverty line (ʿArafa 2011, 12, n. 59), and in the meantime the regime was not only appropriating a greater share of the country's wealth but was also exporting these resources.

Even more importantly, however, it will be necessary to introduce a new development model premised on the need to achieve a fair and dynamic form of

12 The state-of-emergency law (*qānūn al-ṭawāriʾ*) was first introduced in 1958 (Law No. 162 of 1958), and though it was repealed in 1967, it was reinstated in the wake of al-Sadāt's assassination in 1981. This law broadens police powers, suspends constitutional rights, and legalizes censorship (cf. ʿArafa 2011, 21).

development that does not require the breakup of family and community capitalism. For more than three decades Egypt has followed the neoliberal Washington consensus model (CID 2003, quoted in ʿArafa 2011, 27, n. 115), providing conditional loans requiring the government to cut entitlement programmes designed to aid the most vulnerable groups in society, as well as to lower import tariffs and divest itself of ownership interests in state-owned enterprises. This model was supported by the International Monetary Fund (IMF), which was mainly concerned with reaching macroeconomic stability targets regardless of their impact on poverty and the community capitalism making up the fabric of the Egyptian economy. The upshot of this economic policy was a dramatic spike in the unemployment rate.

The new development model will have to be mainly focussed on achieving an equitable distribution of national wealth, while introducing a minimum wage and investing in human resources to improve health care and education. Above all, it will be necessary to make the national budget transparent by disclosing all resources that have been appropriated by the regime, while reporting the revenues that flow from fees levied on the use of the Suez Canal, as well as from natural gas and foreign aid.

9.4 The Egyptian constitutional model

Unlike the transition of power in Tunisia, the one in Egypt needs to be understood by looking at the role played by the army.[13] The armed forces in Egypt have always commanded respect from the population as guarantors of order and stability. After Ḥusnī Mubārak stepped down, the Supreme Council of the Armed Forces (SCAF) issued a statement declaring that it would be in charge of national security. The council subsequently issued a decree (*bayan* no. 5) dissolving both chambers of Parliament (the People's Assembly and the Shoura Council) and suspending the 1971 constitution. Finally, on 30 March 2011, the SCAF issued the Provisional Constitution of the Arab Republic of Egypt (also known as the Constitutional Declaration of 2011),[14] which was

13 On the role played by the army in the processes of political transition, and more generally on the forms of constitutional transition and on democratization processes, see the extensive study undertaken in Mezzetti 2014. On the relation between the republican form of government and the Arab Spring revolutions in Tunisia and Egypt, as well as on the relation between monarchy and reform in Morocco and Jordan, see the interesting analysis offered in Alianak 2014.

14 On the constitutional declaration of March 2011, and on the role the armed forces played in the constituent phase, see the accurate reconstruction in Sbailò 2012, 304ff. The first part of the book provides an extensive analysis of Islamic legal thought, with an emphasis on public law. The second part turns to the Egyptian legal system, offering an in-depth reconstruction of it within the debate on public law in contemporary Islam. The third part traces the development of the Egyptian constitutional system from the Mubārak presidency to the Arab Springs of 2011 and 2012.

to replace the 1971 constitution and remain in effect until a new constitution would be enacted.

The provisional constitution contained sixty-three articles laying out the powers of the state as a presidential system with two chambers—the previously mentioned People's Assembly and Shoura Council (Art. 39)—and an independent judiciary. Egypt was described as "a state with a democratic system" and as "part of the Arab nation working toward achieving its comprehensive unity" (Art. 1). Article 2 made the *sharīʿa* the main source of legislation: "Islam is the Religion of the State. Arabic is its official language. The principles of Islamic Law [*sharīʿa*] are the chief sources of legislation."

Article 60 provided that the People's Assembly and the Shoura Council would elect a constituent assembly tasked with drawing up a constitution that would then be put to a referendum for approval. But on 14 June 2012, only two days before the election for president of the republic was to be held, the Constitutional Court issued two rulings that would have a deeply destabilizing effect.

Indeed, the first of these two rulings invalidated the electoral law on which basis the March 2012 parliament had been elected. This law barred independent candidates from running on party tickets, while allowing candidates on these tickets to also run as independents—a discriminatory distinction on account of which the court found the law to be unconstitutional. At issue in the second ruling was a provision that barred exponents of the old regime from running for president. Here, too, the court found this provision to be unconstitutional, thereby clearing the way for the candidacy of Aḥmad Shafīq, who had served as prime minister under Ḥusnī Mubārak.

The first ruling opened a huge institutional void, especially because it undermined the legitimacy of a constituent assembly appointed by a parliament that had now been declared illegal. On top of that, the legitimacy of the court's rulings was itself challenged on the ground that these rulings were based on the constitutional declaration the SCAF had issued unilaterally on 30 March 2011. In this volatile constitutional imbroglio, the military junta issued a supplement to the constitutional declaration, conferring legislative power on the Supreme Council until a new parliament would be elected (Art. 56/B) and making the same council solely competent to make decisions involving the armed forces (Art. 53). This placed the military junta above the president and the other branches of government (UNIMED 2012), thus setting the stage for an inevitable tug of war between the new president and the Supreme Council.

And in fact on 8 July 2012 President-Elect Muḥammad Mursī issued a decree annulling the ruling through which the Constitutional Court had dissolved the parliament controlled by the Muslim Brotherhood's Freedom and Justice Party and the Salafi al-Nūr Party. And thus was fired the opening salvo that turned the simmering hostility into an open clash. On August 12 President Mursī deposed the two highest-ranking members of the Supreme Council (Ḥusayn al-ṭanṭāwī, minister of defence, and Samī ʿAnnān, chairman of the Joint Chiefs of Staff) and appointed General ʿAbd al-Fattāḥ al-Sīsī as new minister of defence (Gresh 2012). At the same time the *Official Gazette* published a decree annulling a supplementary constitutional declaration through which the Supreme Council granted itself powers greater than those of the president.

In this way the clash between the Muslim Brotherhood and the military junta moved into a new phase that seemed to favour the former. Thus on 29 November 2012 President Mursī called the constituent assembly back into session so as to put the new constitution up for a vote. This was an assembly from which all secular members had resigned so as to deprive it of the quorum needed for the vote to pass; the president therefore packed it with new members so as to fill that gap and thus enable the vote to proceed. On December 15 and 22 the constitutional text approved by the assembly was put to a referendum: it passed with 60 percent of the popular vote, but with a meagre 30 percent of the population taking part in it, and on December 26 President Mursī signed the constitution.

Several aspects of the 2012 constitution seemed especially concerning. Article 2 reiterated the idea that "the principles of Islamic law [*sharīʿa*] form the main source of legislation." Qurʾānic law was accorded absolute primacy as the highest source of law, a feature of the new constitution that was carried over from the one it replaced. This secured the confessional nature of the state.

In the same vein, Article 219 further entrenched the superiority of the *sharīʿa* by specifying the full range of sources on which basis it was to be interpreted: "The principles of Islamic law [*sharīʿa*] include general evidence, the foundational principles of Islamic jurisprudence [*uṣūl al-fiqh*], the reliable sources from among the Sunni schools of thought [*madhāhib*]."

Article 81 stated that "the rights and freedoms that attach to the citizen must not be impaired. No law regulating the practice of these rights and freedoms may narrow their intent and essence." But then it went on to say that these "rights and freedoms are to be practiced in such a way that they do not conflict with the provisions of Part One of this Constitution, which covers the elements of state and society." Among these Part One provisions was Article 10, stating that "the family is the foundation of society. The family's foundations are religion, morality, and patriotism. Both state and society seek to preserve the inherent character of the Egyptian family, its cohesion, stability, and moral character, and to protect the family as specified by law." Furthermore, Article 11 provided that "the state promotes morality, decency, and public order, as well as a high level of education and religious and patriotic values, scientific truths, the Arab culture, and the historical and civilizational patrimony of the People." In combination, these two articles (10 and 11) qualified the enjoyment of rights by setting clear boundaries around them on the basis of religion and cultural identity.

Freedom of religion, for its part, was protected under Article 43 as an "inviolable" freedom. But here, too, this statement was qualified immediately thereafter: "The state guarantees the right to practice one's religious rites and establish places of worship for the heavenly religions. Details are specified by law." This meant that only monotheistic religions could be practiced, nor was any protection afforded to those who practice atheism or espouse nontheistic creeds. And Article 44 reinforced the content of Article 43 by prohibiting blasphemy directed at any Abrahamic messenger or prophet.

Also troubling was Article 33, stating that "citizens enjoy equality before the law. They have identical rights and public duties. There is no discrimination among them." The problem is that the equality so protected was only formal, so it did nothing to address the legacy of substantive inequality baked into the fabric of society, with the social, economic, cultural, and gender disparities it perpetuates. So, too, this constitutional prohibition against discrimination was vague, for unlike Article 30 of the draft constitution approved by the constituent assembly, it made no mention of the possible sources of discrimination, such as gender, native background, language, creed and belief system, social status, and disability.

Worth mentioning, finally, is the Article 10 clause under which "the state provides special protections for female breadwinners, divorced women, and widows." Indeed, implicit in this guarantee was a recognition that many women found themselves in a position of disadvantage. And so an argument can be made here that this clause acted to reinforce the very status quo it was meant to correct for, precisely by representing women through the lens of their condition as dependent subjects.

The picture that emerges from this brief rundown of the articles contained in the 2012 constitution is that of a confessional state—a state that takes it upon itself to act as a steward of morality on the basis of the *sharīʿa* as the highest source of law. It follows that such a state would not have been able to guarantee equal rights when it came to freedom of religion or the position of men and women in society.

9.5 The new Egyptian constitution: The Janus-faced nature of the Egyptian state

On 14 and 15 January 2014 a referendum was held through which the new Egyptian constitution was approved. The referendum was meant to legitimize the coup d'état that had ousted President Mursī.[15] But in reality, even if the constitution passed with an overwhelming 98.1 percent of the popular

15 The coup d'état, staged by the military on 3 July 2013, was billed as "democratic." Why that is a problematic characterization of it is explained in Sbailò 2013, 21ff. The military claimed extraconstitutional powers for itself by declaring a state of exception while invoking Article 84 of the 1971 constitution, which confers the presidency on the speaker of the People's Assembly if the presidential office should become vacant, and on the president of the Supreme Constitutional Court if the assembly should be dissolved, and it was on the latter basis that the military proceeded, vesting the function of interim president in the president of the Constitutional Court.

The military thus acted with the support of the Constitutional Court, whose legitimacy now looks tenuous precisely on account of its role in supporting the coup. What precipitated the ouster of President Mursī was a clash between two opposing camps among the population, independently of any internal tussle on institutional procedures. It is against the backdrop of this *delegitimized institutional framework* that the new Egyptian constitution was approved.

vote, the turnout was much lower: as the *Al Ahrām* newspaper reports,[16] only 38.6 percent of eligible voters cast their ballot.[17]

The constitutional text lays the foundation for two possible forms of government: one based on the rule of law, the other a presidential model that turns on the complex relation which holds between the executive power and the army. The preamble ambivalently contains elements consistent with both of these outcomes, stating that "our patriotic army delivered victory to the sweeping popular will in the 'Jan 25–June 30' Revolution that called for bread, freedom and human dignity within a framework of social justice, and brought back the homeland's free will" (Arab Republic of Egypt 2013, 9). We can see from this politically charged statement that the army claims credit for leading the people to victory. The statement is not just misleading, for it was certainly not the action of the army alone that led to the downfall Ḥusnī Mubārak: it also, and more importantly, underscores how central a role the army came to play once it toppled President Mursī.

The preamble depicts the 2011 revolution in Taḥrīr Square as the historical denouement of a process whose seeds were sown in two previous revolutions. The first was the 1919 revolution, which liberated Egypt from British colonial rule and championed the principles of citizenship and equality. The second was the revolution of 23 July 1952, which was led by Jamāl ʿAbd al-Nāṣir with wide popular support and fulfilled the dream that for generations had been harboured for liberation and independence. "As a result" of this second revolution, the preamble states, "Egypt affirmed its Arab allegiance, opened up to its African continent and Muslim world, supported liberation movements across continents, and took firm steps on the path of development and social justice" (ibid., 10).

While the 25 January Revolution "represents an extension of the revolutionary march of Egyptian patriotism" (ibid.), it

> is a unique revolution, because of the heavy popular participation involved—which was estimated to be in the tens of millions—and the significant role of youth who aspire to a brighter future, the masses who transcended class and ideology to reach out to more expansive patriotic and human horizons, the manner in which the people's army protected the popular will and the blessings granted to it by Al-Azhar and the patriotic church. It is also unique because of its peacefulness and ambition to achieve freedom and social justice together. (Ibid.)

16 "Table: Official Results of Egypt's 2014 Constitutional Referendum," *Ahram Online*, 19 January 2014, http://english.ahram.org.eg/News/91957.aspx

17 In the immediate aftermath of the military takeover, there was a moment of instability that seemed to signal the coming of a military dictatorship, in a climate in which the overthrow of the government led by the Muslim Brotherhood was accompanied by "a xenophobic nationalism that views the Brotherhood as 'terrorists' and a pawn of external enemies" (Alaoui 2014).

The constitutional framework that emerges from these initial observations outlines a democratic form of government with a plurality of political forces competing in an alternating system of power. As Rizk and El Sharnoubi (2013) describe it commenting on the preamble of the amended 2012 constitution: "'We are writing a constitution that completes building a modern democratic state with a civilian government,' which means neither religious nor military." In the same vein, the preamble of the 2013 constitution describes the document as being "in line with the [1948] Universal Declaration of Human Rights, which we took part in the drafting of and approved" (ibid., 11).[18]

However, while Article 4 proclaims that "sovereignty belongs to the people alone, which exercises it and protects it," the preamble also qualifies this tenet by stating that "the principles of Islamic Sharia are the principal source of legislation" (ibid.). In short, *the 2013 constitution sets up a civilian form of government within a confessional state.* Which of these two models, then, is being proposed?

Chapter One of the 2013 constitution sets forth the principles on which the state is based: "The Arab Republic of Egypt is a sovereign state, united and indivisible, [...] and its system is a democratic republic based on citizenship and the rule of law" (Art. 1). This form of government is given further specification in Article 94: "The rule of law is the basis of governance in the state. The state is subject to the law, while the independence, immunity and impartiality of the judiciary are essential guarantees for the protection of rights and freedoms."

The constitutional structure of the rule of law is further specified as well in Article 5: "The political system is based on political and partisan multiplicity, the peaceful transfer of power, *the separation and balance of powers*, authority going with responsibility, and respect for human rights and freedoms, as set out in the Constitution" (italics added). An argument can be made that precisely in the separation of powers lies the true problem with constitutions in the Arab world, for the principle is only *formally* enshrined, resulting not in a separation but in a *web* of powers, in a system where rights cannot truly be protected. *The separation of powers should therefore serve as the main benchmark against which to assess Egypt's constitutional makeup in the post–Arab Spring era.*

Completing the formal statement of the separation of powers in Egypt's constitution is the principle of judicial review, making the Supreme Constitutional Court an "independent judicial body" (Art. 191) "exclusively competent to decide on the constitutionality of laws and regulations" (Art. 192). But then Article 193 gives the Constitutional Court an exclusive power to select its own

18 I should note in passing that the 2013 constitution came as part of the power-transition plan the interim military government put in place in the wake of the July 2013 coup that ousted Muḥammad Mursī. It passed by referendum in January 2014.

members,[19] making it the first constitutional court in the world to have ever been endowed with such authority.

Furthermore, the 2014 constitution provides no clear criteria for appointing judges, thereby insulating the judiciary and favouring the formation of a nepotistic system: "The danger of the immunisation and impenetrability of the judiciary is its transformation into a sect with group interests that do not necessarily coincide with those of the general public" (Chazli 2014, 10).[20] In this sense, it cannot be argued that the conception of judicial power outlined in the Egyptian constitution of 2014 has laid the foundation for the construction of a democratic state, in that this power, so conceived, cannot claim any legitimacy based on its impartiality and transparency.

In a constitutionalist model based on an independent judiciary, with powers of judicial review in a system that maintains a separation among the powers and functions of government, that independent judiciary needs to also be *impartial.* This is a *necessary condition* absent which it would not be possible to guarantee the rights enshrined in Chapter 3 of the 2014 constitution (Arts. 51–93).

And these rights themselves bear comment. We begin with Article 51, on dignity, which describes this as "a right for every person that may not be infringed upon. The state shall respect, guarantee and protect it." What stands out here is the very idea that the state can protect dignity. For in the current Western debate, dignity is primarily understood not as a right per se but as a *foundation* of rights: dignity *precedes* the state's recognition of rights and cannot *itself* be a right granted by the state.

Also at odds with the current Western conception is the Egyptian constitution's framing of personal freedom, which in Article 54 is introduced as "a natural right which is safeguarded and cannot be infringed upon." In the West, the idea of personal freedom as a natural right belongs to the natural law theory of the seventeenth and eighteenth centuries: what took its place was the idea of personal freedom as a *positive* right (legal positivism) and now as a *constitutional* right (resting on a constitutional foundation).

Article 4, on sovereignty, ties this concept to equality by stating that "sovereignty belongs to the people alone," who "safeguard their national unity, which is based on the principle of equality, justice and equal opportunity between citizens, as provided in this Constitution." However, equality is further addressed in Article 11 ("The Place of Women, Motherhood, and Childhood"), providing

19 Article 193: "The Court is made up of a president and a sufficient number of deputies to the president. / The Commissioners Authority of the Supreme Constitutional Court is composed of a president and a sufficient number of presidents in the authority, advisors and assistant advisors. / The General Assembly chooses the Court's President from among the most senior three vice-presidents of the court. It also chooses the vice-presidents and the members of its Commissioners Authority, who are appointed by a decree from the President of the Republic. The foregoing takes place in the manner defined by the law."

20 Compare Brown 2012, arguing that this impenetrability of the powers of the state may lead to a "Balkanization of the Egyptian state."

that "the state commits to achieving equality between women and men in all civil, political, economic, social, and cultural rights." But in enshrining this principle the same article also provides that "the state commits to the protection of women against all forms of violence, and ensures women empowerment to reconcile the duties of a woman toward her family and her work requirements," thus appealing to the traditional view of women as having a defined role in the family, with a corresponding set of duties—a qualification that undercuts the principle of gender equality set forth in the same article.

Similarly illiberal are the limits placed on the freedom to form political parties, the subject of Article 74, which states that "no political activity may be exercised or political parties formed on the basis of religion." Although, on the face of it, this provision seems to align nicely with the principle of the separation of church and state, the reality is that it was introduced specifically to exclude the Muslim Brotherhood from political life, along with the movement's political-party embodiment, the Freedom and Justice Party. This provision appears all the more questionable if we consider that what the 2014 constitution clearly fashions is a *confessional* state. Indeed, echoing the language contained in the preamble—"we are drafting a Constitution that affirms that the principles of Islamic Sharia are the principal source of legislation"—Article 2 provides that "Islam is the religion of the state and Arabic is its official language. The principles of Islamic Sharia are the principal source of legislation."

To be sure, Article 3 does make room for the other monotheistic religions as well: "The principles of the laws of Egyptian Christians and Jews are the main source of laws regulating their personal status, religious affairs, and selection of spiritual leaders." But two points are worth making in this respect. The first is that, while Article 3 does make allowance for the other monotheistic religions, it does not recognize any other religious confession. The second point is that, even in making allowance for the other monotheistic religions, the article limits their scope as sources of law by restricting their application to matters pertaining to the personal status of Christians and Jews: it follows by analogy that Muslims fall subject to the Islamic *sharīʿa* when it comes to their personal status.

But seen through the lens of the Western tradition, the recognition of the Islamic *sharīʿa* undermines the purportedly constitutional character of the state. For in that tradition a constitutional state *cannot* be a confessional state. Indeed, on the Western conception, only a secular or neutral state can be trusted to protect rights and the interests of minorities.

The foregoing considerations illustrate just how far removed the Western constitutional experience is from the model of the state outlined in the Egyptian constitution, nor does it look like the gap can easily be closed. But also worth stressing in this respect is the previously discussed question of the central role of the executive power and its relationship with the army. Article 139 states that "The President of the Republic is the head of state and head of the executive branch of government." This means that it is not the president's role to act as guarantor of the constitution, precisely because that role is executive, not constitutional. This is borne out by the fact that the president, in consultation with the prime minister, can appoint the ministers of justice, the interior, and defence (Art. 146).

The president's legitimacy derives from the direct popular vote needed for the president to take office (Art. 143). Under Article 147, the president "may exempt the government from carrying out its tasks, provided that the House of Representatives approves of such with a majority." In its wording, this provision does not make it possible to understand whether it is the majority vote of the House that determines how the president should act or whether, conversely, it is the president's independent decision that needs to be approved by a majority of the House in order for an exemption to pass.

Unlike the previous constitution of December 2012, the 2014 constitution provides that "the House of Representatives may propose to withdraw confidence from the President of the Republic and hold early presidential elections upon a causal motion signed by at least a majority of the members of the House of Representatives and the approval of two-thirds of its members" (Art. 161).

The president also has broad policymaking powers: "The President of the Republic, jointly with the Cabinet, sets the general policy of the state and oversees its implementation as set out by the Constitution" (Art. 150). So, too, the president, acting in "consultation with the Cabinet," has the authority to declare "a state of emergency in the manner regulated by law. Such proclamation must be submitted to the House of Representatives within the following seven days to consider it" (Art. 154).

There is, finally, the matter of defence and the role the president plays in it as well as in relation to the armed forces. The first point to be noted here is that "the President of the Republic is the Supreme Commander of the Armed Forces" (Art. 152). The second point concerns the National Defense Council, whose functions are governed by Article 203:

> A National Defense Council is established, presided over by the President of the Republic and including in its membership the Prime Minister, the Speaker of the House of Representatives, the Minister of Defense, the Minister of Foreign Affairs, the Minister of Finance, the Minister of Interior, the Chief of the General Intelligence Service, the Chief of Staff of the armed forces, the Commanders of the Navy, the Air Forces and Air Defense, the Chief of Operations for the armed forces and the Head of Military Intelligence.
>
> The Council is responsible for looking into matters pertaining to the methods of ensuring the safety and security of the country, for discussing the armed forces' budget [...]. Its opinion must be sought in relation to draft laws on the armed forces.

What clearly emerges here is the prominent role allotted to the National Defense Council, which is mainly controlled by the military complex and has a say in the process of setting the military budget and forming the laws governing the armed forces (Abd Rabou 2014, 5).

Also worth underscoring is the augmented judicial power accorded to the military courts, which under Article 204 are competent to try civilians charged with carrying out direct attacks against military installations, but these courts' civilian jurisdiction also extends to "whatever falls under their authority." This is an extraordinarily vague description that, as Abd Rabou points out, could also be used against political enemies (ibid.).

The 2014 constitution also assigns a fundamental role to the armed forces. As is stated in Article 200, "the armed forces belong to the people. Their duty is to protect the country, and preserve its security and territories. The state is exclusively mandated to establish armed forces. [...] The armed forces have a Supreme Council as regulated by law."

While Article 201 makes the defence minister "the Commander in Chief of the Armed Forces, appointed from among its officers," Article 234 gives appointment powers to the SCAF (ibid., 4): "The Minister of Defense is appointed upon the approval of the Supreme Council of the Armed Forces. The provisions of this article shall remain in force for two full presidential terms starting from the date on which this Constitution comes into effect." So, even if the framework outlined by the 2014 constitution is that of a presidential—and hence civilian—state, the Article 234 provision "translates as complete independence for the military in the appointment of its leader without any interference or authority from the government or president" (ibid.).

The 2014 constitution can therefore be described as Janus-faced. For on the one hand it supported a democratic, civilian form of government—and though it did so recognizing the sharīʿa *as the "principal source of legislation," it limited the scope of the* sharīʿa *to matters relating to personal status—but on the other hand the same document also invited a presidential form of government, with the complex and problematic dialectic this entailed vis-à-vis an independent military power.* The path this important Arab country would chart was going to depend in large part on how this open-ended constitution would be implemented. As we will see in Section 10.9, however, Egypt would soon turn into a presidential police state.

9.6 Tunisia: A democratic future

A different matter, at the time of the Arab Springs, was the political and constitutional situation in Tunisia, where these uprisings did lead to the democratic form of government that was hoped for.

A few days before the 2014 constitution was enacted, a preview of its main contents was offered by the previously quoted Hamadi Redissi, a brilliant intellectual who teaches at the Faculté de Droit et de Science Politique at the Tunis El Manar University. To begin with, he underscored that the Tunisians had headed off the risk of an Islamic state (Redissi 2014a). But in a subsequent article he observed that the constituent assembly reprised the language of the 1959 constitution, stating that "Tunisia is a free, independent, sovereign state; its religion is Islam, its language Arabic, and its system is republican"

(Art. 1), and that in doing so the assembly did not clarify what the relation is between Islam and the state.[21]

In the second place, Article 2 states that "Tunisia is a civil state based on citizenship, the will of the people, and the supremacy of law." Expressed in this formal statement is the principle that the Tunisian state is not a confessional state and that Islam cannot be deemed a source of law. But this, too, is a statement contained in which is a deep ambiguity. Indeed, as Redissi points out, there is often at work the mistaken assumption that a civil state is not an Islamic state. To see why that is not always the case, we need look no further than al-Nahḍa, whose party platform is based on a civil-state model, and as noted in Chapter 8, the Freedom and Justice Party in Egypt has introduced the idea of an "Islam-inspired civil state" (Redissi 2014b; cf. Avon 2012, 90). As Redissi comments, this "Islam-inspired (Article 1) civil state (Article 2) excludes the theocratic state without being secular; it wears an Islamic garb while styling itself as secular" (Redissi 2014b; my translation). There comes into view here a contradiction whose outcome will be determined by the social and political forces that compete in the making of the material constitution.

Finally, there is the question of the status of women, the subject of Article 21 of the constitution, stating that "all citizens, male and female, have equal rights and duties, and are equal before the law without any discrimination." As Redissi points out, this is only a limited statement of gender equality, for it gives *citizens* equal rights under the law, where it would have been more forceful and complete if it had referred to *men and women* as equal before the law. Even so, the Tunisian constitution of 2014, for all its shortcomings, is judged by Redissi to be a document that can lay the foundation for a "new republic."[22]

The preamble to the 2014 constitution invokes the Tunisian struggle for independence, state-building, and freedom from tyranny and points to the need "to achieve the objectives of the revolution for freedom and dignity, the revolution of December 17, 2010, through January 14, 2011." It also states that the Tunisian people espouse a "commitment to the teachings of Islam and its aims characterized by openness and moderation, and to the human values and the

21 Indeed, the phrase "its religion is Islam" lends itself to *two* interpretations, depending on whether the pronoun *its* is understood to take *Tunisia* as its antecedent or the *state*: Islam could accordingly be understood as the religion of Tunisia or that of the state. In an earlier era, under the Bourguiba presidency, this "constructive ambiguity" of Article 1 made it possible for the country's modernizing elites to secularize the Tunisian state, or, more to the point, it enabled the state to "secularize itself without becoming de-Islamicized." By the same token, however, the same ambiguity can also legitimize Islamists in a push to Islamicize the state (Redissi 2014b; my translation).

22 This constitution was adopted through a collective procedure with participation from oversight bodies like the NGO Al Bawsala (which followed the drafting process day by day), as well as feminist groups and professional and trade associations. The constitution can therefore lay claim to legitimacy on the basis of broad stakeholder support (see Redissi 2014b).

highest principles of universal human rights."[23] Yet *the constitutional text does not support the idea of a confessional state*, for it makes no reference to the *sharīʿa* as a source of legislation and instead expresses a commitment "to building a republican, democratic and participatory system, in the framework of a civil state founded on the sovereignty of the people, exercised through the peaceful alternation of power through free elections."[24]

The preamble also makes it clear that this constitution is based on the rule of law, with its companion "principle of the separation and balance of powers." Under this form of government, "the state guarantees the supremacy of the law and the respect for freedoms and human rights, the independence of the judiciary, the equality of rights and duties between all citizens, male and female [...]." Also emphatically stated in the preamble is the idea of Tunisia's "cultural and civilizational affiliation to the Arab and Muslim nation," and the need to build on a "national unity that is based on citizenship, fraternity, solidarity, and social justice, committed to strengthening Maghreb unity as a step towards achieving Arab unity, towards complementarity with the Muslim and African peoples, and towards cooperation with all the peoples of the world."

What is clearly distinctive about this preamble is that, *even as it invokes the substantive ideals of Islam and allegiance to the Arab and Muslim nation, it unequivocally outlines a democratic form of government based on the rule of law.* This can be appreciated by looking at the body of the constitutional text itself.

Article 3 states that "the people are sovereign and the source of authority, which is exercised through the peoples' representatives and by referendum."

By the same token, and as previously noted, Article 2 states that "Tunisia is a civil state based on citizenship." And in light of that framing we can understand the Article 6 clauses under which the "state is the guardian of religion" and is committed to the "protection of the sacred" (the latter clause was carried over from the previously discussed *Ébauche de Projet de la Constitution* of 14 December 2012). In view of Tunisia's civil-state status, an argument can be made that its constitutional commitment to the "protection of the sacred" is actually meant to support the "freedom of conscience and belief" and "free exercise of religious practices" guaranteed in Article 6. This article "undertakes

23 It is true that the Tunisian constitution stands on the strength of "a consensus [...] that Islam is part and parcel of society, culture, and political life. But this centrality," Olivier Roy (2012, 50) points out, "is expressed more in terms of identity than of *sharīʿa*. This is clearly the case in Tunisia, where al-Nahḍa rejects the imposition of *sharīʿa* but insists on the country's Islamic identity and culture."

24 In this regard the European Commission for Democracy through Law, looking at the final draft constitution for the Republic of Tunisia, highlighted "some tensions between, on the one hand, the predominant position given to Islam, and on the other hand, the civil nature of the Tunisian state and the principles of plurality, impartiality and non-discrimination" (Venice Commission 2013, 7). And indeed this very tension was central to the contentious debate that unfolded in the run-up to the passage of the constitution: Was its unifying element to be found in the religious community or the national community? Were God-given rights to take precedence over civil rights? (Avon and Aschi 2014).

equally to prohibit and fight against calls for Takfīr [apostasy] and the incitement of violence and hatred." Which is a historic first: never has such a clause been introduced in the constitution of any Arab or Islamic country. Even so, the state's "protection of the sacred" could also entail the consequence of *limiting* freedom of conscience and religion.[25]

Title Two of the constitution (Arts. 21–49) covers rights and freedoms. Significant among these provisions is the Article 35 clause guaranteeing the "freedom to establish political parties, unions, and associations," which are bound to "respect the provisions of the Constitution, the law, financial transparency and the rejection of violence." No more are there any of the political and administrative restrictions and control mechanisms put in place under Ben Ali.

Article 39 "guarantees the right to free public education at all levels." It also requires the state to "work to consolidate the Arab-Muslim identity and national belonging in the young generations, and to strengthen, promote and generalize the use of the Arabic language," but at the same time it contains a commitment "to openness to foreign languages, human civilizations and diffusion of the culture of human rights."

Likewise important is Article 46, on women's rights and gender equality. If on the one hand this article requires the state to "protect women's *accrued* rights" (my emphasis on *accrued*), it also guarantees equality of opportunity at "all levels of responsibility in all domains."

Less liberal is Article 49: "The limitations that can be imposed on the exercise of the rights and freedoms guaranteed in this Constitution will be established by law, without compromising their essence." There is cause for concern here particularly as regards the *grounds* on which these limitations can be introduced, which grounds include "public order, national defence, public health or public morals." In fact, even if the provision requires "proportionality between these restrictions and the objective sought," the spectrum of objectives that can conceivably be pursued on these grounds seems quite broad, making it possible to restrict rights almost arbitrarily, and nowhere more so than when "public morals" are adduced.

Despite these concerns, however, what emerges from an analysis of the state's powers is that the Tunisian republic born of the revolution can indeed be described as a constitutional democracy.

Thus, Article 72, on the functions entrusted to the president, makes it a requirement for the officeholder to guarantee the independence of the state and ensure respect for the constitution. The president is elected to a five-year

25 This is a concern raised by Redissi (2014b), who asks: Will lawmakers authorize the construction of non-Islamic places of worship? Will they allow secular Tunisians to request exemptions from religious instruction? Will it be possible for atheist Tunisians to openly express their views? This will all depend on the way in which the elites will shape the institutions of government.

term and may not serve more than two terms (Art. 75). This effectively eliminates the risk of a presidency for life, as had happened under the Ben Ali regime, when a constitutional amendment passed in 2002 repealed the rule providing for a maximum of three five-year terms—a move that cleared the way for him to run for president even after this term limit was set to expire (Nicosia 2011, 114).

Article 95 establishes a parliamentary form of government: "The government is accountable before the Assembly of the Representatives of the People," to which it must "present a summary of its programme [...] with the objective of obtaining the confidence of an absolute majority of its members" (Art. 89).

What the 2014 constitution outlines is a *constitutional democracy* resting on the supremacy of the constitution and on judicial review. The supremacy clause is contained in Article 102: "The judiciary is independent. It ensures the administration of justice, the supremacy of the Constitution, the sovereignty of the law, and the protection of rights and freedoms." Judicial review by the Constitutional Court is instead enshrined in Article 120. This review can be preventive—applying to "draft laws, upon the request of the President of the Republic, the Head of Government, or thirty members of the Assembly of the Representatives of the People"—or it can apply ex post facto to enacted laws whose constitutionality is challenged in cases that work their way up through the appeals process. This is in contrast to the 1959 constitution, which under Article 72 only allowed for preventive judicial review at the president's request.[26]

Despite the innovative thrust of the 2014 constitution, early commentators did not shy away from underscoring its ambiguities and contradictions. An initial proving ground came with the 2014 elections for parliament and the presidency, as well as the gubernatorial and city elections. Also closely watched was the parliament as it set about translating the constitutional principles into statutory law. This work concerned the recognition of Islamic identity under Article 1. Then, too, there was the question of the way the parliament would legislate in regard to Article 39 of the constitution, under which the state "shall also work to consolidate the Arab-Muslim identity and national belonging in the young generations" (see Yahya 2014).

But even more crucial was the question of the parliament's work in legislating on "social justice, sustainable development and balance between regions" (Art. 12) within the framework of the decentralization mandate at Article 14. Decentralization was to be implemented locally at the city, regional, and district levels (Art. 131). Stakeholders at these local levels were to set their own priorities and participate "in promoting development activities that are responsive to local

26 The Article 72 judicial review clause of the 1959 constitution reads as follows: "The Constitutional Council looks into bills submitted to it by the President of the Republic to ensure their conformity with the Constitution."

needs while holding elected officials more accountable" (Yahya 2014).[27] The Tunisian constitution of 2014 held promise as the foundation for an extraordinary democratic development.

As we saw, *it was Tunisia that put the match to the extraordinary season of the Arab Springs. Along the way, the country went through a turbulent revolutionary phase, witnessing the failure of an Islamist government before charting a path to democracy without forsaking its own heritage and cultural identity. The hope is that this may become a model on which to build democracies across the Arab world.*

9.7 Tunisia: At long last the first elections in the new democracy

With much anticipation, the first elections held in Tunisia since the passage of the constitution came on 26 October 2014. This, too, acted as a proving ground for the new democracy, and it turned out to be the only successful outcome of the Arab Springs.

A wide range of parties and coalitions took part in the electoral contest. The main parties were al-Nahḍa, the Islamist party led by Rāshid al-Ghannūshī, which was expected to win over a majority of the electorate; followed by Nida' Tunis ("Call for Tunisia"), a coalition of secular forces led by the elderly Béji Caïd Essebsi (al-Bāji Qā'id al-Sabsī), who had previously served as minister of the interior and as foreign minister under Habib Bourguiba; and the Popular Front, a left-leaning grouping that had formed in 2012. Also on the ballot were, among several other formations, the Republican Party, the Congress for the Republic, and the Democratic Forum for Labour and Liberties, better known as al-Takattul (see Yehia 2014).

The 2014 elections were a free and open contest. By contrast, the elections held on 23 October 2011 for the constituent assembly barred those political figures whose reputation had been tarnished by their affiliation with the Ben Ali regime. This is what had been decided by the Haute Instance pour la Réalisation des Objectifs de la Revolution, chaired by Yadh Ben Achour, though he did not make the ban permanent. And in fact these blacklisted politicians did have an opportunity to run for office in 2014, since the government in office wisely reasoned that these elections had to be about reconciliation and inclusion (see Klaas and Dirsus 2014).

Contrary to expectations, a relative majority of the votes went to Nida' Tunis, which came in ahead of al-Nahḍa, the former taking 86 seats in the Assembly of the Representatives of the People (38 percent of the votes), against the latter's 69

27 The processes and methods used to apply the 2014 constitution were in large part shaped by the new stakeholders who in the period from 2011 to 2014 took an active part in civil society: trade unionists, academics, journalists, and bloggers, as well as a range of organizations. They are to be credited with having raised public awareness and engaged broad swaths of society in ways that cut across party affiliation (Avon and Aschi 2014).

(28 percent), over a total of 217 seats. This outcome certainly had a lot to do with al-Nahḍa's inept governance, but it can also be set down to the bad economy during the transition period. The Nida' Tunis victory is open to more than one interpretation: some have contended that Béji Caïd Essebsi was in reality trying to restore the Ben Ali regime, while his supporters saw him as the only viable alternative to al-Nahḍa (see Amraoui 2014).

However, the proportional electoral system made it necessary to form a coalition government, which indeed is how al-Nahḍa was seeing its political future (see the interview with Rāshid al-Ghannūshī in Cadalanu 2014). A governing coalition was probably the best solution for tackling the pressing and thorny issues that were roiling Tunisian society and politics in its complex postrevolutionary phase: the need to promote foreign direct investment in the country, revive the tourism industry, grow the economy, and bring down unemployment. Another priority for the new government was to stave off the risk of terrorist infiltration from Libya and Algeria (see Yehia 2014).

9.8 The Arab Springs in the destabilized landscape of the Middle East

In an interview released on the heels of the American decision to put together a coalition of states to fight the advance of ISIS in Syria and Iraq, the then Tunisian president, Mohamed Moncef Marzouki, called that strategy a political mistake (quoted in Nigro 2014). He said that the help the West was enlisting from autocratic regimes, especially the Gulf monarchies, would in the first place strengthen those regimes and would in addition prompt the people in the region to cast a fresh eye on extremists and even on the Islamic State itself. Only with steadfast support for the democratic process, he argued, would it be possible to thwart the advance of ISIS.

The American philosopher Michael Walzer took the view that a US war against the Islamic State would be legitimate, considering that a military intervention had been requested by the Iraqi government and that, in his assessment, such an intervention enjoyed popular support. He further argued that this would be a just war, for it would pursue the legitimate war aim of putting an end to the persecution of religious minorities (Flores d'Arcais 2014, 13). But in reality, and like never before, this "just war" was paradoxically poised to yield chiefly *injustice* in its prosecution. To see this, we need only consider the indirect support the military intervention would lend to the repressive Syrian regime that was holding the country in its grip under Baššār al-'Asad, who in fact had already carried out massacres targeting his own people, and whose human rights violations had been widely reported.

There were several mistakes the Western powers made before the Islamic State could find an opportunity to take its hold, ranging from their lukewarm support for the Arab Springs to their unwillingness to intervene in Syria. But the reasons why the Islamic State could expand are broader, ranging from the oppression of the Sunni opposition which the Nūrī al Mālikī regime carried out in Iraq with the backing of Washington to the Syrian government's crackdown on its own people with the backing of Moscow. In this context, ISIS could play on the widespread sense among Sunnis that forces of all sorts across the Middle East were arrayed against them and that, exhausted, they were powerless in the face of this situation.

Then, too, the Gulf monarchies were financing "a semi-clandestine Islamist economy," while Turkey was "allowing free passage to jihadists from much of Europe, and as far as Australia" (Harling 2014). There seemed to be no way out of the quagmire. The only path worth pursuing was to wholeheartedly support the democratic forces and movements that were gaining momentum across the Arab world: although this was a long game, it could well lead to acceptable solutions for coping with the instability that was engulfing the Middle East.

9.9 Tunisia: What prospects for the future?

In order to peer into what the future might hold for Tunisia, we need to first drill deeper into the question of how the democracy that was built in Tunisia can be understood in relation to the revolution that acted as its proximate cause.

In a recent book, *Tunisie: Une révolution en pays d'Islam*, Yadh Ben Achour analyses the revolution that laid the groundwork for the new Tunisian democracy, and correctly argues that this revolution cannot be compared to any of the major revolutions that came before it: the English Revolution of the mid-seventeenth century or the American and French Revolutions of the late eighteenth century: "Tunisia," he comments, "has invented a type of revolution that has absolutely no precedent in history" (Ben Achour 2016, 7; my translation).

The picture we get of the defining features of a revolution is the picture that historians construct in light of their ideologies and assumptions, a case in point being the Marxist reading of the French Revolution as a bourgeois revolution (see, for example, Mathiez 1922 and Soboul 1962). There are multiple causes behind any revolution, and historians key in on those that best comport with their outlook. And so, accordingly, the Tunisian Revolution is amenable to multiple interpretations. As Ben Achour asks:

> Was this the revolution of the economic, social, and political periphery against the centre? Was it the revolution of the tribes moved to action by the Khaldunian esprit de corps grounded in *'asabiyya*? […] Or that of the small landholders and street vendors in the heartland, like Bouazizi, reacting to land expropriation? […] Was it a secular revolution or a religious one? (Ben Achour 2016, 14)

Drawing on Hegel's philosophy, Ben Achour proceeds from a view of history as a dialectical movement in which the present must always reckon with the past. On this approach, the religious phase based on identity ties played a key role in the Tunisian Revolution (ibid., 20). And indeed the revolution put the issue of secularism front and centre. The outcome was a constitution that cannot in any sense be described as theocratic, and it could even be argued that the Islamist parties in Tunisia are themselves pivoting towards secularism.

Every revolution is underpinned by a political logic and dynamic peculiar to itself. In view of the distinctive traits of the constitutional debate in Tunisia—and particularly in view of its concern with the relation between law and religion—it would be fair to say that the Tunisian constitution laid the foundation for what might be described as a "constitutional democracy inflected with an Arab-Muslim identity"—a unique form of government that has no equivalent in the Western canon.

What emerged with force in the Tunisian Revolution was a post-authoritarian Islam whose main thrust came from its rejection of the authoritarian regime. Indeed, as Redissi (2017, 14) comments, "Islam is in its 'essence' anti-authoritarian" (my translation). But while post-authoritarianism led to a break with authoritarianism, it did not break with tradition. Hence the specific brand of Islam-inflected constitutional democracy that emerged from the Tunisian Revolution—a blend of ingredients resulting from a compromise struck between a modernist attitude and a conservative one rooted in Islam.

It has also been suggested that what came into being was a form of government anchored in a new kind of legitimacy: the legitimacy of compromise (Nachi 2017, 33). Compromise was the final point of convergence for all the forces that took part in the Tunisian constitutional revolution, and it is also the answer to the question of why Tunisia is the only country in which the Arab Springs had a successful outcome. Indeed, as mentioned, two projects were competing: a modernizing one and a conservative or Islamist one. It was in the context of this competition that this historic compromise solution was achieved, averting the risk of polarization, and it was achieved through an *active pluralism* (ibid., 20) predicated on the need to recognize difference, taking account of the plural principles and forms of life shaping Tunisian society.

The revolution brought into focus the problem of the relation between Islam and modernity, this on account of the two conflicting forces that have long been shaping Tunisian society: the secularist ones that have progressively been gaining strength, and those that are pushing against them, namely, the forces of fundamentalism and radical Islam. The secularists have had to reckon with the distinctiveness of Tunisian society, with its history and identity, whose roots in large part trace back to Islam and the Islamic civilization.

Two antithetical visions were therefore in contention in the revolution: one that was calling for a radical break with the past, and another that was instead geared towards national reconciliation. So a debate took place in which these two visions were staking out their positions: ranged on one side of the field were those whose project was modernist (*hadathi*)—receptive to Western culture with a view to building a secularist state (*Dawla madaniya*) within a constitutional framework—while on the other stood those whose project looked to Islam and the Arab nation as their lodestars (ibid., 30). The foundation for the compromise was set when the secularists accepted that the Islamist party al-Nahḍa should take part in the political process, and al-Nahḍa in turn accepted the idea of negotiating as way to break the stalemate that lasted from 2011 to 2014 (ibid., 32).

9.10 Can the compromise stand?

So, then, does the Tunisian compromise have lasting power? To answer this question we can consider what Gilbert Achcar writes in regard to the Tunisian model and its limits. In 2013, a political assassination was carried out by Salafi elements targeting "one of the leading figures of the Popular Front" (Achcar 2016, 159). This "led to a huge outpouring of mass anger against Ennahda [al-Nahḍa], which was held responsible for creating the political conditions for the assassination" (ibid.). And then "a few months later [...] another prominent figure of the Popular Front" (ibid.) was assassinated: this "led to the foundation on the next day of the National Salvation Front (NSF), bringing together the Popular Front's key parties as well as Nidaa Tounes ('Tunisia's call') as well as a few centre-left and liberal groups" (ibid., 159–60). In a further development, "the NSF called for a popular anti-Ennahda rally on 6 August 2013, which turned out to be a true Tunisian equivalent of Egypt's 30 June 2013 anti–Muslim Brotherhood mobilisation" (ibid., 160). Despite the parallel, however, "there are important differences between the two processes, the major factor in this respect being Ennahda's attitude" (ibid., 161). As Achcar explains:

> Already quite impressed by the tragic repression of his Algerian co-thinkers, Ghannouchi [the leader of al-Nahḍa] was no doubt appalled by the tragic downfall of his Egyptian fellows only a few weeks before August 6. In striking contrast to the Egyptian Muslim Brotherhood's foolish intransigence, he thus accepted a compromise whereby the Ennahda-dominated government would give way to "technocratic" transitional government in January 2014, which oversaw the elections held in autumn of the same year. (Ibid.)

As Achcar observes, "another key factor facilitating the smooth return of the old regime was the role played by the Left" (ibid., 162). In fact, "a dominant section of the Tunisian Left organized in the Popular Front leaned towards an electoral and political alliance with Nidaa Tounes" (ibid.), which in the October 2014 elections won a relative majority of the votes.

> In fact, the Popular Front contributed decisively to bringing Nidaa Tounes back in from the cold, where it had been confined as a result of being reviled by both the Left and Ennahda, as representing the ousted regime. By entering into the NSF alliance with Nidaa Tounes, the Tunisian Left contributed to the rehabilitation of the latter, as did the assassinations' impact in stoking up fear of Islamic fundamentalism and a longing for a strong state. (Ibid.)

The power transition based on that compromise gave birth to a coalition government in which Nidaa Tounes formed an alliance with al-Nahḍa, rather than with the Popular Front, for they

> share a dedication to a neoliberal socioeconomic perspective—so much so that the mood of reconciliation went so far as to allow the coalition government to draft a "reconciliation law" granting amnesty to businessmen and civil servants who had committed financial crimes or misused public funds. They would be amnestied in exchange for their admission of guilt and willingness to pay back their ill-gotten gains with 5 percent interest—a transaction that undermined the transitional justice procedure that had painstakingly put in place in December 2013. (Ibid., 163)

On top of that came a war on terror designed to drive back the Islamic State with "an 'anti-terrorist' law [of 2015] denounced by human rights organisations as a threat to civil rights and liberties" (ibid., 164). Achcar is therefore unforgiving in forming an overall assessment of the Tunisian transition: "Tunisia is [...] walking back with long strides into a restoration of the old regime, under the presidency of the world's third-oldest head of state after Zimbabwe's Robert Mugabe and Queen Elisabeth II of England" (ibid.). He also takes issue with the government's handling of the economy, noting that "the root causes of the social exasperation that led to the self-immolation of Mohamed Bouazizi on 17 December 2010 to act as a spark setting on an all-engulfing fire have only been aggravated by the pursuit of neoliberal policies against a backdrop of political turmoil" (ibid.). To illustrate, he quotes Anouar Boukhars, who cites the ballooning "size of the informal economy," a problem compounded by "structural determinants [...], chiefly bureaucratic corruption, excessive regulation, high taxes, and exorbitant start-up costs" (Boukhars 2015, 19–20, quoted in Achcar 2016, 165).

Will Tunisia be able to preserve the democratic-constitutional gains of its 2011 revolution? In answering this question, it will first have to be noted that some of the high hopes engendered by the revolution have not materialized, especially in what concerns the prospect of a transitional justice which was supposed to build fairness into the democratic constitutional form of government that had been envisioned.

To be sure, a significant step forward was taken with the 2013 law on transitional justice,[28] making it possible to prosecute violations of socioeconomic rights. But with the coalition government formed by Nidaa Tounes and al-Nahḍa, attention shifted towards reconciliation rather than the prosecution of crimes

28 Loi organique 2013-53 du 24 décembre 2013, relative à l'instauration de la justice transitionnelle et à son organisation, in *Journal Officiel de la République Tunisienne* (JORT) no. 105 of 31 December 2013, 3655–65 (Organic Law 2013-53, of 24 December 2013, Establishing and Organizing Transitional Justice, JORT no. 105, 31 December 2013, 903–11).

(see Ketelaars 2018, 252).[29] This can be appreciated from Organic Law 2017-62 Relating to Reconciliation in the Administrative Field.[30] Although this law was signed by President Mohamed Béji Caïd Essebsi on 24 October 2017, it was 2015 when he first introduced it, and only after it was amended did it pass the Assemblée des Représentants, on 13 September 2017, following an intense day of heated debate in the legislative house amid protests staged outside the building. In fact, as Amna Guellali comments, while the law was aimed at reconciliation, what it did was to give amnesty to civil servants embroiled in scandals involving corruption and embezzlement of public funds: it did so without setting up any real inquiry mechanism, and without consequences for those engaged in the systematic practice of plundering the Tunisian economy under the regime headed by Ben Ali and his family. The result, therefore, was a "reconciliation" which could only add to the mistrust that many Tunisians were already feeling towards a system that had not yet quite managed to chase away the demons of its own past (Guellali 2017). In short, it wouldn't be unreasonable to suggest that the new parties in government, despite the differences that set them apart, struck an alliance designed to protect the interests of the middle classes and elites representing the status quo ante (Ketelaars 2018, 252).

Shadows of uncertainty therefore appear to be looming on the horizon for the young Tunisian democracy. But we should not neglect to consider that the constitutional democracy born of the Tunisian Revolution is the outcome of a long historical process that began with the abolition of slavery in 1846, a full nineteen years before slavery was abolished in the United States (Masri 2017, 128)—a process which in 1861 reached another landmark with the first constitution in any Arab or Muslim country, and which continued to advance when, in 1956, Tunisia gained its independence under the leadership of Habib Bourghiba, who in the same year introduced a code improving the condition of women,[31] and then proceeded to overhaul the education system.[32]

29 Transitional justice in Tunis marks the fourth wave of transitional justice, after the first one at the time of the war crime trials held in Nuremberg and Tokyo in the wake of World War II. The second wave concerned the transition towards democracy in the Eastern Bloc countries after the fall of the Berlin Wall. The third wave came in connection with the war crimes and genocides perpetrated in the former Yugoslavia and in Rwanda (see Ketelaars 2018, 244–45).

30 Loi organique 2017-62 du 24 octobre 2017, relative à la réconciliation dans le domaine administratif, in *Journal Officiel de la République Tunisienne* (JORT) no. 85 of 24 October 2017, 3625.

31 Code du Statut Personnel (promulgated on 13 August 1956), in *Journal Officiel Tunisien* n. 104 du 28 décembre 1956, 1740–80.

32 These are reforms that Bourghiba put into effect with his education minister, Mahmoud Messaadi. In 1958, faced with a surge in enrolment, they reduced both the number of compulsory years in school (from seven to six) and the amount of classroom time (to thirty hours a week), but the reduced workload wound up improving the quality of teaching (Ketelaars 2018, 249). In 1967 Messaadi set up a commission that reinstated the seven-year standard for primary school, with an expanded curriculum that made for a richer education (ibid., 249–50).

As a result of these developments, Tunisia stands out as an anomaly in the Arab Muslim world (Masri 2017, 291ff.), having set the conditions for achieving a "constitutional democracy inflected with an Arab-Muslim identity"—a foundation that, despite the tensions and uncertainties incident to the transitional phase, has set the country on a course it is bound to follow and build on.

9.11 The challenges ahead

When President Mohamed Béji Caïd Essebsi died, on 25 July 2019, Tunisia called for early elections, with a first round on September 15, just before the parliamentary elections of October 6. The runoff for the presidential contest was held on October 13, awarding a landslide 72.71 percent victory to Kais Saied, a professor of constitutional law who put forward a conservative, antisystem agenda calling for radical change and a new slate of incoming leaders for a refreshed power structure in Tunisia.

On the back of an ailing economy that was barely showing any sign of recovery—with high youth unemployment, high inflation, and a rising public debt—the parliamentary elections held on October 6 completed the realignment by unseating the old establishment guard in large numbers (cf. Frettoli 2020, 1), with a blow to the two main parties in the governing coalition, al-Nahḍa and Nidaa Tounes. Despite the setback, the former still managed to win over the largest share of the electorate, with 19.6 percent of the votes and 52 seats. Nidaa Tounes, for its part, having split up, received only 1.5 percent of the votes, while many of those who had previously voted for Nidaa Tounes switched to two of its splinter groups, both centre-leaning, namely, Tahya Tounes and Qalb Tounes, which took in 4.08 percent and 14.5 percent, respectively.

After a first failed attempt, President Kais Saied entrusted the task of forming a new government to Elyes Fakhfakh, who had served as finance minister from 2011 to 2013, and who in the end managed to secure the confidence of the Assemblée des Représentants du Peuple. The new government contains a plurality of heterogenous forces: al-Nahḍa; two centre-left parties, Ettayar (Democratic Current) and Echaâb (People's Movement); Tahya Tounes; and Le Bloc de la Réforme Nationale. Given the array of opposing visions and ideologies gathered under this big tent, it will be essential for the new prime minister to try to hold them together cohesively (ISPI 2020). But the greater challenge will continue to be the economy, with a cash-strapped government, 15 percent unemployment, and inflation at 6.7 percent—a daunting problem to attack which Fakhfakh has introduced an ambitious recovery plan based on a broad social pact.

Tunisia is still looking at an uncertain future, to be sure, a road paved with potential pitfalls, but its ability to overcome the existential crises it has been confronted with since Ben Ali fled the country in January 2011 suggests that it has the resourcefulness it needs to face the challenges looming ahead. Democracy is a learning process, and the Tunisian democracy is learning at a rapid pace.

Works Cited

Abd Rabou, Ahmed. 2014. "Civilian-Military Relations and the Position of Security Institutions in the 2014 Constitution." *Arab Reform Initiative*, March 2014.

Achcar, Gilbert. 2016. *Morbid Symptoms: Relapse in the Arab Uprisings*. London: Saqi Books.

Alaoui, Hicham Ben Abdallah El-. 2014. "Take Back the Arab Spring." *Le Monde Diplomatique*, February 2014. https://mondediplo.com/2014/02/02arabspring. Published in French under the title "Le 'printemps arabe' n'a pas dit son dernier mot" https://www.monde-diplomatique.fr/2014/02/EL_ALAOUI/50074

Alianak, Sonia L. 2014. *The Transition Towards Revolution and Reform: The Arab Spring Realised?* Edinburgh: Edinburgh University Press.

Amraoui, Ahmed El. 2014. "Tunisia's Ennahda 'Faces Defeat' in Elections." *Al Jazeera*, October 28.

Arab Republic of Egypt. 2013. Draft Constitution 2013. New Constitutional Document After Amending the Suspended 2012 Constitution. Draft dated 2 December 2013 of the Constitution of the Arab Republic of Egypt Prepared pursuant the Article 29 of the Constitutional Declaration dated 8 July 2013. Unofficial translation prepared by the International Institute for Democracy and Electoral Assistance (International IDEA).

'Arafa, Mohamed A. 2011. "Towards a Culture for Accountability: A New Dawn for Egypt." *Phoenix Law Review* 5, no. 1: 1–37.

Association Henri Capitant des Amis de la Culture Juridique Française. 1994. *Journées franco-italiennes de Nice et Gènes: La circulation du modèle juridique français*. Travaux de l'association, tome XLIV, année 1993. Paris: Litec.

Avon, Dominique. 2012. "Les Frères Musulmans et l'État civil démocratique à référence islamique.'" *Les Cahiers de l'Orient* 2012/4, no. 108: 81–95.

Avon, Dominique, and Youssef Aschi. 2014. "La Constitution tunisienne et l'enjeu de la liberté individuelle: Un exemple d'accommodement au forceps." *Raison Publique: Forum Philosophique et Littéraire*, June 3.

Ben Achour, Yadh. 2012. "Religion, révolution et constitution: Spécialement d'après l'exemple tunisien." *Leaders*, Notes & Docs, November 13. www.leaders.com. tn/article/9831

Ben Achour, Yadh. 2016. *Tunisie: Une révolution en pays d'Islam*. Tunis: Cérès Éditions.

Ben Mrad, Hédi. 2012. "La problématique constitutionnelle de la transition." In *La Transition démocratique en Tunisie: États des lieux*. Vol. 2, *Les thématiques*. By the Observatoire Tunisien de la Transition Démocratique, edited by Hamadi Redissi, Asma Nouira, and Abdelkader Zghal, 7–22. Tunis: Diwen.

Boukhars, Anouar. 2015. *The Reckoning: Tunisia's Perilous Path to Democratic Stability*. Washington, DC: Carnegie Endowment for International Peace.

Brown, Nathan J. 2012. "Egypt's Judges in a Revolutionary Age." In The Carnegie Papers, Middle East, February 2012. Washington, DC: Carnegie Endowment for International Peace. http://carnegieendowment.org/files/egypt_judiciary.pdf

Cadalanu, Giampaolo. 2014. "Ghannouchi: Il voto in Tunisia è cruciale, in gioco c'è la democrazia." *la Repubblica*, October 27.

Cecere, Giuseppe. 2012. "La primavera incompiuta del liberalismo egiziano." Introduction to *Costituzione egiziana (1923)*. Macerata: Liberilibri.

Chazli, Karim El. 2014. "The Judiciary in the Constitution: Lost Opportunities for Reform and Enshrinement of the Judiciary's Impenetrability." *Arab Reform Initiative*, March 2014.

CEDROMA (Centre d'Études des Droit du Monde Arabe), Faculté de Droit et des Sciences Sociales, Université Saint-Joseph de Beyrouth. 2005. *Les principes généraux du droit: Droit français, droit des pays arabes, droit musulman (dénominateurs communs).* Proceedings of Beirut conference, 4–6 October 2001. Brussels: Bruylant.

CID (Center for International Development at Harvard University). 2003. "Washington Consensus." (Document no longer retrievable.)

Flores d'Arcais, Alberto. 2014. "Walzer: 'È una guerra giusta, non possiamo ignorare massacri e diritti violati. La barbarie va fermata.'" *la Repubblica*, September 28.

Frettoli, Fabio. 2020. "Tunisia: Il difficile cammino per uscire dalla crisi." Focus Mediterraneo Allargato No. 12, February 21. Istituto per gli Studi di Politica Internazionale (ISPI). https://www.ispionline.it/it/pubblicazione/tunisia-il-difficile-cammino-uscire-dalla-crisi-25156

Gresh, Alain. 2012. "Egypt: From Military to Religious Dictatorship?" *Le Monde Diplomatique*, November 2012. https://mondediplo.com/6623

Guellali, Amna. 2017. "La loi sur la réconciliation administrative, dangereuse pour l'avenir de la démocratie tunisienne." *Middle East Eye*, September 21.

Harling, Peter. 2014. "Islamic State Fills Middle East Void; IS Back in Business." *Le Monde Diplomatique*, September 2014.

Houssi, Leila El. 2013. "Tunisia: Rivoluzione in atto." In *Dove vanno le primavere arabe?*, edited by Antonio Cantaro, 53–66. Rome: Ediesse.

Human Rights Watch. 2011. *"Work on Him until He Confesses": Impunity for Torture in Egypt.* New York: Human Rights Watch. https://www.hrw.org/report/2011/01/30/work-him-until-he-confesses/impunity-torture-egypt#412

ISPI (Istituto per gli Studi di Politica Internazionale). 2020. "Un governo per la Tunisia." ISPI *Daily Focus*, edited by Alessia De Luca, February 27. https://www.ispionline.it/it/pubblicazione/un-governo-la-tunisia-25221

Jankowski, James. 2000. *Egypt: A Short History.* Oxford: Oneworld.

Ketelaars, Elise. 2018. "EU Support for Transitional Justice in the Aftermath of the Arab Spring: What Has Become of the Promises of the Fourth Wave of Transitional Justice?" In *North Africa and the Making of Europe: Governance, Institutions and Culture*, edited by Muriam Haleh Davis and Thomas Serres, 243–63. London: Bloomsbury.

Klaas, Brian, and Marcel Dirsus. 2014. "The Tunisia Model: Did Tunis Win the Arab Spring?" *Foreign Affairs*, October 23. https://www.foreignaffairs.com/articles/tunisia/2014-10-23/tunisia-model

Le Roy, Thierry. 2012. "Constitutionalism in the Maghreb: Between French Heritage and Islamic Concepts." In *Constitutionalism in Islamic Countries: Between Upheaval and Continuity*, edited by Rainer Grote and Tilmann J. Röder, 109–119. Oxford: Oxford University Press.

Longo, Pietro. 2013. "Atti di sovranità e politiche costituzionali in Tunisia, Egitto e Libia dopo le Primavere Arabe." *Rivista italiana di studi sull'Islam politico* 0: 13–39.

Masri, Safwan M. 2017. *Tunisia: An Arab Anomaly.* New York: Columbia University Press.

Mathiez, Albert. 1922. *La révolution française: La chute de la Royauté; la Gironde et la Montagne; la Terreur.* Paris: Colin.

Mezzetti, Luca. 2014. "La quarta ondata: Transizioni costituzionali e consolidamento democratico nelle esperienze recenti degli ordinamenti islamici." In *Transizioni e democrazia nei paesi del Mediterraneo e del vicino Oriente*, edited by G. D' Ignazio, N. Fiorita, S. Gambino, F. Raniolo, and A. Ventura, 19–110. Cosenza: Edizioni Periferia.

Nachi, Mohamed, ed. 2017. *Révolution & Compromis: Invention d'une solution aux incertitudes de la transition démocratique en Tunisie.* Tunis: Nirvana.

Nicosia, Aldo. 2011. "La Tunisia dalla rivoluzione alla nuova costituzione." Chap. 5 in *Le rivoluzioni arabe: La transizione mediterranea*, edited by Francesca Maria Corrao. Milan: Mondadori.

Nigro, Vincenzo. 2014. "Marzouki: 'Ma è un errore allearsi con i regimi dell'area.'" *la Repubblica*, September 12.

Redissi, Hamadi. 2014a. "Nous avons conjuré le risque d'un État islamique." *L'Humanité*, January 13.

Redissi, Hamadi. 2014b. "Raison publique et laïcité islamique: La constitution tunisienne de 2014." *Leaders*, July 4.

Redissi, Hamadi. 2017. *L'Islam incertain: Révolutions et Islam post-autoritaire.* Tunis: Cérès Éditions.

Rizk, Mariam, and Osman El Sharnoubi. 2013. "Egypt's Constitution 2013 vs. 2012: A Comparison." *Ahram Online*, December 12.

Roy, Olivier. 2012. "Islamic Revival and Democracy: The Case in Tunisia and Egypt." In *Arab Society in Revolt: The West's Mediterranean Challenge*, edited by Cesare Merlini and Olivier Roy, 47–52. Washington, DC: Brookings Institution Press.

Sbailò, Ciro. 2012. *Principi sciaraitici e organizzazione dello spazio pubblico nel mondo islamico: Il caso egiziano.* Padua: CEDAM.

Sbailò, Ciro. 2013. "Dove va l'Egitto? Riflessioni su un 'colpo di stato democratico.'" *Federalismi.it: Rivista di diritto pubblico italiano, comunitario e comparato* 16 (August 7): 1–24.

Soboul, Albert. 1962. *Histoire de la Révolution française.* Vol. 1, *De la Bastille à la Gironde.* Vol. 2, *De la Montagne à Brumaire.* Paris: Gallimard.

UNIMED (Unione delle Università del Mediterraneo). 2012. "Egitto: Un nuovo presidente nel caso costituzionale politico." June 20.

Vatikiotis, P. J. 1991. *The History of Modern Egypt: From Muhammad Ali to Mubarak.* Baltimore: Johns Hopkins University Press.

Venice Commission (European Commission for Democracy through Law). 2013. "Opinion on the Final Draft Constitution of the Republic of Tunisia," adopted by the Venice Commission at its 96th plenary session, Venice, 11–12 October 2013. Council of Europe, Strasbourg, 17 October 2013, Opinion 733/2013, CDL-AD(2013)032. (Originally written in French under title "Observations sur le projet final de la Constitution de la République Tunisienne.")

Yahya, Maha. 2014. "Beyond Tunisia's Constitution: The Devil in the Details." Carnegie Endowment for International Peace, April 28. https://carnegieendowment.org/sada/55398

Yehia, Karem. 2014. "Tunisia at the Crossroads." *Al-Ahram Weekly*, October 26.

10 The Arab Springs: An analysis of its roots and causes

10.1 The causes of the uprisings

The outbreak of the Arab Springs was an event that no one had seen coming. But while the moment may have been impossible to predict, the conditions that led to it had been extensively analysed. These conditions were in part shaped by demographic and socioeconomic trends.[1] In this connection, Bichara Khader has pointed out the seismic shift that in the last quarter of the twentieth century took place the Arab Maghreb, and to a lesser extent in the Mashriq as well: the population was getting younger, and the youth kept entering the workforce in greater and greater numbers (Khader 2003). In 2007, almost one-quarter of the population in the Middle East and North Africa (MENA) ranged between the ages of 15 and 24 (Assaad and Fahimi 2007). At the time, there were about 100 million people in this age bracket, out of a population of 380 million. If we broaden the age bracket so as to also include people between the ages of 25 and 30, we get a youth population that accounts for 65 percent of the overall population. The MENA region ranks second only to Sub-Saharan Africa in the percentage of youths within this age bracket (Gelvin 2012, 19). This trend is part of a broader trend within the MENA region, where the population soared from 60 to 380 million over the course of the twentieth century.

This picture of the labour market was posing a serious challenge to the Arab countries, considering that the objective was to increase the labour force participation rate by 4 percentage points by 2020. It was unrealistic to expect this kind of performance, with a growing unemployment rate that had already surpassed the 15 percent mark in 2003.

1 As Kneissl (2011, 5) observes, these trends "pointed towards a mounting crisis or even to social explosion. However, nobody could foretell an exact date." Kneissl goes on to comment that "the Arab world might have seen popular democratic uprisings earlier, if the Iraq war had not come in between in early 2003" (attributing that assessment to Volker Perthes), "since the notion of democracy has been connoted with interventionism, instability and anarchy ever since the invasion into Iraq for the sake of regime-change started" (ibid.).

In order to appreciate how a growing population was affecting unemployment, we need only consider that in the decade from 2000 to 2010, 40 million youth entered the labour force (see Ciranda 2010/11, 86; cf. Ciranda 2012), marking a 40 percent spike in the size of the overall labour force. According to a study issued by the World Bank (Kabbani and Kothari 2005, 13), the MENA countries would have had to generate at least 100 million jobs in the two decades from 2000 to 2020 in order to absorb the incoming labour force. But the number of jobs that were being created was woefully inadequate in a bad economic situation further aggravated by the global financial crisis of 2007–2008 and by social trends like the growing number of women moving into the labour force.

But there are also structural reasons that account for the shape of the labour market in the Arab countries. The first of these lies in the government's waning ability to act as an "employer of last resort" (Adams and Page 2002; cf. Ciranda 2010/11, 87).[2] Another lies in an educational system that does not train for the skills needed for the labour market, and another still in a system that does not encourage investment, whether foreign or domestic.

Another structural force worth pointing out lies in the effect of foreign interventions, especially the structural adjustment programs (SAPs) that in the 1980s the International Monetary Fund (IMF) implemented across almost the entire MENA region: under these programmes, the state had to progressively withdraw from the economy, thereby scaling back its own role as a backstop employer of last resort,[3] a role it had specifically been designated for in previous years (Assaad 2008).

Furthermore, economic crisis in countries that cannot count on oil revenues translates into proportionally lower educational budgets, all to the detriment of an already fledgling educational system. The youth in the Arab countries' educational systems fall into two buckets. There is an exclusive body of students who belong to the elite families affiliated with the government: they are trained in foreign schools and universities and will find specially reserved jobs in the high-skill labour market. In the second, much bigger bucket are all the youth who belong to poor and middle-class families, and what they can look to is mass unemployment, especially in small towns and rural areas, where there are no job opportunities, but also in the large metropolitan areas, where

2 As the International Labour Organization reports referring "to 2004 data, in the Middle East and North Africa region, the public sector represented some 29 percent of total employment [...], in sharp contrast to other countries in the world," adding that this was "almost double the world average (excluding China)" (Awad 2009, 8, also cited in Amin et al. 2012, 33).

3 See Romagnoli and Mengoni 2014, 161–62, for a snapshot of the public sector's diminished capacity to absorb the labour force, the slow growth of the private sector, and the imbalance between supply and demand in the labour markets, with its effect on unemployment, particularly on the youth labour force.

unaffordable housing severely hamstrings their ability to find gainful employment (Mouhoud 2012, 40).[4]

If we look at the other side of the Mediterranean, the contrast couldn't be more striking. In Italy, for example, the birth rate sits at 1.3 children for every woman of child-bearing age, whereas in Libya, a former Italian colony, that number jumps to 4. This means that the Italian population is projected to fall by 6 percent by 2028/30, while the Libyan population is expected to double over the same period. In this scenario, migration could act as a safety valve, making it possible to relieve the southern Mediterranean of its excess population by way of migration into Europe. These migratory processes could help to close the population gap—this all to the benefit of the EU, considering that by the year 2050, according to a UN report (UN DESA 2001), the EU will have to gain anywhere from 47.5 million people, on a conservative estimate, to 159 million, on a liberal estimate, if it is to maintain its current levels of social security (Khader 2003, 359).

But the implications of that demographic trend go quite against the grain of public opinion across Europe, where migration continues to be widely perceived as a *threat* to social security,[5] weakening the labour market and diluting national cultural identities. But the data is incontrovertible: according to projections that Khader reported in 2003, the birth rate trend of the time was pointing to 30 million people that Europe would lose by 2025 (Khader 2003, 359). It had also been projected that the labour pool would shrink as the youth stayed

4 As Hollis (2012, 81) observes, "persistent and gross disparities in wealth and high unemployment were among the grievances that triggered the Arab revolts in 2010–11." And precisely in this connection we can see a failure of the EU, with its attempt "to 'export' its model of liberal economics and democracy," a model that "consistently featured accountable government, the rule of law, freedom of expression and assembly, and respect for human rights." For it was on the basis of this model that "for over two decades the EU [had] been promoting and justifying its policies on the grounds that they [would] help create 'shared prosperity' and more jobs for all the countries of the Mediterranean" (ibid.).

5 EU countries have signed bilateral agreements to control migration. Among these is a 2008 agreement between Italy and Libya (Law No. 7 of 6 February 2009, "Ratifica ed esecuzione del Trattato di amicizia, partenariato e cooperazione tra la Repubblica italiana e la Grande Giamahiria araba libica popolare socialista," signed in Bengasi on 30 August 2008, published in *Gazzetta Ufficiale* (GU), Serie Generale, no. 40 of 18 February 2009), whose Article 19 states that "the two parties shall intensify their ongoing cooperation in the fight against terrorism, organized crime, drug trafficking, and illegal migration" (my translation). Cf. Kneissl 2011, 5, n. 11. Similarly, in 2008 France and Tunisia signed an agreement to control illegal migration and the migration of seasonal and permanent workers, while undertaking to develop job skills and human resources in Tunisia (Kneissl 2011, 6, n. 12). See Décret n. 2009-905 du 24 juillet 2009 portant publication de l'accord-cadre relatif à la gestion concertée des migrations et au développement solidaire, du protocole relatif à la gestion concertée des migrations (ensemble deux annexes) et du protocole en matière de développement solidaire (ensemble trois annexes) entre le Gouvernement de la République française et le Gouvernement de la République tunisienne, signed in Tunis on 28 April 2008, published in *Journal Officiel de la République Française* (JORF) no. 0171 of 26 July 2009, 12493ff., text no. 4.

longer in school, and that for every 10 dependent persons in Europe (people younger than 15 or older than 65), there would only be 14 workers in 2020 generating the income needed to support them, as against 23 workers in 1989 (ibid., 360).

In this predicament, even as immigration faces opposition, the process appears to be at once necessary and inevitable: it would help to achieve a demographic balance, and the remittance payments that migrants send back home would help to reduce the economic disparity between poor and rich countries. The resistance that has been mounted against immigration out of fear for security has been contributing to skyrocketing unemployment in the Arab countries, all the while making security itself an actual problem in Europe.

10.2 From revolt to revolution: The people reclaiming their dignity

The sociologist ʿĀdil Jabbār (2011) has claimed that the Arab peoples of North Africa have broken the triangle that for decades has acted as an enclosure of repression and absolute despotism. Making up one side of the triangle was a certain brand of religious fundamentalism that was devoid of vision, clarity, or any coherent plan over the long run. Another side consisted of a system of secular, despotic, family-run, and in large part corrupt governments. And on the third side was the interference of foreign powers that had been propping up these authoritarian and corrupt regimes, all with histories of violating the most basic rights of their own people. These three elements have all fallen apart now, and even the opposition parties have been pushed aside.

But revolt movements do not come bolting out of nowhere. On the contrary, these peoples had millenary histories behind them and have long been engaged in struggles to liberate themselves from colonial rule. Although in the 1960s and 1970s, these Arab states managed to build social safety nets, this social infrastructure has since been eroding. So, too, many government assets have been privatized, and many of them went to the elites and to the clients in the regimes' patronage networks. Finally, in regimes as repressive as these there are no public spaces in which to have an inclusive and open debate, and it is for this reason that text messaging and social media became such important tools for sharing information.

The revolutions that sprang from this confluence of factors took the form of nonviolent civil disobedience, belying the Western stereotype of Muslim societies as inclined to violence. As has been argued, correctly in my view, what transpired in these uprisings is bound to shake the Western prejudice about the Muslim world, and to finally debunk the famous thesis of the clash of civilizations (Roy 2011).

What is more, *those who joined these movements did so not out of religious reasons but to defend their dignity as citizens.* The signs they held up (handwritten) carried messages whose watchwords were freedom, dignity, democracy—all in one way or another saying no to despotism.

This observation has been taken to suggest that Arab societies have transitioned into a *post-Islamist* phase,[6] precisely because the mass movements that unfolded in the Arab Springs were no longer being carried forward in the name of an Islamic state, and they tended to keep the religious sphere separate from the political.[7] But in reality Islam has continued to act as an important force, as can be appreciated from the rise of the religious parties, and so post-Islamism has had to reckon with the resurgence of political Islam, "bent on reinstating the identity between religion and the social system (*al-islām dīn wa-dunyā*) that constitutes a distinguishing trait of the Muslim worldview" (Campanini 2013, 39; my translation).

The Arab revolts have sent shockwaves across the Middle East, and the outside attempts that have been made to reconfigure the political and economic system have been marginal at best, for which reason they will be inadequate to the demands voiced by the youth population (bearing in mind that two-thirds of the population in the Arab world at the time of the revolts was 35 years of age or younger: Jabbār 2011). The answer to these unmet demands will therefore have to be bold, addressing the fault lines in both the political system and the economic one (ibid.).

6 See the account in Bayat 2013, 243, where post-Islamism is described as being "not only a condition but also a project." As such, "it is neither anti-Islamic nor un-Islamic," being "an endeavor to fuse religiosity and rights, faith and freedom, Islam and liberty. It wants to turn the underlying principles of Islamism on their heads by emphasizing rights instead of duties, plurality in place of a singular authoritative voice, historicity rather than fixed scripture, and the future instead of the past," thereby "transcending Islamism in social, political, and intellectual domains" (ibid.). And because "many Muslims may adhere eclectically and simultaneously to aspects of both discourses"—one "marked by the fusion of religion and responsibility," the other instead laying emphasis on "religiosity and rights"—what "in reality we may witness" are "simultaneous processes of both Islamization and post-Islamization" (ibid., 243–44).

In an earlier study, Bayat traces the "post-Islamist turn" to forces that took shape in the 1990s: "The new pluralist strategy of the Lebanese Hizbullah in the early 1990s leading to a split in the movement, the emergence in the mid-1990s of the Al-Wasat party in Egypt as an alternative to both militant Islamists and the Muslim Brothers, the pluralism of Islamic parties in Turkey (Rifah, Virtue, and Justice and Development Parties), the discursive shift in Indian Jamat-i Islami towards more inclusive, pluralistic and ambiguous ideological dispositions, and finally the emergence in Saudi Arabia of an 'Islamo-liberal' trend in the late 1990s seeking a compromise between Islam and democracy, each displays some diverse versions of post-Islamist trends in Muslim societies today" (Bayat 2007, 20; footnotes omitted).

7 As Filiu (2011, 22) observes commenting on those who took part in the Arab revolution, "the unemployed 'martyr,' the principled general and the sophisticated jurist may be pious Muslims or devout believers, but they never put their religious convictions forward to justify their recent decisions, so critical for the fate of Tunisia. Likewise, tens of thousands joined or supported the uprising without ever mentioning Islam. They were incensed, desperate, disgusted, revolted, ashamed, or even furious, but they were not religiously motivated. And what is true in (partially) Westernized Tunisia is also the case in Egypt."

What at any rate is losing ground is Arab-Muslim exceptionalism—the idea that the Muslim world is extraneous to democracy.[8]

We should now look briefly at this new generation of youths. Those who took to Taḥrīr Square in Egypt can be compared to the youth who protested against Mahmoud Ahmadinejad in Iran. Even if many of them were likely to have been believers, this had nothing to do with their political demands: their movement was a *secular* one, separating religion from politics.

What limited these movements was the very characteristic that enabled them to flourish, which is to say that they were leaderless and politically unorganized, and this made it difficult for them to find institutional forms through which to work towards a possible democracy (Roy 2011). But this condition did not mean that a vacuum had thereby been created for Al-Qaeda to exploit, since this terrorist organization's recruitment was mostly targeted at youths who had severed their family and social ties. Al-Qaeda never attempted to build a political structure in the Muslim countries, and its impact in Arab societies remained extremely limited even in its heyday.

This point invites a broader reflection on the politics of Islam, for which I turn to the commentary offered by Olivier Roy (2011), who is worth quoting at length:

> Dictatorships in the Arab world, though not in Tunisia, have often favoured a conservative Islam that is highly visible but not especially political, and that is obsessed with controlling public morals. [...] This has meshed with the "Salafist" movement, which emphasises the re-Islamisation of individuals rather than the development of social movements. What has been perceived

8 Among contemporary political thinkers, the Arab Springs are understood as having marked the "fourth wave of global democratization" (Magen 2012, 10), preceded by a "fourth wavelet" marked by the "transitions in Serbia (2000), Georgia (2003), and Ukraine (2004), together with steady democratic consolidation among the other Balkan states" (ibid., 11, attributing the "fourth wavelet" analysis to McFaul [2002]). "The first, long wave (1774–1926) was rooted in the values of the American and French Revolutions" (Magen 2012, 10), followed by "a second, short wave of democratization (1945–62)" with "the Allied victory in World War II and the early phases of decolonization in Asia and Africa" (ibid., 11). The third wave was sparked by the Portuguese Carnation Revolution of 1974, which quickly spread to the rest of the Iberian Peninsula and Greece and then, in the 1980s, to Latin America, sub-Saharan Africa, and Asia, and then to Central and Eastern Europe with the demise of Soviet Communism in 1989–1991 (ibid.). Magen also notes that, while these political transformations were "sudden," they "resulted from gradual socioeconomic and cultural change. Urbanization, higher levels of literacy, and the internet produced social mobilization, attitudinal change, and expectations for a better life" (ibid., 13).

Analysing the Arab revolts from a theory-of-revolutions perspective, Beck and Hüser (2012, 26) see it as "likely that at least some countries will pass through lengthy transition processes; these will be inconsistent and the results will be open. This could also lead to the emergence of hybrid regimes that cannot be clearly distinguished as consolidated democracies or autocracies for an extended period."

in the west as a great, green wave of re-Islamisation is in fact nothing but a trivialisation of Islam: everything has become Islamic, from fast food to women's fashion. The forms and structures of piety, however, have become individualised, so now one constructs one's own faith, [...] abandoning all interest in the utopia of an Islamic state. [...]

It is also a mistake to see the dictatorships as defending secularism against religious fanaticism [...]; on the contrary, they have reached an accommodation with a neofundamentalist form of re-Islamisation in which the imposition of sharia law is called for without any discussion of the nature of political power. Everywhere, official Muslim institutions, based on an austere conservative theology, have been co-opted by the state. [...]

These developments have also affected Islamist political movements, as is exemplified by the changing face of the Muslim Brotherhood in Egypt [whose share of the electorate in 2011 surpassed 40 percent] and al-Nahda, the "renaissance party," in Tunisia. [...] A new generation of militants has drawn lessons from this, as have such veterans as Rachid Ghannouchi, founder of al-Nahda. They have understood that seeking to take power in the wake of a revolution leads either to civil war or to dictatorship. [...]

Above all, the Muslim Brotherhood no longer advocates an alternative economic and social model. The Brothers have become conservative with regard to morality and liberal on the economy. This is without doubt the most striking evolution in their outlook, because, in the 1980s, Islamists claimed to defend the interests of the oppressed classes and called for state ownership of the economy and redistribution of wealth. Today, the Muslim Brotherhood in Egypt endorses Mubārak's agricultural counter-reforms, which have returned to landowners the right to raise prices and sack tenant farmers. So complete has this transformation been that Islamists are now wholly absent from the social movements active in the Nile Delta, where there has been a resurgence of the "left," particularly of trade union militancy.

However, the embourgeoisement of the Islamists is at the same time an asset for democracy, because it pushes them towards reconciliation and compromise, and into alliances with other political forces. It is no longer a question, therefore, of attempting to establish whether or not dictatorships are the most effective bulwark against Islamism; Islamists have become players in the democratic game.

After the fall of President Muḥammad Mursī, however, the Muslim Brotherhood was outlawed as a terrorist organization. This altered the dynamics of the Islamists' political participation, making the future of Egypt extremely uncertain.

10.3 The civil war in Libya

After the events in Tunisia and Egypt, the Arab revolt spread to Libya, where it toppled the dictatorship of Colonel Muʿammar Gaddafi. What sparked the protest was a commemoration held to mark the Abū Sālim prison massacre of

1996, which according to Human Rights Watch (2006) may have claimed the lives of as many as 1,200 prisoners. These were by and large political prisoners, under the watch of the Internal Security Agency, at whose discretion prisoners considered to pose a security threat could be held in detention indefinitely.

The revolt in Cyrenaica spread to Benghazi and al-Bayḍāʾ and across the entire region. In order to quell the uprisings, Gaddafi recruited mercenary troops from Chad and Uganda, for they had no ties of tribal kinship with the local population, and so had no qualms about opening fire on the protesters. The protesters were demanding an overhaul of the criminal justice system in a country that had made it a crime to object to the aims of the Great Socialist People's Libyan Arab Jamāhīriyya. Contemporary news reports highlight all the obstacles the protest met as it sought to mobilize the population in a harshly repressive environment. No one at first could predict the outcome of the clash, since Libya, unlike Tunisia and Egypt, had severed its ties with the international community, retreating into a state of isolation that enabled it to keep the country under a state of totalitarian control. As a result, the regime could carry out a bloody crackdown campaign despite defections in the Libyan army and air force. And when international pressure was put on the regime, especially from Europe, the regime threatened to ease its border controls, which meant pulling back on its commitment to cooperate on immigration (Guolo 2011, 22).

The strength of the regime rested on a massive security apparatus. The inner circle of Gaddafi's regime consisted of a cadre of free officers, in which were the colonel's sons. Then came three other circles: a second one consisting of a council of comrades, forming a core of a hundred or so high-ranking government officials; a third one consisting of the Basic People's Congress, charged with doling out government aid to the population; and a fourth one consisting of a retinue of people associated with Gaddafi by way of family ties, group interests, or patronage.[9]

There were also two militias: the Revolutionary Guard Corps and the People's Security Organization. It is the latter—with its complex, widely branched apparatus—that makes it possible to explain why the regime acted as it did in response to the revolt movement (Negri 2011, 4).

The challenge the regime was facing was new and entirely unpredictable. What was coming into shape was not a struggle against colonial rule to establish an independent nation or consolidate a religious identity. It was instead a struggle for individual rights, nor could it be assimilated to radical Islamism.

So, too, as the uprisings spread, they began to have repercussions on Libya's economic relations. The country's main trading partner was Italy. Italy was

9 The main characteristic of the Gaddafi regime lay in its lack of classes, tribes, and political parties. It was in this context that the regime could wield power, through a sociopolitical tool consisting of a group built in virtue of and around a leader—or *zaʿim*—on the basis of pledges of personal loyalty (Lahmar 2012, 124). What held together Gaddafi's *zaʿimic* group was a web of ties based on kinship, vicinage, patronage, and alliances of interests, coupled with violence, both symbolic and physical (ibid., 123).

relying on Libya for one-quarter of its energy needs, importing 50,000 metric tonnes of oil a day from Libya. Further, the Italian energy giant ENI (Ente Nazionale Idrocarburi) had a 28-billion-euro contract with the National Oil Corporation (NOC), the national company that manages oil and gas development in Libya: under the agreement, the two companies were exploiting crude oil fields so as to increase gas production (Carlini 2011). The civil war in Libya therefore posed a threat to ENI, whose oil drills were pumping 244,000 barrels a day in the Libyan Desert. Also at risk was Finmeccanica, which had opened a plant to assemble Agusta helicopters and was fulfilling orders worth 1,750 million euros to update the Libyan railway signalling system. The Italo-Libyan Chamber of Commerce was representing 180 firms, with about 1,500 Italian workers in construction. There was, furthermore, the open question of Libyan investment in Italy, with stakes in ENI, Finmeccanica, Iveco, and Impregilo.[10] It is finally worth mentioning that Italy was exporting arms to Libya: in 2008, Libya was the ninth biggest client of the Italian armaments industry, with yearly sales of 93.2 million euros (Carlini 2011). So there were huge questions about the reconstruction that would have to be undertaken in Libya after the civil war that was laying waste to the country.

The secular movements had been crushed under a campaign of violent repression carried out in 1993. The Islamist movements, for their part, formed a complex patchwork with elements of Islamic fundamentalism, regional rivalry, and tribal strife. Compounding these problems was an explosive cocktail in Cyrenaica, where Islamic opposition had always been active. The repression Gaddafi had waged against these groups left a trail of blood that spawned retaliatory vendettas—a force that was posing one of the biggest threats to the future of Libya.

The instability of the Libyan regime was tied to its being divided into three regions—Tripolitania, Cyrenaica, and Fezzan (see Mezran 2011, 54ff.)—whose relations with one another had historically been tenuous. There have always been deep-rooted tribal antagonisms among the tribal components of the three regions. Particularly intractable were the problems stemming from the competing interests that pitted Tripolitania against Cyrenaica—the former a prevalently urban area, the latter deeply tribal in its heritage, and governed by a tightly knit web of mystical orders. It was in this motley cultural landscape that the Sānūsiyya order and clan became a ruling dynasty in 1950, having built its base in the Cyrenaican tribal society.[11]

The allegiances and drivers of action rooted in these traditions remained firmly in place even after the 1969 Libyan coup d'état led by Gaddafi. As has

10 On the financial interests Libya established in Italy by way of Libyan funds invested in Italian banks and government-run entities, and on the ensuing Libyan crisis and the challenging effort to protect Italian interests in Libya, see Varvelli 2012, 129ff.

11 On the history of the Sānūsiyya order in Cyrenaica, where in 1841 Sayyid Muhammad bin ʿAli al-Senussi established his first centre for worship and religious training, see Cricco 2012, 41ff.

been pointed out, this is why "if nothing had moved in Cyrenaica, the uprising would likely not have reached Tripoli and would not have brought about the fall of the regime" (Del Boca 2011; my translation). It was when this delicate balance began to break down that Libya began to descend into chaos, a perilous slide which the country's geopolitical position made even worse for two reasons. The first was that Libya extends into sub-Saharan Africa, making it a privileged channel for migrants moving up from the southern regions of the world. The second had to do with the mobility of al-Qaeda in the Islamic Maghreb (AQIM), for this enabled these terrorist groups to destabilize Libya and use the country as a staging ground from which to expand their operations into sub-Saharan Africa and into the rest of the Arab world (in so doing following the template they had perfected in Afghanistan).

Libya was therefore the Arab country with the greatest exposure to the risk of collapse. As has been commented, Libya was the Mediterranean equivalent of Afghanistan, for the condition it found itself in made it difficult to see how it could possibly transition towards democracy (Allam 2011, 5). In this regard, several options were put on the table when the civil war broke out:

- The first set of options was humanitarian, where the concern was to evacuate Westerners who found themselves stuck in Libya.
- A suite of political-economic options were discussed that included economic and military sanctions, a total embargo on the arms used in the regime's clampdown, and a freeze on the assets belonging to the Gaddafi clan. This led to UN (United Nations) Security Council Resolution 1970 of 26 February 2011, which imposed the arms embargo and the asset freeze and referred "the situation in the Libyan Arab Jamāhīriyya since 15 February 2011 to the Prosecutor of the International Criminal Court" (ICC) in The Hague (UNSC 2011a, item 4).

  This last measure—the legal measure adopted by the UN Security Council—was selected from a menu of options that had been considered. These included creating an ad hoc international court like the ones that had been set up for the former Yugoslavia and for Rwanda, charging the regime with crimes against humanity before the ICC, or bringing the charges before national courts, which would have been able to prosecute the crimes where they had been committed, and would have done so relying on an existing judicial system—to which end, however, the national courts would have had to be flanked by international ones so as to ensure a fair and impartial process. But, as we just saw, it was ultimately decided to refer the matter to the ICC.

  This decision took observers by surprise, considering that China, Russia, and the United States had all objected to these crimes being tried by the ICC. It was the smaller players—Great Britain, France, and Germany—that were making the case for the ICC solution, and yet it was their position that prevailed. As we saw, however, the Security Council restricted the court's mandate by instructing it to only consider the events that had unfolded since 15 February 2011, that is, since the crackdown began, in determining whether they amounted to crimes against humanity (Cassese 2011b, 7). This meant that under the 2011 Security Council resolution, the Gaddafi regime itself fell outside the ICC's personal jurisdiction. As Antonio Cassese (2011a, 41) has commented, then, the court was tasked with trying not the political regimes but the crimes that had been perpetrated: the bombing, the torturing, the abductions and killings. The fate of the regime was instead placed in the hands of the popular uprisings and of the foreign "humanitarian" interventions—which is precisely what ended up happening.

- There was finally a discussion of military options. A no-fly zone was proposed to prevent the regime from bombing its own population, and this needed a resolution to be passed by the UN Security Council. A second option was for the North Atlantic Treaty Organization (NATO) to intervene militarily with the backing of the UN, but this was a more problematic proposition. Indeed, for one thing, Libya was a highly fragmented territory controlled by the disparate forces fighting in the different regions of the country, such as Cyrenaica, and even in the cities, and this was going to make any military engagement challenging. And, for another, there was the matter of how fraught was the whole idea of "humanitarian intervention," for as history had shown, especially looking back on the NATO campaign in Kosovo, these interventions could conceal aims to control the resources of the country where the intervention is carried out. Even so, it was decided to go with the NATO intervention, despite the concerns it would inevitably raise.

The outcome was UN Security Council Resolution 1973 of 17 March 2011, which passed with ten votes in favour and five abstentions. It authorized the international community to establish a no-fly zone over Libya and to use all means necessary to protect the Libyan population except by direct occupation on the ground. The resolution stated "that the widespread and systematic attacks currently taking place in the Libyan Arab Jamāhīriyya against the civilian population may amount to crimes against humanity," and it accordingly expressed the Security Council's "determination to ensure the protection of civilians and civilian populated areas and the rapid and unimpeded passage of humanitarian assistance and the safety of humanitarian personnel" (UNSC 2011b, 1). On this basis the Security Council authorized "Member States [...], acting nationally or through regional organizations or arrangements, and [...] in cooperation with the Secretary-General, to take all necessary measures [...] to protect civilians and civilian populated areas under threat of attack in the Libyan Arab Jamāhīriyya, including Benghazi, while excluding a foreign occupation force of any form on any part of Libyan territory" (ibid., 3, item 4).

The ensuing news reports and the debates preceding and following the military intervention inevitably, once more, made fully apparent the unmanageable ambivalence packed into the idea of humanitarian intervention. Some commentators pointed out the lack of guiding principles in light of which to engage militarily in response to humanitarian interventions such as this one (see esp. Pipes 2011, 9). Others, and in particular the highly regarded Italian philosopher of law Danilo Zolo, contended that the intervention was in violation of the UN Charter, which makes it a prohibition for the "United Nations to intervene in matters which are essentially within the domestic jurisdiction of any state" (Art. 2.7): what was happening in Libya was a *civil war*; it was therefore subject to this provision, and so a matter falling within Libya's exclusive domestic jurisdiction, precluding any military intervention the UN Security Council might authorize on its own. Then, too, UN Security Council Resolution 1973 of 2011 also on several occasions invoked the responsibility-to-protect (R2P) doctrine as justification for intervening. This doctrine (discussed in Chapter 4) was first introduced by the Security Council itself under Resolution 1674 of 2006 (UNSC 2006), and as Zolo argues, it is not within the Security Council's powers to establish new rules of international law. What in this way prevailed—on this R2P basis—was the United States' hegemonic strategy, perpetuating the neocolonial policies promoted by the Western powers (Zolo 2011, 14).

10.4 After the fall of the regime

When the Libyan regime fell, with the killing of Gaddafi on 20 October 2011, the country fell into a state of confusion and disarray which persisted for several years thereafter, and from which the country has yet to fully recover. The central government remained unable to assert its own authority or to disarm the independent militias that continued to clash for control of the territory.

And there was also the question of the Muslim Brotherhood, which, unlike in Egypt and Tunisia, found itself acting in a society that, after the fall of Gaddafi, no longer needed it to carry forward a vision of Islam felt to be right for that society. In fact what the Muslim Brotherhood embraced was a Salafi vision in a society that was already Salafist in the strictest sense of the word, that is, in a nonpolitical, religiously conservative sense (Tinazzi 2013). It would indeed be misleading to view the political dynamics in Libya through the false lens of the clash between Islamists, on the one hand, and liberals and secularists, on the other. For the real problem was that of security, which meant disbanding the paramilitary groups. The tribal councils continued to interfere with the central government's ability to assert its own power, and at the same time it was proving difficult to disarm the militias (ibid.). In short, the biggest hurdle that Libya needs to overcome before it can fully transition to democracy lies in the fact it lacks the conditions needed to build a strong central government.

Libya was a rentier state, meaning a state whose revenues derive in large part from the rent that foreign entities pay for its natural resources. In Libya's case, this meant the income it received from its sale of oil on the international market (Varvelli and Villa 2012, 232). A state so configured has no need for democratic institutions, for it can raise revenue without levying high taxes on the population, and so it does not have to rely on popular consent or participation for its legitimacy. This position of advantage enjoyed by resource-rich countries, and oil-rich ones in particular, helps to explain the predominance of authoritarian regimes in the Middle East and the challenge they face in transitioning towards democracy.

Built into these rentier or "distributive states" (Vandewalle 1998, 7) is the paradox whereby, on the one hand, they have a weak administrative and fiscal apparatus, precisely because they are not highly dependent on tax revenues, but at the same time they have stable forms of government, for they lack the democratic organization that could enable the people to organize and mobilize. Before the civil war, Libya could be described as a rentier state owing to the control it exerted on the inflow of oil revenues, but its institutional makeup was not statelike: as noted, it rather consisted of a patchwork of informal organizations, clans, committees, and militias that all answered to Gaddafi's dictatorial regime. It was *organizationally* a stable system, to be sure, but it did not manage to diversify its own economy, and so it felt the full brunt of the volatility the oil market experienced in 1975 and of the sanctions the United States imposed on Libya from 1986 to 1990. In addition, the Libyan regime was highly dependent on foreign technology and know-how.

The outcome was persistent high youth unemployment (about 20 percent), coupled with significant wealth disparities between the different regions of Libya, Cyrenaica being particularly hard hit. This was the economic picture in the period leading to the outbreak of the uprisings in Tunisia and Egypt, an outbreak that in turn conspired with the economic malaise to make conditions ripe for the revolts that would soon break out against the dictatorial regime in Libya.

The end of Gaddafi changed the situation in profound ways. Which is to say that the challenge confronting Libya was not just one of state-building: it was also, and most crucially, a *nation*-building challenge. Indeed, when the Gaddafi regime fell, what remained was a fractured Libya made up of regional and clan or tribal allegiances—an intricate sociopolitical landscape prone to instability, and with the added peril of militias bearing little or no connection to the central government.

Finally, there was Libya's structural persistence as a rentier or "distributive" state that has not been able to effect an authentic democratic-participation process: this was making unfeasible the prospect of any transition towards democracy (Varvelli and Villa 2012, 247–48). On top of that was the aforementioned clash between armed militias, as well as the fragility of the democratically elected parliament and government, making it difficult to prefigure what the future of Libya might look like.[12]

12 On the Libyan situation, fractured between the "legitimate" government in Tobruk and the "revolutionary" militias that in 2014 joined forces under the Libya Dawn banner to take control of Tripoli, see Toaldo 2015.

10.5 Autumn after spring?

The transition processes that have unfolded in the post-Gaddafi era have sparked much controversy, and there have also been careful analyses that were making predictions about the end of these processes. In an article published just after the fall of Gaddafi, Lucio Caracciolo (2011, 35) warned of the risk that the Arab Springs would grind to a halt. He was drawing attention to two developments—the Saudi-led intervention in Bahrain and the war to overthrow Gaddafi—that in his judgment had acted as the spark for the counter-revolution. The Saudi-led intervention in Bahrain seemed emblematic of the geopolitical relations that were taking shape: its objective was to prevent the region from falling into Iranian hands, and it was allowed to proceed without eliciting any condemnation from the Western democracies. The war to overthrow Gaddafi, for its part, revealed just how crucial a role the Islamist brigades had played in toppling the regime. As Caracciolo pointed out, these brigades were led on the ground by a proper jihadist, ʿAbd al-ḥakīm Belhaj, and their spiritual father was the Islamist cleric Sheikh ʿAlī al-Salabī, an exponent of the Muslim Brotherhood, who called on Prime Minister Maḥmūd Jibrīl to step down along with the other so-called secularists in the National Transitional Council he chaired (ibid.).

Caracciolo analyses the way in which the fall of Gaddafi, in putting an end to a ruthless dictatorship, set in train a "counterrevolution led by the Gulf's petro-monarchies" (ibid.; my translation). With the backing of the United States and the other Western powers, these monarchies acted to prevent the Arab Spring from spreading to the Arabian Peninsula. This led to a series of consequences:

- The secular progressive forces that had taken to the streets in protest ebbed slowly away.
- By contrast, an array of Islamist forces ranging from the Muslim Brotherhood to the Salafi groups gained strength, acting in agreement with the Persian Gulf countries run by Sunni monarchies.
- The armed forces took centre stage as the real locus of power in Egypt.
- Little or no action came from any Western or Arab country in response to the Syrian crackdown on its own people.
- Cairo saw a resurgence of anti-Israeli and anti-Semitic sentiments.

In view of these aftereffects, Caracciolo was inviting us not to get swept up in enthusiasm for the Arab Springs, and to instead take a good, hard look at them. With that said, the Mediterranean continues to hold the contradictions that have always been woven into its fabric: these contradictions originate out of conflict, to be sure, but they can also open windows of opportunity that can be exploited in the effort to forge a "new world." As we cast our eyes across the countries that have been absorbed into the Arab Springs—Tunisia, Egypt, and Libya—we see a highly diversified landscape, yielding outcomes that are highly controversial.

10.5.1 *What peace for Libya?*

The fall of the Gaddafi regime created a scenario where it seemed possible to put relations between Europe and Libya on a new footing. We can set the scene here by going back to UN Security Council Resolution 1973 of 2011 (UNSC 2011b): we saw that this was the legal basis for the intervention in Libya, and we also saw that this document invoked the R2P doctrine, claiming that it was justified to intervene on the basis of a responsibility protect the civilian population. And yet, as has been commented, at no time *after* the fall of the regime did the international community invoke a "responsibility to rebuild" a country that had fallen into disarray (Costantini 2018, 228).

Behind this retreat from the scene in the wake of the intervention were two lines of reasoning: on the one hand it was thought that Libya could manage a political and economic transition on its own; at the same time, there was scepticism about embarking on such projects, considering the failed attempts that had recently been made in countries like Iraq and Afghanistan.

The idea was to stabilize the country by facilitating a process internal to it, to this end relying on the United Nations Support Mission in Libya (UNSMIL). But it proved impossible to achieve this aim in the face of the divisions by which the country was plagued. The first parliament elected after the fall of the Gaddafi regime was the General National Council, which proved incapable of putting together a unitary political and institutional framework. This was because of the fragmentation of the Libyan society—which, as we saw, was parcelled into tribes and families—and because of the form of government that had been set up by Gaddafi, a form based on the idea of a "government of the masses" (Jamāhīriyya) (ibid., 223), under which all efforts to achieve a stable set of institutions had stalled. In 2012 new elections were held that led to the establishment of a House of Representatives, but this was done against the opposition of the General National Council, which held itself up as the country's only legitimate legislative body.

The UN's subsequent support mission opened negotiations that led to what is known as the Libyan Political Agreement, signed in Shkirat, Morocco, in December 2015. Under this agreement, a Presidential Council was established, and then a Government of National Accord was formed, based in Tripoli and headed by Prime Minister Fayez al-Sarraj (UN 2015). But what this setup gave rise to was a bipolar political situation, with one locus of power in Tripolitania, where the Presidential Council was located, and another in Tobruk, Cyrenaica, where the House of Representatives was based, under the leadership of General Khalifa Haftar.

"The prevalence of militias in Libya undermined the authority of the central government and worsened security to unprecedented levels, thereby causing conditions conducive to the emergence of new militias" (Fraihat 2016, 30),[13] which "functioned like a state within a state" (ibid.). In May 2014,

> Khalifa Haftar, a former general who returned to Libya during the uprising to fight against Qaddafi and ultimately became a militia commander [commander-in-chief of the self-proclaimed Libyan National Army], launched what he called Operation Dignity, a campaign to eliminate all Islamist and pro-Islamist militias in Libya. Based in the Eastern part of the country, Haftar's forces started to attack both February 17 revolutionaries [of the Libya Revolt of 2011] who fought against Qaddafi and Ansar al-Sharia, a Salafi jihadi militia based in Benghazi. These groups and others formed an alliance called the Shura Council of Benghazi Revolutionaries. In Western Libya, including Tripoli, Haftar allied with the powerful Zentan militia, which played a prominent role in the fight against the Qaddafi regime but is more tribal than ideological. Another anti-Haftar alliance, Libya Dawn (Fajr Libya), emerged in response, composed of the powerful Misrata militia, Islamist factions called the Libya Revolutionary Operations Room and Libya Shield Force, and tribal militias such as the Zawyan and Sibratan. [...] the outcome of all these developments is that Libya is facing a brutal, two-front civil war [...]. (Ibid., 31)
>
> General Haftar's campaign has defined the intra-revolutionaries' civil war as a struggle between Islamists and non-Islamists. This characterization has not only inflamed domestic tensions along those lines but has also encouraged regional actors to intervene. Egypt and the United Arab Emirates have gone so far as to conduct air strikes" [in support of Haftar's forces, which subsequently also gained the support of Russia], while Libya Dawn is reportedly receiving support from Turkey and Qatar. This regional dimension only adds to the complexity of the transition process and makes Libya's crises particularly difficult to solve. (Ibid., 32–33)
>
> It is very unlikely that Libya's civil war will end in a definitive military victory for either side in the foreseeable future. This only increased the importance of Libya's pursuing a national dialogue sooner rather than later. Its civil war needs a negotiated agreement in which all parties take part. (Ibid., 33)

10.5.2 Europe's role

It is in the context just outlined that Europe decided to intervene. Driving this decision were two key factors: the first was that the European Union's interests in Libya were not in line with those of the United States; the second was the issue

13 As Mieczyslaw P. Boduszynsky and Kristin Fabbe observe, "militias in Libya offer young men power, prestige and money exceeding anything that the official state can provide" (quoted in Fraihat 2016, 30; the quotation in context in Boduszynski and Fabbe 2014).

of migration out of Libya, which became a real concern owing to Libya's proximity to Europe. The military operations in Libya, especially those of France and Italy, were carried out supporting different political forces and in cooperation with different militias (see Toaldo 2016, 2).[14]

There was much evidence suggesting that these interventions were ultimately undertaken with an eye on Libya's oil resources. The problem of oil resources lay at the heart of the struggles for power in Libya, with different political actors advancing different plans: the oil companies were putting pressure on Tripoli for special access to the country's oil; a separate government had been set up in the Eastern part of the country under Ibrahim Jadhran, head of the Petroleum Facility Guard for Central Libya, who in 2013 seized a series of major oil terminals so as to export oil illegally (Costantini 2018, 232); and the governments in Tripoli and Tobruk were clashing over control of the country's main oil entities, among which the National Oil Company. The international community and the European countries only tried to exploit this conflict and havoc that was unfolding in Libya: they did so lending their support to different political actors, but in an extremely volatile context that would not be able to sustain any stable economic and trade relations until a viable political institutional framework was in place.

The political instability in Libya also made it impossible to control the flow of migration off the coast. The EU responded by trying to stem the problem at source, which meant ramping up border security along the Libyan coastline and detaining migrants in containment centres—a policy that translated into a practice amounting to a constant string of serious human rights violation.

Libya's instability is the outcome of a complex intersection of political, economic, and military causes, both domestic and regional (Toaldo 2016, 7).[15] Instead of supporting this or that political actor or force in Libya, the European countries should therefore be working to promote national reconciliation under a broad scheme of cooperation with Libya and the whole of Africa. We have so far seen a variety of security strategies that involve fighting terrorism or trying to stem the flow of migration by supporting the Libyan Coast Guard. But these targeted operations will inevitably be limited in their effect if pursued without looking at the bigger picture, and so are unlikely to lead to any conclusive solution.

14 As of late 2016, the situation on the ground in Libya was one in which thousands of militias were fighting one another pursuing different agendas, but all seeking to gain control of the oil infrastructure (see Toaldo and Fitzgerald 2016).

15 It would indeed be remiss to leave out the role played by regional actors. Emblematic in this regard, Mezran (2018, 2) observes, is the case of Egypt: "The support Cairo has given to Haftar was intended to keep Islamist groups out of power in Libya and away from the border between the two countries. It was also aimed at re-establishing order in Libya so as to initiate the process of economic reconstruction, of which Egypt planned to obtain a lion's share." Also worth underscoring in this connection is the interest that Russia has increasingly been taking in Libya, growing increasingly attuned to the Libyan theatre's role in the regional and international geopolitical game board, in which Russian interests are aligning with those of the main European players (see Stepanova 2018, 108ff.).

In conclusion, if we look at the way the EU responded to the Libyan crisis or the way the Arab Spring worked itself out in Egypt, or again the way Europe showed itself to be ineffectual in the face of the Syrian crisis, we can appreciate the inadequacy of the EU's Euro-Mediterranean policies and the lack of adequate tools for managing these crises, mainly on account of the political divisions within the EU itself. In this age of multipolarity, the EU should instead work with other regional and international actors in tackling the problems affecting the Mediterranean, and should do so by implementing a "new security architecture" in the region (Colombo and Huber 2016, 35–36).[16]

10.6 Revolt and revolution in Tunisia

As we saw, the Arab Spring uprisings came in reaction to unsustainable living conditions owed to a combination of corruption, repression, and economic hardship. We saw in Chapter 9 that what lit the fuse on the Tunisian Revolution was an act of desperation by a twenty-six-year-old street vendor named Muḥammad al-Būʿazīzī. Būʿazīzī had to leave secondary school when his father died, making him the breadwinner for the entire family (his mother and six siblings). It was 17 December 2010 when he set himself on fire in protest, after the produce he was selling to support the family was confiscated by local officials who, in so doing, also subjected him to harassment and humiliation.

What began as an act of protest snowballed into an uprising that spread across Tunisia's entire civilian society, a movement led by students who couldn't see a future ahead of them. The dry kindling that was sparked into flame with these protests was therefore in plain view: it consisted of real conditions that were familiar to all and had been extensively analysed,[17] and they made the revolution inevitable. Which in turn tells us that if the transformation which from Tunisia spread to the Arab world is to be carried through to a successful conclusion, it will have to retain its grassroots origins: its driving force, in other words, will have to reside in society.

Three sets of interlinked factors formed the backdrop against which the Tunisian Revolution took place. First, as noted, were the economic conditions. Despite some optimistic official statistics, the economy had been in bad shape at least since 2009: unemployment was high (14.2 percent) and rising, and was particularly hard (46 percent) on youths just out of school.[18]

16 If political institutions in the area are to gain legitimacy, they need to act within an electoral democratic framework. But there is no way that such a framework can be built without first committing to an institution-building process that will engage the different Libyan communities and the different regional actors. This point is also made in Eljarh 2018, 64ff.

17 See Khader 2003, underscoring the problem of a fast-growing population coupled with widespread joblessness and the European curb on immigration.

18 This economic picture was borne out in subsequent data. In fact, under the first transitional government in 2011, 27 percent of the population was living below the poverty line, while unemployment affected 700,000 people, 70 percent of whom were thirty years of age or younger (Redissi 2013, 67).

The second factor was the widespread corruption ingrained in the Ben Ali regime, which operated on a clientelistic system of quid pro quos in which private monopolies were granted to the clans tied to Ben Ali or to his family. When in 2009 a group of Tunisian economists conducted a study titled "Limites, coûts et fragilités des performances économiques tunisienne," they had to circulate it clandestinely. In it they found that "the size of the fortune one can amass in Tunisia depends on one's closeness to political power. This closeness opens the doors to banks, makes it possible to cut in front of others in line when the assets of privatized state-run companies are sold, and clears the way for monopoly positions to be maintained in certain sectors (Beau and Graciet 2009, 136, quoted in Roggero 2012, 51; my translation).

The third factor lay in the lack of freedom and democratic participation under the repressive dictatorship built by Ben Ali. It was this third factor that built the resentment which fuelled the fire of protest, and which in combination with the other factors enabled a protest on December 17 to grow into a countrywide uprising that turned an entire society "against a regime perceived to be not only authoritarian but also immoral" (Roggero 2012, 54; my translation).

As we saw in Chapter 9, this Tunisian protest movement that developed into a revolution proper gave birth to a new form of government based on broad participation by society; that is, it brought into being a form of democracy distinctive to the Arab world.[19] A prominent role in this revolutionary process was played by labour unions, which helped to organize the protest and support the spread of its grassroots initiatives. Equally significant was the role of nongovernmental organizations (NGOs), which were "disseminating documented information about the casualties and death tolls" (Hanafi 2011) and putting pressure on international bodies to take a clear stance against the regime. This highlights how important was the synergy that was formed in civil society between labour

19 When it wasn't yet at all clear that the Tunisian uprisings were going to usher in a democratic transition, Béatrice Hibou (2011, 5) commented that the true transformation resided in the "disappearance of fear" (*la disparition de la peur*). But in reality—as Hibou herself observes acknowledging the input she received from Hamza Meddeb—the Tunisian transition was marked from the start by the elements we find in every revolution, that is, by the mobilization of society through the spontaneous creation of "local and regional committees for the protection of the revolution" (*comités locaux et régionaux de protection de la révolution*) (ibid., 14). Following Hannah Arendt's ([1963] 1977) seminal analysis of revolution, we might say that these committees enabled citizens to reclaim a public space in which to express their "public freedom" or "public happiness." The Tunisian revolutionary committees, made up of lawyers in the Union Générale Tunisienne de Travail (UGTT) and of ordinary citizens, were formed to keep watch over the revolution: their aim was to make sure that Ben Ali's party—the Rassemblement Constitutionnel Démocratique—would not return to power in any form, to which end they formed a network that undertook to seek out all the party members who were believed to have been complicit in the regime's corruption, demanding that they not be appointed to offices in the new transitional government (ibid., 14–15).

unions and NGOs, while the role played by opposition forces, legal and illegal alike, was marginal at best (ibid.).

The revolution was thus started and carried forward by forces in civil society, and contrary to what happened in Egypt, where the army assumed the country's leadership, the Tunisian army was never brought out during the revolution and did not play a role in shaping Tunisia's postrevolutionary makeup. The Tunisian example can also act as a model for the entire Arab world. For the Tunisians have shown that Arab countries are capable of bringing about revolutions like those that have taken place in Latin America and Eastern Europe (Naïr 2011, 13).

The democratic model that emerged from the Arab revolutions offers insight into the possibilities for democracy itself, specifically in connection with the Arab world. In this new scenario we need to rethink the role of Europe from the ground up. In 2008 French president Nicolas Sarkozy and Egyptian president Ḥusnī Mubārak were heading the Union for the Mediterranean (UfM), an organization committed to providing Arab and North African governments with support under a realpolitik banner. But the policies they were promoting under that banner failed. In fact, when the Ben Ali regime was toppled in Tunisia, on 14 January 2011, and the country plunged into the tumult of revolution, Europe did little to help except by way of token gestures. The Tunisian minister of industry described the EU's support as "laughable" (*ridicule*): "Europe is demonstrating that it has not grasped the full significance of the historical event that has taken place. Even in aiding the birth of a democracy on its own southern shore, Europe conditions its support on the implementation of a free-market scheme and a migration policy premised on the logic of Fortress Europe" (Ben Attia 2012, 74; my translation). As this remark suggests, it is now time for the EU to rethink its entire strategy for fostering cooperation aimed at consolidating democracies along the southern Mediterranean.

In response to the Tunisian Revolution, the EU launched two financial aid programmes totalling 110 million euros to support the country's political and economic transition, with a specific emphasis on improving social conditions and the job market. But this European aid is "a trifling amount compared with the 4,589 billion euros the EU allocated to rescue its own banking system [in the wake of the 2008 financial crisis]—a drop in an ocean of needs!" (ibid.).

The Tunisian case stands out for its complexity. The constituent assembly elections held on 23 October 2011 saw the rise of the Islamist al-Nahḍa (Renaissance) Party, which emerged as the main player in the first phase of the country's transition towards democracy. Al-Nahḍa won 89 seats out of a total of 217, gaining 37 percent of the votes, which bumped up to 41 percent under a proportional electoral system that favours large electoral lists. Moncef Marzouki's Congress for the Republic (CPR), outperforming all secular parties, took 29 seats (Redissi 2013, 69), followed by Pétition Populaire, with 26 seats; al-Takattul (Democratic Forum for Labour and Liberties, or FDTL, short for

Forum Démocratique pour le Travail et les Libertés), with 20 seats; and Parti Démocratique Progressiste, with 16 seats.[20]

The outcome of the 2011 constituent assembly elections reflected Tunisia's composite and syncretic character, offering a snapshot of a country that has retained its Arab Islamic tradition but has not forsaken the experience of its reformist past, either. Al-Nahḍa won the elections running on the message that the country needed to recover its traditional Muslim values of integrity and honesty so as to fight back the corruption of the secularised and Westernized elites that had governed the country until that time. In packaging this message, the party was able to turn to advantage the history of persecutions it had suffered at the hands of the former regime; even more importantly, however, it proved to be particularly adept at organizing and connecting directly with the people.

It also bears pointing out that al-Nahḍa did not campaign arraying itself against the secularist legacy of Habib Bourguiba. The party's charismatic leader, Rāshid al-Ghannūshī, was careful to reassure the electorate that the party was in favour of women's rights—such as the right of women to choose whether they want to wear a Muslim headscarf, as well as the right to seek a divorce—and it was also made clear that the party would not seek to repeal the 1956 Code of Personal Status. In short, as has been commented by Al-Hadi Bulleid, who teaches constitutional law in Tunisia, al-Nahḍa clearly understood that Tunisians are by and large moderate Muslims who embrace progress and the civil and individual rights protected in Europe, even if they claim to be supporters of political Islam (Al-Ahram Weekly 2011, 2). The party that came in second—Moncef Marzouki's secularist CPR—said it was open to forming a coalition with al-Nahḍa but warned that it would at once exit the governing coalition if al-Nahḍa should push policies undermining the civil liberties of Tunisians.

As for the democratic model that was being proposed for Tunisia, al-Ghannūshī has on several occasions compared his own al-Nahḍa to Tayyip Erdoğan's Justice and Development party in Turkey, underscoring al-Nahḍa's

20 I should also point out the presence of Salafism as a political force in Tunisia. The first Salafi party to be legalized in Tunisia was Jabhat al Iṣlāḥ (Tunisian Islamic Reform Front): this happened in March 2012 (Zelin 2012) but the party has yet to gain any seats in the Assembly of the Representatives of the People.

In July 2012 a second Salafi party was legalized, called Ḥizb al Taḥrīr (Party of Liberation), and in its agenda is the establishment of a caliphate.

There is then a third group called Anṣār al Sharīʿa (Supporters of Islamic Law in Tunisia), founded by Abū ʿIyāḍ (see Longo 2013). This group was allied with al-Nahḍa but was banned after the US embassy in Tunis was attacked in September 2012. The group is thought to have subsequently ordered the 2013 assassinations of Chokri Belaïd and Mohamed Brahim, two leaders of the non-Islamic opposition. In connection with these killings, a formal accusation was brought against the group by Prime Minister Ali Larayedh.

pragmatism,[21] as well as its ambition to fortify the rule of law in Tunisia and rebuild the country's economy.

Despite these reassurances, when al-Nahḍa gained power and formed a governing coalition in Tunisia, it embarked on a process to Islamicize Tunisian society,[22] which reacted energetically against this government policy. This response, spelling the failure of the al-Nahḍa-led government, led it to step down, which in turn cleared the ground for the enactment of a new constitution in Tunisia and the creation of a democratic form of government (a process we looked at in Chapter 9).

But the Tunisian reality is much different from what we find in other Arab countries, like Egypt, Libya, Yemen, or Syria, where internal conflicts and regional meddling have effectively stymied the effort to transition towards democracy.

10.7 The crisis of the Arab Spring in Egypt

The 2011 election to the People's Assembly of Egypt, held on November 28, introduced a new political dialectic that set the conditions for the country to break away from the situation of simmering conflict that had hitherto been lurking in the background. Until the election, the opposition had come from the protest movement in Taḥrīr Square or from the army. In the election, the largest share of the votes (38 percent) went, as predicted, to the Freedom and Justice Democratic Alliance affiliated with the Muslim Brotherhood, while the Salafi al-Nūr party beat expectations by gaining 28 percent of the vote. These electoral outcomes effectively sidelined the Taḥrīr Square movement. What came into being was a new rivalry that pit the Muslim Brotherhood against the army, but in a dialectic that initially suggested the possibility of building a constitutional democracy.

21 Paradoxically, the Islamist victories in the Arab world have been construed by Asef Bayat as marking the beginning of a post-Islamist era. Bayat, a professor of sociology, global and transnational studies, and Middle Eastern studies at the University of Illinois at Urbana-Champaign, argues that the Arab Spring revolutions have moved beyond Islamist politics and that "the Iranian experience of 1979 may well remain the first and last Islamic revolution of our time" (Bayat 2011). He makes this argument pointing to the democratic trends and movements that have emerged in the Middle East. "Post-Islamism," he explains, "is not anti-Islamic or secular; a post-Islamist movement dearly upholds religion but also highlights citizens' rights. It aspires to 'a pious society within a democratic state' in which all Muslims and non-Muslims could enjoy access to certain basic rights" (ibid.). In regard to Tunisia, Bayat points out that al-Ghannūshī, the founder of the main Islamist party in Tunisia, has publicly come out against the idea of a state fashioned after the Iranian model.

22 Observing al-Nahḍa's track record in government in postrevolutionary Tunisia, Hamadi Redissi found that there was "no lack of signs pointing to the construction of a new dictatorship" (Redissi 2013, 72; my translation). He was referring to the creation of "organized militias in the ranks of the Leagues for the Protection of the Tunisian Revolution: after the [2011] elections, these militias were legalized by the Islamist interior minister, Ali Larayedh" (ibid.). In this development Redissi saw "the risk of a 'theo-democracy' if the Islamists should win the elections" (ibid.) scheduled for October 2014.

What deserves close attention here is the rise of Islamist parties in the Arab world: in late October 2011, the al-Nahḍa party in Tunisia gained 40 percent of the vote, taking 89 of the 217 seats in the constituent assembly that had enacted the new constitution. A few weeks later the Moroccan Justice and Development party followed suit, gaining a 107-seat majority in Parliament. Then came the Egyptian elections just discussed. And even in Libya the Islamist forces played a prominent role in the civil war, having led the offensive against Gaddafi, and they continue to shape the political scene.

According to the Palestinian journalist ʿAbd al-Bāriʾ ʿAṭwān, these electoral outcomes can be explained by looking at the average Arab voter: a moderate Muslim who places trust in Islamic parties, having long endured the corruption and oppression of the dictatorial regimes that have plundered the country (see UNIMED 2013, 3).

In the Egyptian parliamentary elections of November 2011, the Muslim Brotherhood won 216 seats out of a total of 498, while the Salafist parties of the Islamist Alliance won 125 seats (109 of which were taken by the al-Nūr Party alone). It was this electoral outcome that ushered in the new political phase just mentioned, shoving aside the Taḥrīr Square movement while putting the spotlight on the political standoff between the Muslim Brotherhood and the Supreme Council of the Armed Forces (SCAF).

Here it is worth taking a closer look at the complex composition of the Muslim Brotherhood and the ideological and religious sources of their policies.[23] The movement placed much emphasis on schooling in society through what is known as *daʿwam*, or inviting one to a Muslim education. However, when the Freedom and Justice Party (FJP) was founded in 2011, the Muslim Brotherhood felt compelled to go directly into politics, so as to engage directly with the concrete problems and aspirations of the Egyptian people.

Furthermore, the Arab Springs ushered in a pluralism that was also "reflected within the Brotherhood, which now has a new guard, often more open, alongside the old one, and different Sufi and Salafist orientations" (Dīn ʿArafāt 2012).[24] The new political situation brought about by the Arab Springs exposed and magnified the contradictions inherent in the Brotherhood. Indeed, a new party

23 In an insightful analysis of the political dialectic that set the Muslim Brotherhood against the Ḥusnī Mubārak regime, Massimo Campanini (2011, 19ff.) underscores the latter's shift in attitude, pointing out that in the 1980s the Muslim Brotherhood was tacitly tolerated, only to be labelled a terrorist organization in the 1990s, when it was subjected to political repression and persecution. But the Muslim Brotherhood knew how to ingrain itself into Egyptian society by forming ties with professional associations, like those of doctors, lawyers, and engineers. Looking at the Muslim Brotherhood's time in government, Campanini observes that "its moderate Islamism continues to serve as an essential reference point in Egypt, and the movement's grassroots-Islamification strategy looks all the more interesting in view of how important the relation between Islam and democracy is in the twenty-first century" (ibid., 20; my translation).

24 The term *Salafism* traces its origin to the Arab word *salaf*, meaning "ancestor" and alluding to the conduct of the prophet Muhammad and his companions.

emerged called Al-Wasaṭ (Centre Party) that can be characterized as the Egyptian equivalent of the Justice and Development Party (AKP) in Turkey. Until the Egyptian coup d'état in 2013, Al-Wasaṭ was led by ʿAbū l-ʿAlā' Māḍī, who embraced democratic citizenship under a view of Islam consistent with modernity.

One Al-Wasaṭ leader is the Egyptian thinker Muḥammad Salīm al-ʿAwā, a proponent of moderate Islam whose political view can be captured under six principles as follows: (1) *shūrā* (consulation); (2) *ʿadl* (justice); (3) *ḥurriyya* (freedom); (4) *musāwāt* (equality); (5) *musā'alat al-ḥukkām wa ṭāʿatuhum* (prescribing the accountability of governors and their allegiance to the state); and (6) *al-amr bi-l-maʿrūf wa-l-nahī ʿan al-munkar*, an ethical conception of the state predicated on promoting the good and eradicating evil.[25] In short, this ethico-political conception accepts the nation-state model—a territorial state enclosed within its own borders, and whose citizens are recognized as such independently of their religious beliefs—only so long as it implements the Islamic principles just listed.[26]

25 In a critique of this conception, Massimo Campanini (2013, 46 and 49–52) comments that on the one hand it is overly indeterminate—for it does not specify what the institutional arrangement is under which it ought to be put into practice—but on the other hand it looks flexible enough to support the creation of a participatory form of democracy. This latter path, Campanini argues, can show a way out of the crisis of Western-style representative democracy in the Arab world.

26 As Al-ʿAwā (2007, 280) writes, outlining the main thrust of his conception, "if one recognises the pluralistic nature of humans, and recognises their rights to disagree and differ, one must inevitably, and without much effort, recognise pluralism in the political sphere." In presenting this view, he importantly offers insights into his method by pointing out what he sees as the main distortions of "Islamic political thought" (ibid.). The first of these "is that writings on Islam and Islamic thought continue to be constrained by the unquestioning adoption of ancient writings (*taqlīd*), copying them, building on them and considering them fundamentals and references for analogy (*qiyās*)" (ibid.). He further points out in this regard that, while the Prophet's "companions and their successors did exercise whatever they deemed to serve the interests of the people so long as it did not contradict the Revelation" (ibid., 282), "they did not restrict themselves to the revealed texts alone" (ibid.). He therefore asks: "what do revealed texts or Islamic fundamentals obligate the people to do in the running of their daily affairs, and what do they forbid them from doing?" (ibid., 282–83). We can answer this question, he says, by "emphasising that Islamic references do not outline a specific path for mankind to pursue in order to attain the political objectives stated in the Qur'ān and the Sunnah" (ibid., 283).

Hence the pluralism inherent in his Islamic conception of society: "Islamic fundamentals (sources) provide universal or general values which leave the *ummah* (community) unrestricted and capable of creative thinking and unlimited search for the best means of organisation and re-organisation. These include the means necessary for preserving the *ummah*'s right to live under the banner of Islamic values and for preventing rulers from becoming tyrants and oppressors" (ibid., 284). "It is only common sense," he goes on to comment, "that these means should vary from time to time and from one location to the other. For instance, a community that is under colonial control may have to resort to methods inapplicable to other places, or to means that were never employed by previous generations or other communities. Under certain circumstances, it may be feasible to borrow from the experiences and methods of other cultures if these are thought to guarantee and protect rights and freedoms" (ibid.). Recourse to these methods amounts to the political pluralism advocated by Al-ʿAwā—a pluralism that, as he argues, is not in any way incompatible with Islam.

A second rupture within the Muslim Brotherhood came in July 2011, when Muḥammad Ḥabīb founded the Renaissance Party in Egypt, with a platform close to that of Māḍī's Al-Wasaṭ Party. And a third rupture, in the same year, came when ʿAbd al-Munʿim Abū l-Futūḥ ran for president without the Brotherhood's endorsement. He was part of a breakaway faction that was promoting a moderate agenda premised on a view of the Islamic state as a "civilian state." As discussed in Chapter 8, this is a hybrid form of state that Tariq Ramadan explains by pointing out its double-sided makeup: on the one hand, it is a state based on traditional institutions like the *shura* (consultation), while, on the other hand, operationally, in its actual decision-making, it relies on the authority of its civilian institutions. This decision-making, based on majority voting, in turn operates through the categories of "good and error" rather than through those of "faith and its rejection," in such a way as to ensure harmony with religious and political pluralism (see Ramadan 2011, 168, quoted in Campanini 2013, 49; my translation). Furthermore, the civilian state is a government run not by religious clerics but by popularly elected officials.

Finally, the Muslim Brotherhood participated in the Egyptian presidential election of 2012 by advancing its own candidate, Khayrat al-Shāṭir, who was then excluded from the race, whereupon it put Muḥammad Mursī on the ballot. This shows that in the Brotherhood there existed a pluralism that was naturally going have an impact on the electoral results.

We should then consider the weight of the Salafist groups, who advanced their standing within Egyptian society by doing charity work. After the Egyptian revolution of 2011, they steered a course away from the Muslim Brotherhood by founding their own political parties. Next to the dominant party (al-Nūr), there also emerged other parties, among which was the Construction and Development Party, whose platform can be described as jihadist.

But in Salafist leadership we also find politicians close to the younger generation of the Muslim Brotherhood. This means that even the Salafists are forced to be pragmatic, which in turn suggests that they will probably have to soften up some their hard-line stances, such as their commitment to an Islamic caliphate.

So the political landscape that was shaping up on the eve of the 2012 presidential election was replete with question marks, and two in particular that made for a great deal of uncertainty. For one thing, there had yet to be drafted a constitution, and as a result it was unclear what powers the new president would have. And, for another thing, there was the question of the SCAF, which on the one hand had given assurances that it would definitively relinquish the power it held over civilian authorities, but on the other hand appeared to be still deeply involved in shaping the country's politics (UNIMED 2012).

There was also a deeply polarizing climate of mistrust between the secular front and the Islamist one: even if a charismatic Islamic-leaning candidate like Abū l-Futūḥ was putting forward a liberal vision, people suspected him of sneaking in an agenda of "Islamification by stealth." Although an attempt was made to find some common ground—specifically by ʿAmr Mūsā, who had formerly served as secretary general of the League of Arab States—these appeals were viewed as throwbacks to the earlier regime. As for Muḥammad Mursī, the candidate officially backed by the Muslim Brotherhood, he was advancing a conservative agenda tempered with a great dose of political pragmatism.

Completing this picture of uncertainty was the institutional question of what would happen in the event of election fraud: these cases would be taken up by the National Elections Commission, whose judgment was unappealable, and whose chair was Fārūq Sulṭān, a former army officer and president of the constitutional court that on 10 April 2012 had dissolved the constituent assembly.

On top of that, the military junta fanned the flames of division between the secular parties and the Islamist FJP affiliated with the Muslim Brotherhood by scuttling the parliament's attempts to form a new constituent assembly. In the limbo of this institutional deadlock, the military issued a statement saying that if no constituent assembly could be formed, the military itself would issue a provisional constitution that would give the SCAF control over its own budget and over armaments policy. When military officers retire, they often move on to positions of power as provincial governors, government administrators, and heads of companies belonging to the armed forces, which companies account for much of the Egyptian economy.

In this context, it was inevitable that some should call the Taḥrīr Square movement a failure (see esp. Fukuyama 2012). In fact, the 2012 presidential elections took a course that could not have done more to dash the hopes and expectations which had been raised in Taḥrīr Square. On the ballot in the runoff were the Muslim Brothers' official nominee, Muḥammad Mursī, and Aḥmad Shafīq, who had served as prime minister under Mubārak and as a senior commander in the Egyptian Air Force. The election, then, came down to a choice between an exponent of the conservative wing of the Muslim Brotherhood and an exponent of the old regime, the former winning 51.73 percent of the popular vote and the latter 48.27 percent. Abū l-Futūḥ said he would endorse Mursī so as to avoid a return to the old regime, but at the same time the conservative wing of the Muslim Brotherhood vowed to apply the *sharīʿa*—a prospect that certainly wasn't reassuring to all those who had started the Arab Spring in Egypt.

10.8 The end of the Arab Spring in Egypt

Muḥammad Mursī proved to be totally inept at leading the country, with a presidency marked by an authoritarian governance, an inability to pass any economic plan, bad management of public institutions, and an unrelenting effort to stifle all opposition. It wasn't even a year into his term in office when, in response to this ham-fisted style of leadership, a new grassroots movement was started in Taḥrīr Square called Tamarrud (Rebellion) that gained a huge following, collecting millions of signatures. And so the stage was set for a confrontation that had been brewing between the president—who had won the elections legally by popular vote—and the popular will, with masses of people expressing their disappointment with the president they themselves had elected. This standoff resulted in Mursī being deposed by the army, which installed an interim government that sought to ground its legitimacy in the popular expression of dissent against a legally elected president whose claim to power was now in question, precisely because he no longer enjoyed popular support, the only basis of his legitimacy (Gervasio and Teti 2013, 112–13).

The impasse posed a difficult constitutional problem. *Democracy cannot be reduced to its electoral process: it also crucially turns on the ability of the state to guarantee the rights of citizens, mainly through the separation of powers.* In this latter sense, Mursī's presidency was no longer democratic. Equally undemocratic, however, was the ensuing military coup, for it was carried out to depose a legally elected president with a legitimate mandate based on the popular vote. *Hence the predicament of a clash between a president who had turned antidemocratic and an antidemocratic military response to that development.*

Civil unrest and chaos ensued, and in response the army cracked down on the Muslim Brotherhood and its supporters, killing more than 1,000 demonstrators who had gathered in protest in Cairo on 14 August 2013. In view of this background, it was all but impossible to envision how Egypt might be able to resume its transition towards democracy. The August 14 massacre would persist as a dark stain that would make it difficult for the country to move forward, and the civil strife that followed, like the civil war that had broken out in Algeria in the 1990s, prefigured a devastating scenario for the future of Egypt. The role Egypt plays in the Middle East is huge, and the crisis the country faced in its transition towards democracy—a transition yet to be fully completed—is bound to have deep repercussions across the Arab world.

When Mursī was removed from office on 3 July 2013, some opposition figures in Tunisia's Assembly of the Representatives of the People called on the people of Tunisia to hold peaceful demonstrations to take down the government. But the Tunisian situation was profoundly different from the Egyptian one, for the government in Tunisia was not in the hands of a single Islamist party, as was the case in Egypt, but was led by a coalition that al-Nahḍa had formed with a secular party, namely, President Marzouki's CPR. In addition, whereas in Tunisia the army had withdrawn from politics, in Egypt it had held the reins of power for six decades. The Tunisian constitution of 2014 will serve as a testing ground for the Jasmine Revolution of 2011, for it may set the foundation on which to forge a lasting compromise (grounded in the constitution itself) between the liberal and Islamist forces in the country (Selwan El Khoury 2013).

What would also weigh importantly on the democratic transition in the Arab countries was US policy, which had previously been ambiguous and even contradictory. The United States had accepted the Mursī presidency but did not put pressure on Mursī to make overtures to other political and social forces, thereby giving free rein to Saudi Arabia in its intent to topple Mursī. After his fall, the United States threw its support behind the military government, deciding not to call the ouster a coup d'état, and even though the United States disavowed the military action that led to the August 14 massacre, it did so without depriving the military of its strong financial support, on the mistaken assumption that the United States itself could continue to exert influence on a fundamental ally in the Middle East. In reality, the 1.5 billion dollars the US Congress appropriated for the new transitional government paled in comparison to the 8 billion that Saudi Arabia had already pledged for the generals, not to mention that there was speculation that the latter amount could rise to 12 billion with the contribution of the Arab states of the Persian Gulf.

The fallout from Egypt's internal conflict spread across the Middle East and shaped it in profound ways, giving rise to two camps: on one side, coming out in support of the military government, were Saudi Arabia, Jordan, and the Arab states of the Persian Gulf; on the other side, voicing strong criticism against the military, were Turkey, Qatar, and Syria. As one commentator concluded at the time: "Certainly, the revolution has failed. Perhaps it took its own life. Perhaps one day it will be brought back to life. But the status quo has been broken. The rules of the old game no longer work" (Caracciolo 2013, 33; my translation).

The upshot is that the Middle East remains a deeply destabilized region: the civil war in Syria, the breakup of Iraq and Syria, and the birth and expansion of ISIS have completely redrawn the geopolitical map, with ripple effects being felt across the globe. In this state of affairs—save for the extraordinary exception of Tunisia—the march of the Arab Springs appears to have come to a full stop.

With the trial of former president Mursī in November 2013 and the protests that took place in October of the same year against the Tunisian government, the Islamist parties' experience in government seems to have ended with no chance of its being revived.

As has been rightly observed, where al-Nahḍa and the Muslim Brotherhood went wrong was in misunderstanding the nature of the popular consent they had gained. The votes they captured expressed the popular support which had been coalescing around parties that had not hesitated to fight the repression endured at the hands of the authoritarian governments in both Tunisia and Egypt. But that consent was not tantamount to supporting the project that al-Nahḍa and the Muslim Brotherhood embarked on to Islamicize society (Guolo 2013, 29). Whereas in Egypt the failure of the Islamist parties brought the military back into the fold, in Tunisia it heralded the start a new democratic season.

The Muslim Brotherhood is now outlawed in Egypt, while in Tunisia the al-Nahḍa-led government was replaced in December 2013 by a caretaker government led by Mahdī Jumʿa (a former industry minister) that ran the country until the elections held in October 2014.

At the same time, in a debate that does not seem to be heading towards a resolution, the two Islamist parties have split over the path that needs to be taken going forward, with one side moving towards a new governing vision and the other calling for a return to ideological purity. At any rate, the inability to find any common ground seems to bespeak a crisis of political Islam (ibid).

The Arab Springs have so far had a successful outcome only in Tunisia. Everywhere else in the Middle East they seem to have come to a standstill. But the arc of revolution is long, and every such process proceeds by fits and starts.

10.9 What future for Egypt?

After the coup d'état that in 2013 toppled Mursī under the military leadership of Abdel Fattah Al-Sisi, Egypt saw a startling spike in repression that lurched the country back to its prerevolutionary days. According to Egypt's Interior Ministry, in the period stretching from the coup (3 July 2013) to the day Al-Sisi was sworn in as president (8 June 2014), 22,000 people were placed under arrest—a number the Egyptian Center for Economic and Social Rights (ECESR) puts at 41,000 (see Achcar 2016, 121).[27] At least 547 death sentences were passed against persons affiliated with the Muslim Brotherhood, and many more life sentences were handed down for engaging in political activity, and in October 2014 Al-Sisi expanded the jurisdiction of military courts. What came into being was a presidential police state, unmistakably moving in the direction of entrenching its own power. Indicative of this trend was the debate over the reform proposal introduced soon after the parliamentary elections of 2015 to extend the presidential term of office and enhance the powers of the presidency (Essam el-Din 2017).

In this repressive institutional framework, the Egyptian government continued to pursue the neoliberal policies prescribed by the IMF. The worrisome economic situation Egypt was facing is captured in a report the IMF issued in February 2015, with large capital outflows, falling foreign investment, a troubled tourism industry, rising unemployment (which "peaked at 13.4 percent in 2013/14, with the highest levels found among youth and women"), and widespread poverty (which "rose to 26.3 percent in 2012/13, with another 20 percent of the population estimated to be close to the poverty line") (IMF 2015, 7). Yet the IMF was praising the country's economic policy, commenting that "Egypt has chosen a path of adjustment and reform which, if followed resolutely, will lead to economic stability and growth" (ibid., 24).

Under these policies, the cost of fuel and electricity spiked, triggering an inflationary surge that led to a further impoverishment of the population. The lack of a credible human development project and of responsible government policy led to an increasing scarcity of essential goods and services.[28]

Adding to the strain of this inflation and scarcity was a wage containment policy under which "the government [...] set a ceiling for public sector wages, subjected bonuses to income taxes and discontinued the automatic inclusion

27 See also Nader Fergany 2016, 80, noting that in 2015 the Al-Sisi government "waged a relentless campaign of intimidation against all shades of opposition, especially youth activists, through the ruthless application of an unconstitutional piece of legislation that abrogated the right to peaceful assembly, which now required prior authorization by the police."

28 "On 'Black Thursday,' in September 2014, electricity and water supplies were cut throughout the country for nearly ten consecutive hours, while the government remained silent. It was not until several days later that the president appeared on national TV [...] to blame decades of neglect and ask the people to cough up 100 billion EPs [Egyptian pounds] to fix the utilities problem" (Fergany 2016, 92).

of bonuses in basic wages after five years" (ibid., 19). The government was also planning to introduce a "fully fledged" value added tax (VAT) in 2015. These measures, crimping consumers' spending power, were only partly offset by social spending and investment. And at the same time as the regime was cutting public sector wages, it carved out an exception for the military, the police, and the judiciary, whose pensions received a significant increase, thereby undermining an already compromised social justice.

In short, the Al-Sisi government consistently followed IMF directives implementing a neoliberal economic agenda premised on the need to grow the private sector while neglecting the public sector. But the political instability that continued to fester under Al-Sisi's watch stifled growth in the private sector, which therefore could not make up for the cuts made to the public sector (Achcar 2016, 131), with the exception of the special benefits carved out for the military, the police, and the judiciary, and for the heavy defence spending to buy foreign weapons.

In his presidential campaign, Al-Sisi ran on the *Om eldonya* slogan, promising to make Egypt "the mother of the world." But the deep social and economic inequalities that continued to plague Egypt under his presidency caused the country to become "clearly dependent, indeed subservient to, Saudi Arabia and even the United Arab Emirates (UAE) for financial and political support. [...] The Egyptian economy was soon to be dominated by donations and 'investment' by Saudi Arabia and the UAE" (Fergany 2016, 93). This economic dependence drew Egypt into the war that Saudi Arabia launched against Yemen, an effort to which the Egyptian regime contributes by sending ground troops.

As Gilbert Achcar observes, these pressures, and the regime's response to them, fuelled the growth of a "military-security complex" that has become the instrument of choice for dealing with the country's socioeconomic plight and the attendant protests. In fact, countless strikes have been staged since Al-Sisi took office. Despite the government intensifying its crackdown, strikes have broken out among civil servants, police officers, and factory workers, with hundreds of labour protests throughout 2015 (MEE 2017). I should therefore agree with Achar that this wave of mass demonstrations can be taken as "a further indication, following many others, of the fact that the Egyptian revolutionary process that had begun in January 2011 was far from over" (Achcar 2016, 149).

Works Cited

Achcar, Gilbert. 2016. *Morbid Symptoms: Relapse in the Arab Uprisings.* London: Saqi Books.

Adams, Richard H., and John Page. 2002. "Holding the Line: Poverty Reduction in the Middle East and North Africa, 1970–2000." Paper presented at the 8th annual conference of the Economic Research Forum (ERF), *Building for Future Economic Development,* Cairo, January 15–17.

Al-Ahram Weekly. 2011. "News Analysis: Al-Nahḍa Victory." *Al-Ahram Weekly* 1070, October 27 to November 2.

Allam, Khaled Fouad. 2011. "Il rischio più grave è un Afghanistan nel Mediterraneo." *Il Sole 24 Ore*, February 23.

Amin, Magdi, et. al. 2012. *After the Spring: Economic Transitions in the Arab World.* Oxford: Oxford University Press.

Arendt, Hannah. (1963) 1977. *On Revolution.* London: Penguin Books.

Assaad, Ragui. 2008. "Intergenerational Inequality in MENA: Demographic, Economic and Institutional Determinants." Plenary presentation at the 15th annual conference of the Economic Research Forum (ERF), *Equity and Economic Development*, Cairo, November 23–25.

Assaad, Ragui, and Farzaneh Roudi Fahimi. 2007. "Youth in the Middle East and North Africa: Opportunity or Challenge?" Washington, DC: Population Reference Bureau.

ʿAwā, Muḥammad Salīm al-. 2007. "Political Pluralism from an Islamic Perspective." In *Islam in Transition: Muslim Perspectives*, edited by John J. Donohue and John L. Esposito, 279–87. Oxford: Oxford University Press.

Awad, Azita Berar. 2009. "Growth, Employment and Decent Work in the Arab Region: Key Policy Issues." *Thematic paper written for the International Labour Organization (ILO)*, Beirut, October 19–21. Geneva: ILO Publications.

Bayat, Asef. 2007. "Islam and Democracy: What Is the Real Question?" ISIM Paper 8. *Leiden: Institute for the Study of Islam in the Modern World (ISIM)*; Amsterdam: Amsterdam University Press.

Bayat, Asef. 2011. "The Post-Islamist Revolutions: What the Revolts in the Arab World Mean." *Foreign Affairs*, April 26. https://www.foreignaffairs.com/articles/north-africa/2011-04-26/post-islamist-revolutions

Bayat, Asef. 2013. *Life as Politics: How Ordinary People Change the Middle East.* Stanford: Stanford University Press.

Beau, Nicolas, and Catherine Graciet. 2009. *La Régente de Carthage: Main basse sur la Tunisie.* Paris: La Découverte.

Beck, Martin, and Simone Hüser. 2012. "Political Change in the Middle East: An Attempt to Analyze the 'Arab Spring.'" GIGA Working Paper 203 (August 2012). German Institute of Global and Area Studies.

Ben Attia, Moncef. 2012. "La Tunisie et l'Union Européenne: Une puissante emprise de structure." In *La Transition démocratique en Tunisie: États des lieux.* Vol. 2, *Les thématiques.* By the Observatoire Tunisien de la Transition Démocratique, edited by Hamadi Redissi, Asma Nouira, and Abdelkader Zghal, 67–76. Tunis: Diwen.

Boduszynski, Mieczyslaw P., and Kristin Fabbe. 2014. "Op-Ed: What Libya's Militia Problem Means for the Middle East, and the US." *Los Angeles Times*, September 2014. https://www.latimes.com/opinion/op-ed/la-oe-0923-boduszynski-libya-lessons-20140924-story.html

Campanini, Massimo. 2011. "Egitto: Continuità e cambiamenti." In *L'Africa mediterranea: Storia e futuro*, edited by Karim Mezran, Silvia Colombo, and Saskia van Genugten, 3–26. Rome: Donzelli.

Campanini, Massimo. 2013. "Le rivolte arabe: Verso un nuovo modello politico?" Chap. 1 in *Le rivolte arabe e l'Islam: La transizione incompiuta*, edited by Massimo Campanini. Bologna: il Mulino.

Caracciolo, Lucio. 2011. "Islamismo e petrolio." *la Repubblica*, October 22.

Caracciolo, Lucio. 2013. "L'incendio globale." *la Repubblica*, August 17.

Carlini, Vittorio. 2011. "Da Impregilo a Finmeccanica; dalla Juventus fino a Retelit i titoli che 'soffrono' la rivolta in Libia." *Il Sole 24 Ore*, February 21.

Cassese, Antonio. 2011a. "Chi resta a guardare." *la Repubblica*, February 26.

Cassese, Antonio. 2011b. “Hanno vinto le pressioni europee: Adesso serve una sentenza rapida.” *la Repubblica*, February 28.

Ciranda, Marta. 2010/11. “Identikit di una generazione in rivolta: Chi sono e perché protestano i giovani della ‘primavera araba.’” Dissertation submitted at the Facoltà di Conservazione dei Beni Culturali, Cooperazione Internazionale, University of Bologna, Ravenna Campus. Programme: Tutela dei Diritti Umani e dei Beni Etno-Culturali nel Mediterraneo e in Eurasia.

Ciranda, Marta. 2012. “La ‘primavera araba’ e il rapporto governanti/governati: Un’analisi multidimensionale.” *Scienza & politica: Per una storia delle dottrine* 24, no. 46: 77–91.

Colombo, Silvia, and Daniela Huber. 2016. “The EU and Conflict Resolution in the Mediterranean Neighbourhood: Tackling New Realities through Old Means?” PapersIEMed/EuroMeSCo 27, March 2016. European Institute of the Mediterranean. http://www.iai.it/sites/default/files/euromesco_27.pdf

Costantini, Irene. 2018. “Conflict and Peace in the Mediterranean Space: Europe’s Response to the Libyan Crisis.” Chap. 10 in *North Africa and the Making of Europe: Governance, Institutions and Culture*, edited by Muriam Haleh Davis and Thomas Serres, 223–42. London: Bloomsbury.

Cricco, Massimiliano. 2012. “L’Islam in Libia.” Chap. 3 in *Libia: Fine o rinascita di una nazione?*, edited by Karim Mezran and Arturo Varvelli, preface by Lucio Caracciolo. Rome: Donzelli.

Del Boca, Angelo. 2011. “Ma il colonnello ha sottovalutato i clan delle montagne.” Interview by Tonino Bucci. *Puntocritico*, February 22.

Dīn ‘Arafāt, A’lā’ Al-. 2012. Islamists in the Arab Spring: Egypt’s Muslim Brotherhood Divides. *Le Monde Diplomatique*, May 2012. https://mondediplo.com/2012/05/06brotherhood

Eljarh, Mohamed. 2018. “The Libyan Crisis: Internal Barriers to Conflict Resolution and the Role of Multilateral Cooperation.” Chap. 2 in *The Search for Stability in Libya: OSCE’s Role between Internal Obstacles and External Challenges*, edited by Andrea Dessì and Ettore Greco, 47–66. IAI Research Studies. Rome: Edizioni Nuova Cultura.

Essam el-Din, Gamal. 2017. “Calls for Constitutional Amendment to Extend Egypt’s Presidential Terms Spark Debate.” *Ahram Online,* August 16. http://english.ahram.org.eg/news/275469.aspx

Fergany, Nader. 2016. *Arab Revolution in the 21st Century? Lessons from Egypt and Tunisia.* New York: Palgrave Macmillan.

Filiu, Jean-Pierre. 2011. *The Arab Revolution: Ten Lessons from the Democratic Uprising.* Oxford: Oxford University Press.

Fraihat, Ibrahim. 2016. *Unfinished Revolutions: Yemen, Libya, and Tunisia after the Arab Spring.* New Haven, CT: Yale University Press.

Fukuyama, Francis. 2012. “The Failures of the Facebook Generation in the Arab Spring.” *Daily Beast*, May 21, updated 13 July 2017. https://www.thedailybeast.com/the-failures-of-the-facebook-generation-in-the-arab-spring

Gelvin, James L. 2012. *The Arab Uprisings: What Everyone Needs to Know.* New York: Oxford University Press.

Gervasio, Gennaro, and Anrea Teti. 2013. “I segreti inconfessabili del golpe democratico.” *Limes: Rivista italiana di geopolitica* 7 (August 1): 111–16. https://www.limesonline.com/cartaceo/i-segreti-inconfessabili-del-golpe-democratico?prv=true

Guolo, Renzo. 2011. “La rivolta della Sirte.” *la Repubblica*, February 21.

Guolo, Renzo. 2013. “L’esperimento fallito degli islamisti al potere.” *la Repubblica*, November 5.

Hanafi, Sari. 2011. "Lessons of the Jasmine Revolution." *Aljazeera*, January 23.

Hibou, Béatrice. 2011. "Tunisie: Économie politique et morale d'un mouvement social." Introduction au thème "La Tunisie en révolution?" Dossier, *Politique Africaine* 121, no. 1: 5–22. https://doi.org/10.3917/polaf.121.0005

Hollis, Rosemary. 2012. "No Friend of Democratization: Europe's Role in the Genesis of the 'Arab Spring.'" *International Affairs* 88, no. 1: 81–94.

Human Rights Watch. 2006. "Libya: June 1996 Killings at Abu Salim Prison." June 27. https://www.hrw.org/news/2006/06/27/libya-june-1996-killings-abu-salim-prison

IMF (International Monetary Fund). 2015. Arab Republic of Egypt: Staff Report for the 2014 Article IV Consultation. Country Report No. 15/33 of 11 February 2015. Washington, DC: IMF.

Jabbār, ʿAdil. 2011. "La dignità araba." *Africanews.it*, February 15.

Kabbani, Nader, and Ekta Kothari. 2005. "Youth Employment in the MENA Region: A Situational Assessment." Social Protection Discussion Paper No. 0534, September 2005. The World Bank.

Khader, Bichara. 2003. "L'impact de l'élargissement sur les flux migratoires sud-méditerranéens." In *Le partenariat euro-méditerranéen: Le processus de Barcelone; nouvelles perspectives*, actes de colloque du 14 décembre 2001, Lyon, edited by Filali Osman and Christian Philip. Brussels: Bruylant.

Kneissl, Karin. 2011. "Elements for a Scientific Analysis of the Arab Revolutions in Spring 2011." In *Arbeitspapiere zur Sozialanthropologie (ÖAW)*, edited by Andre Gingrich and Guntram Hazod, vol. 21, 1–17. Vienna: Österreichische Akademie der Wissenschaften.

Lahmar, Mouldi. 2012. "La Libia e il travaglio di una modernità incompiuta." Chap. 7 in *Verso un nuovo orientalismo: Primavere arabe e Grande Medio Oriente*, edited by Giampaolo Calchi Novati. Rome: Carocci.

Longo, Pietro. 2013. "L'ascesa del salafismo in Tunisia ed Egitto: Le sfide per la transizione democratica." *Aspenia Online: International Analysis and Commentary*, January 15.

Magen, Amichai. 2012. "On Political Order and the 'Arab Spring.'" *Israel Journal of Foreign Affairs* 6, no. 1: 9–21.

McFaul, Michael. 2002. "The Fourth Wave of Democracy and Dictatorship: Noncooperative Transitions in the Postcommunist World." *World Politics*, 54, no. 2: 212–44.

MEE. 2017. "Egypt Witnessed Hundreds of Labour Protests in 2015: Report." *Middle East Eye*, March 7. https://www.middleeasteye.net/news/egypt-witnessed-hundreds-labour-protests-2015-report

Mezran, Karim. 2011. "Libia: La fine di un'era?" In *L'Africa mediterranea: storia e futuro*, edited by Karim Mezran, Silvia Colombo, and Saskia van Genugten, 51–77. Rome: Donzelli.

Mezran, Karim. 2018. "Unsustainable Instability in Libya." IAI Commentaries 18/13, March 2018. Istituto Affari Internazionali.

Mouhoud, El Mouhoub. 2012. "Political Economy of Arab Revolutions: Analysis and Prospects for North-African Countries," *Mondes en Développement* 40, 2012/2, no. 158: 33–50. https://doi.org/10.3917/med.158.0035

Naïr, Sami. 2011. "La Tunisia brucia." *Internazionale* 881 (January 21): 12–13. (Orig. pub. in *El País*.)

Negri, Alberto. 2011. "I cerchi del potere del Colonnello." *Il Sole 24 Ore*, February 20.

Pipes, Daniel. 2011. "Lenta la reazione di Washington, ma l'intervento militare è un rischio." By Arturo Zampaglione, interviewing Daniel Pipes in New York. *la Repubblica*, February 27.

Ramadan, Tariq. 2011. *L'Islam et le réveil arabe*. Paris: Presses du Châtelet.
Redissi, Hamadi. 2013. "La sfida della transizione politica in Tunisia." Translated by Massimiliano Trentin (originally titled "La transition politique tunisienne au défi"). *Afriche e Orienti* XV, nos. 1–2: 65–75.
Roggero, Caterina. 2012. "Rivolte e rivoluzioni nella storia contemporanea tunisina." In *La primavera araba: Origini ed effetti delle rivolte che stanno cambiando il Medio Oriente*, edited by Michela Mercuri and Stefano Maria Torelli, with an introduction by Vittorio Emanuele Parsi, 33–55. Milan: Vita e Pensiero.
Romagnoli, Alessandro, and Luisa Mengoni. 2014. "Human Capital and Labour Markets in the MENA Region." Chap. 7 in *The Economic Development Process in the Middle East and North Africa*. London and New York: Routledge.
Roy, Olivier. 2011. "This Is Not an Islamic Revolution." *New Statesman*, February 15, translated from the French by Jonathan Derbyshire. Originally published under the title "Révolution post-islamiste," *Le Monde*, 12 February 2011.
Selwan El Khoury, Bernard E. 2013. "La Tunisia teme l'onda di ritorno." *Limes: Rivista italiana di geopolitica* 7 (August 1). https://www.limesonline.com/cartaceo/la-tunisia-teme-londa-di-ritorno
Stepanova, Ekaterina. 2018. "Russia's Approach to the Conflict in Libya, the East-West Dimension and the Role of the OSCE." Chap. 4 in *The Search for Stability in Libya: OSCE's Role between Internal Obstacles and External Challenges*, edited by Andrea Dessì and Ettore Greco, 89–111. IAI Research Studies. Rome: Edizioni Nuova Cultura.
Tinazzi, Cristiano. 2013. "In Libia la Fratellanza non serve più." *Limes: Rivista italiana di geopolitica* 7 (August 1). https://www.limesonline.com/cartaceo/in-libia-la-fratellanza-non-serve-piu
Toaldo, Mattia. 2015. "Perché la Libia è un caso disperato." *Limes: Rivista italiana di geopolitica* 1 (February 16). https://www.limesonline.com/perche-la-libia-e-un-caso-disperato/73938
Toaldo, Mattia. 2016. "Intervening Better: Europe's Second Chance in Libya." ECFR Publications, policy memo, May 2016. European Council on Foreign Relations. https://www.ecfr.eu/publications/summary/intervening_better_europes_second_chance_in_libya
Toaldo, Mattia, and Mary Fitzgerald. 2016. "A Quick Guide to Libya's Main Players." ECFR Publications, October 2016. European Council on Foreign Relations. http://www.ecfr.eu/mena/mapping_libya_conflict
UN. 2015. "UN Welcomes 'Historic' Signing of Libyan Political Agreement." *UN News*, December 17. https://shar.es/1L2mow
UN DESA (United Nations Department of Economic and Social Affairs), Population Division. 2001. *Replacement Migration: Is It a Solution to Declining and Ageing Populations?* UN doc ST/ESA/SER.A/206. New York: United Nations.
UNIMED (Unione delle Università del Mediterraneo). 2012. "L'Egitto al voto per eleggere il presidente … ma è vera democrazia?" May 23.
UNIMED (Unione delle Università del Mediterraneo). 2013. "Le rivoluzioni arabe e l'ascesa dell'Islam politico." April 22–23.
UNSC (UN Security Council). 2006. Resolution 1674 (2006). Adopted by the Security Council at its 5430th meeting (28 April 2006). UN doc S/RES/1674 (2006).
UNSC (UN Security Council). 2011a. Resolution 1970 (2011). Adopted by the Security Council at its 6491st meeting (26 February 2011). UN doc S/RES/1970 (2011).
UNSC (UN Security Council). 2011b. Resolution 1973 (2011). Adopted by the Security Council at its 6498th meeting (17 March 2011). UN doc S/RES/1973 (2011).

Vandewalle, Dirk. 1998. *Libya since Independence: Oil and State-Building*. Ithaca and London: Cornell University Press.

Varvelli, Arturo. 2012. "Italia e Libia: Storia di un rapporto privilegiato." Chap. 6 in *Libia: Fine o rinascita di una nazione?*, edited by Karim Mezran and Arturo Varvelli, preface by Lucio Caracciolo. Rome: Donzelli.

Varvelli, Arturo, and Matteo Villa. 2012. "L'insostenibile leggerezza della rendita e il caso della Libia." Chap. 14 in *Verso un nuovo orientalismo: Primavere arabe e grande Medio Oriente*, edited by Giampaolo Calchi Novati. Rome: Carocci.

Zelin, Aaron. 2012. "Tunisia's Salafis Are Newly Licensed Political Participants: How Have They Done So Far?" Carnegie Endowment for International Peace, July 18. https://carnegieendowment.org/sada/48885

Zolo, Danilo. 2011. "ONU e guerra 'umanitaria': Un'impostura criminale." *il manifesto*, March 22.

11 Democratization and development in the Arab countries of the Mediterranean area

We have so far looked at the Arab Springs mainly from a southern Mediterranean vantage point, observing this experience from within the Arab countries that went through it, and trying to extract the implications it may have for the future of democracy in the Arab world and for its development. But it is only a partial view that this vantage point can afford. And so in this chapter we will be casting our glance across the Mediterranean, in such a way as to also take Europe into view in carrying the analysis forward. Since the discussion covers a bit of ground, and it seems useful to provide it with some guideposts, the twelve sections making up this chapter have been grouped by subject matter. Hence the five headings that follow, under which we will be analysing (I) the process through which the southern Mediterranean countries have been Europeanized; (II) the complex relation between Islam and democracy; (III) the relation between democracy and development; (IV) the difficulties that Europe has historically faced in fostering democracy along the Mediterranean's southern shore; and (V) what the future of Euro-Mediterranean relations might look like after the season of the Arab Springs.

11.1 The Europeanization of the southern Mediterranean countries

11.1.1 A Short reconstruction of relations between the two shores of the Mediterranean

In the early 1970s the European Commission introduced a Global Mediterranean Policy (GMP) making it possible for the EU to enter into cooperation agreements with Mediterranean countries outside the EU. "The long-term objective was a Mediterranean Free Trade Area" (Zank 2016, 130). In part, this meant "giving the Mediterranean countries access to the EU market for industrial products" and ensuring greater access for "Maghrebi agricultural exports," while lowering customs duties by 20 to 80 percent (ibid.). In 1976 cooperation agreements were signed with the three Maghreb countries—Algeria, Morocco, and Tunisia—and shortly thereafter, in 1977, another one was signed with Egypt (ibid., 131). Under these agreements, "EU tariffs were lowered between 30 and 100 percent for 86–89 percent of the agricultural exports" (ibid.).

However, when Greece joined the EU in 1981, and when Spain and Portugal did so 1986, stricter quotas were placed on agricultural exports out of the Maghreb, considering that their agricultural product was similar to that of the countries that had recently joined the EU. What this arrangement brings clearly into view are the power relations that were coming into shape between the EU and the southern Mediterranean countries, in a dynamic that will continue to mould the interaction between European countries and the Arab countries of the Mediterranean.

By the late 1980s, events in Europe were developing in such a way that the southern Mediterranean could no longer maintain its status as a top policy priority, the focus in Europe now shifting to the Maastricht Treaty, monetary union, and the outbreak of the 1989 Autumn of Nations unfolding in central and Eastern Europe (ibid., 132). "In the 1990s, the EU opened negotiations with Morocco and Tunisia for a new generation of agreements, the Euro-Mediterranean Association Agreements," covering "energy policy, transnational crime, and immigration. The problem of more access for agricultural exports into the EU provoked, as usual, protracted controversies within the EU" (ibid., 133), with issues being raised in particular by Germany, the Netherlands, and Portugal.

"In November 1995, the Barcelona Conference opened a new multilateral approach" (ibid.) designed to make for a stronger partnership with the southern Mediterranean countries. On the agenda were three main items: (1) "political and security partnership: establishing a common area of peace and stability"; (2) "economic and financial partnership: creating an area of shared prosperity"; and (3) "partnership in social, cultural, and human affairs: developing human resources, promoting understanding between cultures, and exchanges between civil societies" (ibid.). In short, the Barcelona Process, as it came to be known, sought to "promote democracy, human rights, rule by law, and close economic cooperation built on open market economies" (ibid.). Subsequently, in April 2002, "a Euro-Med conference of foreign ministers in Valencia [...] enlarged the list by the themes of combating terrorism and migration" (ibid.), showing how the EU clearly pivoted to security as its main area of concern. This pivot reflected the failures of the Barcelona Process, analysing which we will be able to shed light on the current situation and what the future might hold.

11.1.2 Beyond Barcelona

As just mentioned, the important Barcelona Process has fallen short of its objectives. These shortfalls can be distilled down to the fact that decisions made in Europe were to apply to all signatories to the process (Mohsen-Finan 2009, 96) and that Arab societies were not involved, even if they were featured prominently in the objectives set out in the Barcelona Declaration of 1995. But there were also other issues, such as the problem of getting governments to commit to the principles established in 1995 (the rule of law, human rights, democracy), as well as a limited cross-border movement of goods and persons, especially in connection with the agriculture sector.

Another failure of the Barcelona Process is that it was hampered in its attempt to enforce a common security policy. This was due to the breakdown of peace talks in the Middle East.[1] Even the attempt made to arrive at a shared definition of terrorism came to nothing, considering the divergent assessments that European and Muslim countries had of terrorism. Despite these differences, however, as Annette Jünemann (2005, 8) underscores, a vast and deep network of relations was created, leading to a socialization effect that in turn engendered a spirit of partnership (*Partnerschaftsgeist*).

A turning point in relations between the EU and North Africa came with the European Neighbourhood Policy (ENP), introduced in 2003. According to Javier Solana, the EU's first high representative for the Common Foreign and Security Policy (CFSP), one of the chief EU objectives in this policy area was to achieve stability: "The prospect of enlargement is a powerful incentive. An enlarged Union will impact on our relationship with our neighbours: the Balkans, Russia, Ukraine, and to the south the countries of North Africa and the Middle East. If these regions are unstable, Europe will not be able to live in security" (Solana 2001; cf. Gomez 2018, 1).

Under the ENP, relations between the EU and the North African countries are essentially measured against the Barcelona Process, in that relations with these countries are managed through action plans which the EU works out with each of the countries in question, identifying reforms for which the EU will provide financial aid. "The most novel aspect of the ENP is the offer of a 'stake in the internal market' and the participation in EU programs" (Zank 2016, 137), where "stake in the internal market" means "assistance in adapting to the complex market regulations of the EU, in joining standardization bodies, and in improving the exchange of information" (ibid.). The first actions plans came in December 2004, addressing "Morocco and Tunisia, the traditional frontrunners in cooperation with the EU" (ibid.).

1 On Bichara Khader's analysis (2008, 137–38), the Barcelona Process was aimed at three objectives. The first of these is what she calls the *cliquet* effect, a sort of open door effect that would expose southern Mediterranean countries to international competition by taking down trade barriers, thereby prodding these countries to reform their institutions, administration, and governance, as well as to privatize the productive apparatus and make it more dynamic, while also enhancing regional cooperation and refashioning the regulatory and distributive state into an entrepreneurial state. In the second place, the Barcelona Process was intended to achieve a spillover effect under which economic stability would lead to greater democratic stability. Under the rubric of the first two effects, international competition, foreign investment, privatization, and the creation of salaried jobs were to expand the middle class, which acts as a driver of democratic transformation.

The third objective was to achieve a "contagion" effect that would lead to peace. The idea here was that economic development would propel the process towards democracy, which in turn would help along the Arab-Israeli peace process.

In reality, Khader comments, the easing of trade restrictions was modest, as were foreign investment, job creation, and the growth of the middle class. All the while, the peace process went nowhere.

But adapting to EU market regulations is not just about achieving a streamlined market: it also carries significant economic and political implications with controversial outcomes. On the economic side, "proper integration into the EU's market presupposes ending state aid to companies, and this will presumably cost jobs" (ibid.). On the political side, "there is a fundamental *asymmetry* in this construction because the rule-makers for this market, the main supervisory bodies, and the dispute-settlement institutions such as the European Court of Justice are all EU institutions. Countries outside the EU have to adapt" (ibid., 138; italics added).

11.1.3 The Europeanization of North African countries

As of 2008, the process of adapting to EU regulations was continuing "systematically, albeit with differences from country to country" (ibid.). The "fastest mover" (ibid.) seemed to be Morocco, with "numerous initiatives" (ibid.) aimed at modernizing the state and the justice system and implementing a "national action plan on human rights" (ibid., 139). On the economic front, these initiatives included "liberalizing trade in services and the right of establishment and likewise further liberalizing trade in agricultural products, processed products, and fisheries" (ibid.). Cooperation on foreign policy was also intensifying (ibid.). Tunisia was "a consistent reformer in the economic field but not so in the political sphere. Budgetary and monetary policies [were] prudent," and progress was being made on "regulatory convergence with the EU" (ibid.), as well as on the elimination of tariff barriers (ibid.) and on consumer protection (ibid.). What could be observed, in short, was a "gradual Europeanization of North Africa" (ibid., 109), a process carried forward by promoting "much closer cooperation between North Africa and the EU countries" (ibid., 141) and by bringing South African countries on board with EU regulations.

But what are we to make of this Europeanization process? It cannot be described as an across-the-board alignment, considering that little progress has been made in the way of human rights and political liberties. In short, despite the headway made in adapting to the European economic system, the authoritarian chokehold that continued to be kept on rights and freedoms until the Arab Springs meant that little could be achieved in this latter sphere, in a condition of political suppression that, as we will see, has always stifled economic development as well. But the Arab Springs did act as a catalyst for transitioning towards democracy in the North African countries, especially in Tunisia, and these processes are surely bound to create new political conditions for economic development. Let us therefore take a closer look at these problems.

These transformations hinge in part on the complex dialectic of the Arab world, where the Europeanization process has faced backlash from a variety of Islamist movements. As a result, several Arab regimes have introduced limits on the forms of democratic government they will countenance, justifying these measures on the ground that they are essential to the fight against terrorism and Islamism (though it is not hard to see that the same restrictions are instrumental to the ability of these regimes to hold on to their own power). And while the

Europeanization policy is facing strong headwinds—having triggered push-back from the Islamic movements, and having provided as well an opportunity for autocratic governments in the Arab world to tighten their grip on the population—there is little that the Union for the Mediterranean (UfM) has been able to do in response, despite its commitment to inaugurating a new season in Euro-Mediterranean relations.

11.1.4 New prospects for cooperation

In Toulon in 2007, a French Mediterranean Union project was launched within the framework of the Barcelona Process. Fully aware of the limits of that process, the Mediterranean Union outlined four main objectives: to control and manage migration; protect the environment; promote joint development so as to close the gap between the two shores of the Mediterranean; and fight corruption, organized crime, and terrorism (Henry 2008, 38). Politically, however, the Mediterranean Union was primarily aimed at mending the fraught relationship that had evolved between France and the Arab world over the course of their postcolonial interactions, particularly when it came to Algeria, and to correct the perception that French foreign policy was tilted in Israel's favour and geared towards the Atlantic (Mohsen-Finan 2009, 98).

Over time, the French project went through several revisions. Thus, in a speech delivered on 23 October 2007 in Tangiers, French president Nicolas Sarkozy emphatically stated that "the future of Europe [...] lies in the south," and that only by going back to its Mediterranean roots can the European project "recover the sense it should never have lost, which is that of a civilizing project."[2] At the same time, he introduced a new vision that saw a common horizon for both Europe and Africa: "Eurafrica" he called it—*le pivot de l'Eurafrique* (Sarkozy 2007)—and it would favour an opening to the East.[3]

2 Translated from the French original: "Car l'avenir de l'Europe, je n'hésite pas à le dire, il est au Sud. En tournant le dos à la Méditerranée, l'Europe se couperait non seulement de ses sources intellectuelles, morales, spirituelles, mais également de son futur. Car c'est en Méditerranée que l'Europe gagnera sa prospérité, sa sécurité, qu'elle retrouvera l'élan que ses pères fondateurs lui avaient donné. / C'est à travers la Méditerranée que l'Europe pourra de nouveau faire entendre son message à tous les hommes. C'est par la Méditerranée, dans la prise de conscience de ce qu'elle lui doit, que l'Europe retrouvera son identité, que son projet retrouvera le sens qu'il n'aurait jamais dû perdre, qui est celui d'un projet de civilisation" (Sarkozy 2007).

3 The European Union project of 2008 was meant to work in parallel with the 1995 Euro-Mediterranean Partnership (EUROMED), or Barcelona Process. So conceived, it sought to revive a multilateral partnership encompassing forty-three countries in Europe and the Mediterranean basin: the EU's twenty-seven member states and sixteen Mediterranean partner countries from North Africa, the Middle East, and the Balkans (Kneissel 2011, 6). "During his electoral campaign, Nicholas Sarkozy said that the Mediterranean Union would be modelled on the European Union with a shared judicial area and common institutions. Furthermore, he saw Turkish membership of the Mediterranean Union as an alternative to membership of the European Union. The first secretary-general of that very Union, Ahmed Masadeh, quit his post on January 26, 2011, stating that 'the general conditions against which he accepted to assume the job have changed'" (ibid., quoting from Jordan Times Editor 2011).

Furthermore, and this was certainly the most innovative aspect of the French policy proposal, Sarkozy (2007) underscored the essence that is common to Judaism, Christianity, and Islam, locating this kernel in a culture of love, peace, and fraternity.[4] And, finally, anticipating the resistance the French initiative might have faced from other EU countries, Sarkozy took care to point out that "this Mediterranean Union project will not be a French project: it will be a project for us all, developed by us all."[5]

Yet, despite this broad, inclusive appeal, the French project did meet with resistance, especially from Spain and Germany. This led to a new, jointly developed project being put together, which happened in Hannover in March 2008, when the proposal was submitted to the European Council (Mohsen-Finan 2009, 99).

> This document, which allowed 27 EU Member States and the European Commission to join the project, proposed the creation of a Union for the Mediterranean (UfM), conceived according to the German Chancellor as "an EU project with the South Mediterranean Countries." It therefore consisted of extending the Barcelona Process by lending it new impulse. (Ibid.)

And "instead of defining general spheres of cooperation," it would allocate aid to support the development of the southern Mediterranean countries by way of "concrete projects" (ibid., scare quotes in the original) to fight pollution, build new roadways, and create a Mediterranean energy market, among other initiatives.

But development aid cannot be reduced to financial aid: for even more important to its outcome is the form of government under which it is implemented. And with that recognition we are brought back to the basic problems of development policy, which need to be probed more deeply before we can hope to level off the asymmetry between North and South and close the development gap separating the two shores of the Mediterranean. Our investigation, in other words, will try to show that economic development hinges on the ability to

4 In making the point that these three monotheistic religions share a common core in the message of love, Sarkozy quoted Antigone: "I was made for fellowship in love, not fellowship in hate" (Sophocles 1906, 17 [line 523]). The French original: "C'est un effort pour que chacun cesse de transmettre la haine pour transmettre l'amour, cet amour qui est déjà dans le cri d'Antigone, il y a 2500 ans: 'Je suis née pour partager l'amour, non pour partager la haine.' Cet amour qui est l'essence du judaïsme, cet amour qui est l'essence du christianisme, cet amour qui est l'essence de l'islam et que les fanatiques n'ont eu de cesse de vouloir étouffer, cet amour qui est dans notre culture, qui est dans notre pensée, qui est dans notre religion, dans notre art, dans notre poésie mais qui n'est pas assez dans les cœurs parce que ce sont des cœurs blessés que les cœurs des peuples de la Méditerranée, des cœurs déchirés par d'horribles souffrances et le souvenir d'atroces douleurs" (Sarkozy 2007).

5 The French original: "Ce projet de l'Union de la Méditerranée ne sera pas le projet de la France. Ce sera le projet de tous. Élaboré par tous" (Sarkozy 2007).

push the Arab regimes' forms of government towards democracy. To this end, however, we will first have to understand the challenges faced in bringing about this transformation.

11.2 The complex relation between Islam and democracy

11.2.1 Democracy and Islam in the Mediterranean

The working assumption in this discussion will be that the challenges confronting the southern Mediterranean countries cannot be boiled down to a lack of resources: they are even more crucially tied to their forms of government. Indeed, when the rule of law is tenuous, the elites in power cannot be held accountable, and the corruption they thrive on cannot be stamped out. It was this corruption that became the target of the Arab Spring revolts.

Closely connected with these problems is that of the weak legal system, making it difficult to enforce contracts and ensure the reliability of economic transactions. For this reason businesses are not too eager to invest in these countries. And the lack of investment in turn does nothing to mitigate the problem of high unemployment we saw in Chapters 9 and 10. Hence the downward economic spiral the system seems to be locked into as a result of its weak institutions.

Making matters even worse is the lack of trust between the two shores of the Mediterranean: in the Arab countries, EU policy is viewed as serving the interests of European companies looking to expand their reach in the southern Mediterranean market, and as instrumental to the effort to control migration and fight terrorism; in Europe, the Arab countries are suspected of using the EU to favour the elites in their own regimes.

Now, this whole complex of problems needs to be viewed in light of the crucial assumption informing the Barcelona Process. Indeed, in setting out to achieve forms of democracy and secure the protection of rights in the southern Mediterranean countries, this process proceeded from the premise that only in a democratic environment can there be economic development: without the backing of democratic institutions, no amount of aid can relieve the people of poverty or reduce economic disparity. Having laid out that context, we can ask two crucial questions: *can development be achieved even without democratic institutions?* And, if not, *are there forms of democracy other than those of the West that can support development?*

In order to answer these questions, we will first take up anew the problem of democracy in Muslim Arab countries, and then we will turn to the problem of how the forms of government in the Arab countries affect the objective of development.

There is a basic tension and problem that we can find at the heart of Muslim societies. It lies in the fact that simultaneously embedded in these societies are two overlapping communities: a *community of believers* and a *community of citizens* (Ben Achour 1992, see esp. chap. 11). This means that no government in the Muslim world can establish its legitimacy without a religious foundation. In Western liberal democracies, by contrast, the legitimacy of government rests on secular foundations, and in particular on its protection of the basic liberties: freedom of thought, religion, assembly, and the like. To make these the founding principles of democracy is to guarantee that various minorities can exercise the same right as the majority and are recognized as having equal dignity with it. And it is also to recognize *relativism* as the basic philosophy of democracy.[6] As can be appreciated, this is not a conception that sits comfortably with the Arab countries' prevailing forms of government.

In describing these forms of government, Daniel Brumberg (2002, 56) introduces the idea of a liberalized or partial autocracy, a "trademark mixture of guided pluralism, controlled elections, and selective repression," referring to political systems that control the forms of political participation and prevent the formation of authentic political society, in which any person or group is free to engage politically with any other person or group.

Some liberalized autocracies, Like Morocco and Jordan, "derive their legitimacy at least partly from their purported lineage ties to Mohammed" (ibid., 62); for others, like Egypt until the outbreak of the Arab Springs, "the legitimacy of the [...] state still rests partly on its role as a defender of communal Islamic values" (ibid.). These autocracies need to be distinguished from total autocracies, based on "the idea that the state's mission is to defend the supposedly unified nature of the Arab nation or the Islamic community" (ibid., 58). "Total autocracy," Brumberg notes, "is the exception rather than the rule in the Arab world. Most Arabs live under autocracies that allow a measure of openness," as is the case with "Morocco, Egypt, Jordan, Kuwait, and Lebanon," which

> have not tried to impose a single vision of political community. Instead, they have put a certain symbolic distance between the state and society in ways that leave room for competitive or *dissonant* politics. By not nailing the state's legitimacy to the mast of one ideological vessel with a putatively sacred national or religious mission, they have helped to short-circuit the growth of counterhegemonic Islamist movements. (Ibid., 61; italics in the original)

As Brumberg also notes, however, it is central to the "survival strategies" of some liberalized democracies that their

> rulers [...] are both the chief arbiters within society and the major patrons of religious institutions [...]. As arbiters, those who hold power in Egypt, Morocco, and Jordan use cultural, religious, and ideological dissonance to divide the opposition. As patrons of religion, these same powerholders

6 This is a point that Ben Achour (1992, 270) makes vivid by commenting that democracy can begin only with the end of absolutes.

> use their ties to Islamic institutions to limit the influence of secular political forces. Over time, this Islamization strategy has led to acute dilemmas. For in their efforts to coopt conservative Islamic ideas these regimes have hindered the creation of alternatives to the illiberalism that is characteristic of *mainstream* (and not merely radical) Islamism. (Ibid., 62; italics in the original)

The rise of Islamist forces has been clear to see at the polls: the Muslim Brothers in the 1980s, the Algerian Islamic Salvation Front in 1991, the Justice and Development Party in Morocco in 2002, Hamas in January 2006 (Cavatorta 2016, 36). And yet one does not have to look far to see Islamist movements working with antiauthoritarian secularist forces: this happened in Algeria, Morocco, Egypt, Jordan, Tunisia, and Syria. Other factors, however, tend to instead favour competition and conflict between the two movements. For one thing, there are deep ideological divisions over the question of democracy and human rights. And, for another thing, there is the practical work of Islamist movements setting out to build institutions offering an alternative to those of the secular state, with a view to demonstrating the superiority of Islamism. As noted, these are divisions the autocratic regimes of the Arab world have sought to turn to their advantage, and successfully at that until the outbreak of the Arab Springs.

But the lack of democracy is not just a function of the divisions that run through Arab societies. For on top of these divisions comes the added layer of complexity owed to the role of Europe and the United States, which tend to back groups that hold secular views, while pushing Islamist groups out of the picture, even if they oppose the autocratic regimes. In fact, Europe and the United States reject out of hand the notion that it may be possible to build an Islamic democracy (ibid., 38).

Western donors, for their part, tend to devote their contributions to causes aligned with Western values, even if in so doing they limit their ability to work for the betterment of society. This is what happened, for example, in Morocco and Tunisia, where Islamist movements have been able to make a compelling case that groups tied to the West lack independence—all of which makes for heightened divisions in society, playing into the hands of authoritarian regimes.

Western countries seem unable to find an appropriate response to the rise of Islamism, even when dealing with nonviolent movements. They would rather support liberal secularist groups, which frequently respond to the threat of Islamism by backing autocratic regimes. The EU has so far shown itself to be unable to enter into dialogue with political Islam, despite the fact that Turkey might have offered an example of how Islam could be made consistent with democracy.[7]

7 I am using the cautious, backward-looking *might* here owing the antidemocratic turn that Turkey has recently taken under Tayyip Erdoğan, whose regime seems to be increasingly moving in the direction of an Islamized state.

And so there is also serious blame that can be placed on the European countries, as well as on the United States. For in the lead-up to the Arab Springs, they consistently backed autocratic Arab regimes, like Ben Ali's regime in Tunisia and Mubārak's in Egypt, viewing them as bulwarks against radical Islamism, and willing to rely on them in the service of that fight even if that meant forsaking democracy and human rights. Support for Arab autocracies was maintained even when the Ben Ali regime was on the brink of collapse (Alaoui 2011),[8] and it was maintained to the very end of the Mubārak regime, with only the occasional gesture made to the popular movements that were springing up. This support by the European countries and the United Stated shows that their concern with democracy and human rights is entirely abstract at best, and it even suggests an ideological facade functional to the interests of realpolitik. As Rosemary Hollis (2012, 94) comments, "EU policies have actually betrayed the professed European values of freedom, democracy and the rule of law rather than exporting them."[9]

11.3 The relation between democracy and development

11.3.1 Democracy as a condition of economic development

Before the Arab Spring revolutions broke out, bringing about deep transformations in the Arab countries of North Africa, the complex dynamic at work in these societies had helped autocratic forms of government establish a stable foothold and foreclose the possibility of any movement towards democracy. With that understanding in the background, we can go back to the question of how authoritarian forms of government work not only against democracy but also against economic development.

As Gema Martín Muñoz (2010, 27) points out, the relation between economic development and democracy has often been analysed as one in which the latter *follows* from the former: economic development fosters democracy, which cannot take hold without economic development as a necessary background condition. But an analysis of Arab societies suggests that "this so-called 'virtuous circle' will not produce the hoped-for results" (ibid.), and that what holds is actually the *inverse* of this relation, meaning that *there can be no economic development except against the backdrop of democratic institutions*, which therefore act as a necessary condition of economic development.

8 France, for example, remained loyal to Ben Ali until the end of his dictatorship, even if the West's backing of dictatorships has always raised criticism in the Arab world, where it is seen as colonialism and imperialism perpetuated by other means (Alaoui 2011).

9 Europe was essentially interested in fighting terrorism and stemming the flow of immigration (see Nicosia 2011, 115), carrying forward a policy that has been characterized as an exercise in "criminal hypocrisy" (Bensedrine and Mestiri 2004, 9).

To see this, we can turn once more to Martín Muñoz, whose analysis is worth quoting in full:

> Authoritarianism has engendered clientelist behaviour, systems of patronage and networks of corruption. For this reason, economic liberalisation processes tend to be imperfect and incomplete. Liberalisation in the strict sense of the word, which would mean the independence of economic actors from politicians, the rule of competition, transparency, and the suppression of monopolistic practices, is obstructed because traditional elites seek to protect themselves from transparency and from the emergence of new autonomous elites that could challenge them politically.
>
> Consequently, there has been resistance to introducing the necessary juridical changes [...]. So efforts are made to maintain the economic role of the state, while increasing the private sector, which leads to a worrying bifurcation of economic policies, because the private sector forms a parasitical relationship with the public sector, or privatisation is limited to selective, less productive, economic sectors [...]. This way, the state preserves its power and autonomy while selectively offloading economic decision-making to a protected market. As a result, although some macroeconomic indicators may have improved, the benefits have not been distributed among the general population.
>
> On the other hand, the interplay between population growth, political authoritarianism and the unequal distribution of wealth is producing a vicious circle of political alienation and economic marginality that progressively fuels support for resistance movements, including violent ones. Because of this potentially unstable situation, the region attracts very little foreign investment (only 5 percent of European investment in emerging countries goes to southern Mediterranean countries as a whole, and only 1.5 percent of world investment enters emerging countries). This reflects the mistrust felt by potential foreign investors about a region they regard as blighted by political instability and poor governance, not to mention poverty and illiteracy, and where political methods of managing tensions have tended to be superseded by military methods. (Martín Muñoz 2010, 27–28; footnotes omitted)

11.3.2 Immigration, development, and European policies

The structural conditions just described clearly cannot support a thriving economy. In fact, what they sustain is a *dependent* economy, one in which people cannot make ends meet without support from migrant workers in the EU, whose remittances account for a hefty share of the national income. In Morocco and Tunisia, for example, these payments in 2005 accounted for 85 to 90 percent of gross domestic product (Gallina 2007, 303), outweighing foreign direct investment by a ratio of three to one.

Immigration is therefore closely bound up with the reality of countries of origin, making it possible to solidify economic relations sustained by community networks (what Bruno Amoroso refers to as *anelli di solidarietà*). These networks are "much more effective than any aid provided by international organizations or by way of foreign direct investment: they act as lifeblood for communities all across the world, and particularly in the Mediterranean" (Amoroso 2007, 511; my translation); they support economic initiatives and forms of cooperation, which in turn generate investments in infrastructure (rural power grids, roadways, water resource management) or local cooperation projects, as in the countries of the Maghreb.

In the Barcelona Declaration of 1995 these same community networks became integral to a novel codevelopment strategy aimed at achieving "increasing cooperation among different areas in such a way as to empower rather than sap them" (ibid., 504). But this grand vision did not pan out. Ten years into the Barcelona Process, the codevelopment goal had already been reduced to the idea of creating a free-trade area, and hence to a strategy for advancing the interests of the European economic powers by way free-market policies and within the scaffolding of the United States' military hegemony.

What in particular played a large role in hindering the progress of the codevelopment policy was European protectionism, which came in various forms, including agricultural subsidies and import quotas. This takes us to the shortcomings of the European policies for democratizing the Mediterranean's southern shore.

11.4 Europe's challenges in fostering democracy along the Mediterranean's southern shore

11.4.1 The European Union, human rights, and democracy

The Barcelona Declaration of 1995 proceeded from the conviction that by pursuing policies designed to strengthen human rights and democracy, it would be possible to establish an area of peace and stability across the southern Mediterranean. This was an innovative policy vision, for it sought to reframe development cooperation by *tying development to human rights and democracy.* At the same time, the 1995 declaration placed a strong emphasis on the role that human rights and democracy could play in laying the groundwork for *peace and stability.* But for all these statements of principle, the declaration had to recognize that the status of its own human rights proclamations was merely declaratory.[10]

Integral to the Euro-Mediterranean association agreements was an "essential clause" under which relations among the signatories were contingent on their pledge to respect human rights and uphold democratic principles (ibid., 353–54). On this basis a *conditionality principle* was introduced to deal with

10 This is an assessment that in 2005, looking back on ten years since the Barcelona Declaration, the Euro-Mediterranean Human Rights Network (now EuroMed Rights) made in a position statement in which it concluded: "Néanmoins, au niveau régional, les mentions des droits de l'Homme conservent un caractère purement déclaratif" (position du Réseau euro-méditerranéen des droits de l'Homme sur Barcelone + 10 et les droits de l'Homme, 1 March 2005, quoted in Angioi 2006, 344).

cases involving human-rights or minority-rights violations, "but no penalties were provided for any such violations, much less did these penalties include a voiding clause" (ibid., 355). The reason for such a concessive approach was that the EU did not in such cases intend to void the agreements *in toto*: for the most part, the idea was rather to suspend only some of their provisions, especially those relative to the disbursement of European funds.

Furthermore, the 1995 Barcelona Declaration contained a principle requiring respect for the cultural and historic specificities characterizing each partner country. But recognizing such specificities where Arab countries are concerned meant legitimizing some manifestly authoritarian forms of government. In this way, the Mediterranean's two shores remained separated by distant positions, and democracy proved to be impracticable where it was viewed by the dominant elites as posing a threat to their power. Under the Barcelona framework, then, authoritarian policies were enabled to move forward unimpeded, thereby hampering the democratization process and highlighting the crisis in relations between the northern and southern shores of the Mediterranean.

So only two other paths remained open as viable alternatives. One was to promote new forms of cooperation by integrating the Muslim world into European societies (so-called Euro-Islam): this was seen as contributing to *a model of democracy through which Europe could establish a dialogue with the Arab countries and thereby foster democratic transformation in those countries.* The other was to support the transition that Arab countries were making on their own towards possible forms of democracy sensitive to their own needs and heritage.

As far as the first path is concerned—where the problem is to forge a new democratic model on which basis the European societies might be able to integrate the specificities of the Islamic world—it is essential that we move beyond the notion of "exporting" our current democratic model, for that would amount to no more than a modern version of the colonial project (neocolonialism). Our relation with the Arab countries should instead proceed from a deep transformation of our Western societies, a transformation effected by bringing integration policies to a successful completion. Indeed, I would argue that *development-cooperation policy cannot be severed from integration policies grounded in a principle of diversity recognition*: a development-cooperation policy, in other words, can succeed only in a society capable of guaranteeing forms of integration premised on the need to recognize differences.

It therefore seems imperative to create a new multicultural space capable of protecting different religions and cultural traditions (Panebianco 2003, 17), all the while fostering their interchange and cooperation. To this end, I submit, a deeper and closer social dialogue needs to be fostered among civil societies. Indeed, it is a model of decentralized cooperation that the Barcelona Declaration envisioned as the foundation on which to promote interaction among civil societies in the Mediterranean, a model on which initiatives and responsibilities would start from local institutions, NGOs, universities, trade unions, and enterprises as actors carrying out functions that complement a range of governmental activities (cf. Reinhardt 2002).

Through these forms of cooperation, different civilizations and cultures can find common ground and engage one another. This can be achieved without discounting the transformations that may originate from within Arab societies themselves. Let us therefore consider what these transformations might be and what potential they disclose.

11.4.2 The state's security and human security as a new prospect for cooperation

The *Arab Human Development Report 2004* introduced a definition of authoritarian governance in Arab countries as a term designating forms of government where the balance of power is skewed towards the executive, in such a way as to effectively undermine or extinguish the separation of powers, thereby depriving citizens of their freedoms and protections. In reply to the question as to what the prospects for reform might be among Arab regimes, the 2004 report found that significant progress could be made by way of cooperation with outside forces, but only so long as a number of principles were observed, among which the following:

1 "freedom for all and complete adherence to international human rights law, in particular the right to national liberation" (UNDP 2005, 20);
2 "absolute respect for the tenet that Arabs should find their own way to freedom and good governance through innovation by Arab social forces, without pressure to adopt ready-made models, as the firm guarantee of a successful and sustainable historic transformation" (ibid.);
3 "guaranteeing the independence of the judiciary" (ibid.); and
4 "abolishing the state of emergency" (ibid.).

In the *Arab Human Development Report 2009*, the problem of reforming Arab regimes is attacked from a different angle, that of ***human security***. Indeed, human security is viewed as a necessary background condition for achieving human development, which in turn is understood as necessary for economic development. In the 2009 report, human security is defined as the "liberation of human beings from those intense, extensive, prolonged, and comprehensive threats to which their lives and freedoms are vulnerable" (UNDP 2009, 2). This definition lays emphasis on "environmental resources and the state's role in guaranteeing or undermining human security, as well as its role in relation to the insecurity of vulnerable groups, poverty [...], and general insecurity tied to employment and to foreign military interventions" (Saaf 2010, 31; my translation).[11]

11 The French original: "Ces définitions mettent en évidence les pressions sur les ressources environnementales, la performance de l'État en termes de garantie ou d'atteinte à la sécurité humaine, l'insécurité propre aux groupes vulnérables, la pauvreté et le chômage, la sécurité alimentaire et la nutrition, la santé et la sécurité humaine, l'insécurité généralisée liée à l'occupation et aux interventions militaires étrangères."

It is a significant turning point that this policy vision signals, since in many cases the state seems to act more as a threat to human security than as its main guarantor (ibid., 33).

The 2009 report is sceptical of government-sponsored reform initiatives: instead, the point is emphatically made that democratic change in the Arab world needs to originate from society itself,[12] underscoring how the Arab world is home to a wealth of civil-society organizations, such as human-rights organizations, NGOs, and other community groups.[13] The report is accordingly clear about the path to be followed: "Reform from within remains its first and best hope for meaningful security in Arab countries, starting with the essential rights of the people. This reform cannot be imposed from outside; neither can democratic models be imported wholesale. Arab countries need to adapt different institutional forms suited to the context of each of them" (UNDP 2009, 76).

The 2009 report identifies "four forces that could have a role" in bringing about democratic transformation in the Arab world: "political opposition groups (with the Islamic movements to the fore), civil society organisations, business people and, lastly, citizens, when they are allowed to participate through the ballot box" (ibid., 70–71).

Especially active among these are the "civil society movements," which "in several Arab states [...] have developed a political identity and have begun to make their views felt" (ibid., 71). These movements can foster democratic development through several initiatives, such as calling for stronger protections of basic freedoms, or putting out reports monitoring the progress of human rights in each country, or appealing to the law and the courts when the opportunity arises to put an end to human-rights violations. The 2009 report mentions, by way of example, the tactics adopted in Egypt by the grassroots coalition called Kifāya ("Enough!"), which "inspired citizens to use mass protest to press their demands on the government" (ibid.). In fact this group can be reckoned among the forces whose action contributed to the outbreak of the Arab Spring in Egypt. And this can be taken as evidence supporting the view expressed in the report that if democratic change is to sweep across Arab countries ruled by a regime, that change needs to work its way up from the bottom, that is, it needs to be located in civil society.

12 An assumption the 2009 report makes in this connection is that of a civil society. But in the Western philosophical canon, as is known, this concept designates a society essentially made up of *individuals* (with their individual needs), and so, in a strict sense, the concept cannot be applied to Arab societies, which instead tend to be rooted in a communitarian tradition.

13 As is pointed out in the *Arab Human Development Report 2004*, there were at the time more than 130,000 civil-society organizations in the Arab world. However, they tended to be concentrated in certain countries (18,000 in Egypt, 25,000 in Algeria, 7,000 in Tunisia, 4,600 in Lebanon, 1,500 in Jordan), with only a negligible presence in other countries (UNDP 2005, 133).

According to the 2009 report, the human-security approach offers a promising opportunity for countries in the Euro-Mediterranean area to cooperate. In fact, the approach was set out with a view to working it into the region's economic, social, and cultural project (Saaf 2010, 31).

Worthy of mention as a European cooperation effort is the Instrument for Stability, introduced by the European Parliament and the Council of Europe: the purpose of this instrument, effective from 2007 to 2013, was to make it possible to deliver economic, financial, technical, and humanitarian aid to third countries. This principled goal was stated in the very opening of the instrument's underlying regulation: "The promotion of stable conditions for human and economic development and the promotion of human rights, democracy and fundamental freedoms remains one of the prime objectives of European Union [...] external action to which Community instruments for external assistance contribute."[14] But while this language comports with the European Union's self-understanding as a civil power, it stands in contrast to the policies pursued by the European states, for which stability essentially means implementing measures aimed at security and migration control.

It is the first approach that needs to prevail, in such a way that the EU will no longer back autocratic Arab regimes. Indeed, if there is any lesson that in this regard can be learned from the Arab Spring revolutions, it is that there is always a latent energy in the people, and when this energy turns effervescent, it makes for an opportunity that the EU can seize on to move beyond its instrumental approach to foreign policy in the Mediterranean's southern shore.

11.4.3 A new development model

In the *Arab Development Challenges Report 2011*, issued by the United Nations Development Programme (UNDP), the conclusion is reached that "Arab countries need a new development model" (UNDP 2011, 1). The report proceeds from the core idea of human development espoused by the UNDP, and it accordingly proposes a model aimed not so much at increasing incomes as at building capabilities, on what Amartya Sen and Martha Nussbaum call the capability approach. This means eradicating poverty while creating conditions under which every human being can flourish, which can be achieved by enabling everyone to authentically enjoy a full range of basic rights—to health, education, political participation, and the like.

The Arab countries are richer than they are developed, for the elites that control government and the economy have used their position to appropriate vast resources, all the while progressively reducing the population to poverty. Compounding the problem, especially in rural and suburban areas, is an

14 Regulation (EC) No 1717/2006 of the European Parliament and of the Council of 15 November 2006 Establishing an Instrument for Stability. OJ L 327, 24.11.2006, p. 1, whereas 1.

inflationary trend that has been pushing up food prices, both domestically and internationally, since 2007.

In 2000 the United Nations held a Millennium Summit out of which came the millennium development goals (MDGs) for the year 2015. If we take these goals as a benchmark against which to measure development in the Arab countries, we will see that progress has been very slow when it comes to eradicating hunger, reducing child mortality, fighting illiteracy, and providing access to health care (see UN 2015). On top of that, there is the problem that while 50 percent of the population is rural, agriculture accounts for no more than 15 percent of Arab GDP. Furthermore, youth unemployment in 2009 stood at 24 percent—more than double the global average, at 11.9 percent. Finally, there is a staggering rate of unemployment among women: in nonagricultural sectors, less than 20 percent of women are employed—the lowest rate among developing countries.

As the 2011 report finds, it is therefore necessary to work towards a "developmental state [...] capable of transforming the enormous potential and natural resources of the region into an inclusive growth base that respects human rights, reduces poverty, creates decent work opportunities and views social expenditure as a real investment in the future" (UNDP 2011, 1).

But there are two basic conditions that need to be met before such a developmental state can be achieved. First, there need to be "political, social and administrative accountability mechanisms that promote inclusive development in both political and economic spheres" (ibid., 1–2). Second, and even more "importantly, the move to a developmental state requires extensive efforts for the proper management of four critical resources, namely: energy, water, agricultural land and human resources. Of the four critical resources, other than finite oil and gas, two are in great abundance and hold significant potential (renewable energy sources and human resources) and two (water and agricultural land) present tough and limiting constraints" (ibid., 2).

Essential to the project of building a developmental state, the 2011 report finds, is regional integration. For "a national developmental state that is regionally integrated will preserve its national security more effectively than a rentier state that is economically and politically dependent on the interplay of geopolitical forces controlled by countries outside the region" (ibid., 8). The goal, then, is to "build a critical number of regionally integrated developmental states" (ibid.). But this can only be achieved by way of "structural transformations" in the form of "stable, constitutional and popular governments"—a necessary condition "for policy objectives to be properly designed and planned" (ibid.). Under these policy objectives it will be necessary to (a) create "decent work opportunities for youth and genuine improvement in democratic governance" (ibid.); (b) "revamp fiscal space by examining issues such as sustainability of public debt and public investment," while "monitoring [...] and evaluation of the impact of fiscal policy on development results (including the thorny issue of food and fuel subsidies)" (ibid., 9); and (c) gain "a more in-depth understanding of labour market dynamics with a view to reducing supply- and demand-side bottlenecks that impede attempts to create and access jobs" (ibid., 10), while also (d) "revising labour laws to ensure worker's rights, encouraging formal and regulating informal employment, creating demand-oriented training programmes and extending social protection to all workers" (ibid., 10).

But in offering these policy prescriptions, the 2011 report is emphatic about the need for accountability, noting that "one main underlying cause of poor development outcomes has been the lack of effective mechanisms by which the people could hold those in power accountable for their actions and demand course correction when policies had adverse impacts" (ibid., 12). And this means that the solution to the problem of development will crucially have to be institutional as well. Which in turns means an independent judiciary, with a clear separation of judicial and executive and powers.

Also receiving emphasis in the 2011 report is the role that civil society and local actors and communities can and should play: these are identified as indispensable partners in the project of building the developmental state.

But these transformations cannot be separated from the process that was set in motion with the Arab Springs: only when this process is complete can the transformations envisaged in the 2011 report take place, and they are bound to shape Euro-Mediterranean relations in profound ways.

The foregoing analysis can be deepened by looking at the World Bank development policy review titled *The Unfinished Revolution*. This report, issued in May 2014, asks why any real development had yet to materialize in Tunisia almost four years after the January 2011 Jasmine Revolution, noting that "Tunisia holds enormous potential, but poor economic performance" (Word Bank 2014, 16). Analysing the Tunisian economic model going into the revolution, the report found that

> pervasive restrictions to the number of firms allowed to operate in the domestic market (the so-called "onshore sector"), coupled with many legal (public) monopolies and undue regulatory constraints, severely limit competition, such that investment faces restrictions in over 50 percent of the economy. These barriers to market entry and contestability [...] stifle economic growth by hampering private initiative and discouraging innovation and productivity. (Ibid.)

The World Bank report "also found evidence that the regulations themselves were [...] being adjusted in response to personal interests and corruption," in "an environment, still largely in place three years after the revolution, where cronyism and rents extraction (rather than competition and performance) drive economic success" (ibid.). It cites "strong evidence that these problems may even have worsened since the revolution" (ibid., 17), which in turn "reflects the failure of this economic model" (ibid., 18).

Despite "significant progress on the political front, with the consensual adoption of a new constitution and the emergence of a vibrant civil society [...], the economic system that existed under Ben Ali has not been changed significantly—and the demands of Tunisians for access to economic opportunity have not yet been realized" (ibid.). Even so, "the post-revolution transition still represents a unique opportunity for Tunisians to revisit their economic system and agree on bold changes to open up economic opportunity to all Tunisians, accelerate shared growth, create quality jobs, and promote regional development" (ibid., 18–19). The report accordingly

> articulates a vision for a different development model—to move Tunisia from a system based on privileges to one based on competition, bringing good quality jobs and prosperity to all Tunisians. It argues that, in order to fulfill its economic potential, Tunisia needs to create a level playing field by opening up the economy and removing Tunisia's three dualisms, namely the onshore-offshore division, the dichotomy between the coast and the interior, and the segmentation of the labour market. A strong social policy is also necessary, of course, and should be designed to accompany private sector-led growth. (Ibid., 19)

In light of that analysis, the 2014 World Bank report outlines policy recommendations that include actions to be taken as follows:

- i "Reform the financial sector to enable resources to be channeled to the most productive projects and increase the quantity of financing available to the private sector for investments: better performance in the banking sector could increase the level of credit to the private sector" (ibid.).
- ii "Strengthen the social protection system, reform the tax system, and adopt a package of policies attacking regional disparities in order to share fairly the benefits of economic growth and ensure that no one is left behind: The current social protection model relies mostly on untargeted fuel subsidies, which are expensive and inequitable—because they largely benefit the rich" (ibid., 20).
- iii Address the problem of "regional disparities," entailing "a rethinking of Tunisia's regional development policies" (ibid.).
- iv Enact reforms aimed at "improving labor market rules and institutions, revamping the industrial policy, including policies to foster innovation, changing the strategy for services sectors, and reorienting the agricultural policy" (ibid.).
- v Undertake a "reform of agricultural policies [that] could unleash the potential of agriculture in interior regions by refocusing agricultural support toward labor-intensive Mediterranean products" (ibid.), in which connection the report finds that "the potential for Tunisia to expand its exports to the EU remains far larger than the potential to MENA or Africa" (ibid., 21).

Clearly, it is still very much an open question whether these policy goals can be achieved. But the transformative potential is there, and so we now have to ask: how might Euro-Mediterranean relations be reshaped if the process of change set in train by the Arab Spring revolutions runs its full course?

11.5 What next?

11.5.1 The Arab Spring revolutions and the possible future of Euro-Mediterranean relations

It was commented earlier that the transformations wrought by the Arab Springs are far from over. And in fact I would argue that they are bound to effect deep change in Euro-Mediterranean relations.

Until the Arab Springs, the southern Mediterranean states had sought to gain international legitimacy by entering into free-trade agreements with the EU, but these agreements were asymmetrical, working to their disadvantage. As a result, their exports declined, their manufacturing became less competitive, and their agricultural products faced EU trade barriers (Mouhoud 2012, 44). "In exchange for political recognition by the EU," these states also "pledged to lead an emigration policy of repression against their citizens and those of sub-Saharan Africa transiting through their respective territories" (ibid.).

The Arab Springs changed the lay of the land in such a way as to delegitimize both the ENP and the UfM, for they both stood on the authority of the old ruling elites. What, then, is coming into sight on the horizon for the Arab states of the Mediterranean region?

As concerns the prospect of economic growth within the Arab world, it is worth mentioning the Greater Arab Free Trade Area (GAFTA), formed in Cairo in 1996, and now comprising seventeen Arab countries: "Over the period 1997–2009, the GAFTA resulted in a 26% (Abedini and Péridy 2008) increase in intraregional commerce" (Mouhoud 2012, 45).[15]

But the deepest changes will concern Euro-Mediterranean relations. The Arab Spring revolutions of 2011 enabled the EU to fully appreciate the challenges the authoritarian governments of the southern Mediterranean countries were facing from their own people. This led the EU to reconsider its relations with these Arab countries, setting new priorities for its own action. Euro-Mediterranean policies had been following a specific order of priorities (Cassarino 2012, 19ff.): at the top of the agenda was illegal immigration into the EU, under whose pressure the southern Mediterranean countries took measures to stem that flow of migration; next came the issue of security in response to the September 11 attacks, which led the southern Mediterranean countries to take up the fight against terrorism, even if this meant loosening their commitment to democracy and human rights; and in the third place was stability, a concern that played into the hands of authoritarian regimes, which managed to use stability as a proxy for good governance—an idea that in turn translated into government control

15 GAFTA was meant to chart a course towards a greater internationalization of economies confined within the boundaries of a limited regional integration. To this end it eliminated tariff as well as nontariff trade barriers, but in the end it didn't break out of the mould of a conventional trade agreement centred on the exchange of goods and services. See Romagnoli and Mengoni 2014, 209.

of the economy, thereby foreclosing the possibility of fostering an open market economy. Let us therefore look at what happened to these Euro-Mediterranean priorities in the wake of the Arab Springs and the transformations they set in motion, or what new set of policies took their place.

The core of the EU's policy response to the Arab Spring revolutions is laid out in two communications issued in 2011 by the European Commission and the High Representative of the European Union for Foreign Affairs and Security Policy: "A Partnership for Democracy and Shared Prosperity with the Southern Mediterranean" (EC 2011a) and "A New Response to a Changing Neighbourhood" (EC 2011b), providing a review of the ENP.

In the first place, the ENP review recognized the need for the EU to devote greater resources to its neighbours. Financial aid was to increase to 1.2 billion euros by 2013, with an additional 1 billion euros in loans from the European Investment Bank (EIB), and the European Bank for Reconstruction and Development (EBRD) was to earmark an initial 1 billion euros for operations to begin in the Mediterranean area. This aid was aimed at fostering economic and social development, supporting small and medium-sized enterprises (SMEs) and microcredit, reducing economic disparities, and starting pilot projects for agricultural and rural development. Furthermore, the southern Mediterranean countries were offered the opportunity to enter into Deep and Comprehensive Free Trade Agreements (DCFTAs), designed to make good on the ENP promise to enable neighbouring countries to participate in the European single market (Colombo and Tocci 2012, 87).

In the second place, the ENP review called for "stricter conditionality and incentives for best performers" (EC 2011b, 21), with a view to achieving "deep democracy" (Balfour 2012, 64), under which neighbouring countries were to ensure free and fair elections, the enjoyment of basic freedoms (such as freedom of expression and peaceful assembly), the rule of law, and an independent judiciary, while committing to the fight against corruption, among other actions. The incentives for embarking on these reforms were part of a package in "assistance, trade, and mobility" (ibid.).

However, there is also an underbelly to conditionality. As Rosa Balfour aptly comments:

> It is questionable whether the focus on conditionality is appropriate. Not only is it notoriously hard for the EU to deliver on the conditions it sets, but the premises upon which conditionality is based do not reflect the post-Arab Spring context as they rely on asymmetrical relations between the EU and North Africa and the Middle East and on the assumption that the European model is attractive and relevant to these societies. (Ibid.)
>
> It is also questionable whether the focus on conditionality is relevant in itself. Sovereignty has always been an important principle in the post-colonial Arab world, seen as part of national identity, and the notion of "dignity"—personal and national—has been a recurring theme in revolutionary North Africa and the Middle East. (Ibid., 76)

Furthermore, there are "many ways [in which] the revision of conditionality seems to reflect an internal demand for a redefinition of 'ethical' standards for engagement, following the exposure of contradictions in the EU's relations with dictators" (ibid., 68). Balfour accordingly argues for

> a more equal relationship [...], moving away from the enduring "unacknowledged cultural legacy of colonialism" (Halliday 2011, 52) and understanding the national "dignity" that moved so many in North Africa and the Middle East to get rid of their perennial leaders. Interdependence, rather than conditionality based on an asymmetry of power, and reference to universal principles, rather than to standards of democracy, make it legitimate to support them abroad, notwithstanding the accusations of double standards that the EU often encounters. And identifying common interests and concerns that reflect the demands of the people in this common Mediterranean space may be a way to establish a new dialogue with a changing Arab world. (Balfour 2012, 68)

In the third place, the EU's communications of 2011 underscore the need for a greater commitment to developing relations with civil societies, private actors in the socioeconomic space, and youth and women's groups in the southern Mediterranean countries. This new awareness comes from the EU having understood that a transition away from the authoritarian regimes of the past inevitably means working with nonstate actors, that is, with people and organizations in civil society.

However, the revised criteria that formed the basis of the ENP have their shortcomings. In the first place, as has been correctly observed, the ENP continues to be straitjacketed within the boundaries of a security policy (Colombo and Tocci 2012, 91).

In the second place, the DCFTAs continue to require compliance with the criteria for participating in the European single market, whereas it would make more sense to deregulate this market, especially in agriculture. In this connection, the crisis the EU is currently undergoing should not be considered separately from the transformation the Arab countries are themselves undergoing: if this latter (still incomplete) transformation moves forward, it would enable the MENA (Middle East and North Africa) countries to "renegotiate the free trade agreement with the EU, demanding both the opening of EU agricultural markets and temporary asymmetry to the benefit of [those] countries" themselves (Mouhoud 2012, 44).

Furthermore, Euro-Mediterranean policy continues to insist on conditionality without clarifying how this mechanism might me made operational. And, finally, the revised ENP is premised on the idea of *bilateral* relations even if it is on a *multilateral* basis that policy in areas such as infrastructure, communications, and the fight against organized crime is best framed (Colombo and Tocci 2012, 94).

So, although the revised ENP could signal a new season on the horizon for Euro-Mediterranean relations, its shortcomings suggest otherwise. Lending support to that assessment is the turmoil that swept across much of the Middle East in the aftermath of the Arab Springs, not only in Egypt—the disarray it was thrown into with the 2011 revolution and the ensuing move to outlaw the Muslim Brotherhood as a terrorist organization—but also in Syria, with a civil war whose devastating effect has destabilized the entire region, making its future highly unpredictable. Only Tunisia's democratic constitution of 2014 gives reason for hope, offering a model for an authentic democracy across the Arab world.

On the other hand, while the Arab Spring revolutions have made for an extraordinary opportunity to set Euro-Mediterranean relations on a new footing, the EU's ability to effect authentic change in the southern Mediterranean has been constrained by constant economic headwinds, first under the protracted effect of the global financial crisis of 2007–08 (Paciello 2013, 83), and now under the COVID-19 recession.

The global financial crisis had the effect of intensifying competition among EU member states, while calling into question the EU's common commercial policy. It also stalled progress on trade negotiations with the southern Mediterranean countries, the only exception being Morocco, with which negotiations on a DCFTA were started early in 2013. At the same time, however, the economic slump in Europe prompted some of these countries, and in particular Egypt and Tunisia, to look for other trading partners. As a result, they built closer economic ties with Turkey and the Persian Gulf countries, mainly Qatar and Saudi Arabia (ibid., 86).

Seemingly unable to learn from its own past failures, the EU continues to soldier on with its traditional trade policy. Even its conditionality policy, severed from any economic incentives, hampers the EU's ability to influence the political process abroad, especially considering that non-European states like Qatar, Saudi Arabia, and Turkey offer aid without strings attached, and in particular without requiring political reform (ibid., 88).

In summary, Europe is confronted with the practical paradox of having to recognize that it is imperative to overhaul Euro-Mediterranean relations, while at the same time having to deal with an underperforming economy that is crippling its ability to present the southern Mediterranean countries with a mutually advantageous economic partnership proposal.

11.5.2 Migrations across the Mediterranean and Europe: What does the future hold?

The Arab Spring revolutions have cast a stark light on the authoritarian nature of the regimes with which the EU had been working for years to stem the flow of migration from the Mediterranean's southern shore to the countries of Europe. A particularly tense and critical moment in this effort, before the transformations that would overtake North Africa, came in the summer of 2005, when the Spanish border patrol and Moroccan authorities used force on migrants storming the border fences surrounding the Spanish exclaves of Ceuta and Melilla in Morocco: several were killed in the incident, and the migrants were then deported to locations in the Moroccan desert (Cassarino and Lavenex 2012, 284). But the incident also set off a broad debate that in December of the same year prompted the Council of the European Union to put out a policy statement outlined in a document titled "Global Approach to Migration: Priority Actions Focusing on Africa and the Mediterranean."

"The European Council," the policy statement says, "agrees to initiate priority actions with a focus on Africa and the Mediterranean countries," and does so on "an integrated and global approach" that in the short term is designed to "reduce illegal migration flows and the loss of lives" and "ensure safe return of illegal migrants" but in the long term seeks to form a "genuine partnership" with the same countries, looking to "strengthen durable solutions for refugees and build capacity to better manage migration, including through maximising the benefits to all partners of legal migration, while fully respecting human rights and the individual's right to seek asylum" (Council of the European Union 2005, 1). Among other things, this entails the need "to promote cheaper and more easily available remittance services and support ongoing efforts by international organisations to improve data on remittance flows," as well as to "consider supporting efforts of African states to facilitate members of diasporas to contribute to their home countries, including through co-development actions, and explore options to mitigate the impact of skill losses in vulnerable sectors" (ibid., 6).[16]

In short, what the Council issued was a two-pronged policy statement. For on the one hand it stressed migration control and the need to return migrants to their countries of origin, but on the other hand it introduced the idea that *the problem of migration cannot be attacked separately from that of development.* The Council accordingly embraced a codevelopment vision that supported a policy of integrating migrants and creating the conditions that would enable them to participate in the labour market.

The Council's 2005 policy statement also stressed the need to "work with neighbouring countries" (ibid., 6). More to the point, the idea was to negotiate with Morocco, Algeria, and Libya in order to find schemes under which to

16 The concept of codevelopment was introduced by the Algerian-born French political scientist Sami Naïr, who described it as a proposal aimed at integrating immigration with development in such a way that the country of origin, no less than the host country, can draw benefit from the migratory flow. This means that the two countries need to establish a consensual arrangement under which the contribution that migrants make to the host country does not translate into a loss for the country of origin (cf. Naïr 1997). Following France's lead, Spain worked the idea of codevelopment into its own migration policy. As Carlos Giménez explains the idea, "codevelopment involves initiatives that two or more organizations in two or more countries linked by a migratory flow undertake for the mutual benefit of those countries under a scheme of mutual support. These initiatives are carried out both in the country of origin and in the host country. Their main thrust comes from a group of migrants in the host country" (Giménez 2004; my translation). See also Gozzi, Venturi, and Furia 2011, 5ff.

cooperate in the fight against human trafficking and in readmitting migrants to their home countries. As Hugo Brady (2012, 278) points out, however, "related negotiations have failed in the past because 'a country with 2,000 nationals illegally resident in the EU, sending money back home, is infinitely better off than a country with 2,000 extra unemployed people,' according to a senior official working in the JHA [Justice and Home Affairs] Council." Implicit in that remark is the recognition that the problem of migration cannot be solved without first addressing the need to redefine Euro-Mediterranean relations in the new landscape that was formed in the wake of the Arab Springs.

The EU carried on with its policy of closing up its borders and clamping down on so-called illegal migration. The question now is whether it is sustainable for the EU to continue along the same course after the dramatic events of the Arab Springs and the surge in migration that followed.

In 2011, while serving as European Commissioner for Home Affairs, Cecilia Malmström put forward a policy proposal to form mobility partnerships with the southern Mediterranean countries, describing this policy as built around migrants and designed to ensure that human rights are protected both in Europe and in third countries. In that spirit, she stressed the need for closer cooperation with these countries, in such a way that both sides stand to benefit. And the mobility partnerships themselves she envisioned as playing an important part in the process through which to democratize the North African countries (Malmström 2011).

What exactly would go into these mobility partnerships was not immediately clarified. In November 2011 the European Commission issued a communication titled "The Global Approach to Migration and Mobility" (GAMM), stating that "The Arab Spring and events in the Southern Mediterranean in 2011 further highlighted the need for a coherent and comprehensive migration policy for the EU" (EC 2011c, 2). "The Commission," the document goes on to state, "has already presented a range of policy proposals and operational measures on migration, mobility, integration and international protection [...]. Those proposals were fully endorsed by the European Council in June," and the EU has since

> taken immediate action by launching dialogues on migration, mobility and security with Tunisia and Morocco [...] and making the necessary preparations to start the dialogue with Egypt. Similar dialogues will follow with other countries in the Southern Mediterranean region, notably with Libya [...]. The dialogues allow the EU and the partner countries to discuss [...] all aspects of their possible cooperation in managing migration flows and circulation of persons with a view to establishing Mobility Partnerships. (Ibid.)

In the document, the GAMM is described as resting on "four equally important pillars: "(1) organising and facilitating legal migration and mobility; (2) preventing and reducing irregular migration and trafficking in human beings; (3) promoting international protection and enhancing the external dimension of asylum policy; (4) maximising the development impact of migration and mobility" (ibid., 7).

Under the first pillar, the GAMM was focussed on a number of priorities that included facilitating the mobility of youth, students, and researchers; streamlining the visa programme; and making it easier to find information about job openings (ibid., 15).

Under the second pillar, the GAMM priorities included (a) the "transfer of skills, capacity and resources to partners to prevent and reduce trafficking, smuggling and irregular migration, to ensure return and readmission, and to strengthen integrated border management"; (b) "cooperation on document security, paving the way for visa facilitation for frequent travellers from priority partner countries"; and (c) "initiatives to provide better protection for and empower victims of trafficking in human beings" (ibid., 17).

Under the third pillar, the document reads, "the EU needs to enhance solidarity with refugees and displaced persons and such efforts should become an integral part of the GAMM. The EU should increase cooperation with relevant non-EU countries in order to strengthen their asylum systems and national asylum legislation and to ensure compliance with international standards. This could enable these countries to offer a higher standard of international protection for asylum-seekers and displaced people who remain in the region of origin of conflicts or persecution. The EU should encourage its partner countries to incorporate this dimension in their national poverty reduction strategies" (ibid.).

On 12 June 2013 the European Parliament approved an asylum package establishing a framework legislation for building a common European asylum system (outlined in EC 2014). Under this system, effective from the fall of 2015, all EU member states can rely on a common framework for granting asylum, enabling "more countries [...] to take responsibility for the people who come for protection in Europe" (Malmström 2013).

Finally, under the fourth pillar, the GAMM priorities include (a) "diaspora investment vehicles that could channel the voluntary contributions by the diaspora and adding EU resources to boost the development-oriented initiatives and investments in priority countries, such as in the Southern Mediterranean"; (b) "private-public partnerships to engage migrant entrepreneurs and SMEs in trade, investment and skills transfers between EU Member States and partner countries," with a view to capacity-building in these countries; and (c) "assistance to partner countries to identify and monitor *bona fide* recruiters in order to empower migrants, notably with a view to facilitating circular migration" (EC 2011c, 20).

However, despite these principled policy statements, the EU has yet to commit to a global approach to migration and mobility: its focus continues to be aimed at clamping down on migration and stemming its flow (Lavenex and Stucky 2011, 136). Indeed, "Schengen countries have reintroduced border controls on around 70 different occasions since border controls first came down in 1995" (Brady 2012, 275). In June 2011 the European Council met to discuss migration with a view to renegotiating the Schengen principles. In its conclusions to this meeting, the Council stated that "a safeguard clause could be introduced to allow the exceptional reintroduction of internal border controls in a truly critical situation where a Member State is no longer able to comply with its obligations under the Schengen rules" (European Council 2011, p. 8, § 22).[17]

To be sure, the Schengen Borders Code, of 2006, did include language under which "Member States should also have the possibility of temporarily reintroducing border control at internal borders in the event of a serious threat to their public policy or internal security,"[18] and so the European Council conclusions of 2011 had a legal basis in their intent to make border controls easier in the face of the perceived threat posed by migration. But the "Schengen rulebook" has become an object of debate in the wake of the Arab Springs, and a wide range of positions have taken shape in this regard across Europe. Hugo Brady identifies four camps: we have (*i*) the "nervous policemen" of Northern Europe, "including France and Germany, for which Schengen's border and policing arrangements do not guarantee enough security"; (*ii*) the "disgruntled border guards" of southern Europe, who "want the right to make exceptions to the EU's 'Dublin regulation' on asylum, which stipulates that they must care for all asylum seekers who reach their shores first without sending them on to richer countries further north," but who "have no wish to see reform damage the rights of their own citizens to move around freely"; (*iii*) the "idealistic free movers [...] of the Schengen area to the east," who "hugely value passport-free travel and are therefore suspicious of any changes to the Schengen system"; and (*iv*) the "libertarian legal eagles," who "are not states but EU institutions such as the European Commission, Parliament and Court of Justice," and whose "mission [...] is to maintain the openness of national frontiers to goods, services, capital and people," considering as well that they are "largely immune from anti-immigration politics" (Brady 2012, 276).

These divergent views and competing interests explain the European impasse on immigration and Europe's inability to coalesce around a coherent policy vision on which basis to address the challenge posed by the flow of immigrants coming into Europe. To this end, as suggested, there needs to be an appreciation that the challenge can no longer be framed exclusively as an emergency situation or a security problem but is tied in with broader trends that are bound to have a lasting effect. It is for this reason that Euro-Mediterranean relations need to be set on an entirely new basis, proceeding from an understanding of migrants as transnational actors capable of contributing to the development of the countries they leave behind as well as the countries they find refuge in.

17 Compare the language in the motion for a joint resolution subsequently introduced in the European Parliament: "Member States want, as a very last resort, in the framework of this mechanism, the introduction of a safeguard clause to allow the exceptional reintroduction of internal border controls in a truly critical situation where a Member State is no longer able to comply with its obligations under the Schengen rules" (European Parliament 2011, 3, whereas M).

18 Regulation (EC) No 562/2006 of the European Parliament and of the Council of 15 March 2006 Establishing a Community Code on the rules Governing the Movement of Persons Across Borders (Schengen Borders Code). OJ L 105, 13.4.2006, p. 2, § 15.

Works Cited

Abedini, Javad, and Nicolas Péridy. 2008. "The Greater Arab Free Trade Area (GAFTA): An Estimation of Trade Effects." *Journal of Economic Integration* 23, no. 4: 848–72.

Alaoui, Hicham Ben Abdallah El-. 2011. "Egypt Catches Tunisia's Fire: The Arab Wall Begins to Fall." *Le Monde Diplomatique*, February 2011. https://mondediplo.com/2011/02/03uprising. Published in French under the title "Tunisie, les éclaireurs." https://www.monde-diplomatique.fr/2011/02/EL_ALAOUI/20111

Amoroso, Bruno. 2007. "Politica di vicinato o progetto comune?" In *L'alternativa mediterranea*, edited by Franco Cassano and Danilo Zolo, 493–515. Milan: Feltrinelli.

Angioi, Silvia. 2006. *Il principio di condizionalità e la politica mediterranea dell'Unione Europea*. Naples: Edizioni Scientifiche Italiane.

Balfour, Rosa. 2012. "New Paradigms for the EU-South Mediterranean: Rethinking Conditionality?" *Med. 2012* (IEMed: European Institute of the Mediterranean): 64–68.

Ben Achour, Yadh. 1992. *Politique, religion et droit dans le monde arabe*. Tunis: Cérès Productions.

Bensedrine, Sihem, and Omar Mestiri. 2004. *L'Europe et ses despotes: Quand le soutien au "modèle tunisien" dans le monde arabe fait le jeu du terrorisme islamiste*. Paris: La Découverte.

Brady, Hugo. 2012. "The Schengen Crisis in the Framework of the Arab Spring." *Med. 2012* (IEMed: European Institute of the Mediterranean): 275–78.

Brumberg, Daniel. 2002. "Democratization in the Arab World? The Trap of Liberalized Autocracy." *Journal of Democracy* 13, no. 4: 56–68.

Cassarino, Jean-Pierre. 2012. "Reversing the Hierarchy of Priorities in EU-Mediterranean Relations." In *The European Union and the Arab Spring: Promoting Democracy and Human Rights in the Middle East*, edited by Joel Peters, 1–15. Lanham, MD: Lexington Books.

Cassarino, Jean-Pierre, and Sandra Lavenex. 2012. "EU-Migration Governance in the Mediterranean Region: The Promise of (a Balanced) Partnership?" *Med. 2012* (IEMed: European Institute of the Mediterranean): 284–88.

Cavatorta, Francesco. 2016. "A Clash of Civilizations inside the MENA Countries? Islamist versus Secular Civil Society and the Failure of Pro-Democracy Policies. In *Clash or Cooperation of Civilizations? Overlapping Integration and Identities*, edited by Wolfgang Zank, 27–42. London and New York: Routledge.

Colombo, Silvia, and Nathalie Tocci. 2012. "The EU Response to the Arab Uprising: Old Wine in New Bottles?" In *Rethinking Western Policies in Light of the Arab Uprising*, edited by Riccardo Alcaro and Miguel Haubrich-Seco, 71–96. Rome: Nuova Cultura.

Council of the European Union. 2005. "Global Approach to Migration: Priority Actions Focusing on Africa and the Mediterranean." Doc. No. 15744/05. Brussels, 13 December 2005.

EC. 2011a. European Commission and the High Representative of the European Union for Foreign Affairs and Security Policy. "A Partnership for Democracy and Shared Prosperity with the Southern Mediterranean." COM(2011) 200 final. Brussels, 8 March 2011.

EC. 2011b. European Commission and the High Representative of the European Union for Foreign Affairs and Security Policy. "A New Response to a Changing Neighbourhood." COM(2011) 303 final. Brussels, 25 May 2011.

EC. 2011c. European Commission. "The Global Approach to Migration and Mobility." COM(2011) 743 final. Brussels, 18 November 2011.

EC. 2014. European Commission, Home Affairs. "A Common European Asylum System." Luxembourg: Publications Office of the European Union.
European Council. 2011. From the General Secretariat of the Council to the Delegations. Subject: European Council, 23–24 June 2011, Conclusions. EUCO 23/11. Brussels, 24 June 2011.
European Parliament (plenary sitting). 2011. "Motion for a Resolution to Wind up the Debate on the Commission Statement pursuant to Rule 110(2) of the Rules of Procedure on changes to Schengen." Drafted by Carlos Coelho, Manfred Weber, Roberta Angelilli, Giovanni La Via, and Salvatore Iacolino on behalf of the European People's Party Group. Doc. No. B7-0393/2011, 4 July 2011.
Gallina, Andrea. 2007. "From Security to Development: Migration Contribution to Euro-Mediterranean Cooperation." *Mediterranean Journal of Human Rights* 11, no. 2: 283–313.
Giménez, Carlos. 2004. *Migraciones y desarrollo: Estudio de dos casos particulares; Ecuador y Marruecos.* Madrid: Centro de Estudios de Cooperación al Desarrollo (CECOD).
Gomez, Ricardo. 2018. *Negotiating the Euro-Mediterranean Partnership: Strategic Action in EU Foreign Policy?* Abingdon, Oxon: Routledge.
Gozzi, Gustavo, Bernardo Venturi, and Annalisa Furia. 2011. *Migration, Development and Human Rights: AMITIE Context Report.* Comune di Bologna/University of Bologna. Available at http://www.comune.bologna.it/amitie/documents.php
Halliday, Fred. 2011. "The Age of the Three Dustbins" (2005). In *Political Journeys: The Open Democracy Essays*, edited by David Hayes, 49–54. London: Saqi Books.
Henry, Jean-Robert. 2008. "French Initiative in the Mediterranean Region: Back to Square One?" *Med. 2008* (IEMed: European Institute of the Mediterranean): 37–43.
Hollis, Rosemary. 2012. "No Friend of Democratization: Europe's Role in the Genesis of the 'Arab Spring.'" *International Affairs* 88, no. 1: 81–94.
Jordan Times Editor. 2011. "Masadeh Quits Mediterranean Union Top Post." *Jordan Times*, January 28. https://mideastenvironment.apps01.yorku.ca/2011/01/masadeh-quits-mediterranean-union-top-post-jordan-times/
Jünemann, Annette. 2005. "Zehn Jahre Barcelona-Prozess." *Aus Politik und Zeitgeschichte* (APuZ) 45: 7–14.
Khader, Bichara. 2008. Introduction to "Barcelone 2010 et l'Union pour la Mediterranée: Quelles perspectives?" In *Europe – Méditerranée: Enjeux, stratégies, réformes*, 137–41. Barcelona: IEMed (Institut Europeu de la Mediterrània).
Lavenex, Sandra, and Rachel Stucky. 2011. "Partnering for Migration in EU External Relations." In *Multilayered Migration Governance: The Promise of Partnership*, edited by Rahel Kunz, Sandra Lavenex, and Marion Panizzon, 116–42. London: Routledge.
Malmström, Cecilia. 2011. "Partnerships for Mobility." Blog post, 18 November 2011. http://blogs.ec.europa.eu/malmstrom/tag/mobility-partnership (archived on 18 November 2014).
Malmström, Cecilia. 2013. "A Common European Asylum System Is Here." Blog post, 12 June 2013. Archived on 18 November 2014, now available at https://cecilia196.rssing.com/chan-12001148/all_p1.html
Martín Muñoz, Gema. 2010. "Democracy and the Arab World: The 'Islamist Dilemma.'" In *Why Europe Must Engage with Political Islam: 10 Papers for Barcelona 2010* (Paper 5, February 2010), edited by Amr Elshobaki and Gema Martín Muñoz, with an

introduction by Bassma Kodmani, 21–33. Paris: EU Institute for Security Studies; Barcelona: European Institute of the Mediterranean.

Mohsen-Finan, Khadija. 2009. "The Union for the Mediterranean: The Difficulty of 'Managing Proximity.'" *Med. 2009* (IEMed: European Institute of the Mediterranean): 96–100.

Mouhoud, El Mouhoub. 2012. "The Arab Economies in the Face of Crisis: Assessment and Perspectives since the Tunisian Revolution." *Med. 2012* (IEMed: European Institute of the Mediterranean): 39–44.

Naïr, Sami. 1997. "Rapport de bilan et d'orientation sur la politique de codéveloppement liée aux flux migratoires" (1 January 1997). Mission interministérielle au codéveloppement et aux migrations internationales. Paris: Ministère des Affaires Étrangères. https://www.vie-publique.fr/rapport/24358-rapport-de-bilan-et-dorientation-sur-la-politique-de-codeveloppement-li

Nicosia, Aldo. 2011. "La Tunisia dalla rivoluzione alla nuova costituzione." Chap. 5 in *Le rivoluzioni arabe: La transizione mediterranea*, edited by Francesca Maria Corrao. Milan: Mondadori.

Paciello, Maria Cristina. 2013. "The Euro Crisis and Euro-Mediterranean Relations." *Med. 2013* (IEMed: European Institute of the Mediterranean): 83–88.

Panebianco, Stefania. 2003. "The Euro-Mediterranean Partnership in Perspective: The Political and Institutional Context." In *A New Euro-Mediterranean Cultural Identity*, edited by Stefania Panebianco, 1–20. London, Frank Cass.

Reinhardt, Ulrike Julia. 2002. "Civil Society Cooperation in the EMP: From Declarations to Practice." EuroMeSCo Papers 15, May 2002. https://www.euromesco.net/publication/civil-society-co-operation-in-the-emp-from-declarations-to-practice/

Romagnoli, Alessandro, and Luisa Mengoni. 2014. "Human Capital and Labour Markets in the MENA Region." Chap. 7 in *The Economic Development Process in the Middle East and North Africa*. London and New York: Routledge.

Saaf, Abdallah. 2010. "La sécurité humaine comme nouvelle perspective de coopération." In *Human Security: A New Perspective for Euro-Mediterranean Cooperation: 10 Papers for Barcelona* (Paper 3, February 2010), edited by Roberto Aliboni and Abdallah Saaf, with an introduction by Atila Erlap, 29–36. Paris: EU Institute for Security Studies; Barcelona: European Institute of the Mediterranean.

Sarkozy, Nicolas. 2007. Discours du Président de la République M. Nicolas Sarkozy sur le thème de l'Union de la Méditerranée. Palais Royal Marshan, Tangiers, 23 October 2007. Ministère de l'Europe et des Affaires Étrangères. https://jo.ambafrance.org/Discours-de-M-Nicolas-Sarkozy.

Solana, Javier. 2001. "Europe: Security in the Twenty-First Century." The Olof Palme Memorial Lecture, Stockholm, June 20. https://www.consilium.europa.eu/uedocs/cms_data/docs/pressdata/en/discours/ACF332.htm

Sophocles. 1906. "Antigone." In *The Dramas of Sophocles Rendered in English Verse Dramatic & Lyric by Sir George Young*. Everyman's Library, edited by Ernest Rhys, 1–41. London: J. M. Dent & Sons.

UN. 2015. *The Millennium Development Goals Report 2015*. New York: United Nations.

UNDP. 2005. United Nations Development Programme (UNDP), Regional Bureau for Arab States (RBAS). *Arab Human Development Report 2004: Towards Freedom in the Arab World*. New York: United Nations Publications.

UNDP. 2009. United Nations Development Programme (UNDP), Regional Bureau for Arab States (RBAS). *Arab Human Development Report 2009: Challenges to Human Security in the Arab Countries*. New York: United Nations Publications.

UNDP. 2011. *Arab Development Challenges Report 2011: Towards the Developmental State in the Arab Region*. United Nations Development Programme (UNDP), Regional Centre for Arab States, Cairo.

World Bank. 2014. *The Unfinished Revolution: Bringing Opportunity, Good Jobs and Greater Wealth to All Tunisians*. Report No. 86179-TN, May 2014. Washington, DC: World Bank Group.

Zank, Wolfgang. 2016. "The Gradual Europeanization of North Africa." In *Clash or Cooperation of Civilizations? Overlapping Integration and Identities*, edited by Wolfgang Zank, 109–146. London and New York: Routledge.

Index

'Abd al-Nasir, Jamal 112, 114, 149, 154
Abd Rabou, Ahmed 159
'Abduh, Muhammad 84, 118, 130, 135–36
Abu Salim prison massacre 181–82
Abu Zayd, Nasr Hamid 128–30
Achcar, Gilbert 168–169, 204
Action Tunisienne 85n8
Aflaq, Michel 87
Ahmadinejad, Mahmoud 180
al-Afghanı, Jamal ad-Din 118–19, 135
Al Ahram newspaper 154
al-Asad, Baššar 165
al-Awa, Muhammad Salim 131, 198
al-Banna, Hasan 118–19, 137
al-Buazizi, Muhammad 144, 192
al-Din, Khayr 135–36
Algeria: colonial government of 97–99; colonization of 24–26; concept of nation 81; domination by France 24–26; nationalism 82; nationalist mission 82–83
Algerian Islamic Salvation Front 218
al-Ghannushi, Rashid 121, 132–35, 146, 164, 195
Alianak, Sonia L. 150
al Maliki, Nuri 165
al-Mawdudi, Abu al-Ala 122–24, 137
Al-Qaeda 180, 184
al-Qaradawi, Sheikh Yusuf 120–21
al-Sadat, Anwar 112, 114–15, 149
al-Sanhuri Abd al-Razzaq 116
al-Sarraj, Fayez 189
al-Shatir, Khayrat 199
Al-Sisi, Abdel Fattah 203–4
al-Wahhab, Muhammad ibn Abd 135
Amoroso, Bruno 221
anticolonial nationalism 79–81; and nation 81–82; and state 81–82
Arab countries of Mediterranean area: democratization in 210–36; development in 210–36
Arab Development Challenges Report 2011 225
Arab Human Development Report 2004 223, 224
Arab Human Development Report 2009 223
Arab-Islamic nationalism 80n2
Arab-Muslim exceptionalism 180
Arab nationalism 83–87
Arab Springs 79, 108, 143–44; after fall of the regime 186–87; autumn after spring 188–92; causes of uprisings 175–78; civil war in Libya 181–86; crisis, in Egypt 196–200; in destabilized landscape of Middle East 165–66; end of Arab Spring in Egypt 200–2; Europe's role 190–92; future for Egypt 203–4; peace for Libya 189–90; people reclaiming their dignity 178–81; and possible future of Euro-Mediterranean relations 229–32; revolt and revolution in Tunisia 192–96; from revolt to revolution 178–81
Arab states: *Code Morand* 101, 102–5; nation-state building 89–91; reception of French law in 99–102; system of 88–89; traditional structures 89–91
'Arafa, Mohamed A. 148
Arkoun, Mohammed 135
Arnaud, Alain 94–95
Arntz, E. R. N. 7–8
ar-Raziq, Ali 'Abd 118
assimilation 95, 105–6
Atwan, 'Abd al-Bari 197
Augustine, Saint 42
authoritarian institutional system 96

autonomy 95; administrative 14n13, 17, 95; ethnic 14n13; individual 127; political 14n13, 17
Avant-Projet de Code du Droit Musulman Algérien 102–103

Bahlul, Raja 126–28
balance politique 66
Balfour, Rosa 230–31
barbarism 6, 42–43
barbarous humanity 6
Barcelona Conference 211
Barcelona Declaration of 1995 211, 221–22
Barcelona Process 211–12, 214, 216
Ba'th Party 87
Battle of Navarino 12
Bayat, Asef 179n6, 196n21
Béji Caïd Essebsi, Mohamed 164–65, 170, 171
Ben Achour, Yadh 105–6, 137–38, 145, 164, 166, 217n6
Ben Ali, Zayn al-Abdin111, 135, 145, 162–65, 170–71, 193–94, 219, 219n8, 227
Berlin Congress of 1884–85 48
Berlin Wall, fall of 170
Berman, Nathaniel 56–57
Black Skin, White Masks (Fanon) 33
Bled Makhzen 89
Bled Siba 89
Bluntschli, Johann Caspar 11, 15
Boduszynsky, Mieczyslaw P. 190
Bouazizi, Mohamed 169
Boukhars, Anouar 169
Bourguiba, Habib 85–86, 111, 164, 170, 195
Brady, Hugo 234, 236
British India 122
Brown, Nathan J. 108n1, 109–10, 113, 114n4, 116, 156n20
Brumberg, Daniel 217
Bull, Hedely 73
Bulleid, Al-Hadi 195
Byzantine Empire 17

Campanini, Massimo 131, 197–99
cannibalism 42–43
Caracciolo, Lucio 188
Carothers, John Colin 31
Carr, E. H. 10
Cassese, Antonio 185
Catherine the Great of Russia 17
Charles VII 25
Chomsky, Noam 58, 67
Christianity 17, 17n17, 69, 215
civilization 46–47; Western 47–48
civilized humanity 6
civil religion 121
civil state: ethics and religion 120–22; Islamic concept of 120–22
civil war: in Libya 181–86; in Syria 7, 14
civitas maxima 65–66
Code de droit international (Bluntschli) 11
Code des Obligations et des Contrats 105
Code Morand 101, 102–5
Cohen, Jean L. 54
colonial domination 21n1
colonialism 133–135; and inferior humanity 34–36
colonial law 92–94
colonial psychiatry 29
colonial science 93
colonization: of Algeria 24–26; and Muslim psychiatry 29–30
Commission de Codification du Droit Musulman Algérien 102
Common Foreign and Security Policy (CFSP) 212
common sense 42–43
compassion 46
The Concept of the Political (Schmitt) 73
Concert of Europe 16–17
conditionality principle 221
"consension" 101
"Considérations ethno-psychiatriques" (Fanon) 30
Constitutional Charter of 1814 96
Constitutional Declaration of 2011 150
constitutional democracy 117, 162–63, 167, 170–71, 196
constitutionalism: Egypt 143–44; and hegemonic techniques 65–68; and international law 65–68; Tunisia 143–144
Constitutional Liberal Party 110
constitutional transformations 108–10
constitutions: Al-Sadat's "Permanent Constitution" 112–15; independence and 110–15
"cosmopolitan" law 55
Council of Europe 225
COVID-19 recession 232
Crimean War 13
cross-fertilization 105–6

cultural diversity 48–51
cultural plurality 48–51
cultural relativism 31
"culture of formalism" 55n2

Deep and Comprehensive Free Trade Agreements (DCFTAs) 230–32
Dehio, Ludwig 66
De Hominis Dignitate (Pico della Mirandola) 69
De Indis insulanis relectio prior (Vitoria) 3
De Jure Belli ac Pacis 4–5
democracy: complex relation between Islam and 216–19; as a condition of economic development 219–20; and European Union 221–23; and human rights 221–23; of interpretation 123; in Islam 108–39; in the Mediterranean 216–19; relation between development and 219–21; and *shura* 131–33; Tunisian case as model for a path towards 144–47; Western 108–39
democracy in Islam and Western democracy 108–39; colonialism, nationalism, secularization 133–35; constitutional transformations 108–10; democracy and *shura* 131–33; divergences 122–25; ethics and religion 120–22; independence and constitutions 110–15; interpretation 128–30; interpretation of Islamic reformism 135–37; Islam and democracy 117; Islamic concept of civil state 120–22; Islamic constitutionalism 116; Islamic reformism 117–20; legitimacy and validity 126–27; liberal and democratic reformism 137–39; Muslim law and religion 130–31; sovereignty 127–28; sovereignty of God 125–26; sovereignty of people 125–26
Democrates Secundus (Sepúlveda) 41, 42
democratic reformism 137–39
democratization: in Arab countries of Mediterranean area 210–36; of external sovereignty 54
development: in Arab countries in Mediterranean area 210–36; and European policies 220–21; relation between democracy and 219–21
Devereux, Georges 50–51
d'Hautpoul, Beaufort 14n12
"diencephalic dominance" 31
dignity and humanity 68–72
direct participation 117
Doe, Samuel 61n10
domestic sovereignty 64
droit de la civilisation 11
Duguit, Léon 10
Dworkin, Ronald 49

Eastern Question 11–17, 118; and Tocqueville 21–24
Ébauche de Projet de la Constitution 147
Economic Community of West African States (ECOWAS) 61
economic development: democracy as a condition of 219–20; human and 225; political conditions for 213
Egypt 143–71; Arab Springs in Middle East 165–66; challenges ahead 171; constitutionalism and revolutions 143–44; Consultative Council of Delegates 109–10; crisis of Arab Spring in 196–200; Egyptian constitutional model 150–53; end of Arab Spring in 200–2; Fundamental Ordinance 109; future for 203–4; Janus-faced nature of Egyptian state 153–59; new Egyptian constitution 153–59; postcolonial revolution 148–50
Egyptian Center for Economic and Social Rights (ECESR) 203
Egyptian Christians 157
Egyptian constitutional model 150–53
Egyptian Jews 157
Egyptian state, Janus-faced nature of 153–59
El Sharnoubi, Osman 155
English Revolution 166
ENI (Ente Nazionale Idrocarburi) 183
Erdoğan, Tayyip 195
Esposito, John L. 122, 125
Essay on Government (Mill) 47
Estlund, David 127
ethics and religion 120–22
Euro-Mediterranean Association Agreements 211
Euro-Mediterranean Human Rights Network 221; *see also* EuroMed Rights
Euro-Mediterranean relations: Arab Spring revolutions and possible future of 229–32; and ENP 231–32
EuroMed Rights 221; *see also* Euro-Mediterranean Human Rights Network
Europe: challenges in fostering democracy along Mediterranean 221–28; and development 220–21; and European

policies 220–21; and immigration 220–21; migrations across 232–36; role in Arab Springs 190–92
European Bank for Reconstruction and Development (EBRD) 230
European Commission 210, 230, 236
European Commission for Democracy through Law 161
European constitutionalism 109
European Council 215, 234
European Court of Justice (ECJ) 54, 213
European humanity 71
European Investment Bank (EIB) 230
Europeanization: of North African countries 213–14; of southern Mediterranean countries 210–16
European Neighbourhood Policy (ENP) 212, 229–31
European Parliament 225, 235, 236
European peoples: civilization of 5–9; conscience of 6
European policies: development and 220–21; immigration and 220–21
European protectionism 221
European Union (EU) 190, 225; communications of 2011 231; and democracy 221–23; "Dublin regulation" 236; Euro-Mediterranean policies 192; Greece joining 211; and human rights 221–23
Ezzat, Heba 121

Fabbe, Kristin 190
facultas 4
Fakhfakh, Elyes 171
Fanon, Frantz 30–34, 71–72
Fatimid Caliphate 89
Febvre, Lucien 46
Fergany, Nader 203
Filiu, Jean-Pierre 179n7
First Geneva Convention 72
first-wave fundamentalism 136
Freedom and Justice Party (FJP) 120, 157, 160, 197
Free Officers' Revolution 149
French colonies: administrative organization 94–97; Algeria 24–26, 97–99; political organization 94–97; Tunisia 97–99
French Mediterranean Union project 214–15
French Revolution 68, 117, 166
function of law: and humanitarian intervention 56–57; and war 56–57
Fundamental Ordinance of 1882 110

Gaddafi, Muammar 181–89, 197
Gautier, Émile-Félix 88
Gellner, Ernest 90
Ghannouchi, Rachid 181
Girault, Arthur 97–98, 104n13
"The Global Approach to Migration and Mobility" (GAMM) 234–35
"Global Approach to Migration: Priority Actions Focusing on Africa and the Mediterranean" 233
Global Mediterranean Policy (GMP) 210
God, sovereignty of 125–26
Government of National Accord 189
Greater Arab Free Trade Area (GAFTA) 229
Grotius, Hugo 4–5, 8–9, 70
Guellali, Amna 170
Guizot, François 23

Habermas, Jürgen 127
Haftar, Khalifa 189–91
Hague Convention of 1899 72
Hamas 218
Haute Instance pour la Réalisation des Objectifs de la Révolution 164
Hegel, Georg Wilhelm Friedrich 166
hegemonic logics 59–63
hegemonic techniques 12; and constitutionalism 65–68; and international law 65–68; responsibility to protect as 62, 68
Hibou, Béatrice 193
High Representative of the European Union for Foreign Affairs and Security Policy 230
History of British India (Mill) 47
Hobbes, Thomas 64
Hollis, Rosemary 177, 219
Hourani, Albert 84, 85n7, 86n9
human egoism 47
humanitarian intervention: described 4; and function of law 56–57; legal construction of 59; legitimation for 3–5; origins of 3–18; and responsibility to protect 57–58; theory of 5–9; and war 56–57
humanitas romana 68–69

humanity: barbarous 6; civilized 6; conquest of 41–42; and dignity 68–72; and international law 72–73; savage 6
Human law 9–11
human life 48–51
human nature: and human egoism 47; as identification with the other 45–46; and science of man 43–45; and Western hegemony 40
human rights: and democracy 221–223; and European Union 221–23
Human Rights Watch 147, 182
human security 223–24; defined 223; as new prospect for cooperation 223–25
human society 9–10
human solidarity 10–11
Hume, David 43–45

Ibadi Islam 102
immigration and European policies 220–21
Imperial Reform Edict 13n10
importation 105–6
independence and constitutions 110–15
Indian Muslims 123
indigenous mentality 32
Indios and slavery 41
inferior humanity and colonialism 34–36
"In Larger Freedom: Towards Development, Security and Human Rights for All" (UNGA) 57, 59
Instance Supérieure Indépendante pour les Élections (ISIE) 145
interdependence sovereignty 64
International Commission on Intervention and State Sovereignty 57–58
international community, and sovereignty 53–55
International Criminal Court (ICC) 54, 184
international human rights law: and humanity 72–73; and international law 72–73
International Labour Organization 176
international law: and constitutionalism 65–68; and hegemonic techniques 65–68; and humanity 72–73; and international human rights law 72–73; and Western civilization 47–48
international legal sovereignty 64
International Monetary Fund (IMF) 150, 176, 203–4
international society 10
interpretation 128–30
intrinsic value 49
Iranian Revolution of 1979 137
ISIS 165–66, 202
Islam 27–28, 215; complex relation between democracy and 216–19; and democracy 117; democracy in 108–39; in the Mediterranean 216–19
Islamic concept of civil state 120–22
Islamic constitutionalism 109, 116
Islamic democracy 123, 125; construction of 124; divergences 122–25
Islamic democratic secularism 121
Islamic fundamentalism 183
Islamic reformism 117–20; interpretation of 135–37
Islamist al-Nahda (Renaissance) Party 194
Italo-Libyan Chamber of Commerce 183

Jabbar, Adil 178
Jadhran, Ibrahim 191
January Revolution 148
Jasmine Revolution 227
Jeanson, Francis 33n19
Joseph II of Austria 17
Jouannet, Emmanuelle 62
Judaism 215
Juma, Mahdi 202
Jünemann, Annette 212
jus ad bellum 56
jus gentium 3–4, 8
jus humanae societatis 8
jus in bello 56
"just causes" 4
Justice and Development Party: Moroccan 197, 218; in Turkey 195, 198
"just war" 4

Kamarowsky, Comte L. 18
Kant, Immanuel 70–71
Keene, Edward 44
Kelsen, Hans 126, 133
Khader, Bichara 175, 177, 212
Khalid, Muhammad Khalid 86
Khomeini, Ayatollah 137
King Pyrrhus of Epirus 43
Kneissl, Karin 175n1, 177n5
Koskenniemi, Martti 10, 12, 55n2, 62
Krasner, Stephen D. 64–65, 67

"The Lady Doth Protest Too Much" (Koskenniemi) 55n2

La Haute Instance 145
Lapie, Pierre-Olivier 34
La Tunisie martyre 85
Lauterpacht, Hersch 70
"laws of humanity" 5, 7, 71
League of Nations 5, 34
legislative democracy 117
legitimacy and validity 126–27
Le Roy, Thierry 143
Le Tunisien 84
Lévi-Strauss, Claude 45–46
liberal reformism 137–39
Libya: and Arab Springs 189–90; civil war in 181–86; peace for 189–90
Libyan Coast Guard 191
Libyan Political Agreement 189
Locke, John 64
Lorimer, James 5–6
Louis Philippe I 23

Maastricht Treaty 211
Mahmud II 22–23
Majalla 100, 100n7
Malmström, Cecilia 234
Mannoni, Octave 33
Martens, Friedrich 15n14, 17n17
Martín Muñoz, Gema 219–20
Marzouki, Mohamed Moncef 146, 165, 201
Mediterranean: democracy and Islam in 216–19; migrations across 232–36
Mediterranean's southern shore: and democracy 221–23; European Union 221–23; Europe's challenges in fostering democracy along 221–28; and human rights 221–23; new development model 225–28; state's security and human security 223–25
Mediterranean Union 214
Menon, Krishna 57
Méray, Henry 94–95
Metaphysics of Morals (Kant) 70–71
Mezran, Karim 60n7
Mezzetti, Luca 150n13
Middle Ages 89, 131
Middle East: and Arab revolts 179; Arab Springs in destabilized landscape of 165–66; nationalism in 83–84
Middle East and North Africa (MENA) 175–76, 228, 231
migrations, across Mediterranean and Europe 232–36
Mill, James 47
millennium development goals (MDGs) 226
Millet, René 35n20
"modern Islamism" 118
Moncef Marzouki, Mohamed 146, 165, 194–95
monotheistic religion 27, 157, 215n4
moral causes 45
"A More Secure World: Our Shared Responsibility" (UNGA) 57
Mount Lebanon Civil War; *see* civil war in Syria
Mousseron, Jean-Marc 99
Mubarak, Husni 115, 119, 148–51, 154, 181, 194, 197, 219
Mugabe, Robert 169
Muhammad Al, pasha of Egypt 22
Mursi, Muhammad 120, 137, 151–54, 181, 199, 200
Muslim Brotherhood 114n4, 118–22, 136–37, 151–52, 154n17, 157, 168, 181, 186, 188, 196–97, 199–203, 232
Muslim humanity 29
Muslim law: codify 102–4; and French codes 100; principles of 104; and religion 130–31; and Western European law 99
Muslim psychiatry 29–30
mutasarrifiyya 14n13

Naïr, Sami 233
Napoleon 148
Napoleon III 14
nation: and anticolonial nationalism 81–82; concept and Algeria 81; and Muslim world 88
National Elections Commission 200
nationalism 106, 133–35; Algeria 82; anticolonial 79–81; Arab 83–87; Arab-Islamic 80n2
"nationalist sacred" 81
National Oil Company 191
National Oil Corporation (NOC) 183
National Salvation Front (NSF) 168
national society 10
nation-state building, and Arab states 89–91
native primitivism 31
natural law 9–11
natural liberty of nations 65
"natural or mere human recognition" 6
neocolonialism 59–63
Neo-Destour 110–11

new development model 225–28
new Egyptian constitution 153–59
"A New Response to a Changing Neighbourhood" (EC) 230
New World peoples 3–4
Nicholas I of Russia 17
Noble Edict of the Rose Chamber 13n10
nongovernmental organizations (NGOs) 193–94, 222, 224
North African countries: Europeanization of 213–14
North Atlantic Treaty Organization (NATO) 185
"Notes de psychiatrie musulmane" 29
Nussbaum, Martha 225

Obama, Barack 148
Observatoire pour les Droits de l'Homme 147
Old Testament 27
Orford, Anne 60n6
Organization of American States (OAS) 54
organized hypocrisy 64, 67
Örücü, Esin 13n11
Ottoman Civil Code 102
Ottoman Empire 7, 11–15, 108, 117, 118, 130; partitioning 17–18
Ottoman-Persian Wars 117
Ouzara 97

"partial political recognition" 6
"A Partnership for Democracy and Shared Prosperity with the Southern Mediterranean" (EC) 230
Pasha, Ibrahim 12
Pasha, Ismail 109–10
Pasha, Muhammad Tawfiq 110
"passional relationships" 79–80
Peau noire, masques blancs (Fanon) 33
people, sovereignty of 125–26
People's Security Organization 182
Peters, Anne 73
philosophy of relativism 133
physical causes 45
Pico della Mirandola 69
Pillet, Antoine 10
"plenary political recognition" 6
political expansion 93
political legitimacy 82–83
popular sovereignty 117
Porot, Antoine 29, 30
postcolonial revolution 148–50
practical doctrine 94
primitivism 31
Principes (Girault) 98
Principes de colonisation et de législation colonial 97
principle of nonintervention 7
Prophet Muhammad 123, 130
Provisional Constitution of the Arab Republic of Egypt 150
psychic unity 48–51
psychic universalism 48–51
Psychologie de la colonisation (Mannoni) 33

Queen Elisabeth II of England 169
Quran 27–28, 97–98, 118, 128–30
Qutb, Sayyid 119, 119n9

Ramadan, Tariq 121, 135
Rashid, Rida, 116
Rassemblement Constitutionnel Démocratique (RCD) 145
Ratzinger, Joseph 127
"reason of humanity" 7, 71
Rechtsgemeinschaft 68
Redissi, Hamadi 131, 135–36, 137, 159–60, 167
reformism: democratic 137–39; Islamic 117–20, 135–37; liberal 137–39
Règlement Organique 14n13
Relectiones Theologicae (Vitoria) 41
religion: civil 121; ethics and 120–22; European wars of 117; freedom of 152–53; monotheistic 27, 157, 215n4; Muslim law and 130–31; state 138, 148n11
"religious sacred" 81
representative government 117
responsibility to protect (RtoP) 53, 54; defined 61n8; as hegemonic technique 62, 68; and humanitarian intervention 57–58; legitimizing humanitarian intervention 59; legitimizing neocolonial policies 59–60; regional solutions 61
respublica christiana 5
revolt and revolution in Tunisia 192–96
Revolution 23 July of 1952 149
Revolutionary Command Council (RCC) 111
Revolutionary Guard Corps 182
revolutions: Egypt 143–44; Tunisia 143–44, 192–96

Revue de Droit International et de Législation Comparée (Rolin-Jaequemyns) 7, 11
Rida, Rashÿd 84
Rizk, Mariam, 155
Rolin-Jaequemyns, Gustave 7–9, 11–12, 15–16
Romano, Santi 92–94
Rougier, Antoine 5, 11
Rousseau, Jean-Jacques 45–46
Roy, Olivier 180
rule by decree 96

"sacred" 81
Saied, Kais 171
Salafism 197
Sarkozy, Nicolas 194, 214–15
savage humanity 6
Sayad, Abdelmalek 79–83
Scelle, Georges 5
Schengen Borders Code 236
Schmitt, Carl 55, 71, 73
Scottish Enlightenment 43
second-wave fundamentalism 136
secularization 99, 133–35
Security Council Resolution 60
Sen, Amartya 225
Sepúlveda, Juan Ginés de 41, 42
Shafīq, Ahmad 151, 200
Sharif, Muhammad 109
Sharia 105
Shia Islam 117
shura and democracy 131–33
Slaughter, Anne-Marie 53
slavery: abolition of 170; condition in Indios 41; natural 41
small and medium-sized enterprises (SMEs) 230, 235
social legitimacy 82
Solana, Javier 212
southern Mediterranean countries: beyond Barcelona 211–13; Europeanization of 210–16; Europeanization of North African countries 213–14; new prospects for cooperation 214–16; short reconstruction of relations between 210–11
sovereignty: domestic 64; of God 125–26; interdependence 64; and international community 53–55; international legal 64; of people 125–26; redefining 63–65; Westphalian 64–65
Sovereignty: Organized Hypocrisy (Krasner) 64
special law 94
Spinoza, Baruch 139
state: religion 138, 148n11; security as a new prospect for cooperation 223–25
Stoic philosophy 3
structural adjustment programs (SAPs) 176
Suez Canal 150
Sultan, Faruq 200
Sunnah 118, 138
Sunni Islam 117
Sunni reformism 136
Supreme Council of the Armed Forces (SCAF) 109, 150–51, 159, 197, 199–200
Sutter, Jean 31

Tanzimat 13n10
Taylor, Charles 61n10
Ten Commandments 27
territorial patriotism 83
Theologico-Political Treatise (Spinoza) 139
Thiers, Adolphe 23
Thomas, A. J. 67
Thomas, Ann Van Wynen 67
Tibi, Bassam 81, 88
Tocqueville, Alexis de 21–24, 96; and Algeria 24–26; Quran 27–28
Todorov, Tzvetan 3
Treatise of Human Nature (Hume) 44
Treaty of Bardo 97
Treaty of Berlin 18
Treaty of Casr-Said 35
Treaty of Fez 35
Treaty of Hünkâr İskelesi 22
Treaty of London 12
Treaty of Paris 13–14
Tunisia 143–71; Arab Springs in Middle East 165–66; Assembly of the Representatives of the People 201; challenges ahead 171; colonial government of 97–99; and compromise 168–71; constitutionalism and revolutions 143–44; a democratic future 159–64; first elections in new democracy 164–65; model for a path towards democracy 144–47; prospects for future 166–68; revolt and revolution in 192–96
Tunisian Human Rights League 145
Tunisian Revolution 166–67, 170

Tunisie: Une révolution en pays d'Islam (Ben Achour) 166
Turks as Shiites 11

umma 88
UN Charter 186
The Unfinished Revolution report 227
Union for the Mediterranean (UfM) 194, 214, 229
United Nations: millennium development goals (MDGs) 226; Millennium Summit 226
United Nations Development Programme (UNDP) 225
United Nations Support Mission in Libya (UNSMIL) 189
United States Senate 148
Universal Declaration of Human Rights 67, 72, 155
UN (United Nations) Security Council 184–85; Resolution 1674 186; Resolution 1970 184–85; Resolution 1973 60n7, 185–86, 189
US Congress 201
utilitarianism 47

validity and legitimacy 126–27
Vattel, Emer de 8–9, 65–66
Vitoria, Francisco de 3–4
Voll, John O. 125

Wahhabism 135
Walzer, Michael 126, 165
war and humanitarian intervention 56–57
Western civilization and international law 47–48
Western constitutional history 117
Western democracy: and democracy in Islam 108–39; divergences 122–25
Western hegemony and human nature 40
Western humanity 11
Western liberal democracies 217
Westphalian sovereignty 64–65
which sovereignty 127–28
Wolff, Christian 65
World Bank 176, 227–28
"World Summit Outcome" (UNGA) 57, 61
World War II 170

Zghal, Abdelkader 89, 90
Zolo, Danilo 186

For Product Safety Concerns and Information please contact our EU
representative GPSR@taylorandfrancis.com
Taylor & Francis Verlag GmbH, Kaufingerstraße 24, 80331 München, Germany

www.ingramcontent.com/pod-product-compliance
Ingram Content Group UK Ltd.
Pitfield, Milton Keynes, MK11 3LW, UK
UKHW020011200926
475702UK00014B/1822

* 9 7 8 0 3 6 7 7 5 5 2 4 9 *